CLARK'S

FOREIGN

THEOLOGICAL LIBRARY.

MÜLLER

ON

The Christian Doctrine of Sin.

VOL. II.

THE

CHRISTIAN DOCTRINE OF SIN.

BY

DR JULIUS MÜLLER,

PROFESSOR OF THEOLOGY IN THE UNIVERSITY OF HALLE.

Translated from the German of the Fifth Edition

BY THE

REV. WILLIAM URWICK, M.A.

IN TWO VOLUMES.

VOL. II.

WIPF & STOCK · Eugene, Oregon

Wipf and Stock Publishers
199 W 8th Ave, Suite 3
Eugene, OR 97401

The Christian Doctrine of Sin, Volume 2
By Müller, Julius and Urwick, William
Softcover ISBN-13: 979-8-3852-1477-8
Hardcover ISBN-13: 979-8-3852-1478-5
eBook ISBN-13: 979-8-3852-1479-2
Publication date 1/25/2024
Previously published by T. & T. Clark, 1876

This edition is a scanned facsimile of the original edition published in 1876.

CONTENTS

OF THE SECOND VOLUME.

BOOK III.

THE POSSIBILITY OF SIN.

	PAGE
INTRODUCTION, ...	1

PART I.

MAN'S FREE WILL.

CHAPTER I.

FORMAL AND REAL FREEDOM.

§ 1. Real freedom, ...	6
§ 2. Formal freedom, ...	14
§ 3. Development of the conception of formal freedom, . .	22
§ 4. Meaning of the terms "possibility" and "ability," . .	29
§ 5. Germ of this theory in Augustine, ...	35

CHAPTER II.

THE FREEDOM OF THE WILL IN MORAL DEVELOPMENT.

§ 1. The Pelagian view of freedom, ...	37
§ 2. Determinism, ...	44
§ 3. Moral Development, ...	54
§ 4. Epochs of Moral Development, ...	62

CHAPTER III.

Transcendental and Empirical Freedom.

	PAGE
§ 1. Freedom traced beyond the boundaries of time,	67
§ 2. Theories of transcendental freedom; Kant,	76
§ 3. Developments of Kant's philosophy; Schelling,	94

CHAPTER IV.

Freedom as the Possibility of Sin

§ 1. The true idea of God,	113
§ 2. God's freedom the principle of other existence,	133
§ 3. Primary self-decision extra-temporal,	147
§ 4. Non-temporal self-decision pertains only to personal beings,	157
§ 5. The possibility of evil put an end to,	160
§ 6. Supposed necessity for the fact as well as possibility of evil,	162
§ 7. Can we thoroughly understand evil?	167
Note A. Rothe's criticism,	176
Note B. Explanation of the terms *Grund* and *Ursache*,	177

PART II.

HUMAN FREEDOM COMPATIBLE WITH GOD'S INFINITE WILL AND KNOWLEDGE.

CHAPTER I.

The Relation of Human Freedom to the Divine Omnipotence.

§ 1. Statement of the question,	180
§ 2. Self-limitation of God's will,	188
§ 3. Self-limitation of the Divine will vindicated,	192
§ 4. Is the final triumph of evil possible?	197
§ 5. Divine permission of evil,	201

CHAPTER II.

The Relation of Human Freedom to the Divine Omniscience.

§ 1. The fact of God's foreknowledge,	203
§ 2. Proposed solution of the problem,	205
§ 3. God's objective knowledge,	214

BOOK IV.

THE SPREAD OF SIN.

	PAGE
INTRODUCTION	226

CHAPTER I.

THE UNIVERSALITY OF SIN AS A MATTER OF EXPERIENCE.

§ 1. Extent of human depravity, ...	227
§ 2. Definitions of the *Formula Concordiae*, . . .	228
§ 3. Supposed criterion of man's salvation, . .	233
§ 4. Modern theories concerning nature and grace, . .	243
§ 5. Varieties of moral character, ...	243
§ 6. Scripture regards sin as universal, ...	255

CHAPTER II.

SIN AS A CORRUPTION OF HUMAN NATURE.

§ 1. Impurity of the human heart, ...	259
§ 2. Origin of this impurity, ...	263
§ 3. Phenomena confirming this view, ...	268
§ 4. Witness of Holy Scripture, ...	274
§ 5. What constitutes inborn sinfulness, . . .	281
§ 6. The connection between Sin and Death, . .	287

CHAPTER III.

THE DOCTRINE OF HEREDITARY SIN.

§ 1. Statement of the problem, ...	307
§ 2. Modification of the doctrine, ...	320
§ 3. A *via media* devised, ...	326
§ 4. Participation of all men in Adam's sin, . . .	328
§ 5. Testimony of Holy Scripture, ...	343

CHAPTER IV.

The Origin of Inborn Sinfulness.

	PAGE
§ 1. Sin must be traced back to an extra-temporal act,	357
§ 2. Nature of this non-temporal state,	360
§ 3. This extra-temporal self-perversion not universal,	366
§ 4. Human individuality,	372
§ 5. Man's primitive state in time,	380
§ 6. Relation of our theory to Scripture and theology,	392
Appendix. Criticisms of Rothe and Dorner examined,	397

BOOK V.

THE AGGRAVATION OF SIN IN INDIVIDUAL LIFE.

§ 1. Introduction,	402
§ 2. Growth of a permanent state from actual sin,	403
§ 3. The doctrine of various stages of depravity,	408
§ 4. Degrees of culpability in sin,	415
§ 5. The sin against the Holy Ghost,	418
§ 6. The restoration of all things,	425
Conclusion,	430

INDEXES.

I. Hebrew words referred to,	433
II. Greek words referred to,	433
III. Texts of Scripture,	434
IV. Subjects,	436

BOOK III.

THE POSSIBILITY OF SIN.

INTRODUCTION.

Results of former inquiries. THE topic of inquiry which the conclusions we have arrived at set before us is very obvious. The presence of evil in human life as the positive antithesis of good, is a fact which cannot be denied; neither can it be explained as a necessity arising from the divine government of the world; such a supposition would only be another way of denying the existence of evil altogether. This antithesis to good exists not only as a fact of consciousness, or as an illusion which vanishes upon the standing-point of the Absolute; it is manifest to the eye of God Himself; for He it is who condemns evil by the voice of conscience and the world's judgment, and who is destroying it by His Redemptive work in the hearts of all who yield to His gracious rule. Yet this very fact that God condemns evil and negatives its power, witnesses that the antithesis is not caused nor ordained by Him. Sin is to be found only in the creature, and can have its being only through the creature.

Principle to account for evil to be sought in the creature. But the creature, as the very name denotes, is wholly dependent upon God; and accordingly it would seem that whatever the creature does, must ultimately, and of necessity, have its foundation in the will of the Creator. This argument may be applied to the case of evil, and we are thus brought back to the very point which we have been endeavouring to leave far behind us. The only way of avoiding this circle manifestly is to discover and point out, in the nature of the creature in whom evil is, such a principle of independence as may account for and originate a new beginning; so that thus a limit may be established, beyond which the origin of sin must not be looked for. Such a principle is not to be found in any of the theories in explanation of sin which we have thus far examined, because in all of them evil is regarded, not as wanton defection on the creature's part, whereby he sets himself at variance with the divine order, but (so far as they do not dualistically explain it) as the consequence or the necessary condition of certain parts of this order itself. They thus obtain an explanation of sin by destroying the very essence of it.

Nothing is easier than to abide by the seeming contradiction between the two ideas of created being on the one hand, and independence on the other, a contradiction after all apparent to the dullest eye, and then at once to assert that any such independence is wholly incompatible with our conception of created being. In the following investigations it will be shown that such a conclusion not only deprives human personality of its true import, but seriously dishonours God's omnipotence and love. It is a far more fruitful, though incomparably more difficult task, to discover a principle in human nature which will explain and justify our consciousness of sin, without excluding a personal Creator from the world. All modern speculative endeavours which do not regard the absolute process of mere logic as the highest, are simultaneously directed to this end. We need only call to mind SCHELLING's profound Dissertation upon Freedom, STEFFENS's *Christliche Religionsphilosophie*, and the writings of BAADER, especially his *Fermenta cognitionis* and his *Lectures upon Speculative Theology*. The same effort is made, though in different directions, by J. H. FICHTE in his *Vorschule der Theologie;* WEISSE in his *Idee der Gottheit* and his *Philosophische Dogmatik*; FISCHER in his *Idee der Gottheit* and other works;[1] A. GUNTHER in his works on the Philosophy of Religion; STAHL upon the *Fundamenten einer Christlichen Philosophie;* WEISSENBORN in his *Lectures on Pantheism and Theism;* ULRICI in his treatise *Gott und die Natur*, and others.

Marginal notes: True problem to be solved. Works upon the subject.

If there be any such principle as we require, which shall serve at once as the basis of our consciousness of guilt and as a barrier against attributing sin to the divine causality, it must certainly be the WILL; and the independence which must attach to its power of causation, if it is to meet the case, is clearly what we are wont to call its FREEDOM. If freedom be the highest assertion of the *ego* or self, and if sin (as our inquiry in the first book of this treatise showed) be in its essence selfishness, what else must sin be but an abuse of freedom? Our inquiry accordingly must now be directed to the freedom of the human will, the true conception of it, its inner power, and its connection with evil.

This principle is the freedom of the will.

From the position which Schleiermacher's theory of sin occupies in our inquiry, it is clear that it cannot serve us in the solution of the proposed problem. According to it, freedom is only the lively activity of temporal causality in its highest stage, differing from the vital activity of other natural existences only in degree; and freedom thus viewed, in connection with the origin of evil, only presents this alternative; we may regard sinful conduct either as produced by some external influence, or as the mere outgo of human nature as such.* Human freedom, according to Schleiermacher, possesses power of its own only in relation to other finite causes; in relation to God, free agents are as utterly dependent upon Him, as are the causes and agencies of nature.† Human freedom, thus viewed, is of no avail to prevent our attributing the origination of evil to God, nor does it explain our consciousness of guilt. In order to this the independence of the human will must be recognized as having some reality in relation not only to the world, but to God.

Schleiermacher's theory insufficient.

The same remark applies to the idea of freedom developed by Ritter in his work *Ueber das Böse* in reply to this treatise of mine. What is free (we are told p. 24, 25) in the true sense of the term is to be found only in acts or conduct, it has to do only with the relation between subject and predicate, in propositions which speak of actions or actual things. The proposition "an act is free," attributes

Ritter's view.

---

* *Glaubenslehre*, § 81, 2 (vol. i. 491).   † *Ibid.*, § 49 (vol. i. 272).

the act in question to the Subject, it implies that the act so attributed could be assigned to nothing else but simply and truly to him alone. These simple definitions seem at first sight to grant all that we require, not only a freedom which provides a fit basis for accountability or imputation, but a freedom which is really identical with imputation. But the fact is, what seems more than we want is really less. For when we are told "an action is free so far as it can really and truly be attributed to the Subject of whom it is predicated," it must be explained upon what grounds the act can thus be attributed to him; we must understand the possibility or rather the necessity of thus "attributing" it in the full sense of the word, and this is a matter of great difficulty in the case of a being dependent both as to existence and state. Our inquiry therefore concerning freedom has to do not merely with the formal relation of the predicate to the subject, but to the way and manner in which the predicate, *i.e.*, the act, proceeds *realiter* from the Subject. This inquiry alone can lead us to a conception of freedom which will form a substantial basis and principle of explanation for the fact of imputation of guilt on the part of conscience.

When Ritter, on the contrary, in various connections (pp. 29, 47, 52, 60), represents freedom merely in this relation of predicate to subject, he really makes no essential distinction between it and spontaneity in the sphere of nature; he makes it nothing more than what might with equal propriety be predicated of living beings in nature, regarding whom no mention can be made of guilt. That the tree bears blossoms and fruit, that the wild beast lies in wait for his prey, and the herbivorous beast seeks the pasture—these are all predicates which, upon Ritter's standing-point, seem to belong, and may be attributed to their subjects with equal correctness, and just in the same way as a man's acts are to be predicated of him. Ritter, however, goes beyond the range of these analogies when he calls man "the transcendental cause" of his actions (p. 51). But if the new range thus opened up before us were meant to include that peculiar significance of freedom which forms the basis of our consciousness of guilt and excludes evil from the divine causation, it would not be mentioned so cursorily, and without any reference to freedom. It is, moreover, directly contradictory to Ritter's theory to suppose that anything could proceed from human freedom independently of the divine causality. For he takes pains to prove, by a special argument (p. 48, 49), that to refer a definite act as predicate both to the human and the divine will as its subject, involves no contradiction.

PART I.

MAN'S FREE WILL.

CHAPTER I.

FORMAL AND REAL FREEDOM.

§ 1. REAL FREEDOM.
—External necessity.

MAN is usually conscious of an obliging or constraining force at those points only in his life when the determining power is external to him. It is only when he meets with some check, and finds himself hindered in some effort, when he is acted upon rather than an actor, that he feels the power of any necessity influencing his life. Necessity becomes a matter of consciousness to him only when it is constraint.

Internal necessity.

A narrow acquaintance only with the phenomena of human life apparent on every hand will suffice to convince us that, besides this outward necessity there is also an inner one, arising from the Subject of it himself. The soul of man is not, to begin with, a *tabula rasa*, as Locke's empiricism, following Aristotle, took it to be; it may more correctly be compared to a closed volume, as Herbert of Cherbury called it, containing within itself from the outset a plenitude of determining principles. This determinateness is not the same in all; it varies with sex, race, nation, individuals. It is an inner necessity whereby even in the play of children difference of sex and individuality of character are manifest. When the young man decides upon his calling in life, he is counted happy if he has been led thereto, not by comparison and reasoning, but by the assurance of a higher instinct and an unhesitating consciousness of his appropriate sphere. The artist or the poet does not first hesitate and then choose what shall be the original conceptions of his creations; on the contrary, he feels himself penetrated and impelled by the secret necessity of his nature wherewith genius inspires him. The more perfectly he succeeds in his design, the less likely is it to occur to him that he might have done it differently. Those characters are the strongest who early in life devote themselves, as if it were a needs be, to some definite end, and keep to it through life with an energy undivided and unswerving. In society generally and national life, those constitutions and forms of government are the best which grow naturally and unconsciously from the historical impulses of the people's life, or which owe their legislative code to the inspiration of some great man who feels himself to be the organ of the divine will, and the embodiment and representative of the national spirit.* Widely different from these are the forms of government which reason has manufactured, weighing and balancing everything, and selecting each conclusion from many equally possible ones.

While we recognize such a necessity as this on every hand, excluding neutrality and all hesitation between opposite courses; it is nevertheless clear that this necessity must in the main be regarded as FREEDOM. Primarily and originally the real antithesis to freedom—that with which it cannot co-exist in the one Subject at the same time and in the same circumstances—is DEPENDENCE, in so far, of course, as this is not imposed or sanctioned by the Subject himself. But can we discover any such dependence in the mode of action we have been describing? It is not anything foreign to the man, it is his own nature which prompts him thus to choose and decide. This nature of his, indeed, according to which he lives and works, is something fixed—defined in some particular manner in him as an individual, but this distinctiveness constitutes his personal idiosyncrasy. Were he to withdraw himself from this he would regard his true self, his individuality, as if it were not. So far as he determines himself according to this idiosyncrasy, he unquestionably exercises freedom of will, a freedom which consists in the power of the Subject to realize his own nature in his own acts. But in so far as he is controlled and determined by a power foreign to himself, man is not free. In

Inner necessity one with freedom.

---

* Not of the national WILL as some now a-days demand. If we except those eras so seldom occurring in history, when the people are filled with universal enthusiasm for some particular idea, it is a pure fiction to suppose that any nation has anything like one united will, least of all in the matter of legislation. Still one national spirit may live beneath its will and consciousness, and may operate thereupon.

the cases supposed, however, freedom and necessity, I mean inner necessity, are one.

This conception of freedom is to be found even in Spinoza:
Spinoza's view. —*ea res* LIBERA *dicetur, quae ex sola suae naturae necessitate existit et a se sola ad agendum determinatur, Ethices,* pars. i., def. 7.* Not a few in more recent times are content to stop short at this point, fancying that they can zealously maintain the doctrine of freedom, and look down upon the pantheism of substance as quite beneath them.

Let us now endeavour to apply these principles to the sphere of Morals. First, we call an act free which is the spontaneous outgo of the moral nature of the Subject, and embodies the distinctive character of his moral being, whatever this may be. On the other hand, when any one, constrained by some power either exercised or threatened, acts better or worse than his own feelings and intentions prompt, he is not in such behaviour free. This want of freedom, indeed, is never total; a " forced *act,*" strictly speaking, involves a *contradictio in adjecto,* for so far as the constraint goes the Subject is only acted upon, and not an actor; and the depth of the psychological impression produced by the constraint depends somewhat upon the moral condition of the individual. Still, by powerful influences brought to bear upon the sensuous nature, the product, the thing done, may be something deranged or perverted, something different from what the moral nature of the Subject—if suffered to manifest itself without hindrance—would have produced.

Moral reedom.

But it may further be asked, does this *actual moral condition* of the man in any given case correspond with his *true nature* in such a manner that the conduct which without hindrance expresses the

Harmony of will and act with moral nature.

* This *res* is by Spinoza regarded as the only substance, God as *natura naturans,* P. i., prop. xvii., coroll. 2. Compare prop. xxix., schol. Will, on the contrary, be it regarded as finite or infinite, cannot, according to Spinoza, be called free, but is only "a necessary or constrained cause, because it is determined to life and action by another cause." P. i., prop. xxxii.; compare P. ii., prop. xlviii.; P. v., *præfat.* According to Spinoza's mechanical view of the world, determination through something else is to be found everywhere except in God when He is contemplated, not in His manifestations as *natura naturata,* but as *natura naturans.* Will, therefore, according to Spinoza, belongs to the nature of God as little as knowledge; P. i., prop. xvii., schol. prop. xxxi,, xxxii., coroll. 2.

former is the faithful reflection of the latter? At the very outset of our inquiry we found that sin, as a co-determining element of human life, is really a hindrance and disturbance to the realization of man's true nature in its temporal growth. We cannot, therefore, abide by this or that determinate moral condition, as if the unhindered self-manifestation of this were an adequate conception of freedom. The man's conduct, and indeed his actual moral condition—for this usually is the exact counterpart of his conduct, and is embodied therein—must correspond to his true moral nature, if free will in this sense can fairly be attributed to him. Freedom, accordingly, requires that the true nature of the man as a moral personality shall manifest itself without let or hindrance both in will and deed. But evil cannot form part of the true moral nature of man, for otherwise it could not produce any variance in the man himself; neither, therefore, can that nature be an *aequilibrium* between good and evil. Its essence must be moral good only, love to God and harmony with His holy will. Man is not really free if his will be turned away from God, and if he be attracted and influenced by evil—which is alien to his nature—as well as by good. He is not really free indeed if his will be still undecided, morally indifferent, and unbiassed either way. Then only is he in the highest sense FREE when without hesitation *he wills only what is good*, and carries out in action that inner necessity of his nature, which excludes even the thought of the possibility of evil.

Even our ordinary moral judgment, while maintaining the conception of freedom of choice, pronounces it to be by no means the best and most perfect state when man chooses hesitatingly between good and evil, and when a doubtful conflict between these is being waged within. On the contrary, it regards that state to be not only the happiest but the noblest, wherein there is no hesitation—good having become a second nature to the man—wherein he promptly obeys the voice of conscience in will and deed; not as if he were doing something special, but as if it were quite a matter of course to him. And when this state is so perfect that there is no longer any "ought," because our will is so thoroughly one with duty that the state-

(margin note: Freedom identical with holy necessity.)

ments "Do what you like," and "Do what is right," are identical, who will venture to assert that our will is no longer free? We cannot here consider the true idea of freedom as an attribute of the *divine* nature, and as predicated of God. But if (as is certainly so) we must ascribe the highest freedom to the blessed whose redemption is subjectively complete, freedom in this sense must be identical with a holy necessity. We have already seen (vol. i., p. 109) that the essence of Christian virtue, and its ever abiding element, is LOVE. But where is this identity of freedom and necessity so apparent as in love? Whereas, when virtue appears only as submission to the call of duty, is not the possibility of its opposite—of vice—ever side by side with it in consciousness?

With this view of moral freedom, that of Jacobi, which
Jacobi's has so many advocates among rationalistic theo-
view logians, seems essentially to agree. According to it, freedom consists in the will being independent of desire, or, as the same thought has otherwise been well expressed, in the ability to determine oneself according to the principles of reason, unbiassed by sensuous impulses.* Both views coincide in one essential point, namely, that freedom can have nothing to do with evil, but is associated only with good; if freedom be what either the one or the other of these views represents it to be, then evil can have its origin only in the absence of
Differs from freedom, or its limitation. But side by side with
ours. this coincidence there is a difference between these views which is not to be overlooked. The advocates of the latter view fancy that they separate freedom from fellowship with evil by defining it as " independence of sensuous impulses ; " but from what we have already discovered concerning the relation of sin to sensuousness, it is clear that we cannot adopt such a definition. And this latter view differs from our own in another point, namely, in the fact that it usually attributes

* *Ueber die Lehre des Spinoza* (1789), p. xxxvii., xxxviii. Compare *Von den göttlichen Dingen und ihrer Offenbarung* (1811), p. 97. When Jacobi describes his conception of freedom as "the dominion of the intellectual over the sensuous nature," it only shows more plainly (as Schelling rightly thinks) that such a theory may—not only "possibly"—but easily, and with greater definiteness, be deduced from Spinoza himself, *Sämmtl. Werke*, part i., vol. vii. 345. It is evident, from the Appendix to Book II. Chap. ii. of this work, that Kant's conception of freedom, though apparently akin to this, is really very different.

this independence of will, in its relation to desire, to man as he is; whereas the conclusions at which we have arrived oblige us to regard man's independence of the controlling power of desires contradictory to his ideal will, as in man's present state an achievement still to be performed, a conquest still to be made.

The conception of freedom which we have here developed is confirmed by several statements of Holy Scripture. In the New Testament, whenever the terms ἐλεύθερος, ἐλευθερία are applied to the inner sphere of life, they refer to something not possessed by mankind generally in their state by nature, but to a possession which man acquires only by appropriating the blessings of Redemption. The essential thought expressed by the words is the self-dependence of the Christian life as it develops itself from within, its independence of every foreign power, and its superiority to every thing merely outward. But this inward power which frees man from the tyranny of the outward is not a state of mere emptiness, nor a fulness of capricious resolves,—such as that abstract freedom, that unbridled wilfulness which has often borrowed a sanction from its own misinterpretation of the scriptural doctrine of freedom,—it consists in communion with God, wrought by the agency of the Holy Spirit, and in unison with His holy will. This freedom of the Christian, viewed negatively as independence, and in relation to the letter of external law, is called "freedom from the law"—from the outward command, because the man now possesses within himself the germinating principle of universal obedience. This freedom is not attained by a mere γνῶσις (1 Cor. viii. 1-4, 8-13), but by an act of love, and by a self-surrender to God, leading the Christian to minister by self-sacrifice to the welfare of his weaker brethren. We find references to this freedom (regarding which no one besides St. Paul has expressed himself with such force and clearness as Luther) in 1 Cor. x. 29; 2 Cor. iii. 17; Gal. ii. 4, v. 1, 13; 1 Peter ii. 16. We have now, however, to do more particularly with that aspect of Christian freedom which implies the removal of the dominant power of sin. Thus we find it represented in John viii. 32, 36, where the ἐλεύθερος stands in direct contrast with the δοῦλος τῆς ἁμαρτίας (see Rom. viii. 2). Christ tells us that he only possesses this freedom to whom He gives it. In like manner St James calls the law as fulfilled through Christ νόμος ἐλευθερίας (i. 25, ii. 12), because it makes him who obeys it free, liberating him from the servitude of sin.* But this aspect of Christian freedom is closely connected with the other; indeed they reciprocally and necessarily imply each other. The Christian cannot be free from the outward yoke of the law unless he is free from the prevailing power of sin. He cannot be free from the power of sin if the law stands over against him as a merely external authority. The redeemed possess the principle of this freedom already in the conflict of this present life; but it will be experienced in its fulness when the body also shall be delivered from "the bondage of corruption," in the kingdom of glory, Rom. viii. 21, 23. But as freedom from sin is really self-surrender to God, and obedience to His will springing from an inner impulse, the New Testament often describes this state positively as δουλεία τοῦ θεοῦ,—'Ἰησοῦ Χριστοῦ, —τῆς δικαιοσύνης,—and adopts both expressions, side by side, as perfectly compatible, 1 Cor. vii. 22 (ἀπελεύθερος κυρίου—he whom the Lord has liberated from the slavery of sin—is in another sense δοῦλος Χριστοῦ); 1 Peter ii. 16. Now, a power of choice is not thought of in this freedom, but a state of the most fixed and settled decision for God. And the identity of this with the inner necessity of which we have spoken, is ratified by the New Testament doctrine that the true principles of sanctification, if received into the inner life, must necessarily produce corresponding conduct (Matt. vii. 17–20, xii. 33; 1 John iii. 9). This conduct, accordingly, is truly free, and at the same time necessary.

But however profound and suggestive this conception of freedom may be, it is obvious that, taken by itself, it will not suffice for our present purpose, which is to find out the essential condition of the origin of evil in man, or more generally, to discover in beings possessed of personality some condition of sufficient strength and independence to enable them to make an entirely new beginning in action; and thus to exempt evil from the

This view of freedom inadequate for our problem.

---

* Romans vi. 18, 20, 22, does not bear upon this point, because there the words ἐλεύθερος, ἐλευθεροῦν are used in a formal sense, and with reference alike to righteousness and to sin.

divine causation. In order to meet this demand there must (it would seem) be proved to exist in the freedom of the will, some power whereby evil, as well as good, can be produced. But in the above conception of freedom the possibility of evil is excluded.

Those philosophers seem not to have fully weighed the great interests involved in the question here treated of, who will recognize no other kind of freedom save this real freedom, in the view of it which we have given, or in the corresponding description of it as independence of sensuous impulse. If they cannot surrender themselves to the doctrine of Dualism nothing remains for them but to soften down evil so that it may be derived from a necessity in the divine order. We find that Bretschneider, for example, does this, for in opposition to the freedom here required, he makes it to consist " in man's determining himself by the law or will of God," * or as he elsewhere expresses it, " in the power of man to determine his conduct according to the dictates of Reason" (*i.e.*, in distinction from sensuous impulses, vol. ii., p. 19, 20).† But whence comes evil ? Bretschneider answers, " As human reason is not so perfect as the divine, man's will cannot absolutely coincide with God's. Man, therefore, according to the independence (?) with which he is endowed, acts—sometimes in perfect conformity with God's will, but sometimes contrary thereto—through the influences of other impulses, instead of reason,—and this constitutes his unworthiness and guilt." ‡ If the "therefore" in this statement has any force, the only reason for sin would be that man is man and not God, and thus though the word be retained the true conception of guilt is essentially destroyed. In the section " *Ueber die Theodicée,*" sin is more accurately derived from "the gradual development of man towards freedom, " " the product of moral development in its realization—a transition point for virtue—a means towards an end, passing and transitory." § Even when the process of development does not attain to freedom, it still tends thither if we take immortality into the account, for " sin

<small>Bretschneider's doctrine.</small>

---

* *Handbuch der Dogmatik,* vol i., 645 (3rd ed).
† *Ibid.*, p. 407. Here this ability is expressly said to be "one-sided" or partial.
‡ *Ibid.,* 412, 413.
§ *Ibid.,* 639, 640. See his *Grundlage des evang. Pietismus,* p. 424.

viewed objectively and as part of the development ordained of
God, is not evil ; it, equally with obedience, is a path to freedom ;
the only difference being that it leads through thorns, but
obedience through roses, to the final goal."* If we examine
the principle which lies at the basis of this view we are not in
the least surprised to find that this "thorny path" ends, like
Spinoza's doctrine, in the recognition that "sin does not belong
to the act itself, but is merely relative ;" that "in the region of
objective reality an act is neither virtuous nor sinful, but ranks
as cause or effect in the continuous series ;"† but we are
indeed at a loss to understand how a man who has adopted
such a persuasion can take the field in behalf of Theism and
Morality against pantheistic philosophy.

§ 2. FORMAL FREEDOM. Now there is another view of man's moral freedom, as deeply rooted in our common consciousness as it is ratified on scientific principles, which seems fully to meet the want left unsatisfied by the conception of it which we first described. Freedom may be regarded as that power of choice between good and evil which essentially belongs to human nature ; or, as it may otherwise be expressed, it is essential to freedom that the act called free might either have been left undone or might have been substituted by another, even the opposite, and that the choice between these possibilities rests solely with the acting Subject. The essence of this conception of freedom is the exclusion of necessity, inward as well as outward. It is not so contradictory to this view as some fancy, to speak of a freedom towards evil alone, or towards good alone, because even in such cases a power of choice and decision rests with the individual in particulars, and between various alternatives equally possible (*libertas specificationis*). It is beyond doubt, however, that this view of

---

* *Handbuch der Dogmatik*, 642. Accordingly this theologian describes sin to be "the pains of travail by means of which morality is born," p. 640 ; whereas Holy Scripture teaches that the pains preceding the birth of true piety are the godly sorrow for sin and conflict against it, which are included in the word μετάνοια, and that *death* is the only product of the travail pains of sin, James i. 15.

† *Ibid.*, p. 641. Notwithstanding all this, Bretschneider does not hesitate in other places (*e.g.*, vol. ii., p. 7), to make human freedom,—or the "self-power" of man (p. 21), which is only another name for formal freedom,—the basis of accountability and guilt. (We have noticed this already in vol. i., p. 350.)

freedom is of significance chiefly in relation to the antithesis of good and evil, and philosophy takes cognizance of it only as it in any degree throws light upon the moral dualism traceable in human life.

This conception of freedom does not seem to be confirmed by Holy Scripture as fully as is the other. The circumstance that Scripture does not designate the power of choice between good and evil by the term *freedom* is of but little importance; without using the name it may furnish instruction concerning the thing itself, concerning the nature of this power and its bearing upon the origin of sin. But we seek in vain for any such express instruction. Yet even this may be accounted for from the practical character of the Gospel which, as it finds man already the slave of sin, does not first offer to him the choice between good and evil, but brings to him redemption from the sad consequences of a perverted choice. It constantly appeals to the consciousness of guilt in man as an undeniable fact of his inner life, and it leaves it to the further development of Christian thought to show what this consciousness of guilt necessarily presupposes. This is nothing less than that *freedom of will*, in virtue of which alone man can be the responsible author of his own sins; and all those particulars of Scripture teaching which (as we saw in Book I., part ii.), confirm the truth of our consciousness of guilt are at the same time proofs of this conception of freedom. In this sense we maintain with Nitzsch that the Gospel affords the strongest testimony to the fact of that original freedom in the possession of which God created man.*

<small>Implied only in the Gospel.</small>

But if a direct confirmation of this conception of freedom in Holy Scripture be asked for, we may find the clearest recognition of it in the account of the Fall in the book of Genesis. Not only the command which preceded the Fall and the punishment which followed, but the transaction itself, the reaction against the temptation to disobedience in the clear consciousness of the divine command, and the committal of the sin notwithstanding this, presents man to us as a being endowed with the power of choosing between good and evil. But Holy Scripture, while in announcing redemption it teaches the fact of a relative enslavement of the will

<small>Direct scripture proof.</small>

* *System der Christl. Lehre*, p. 217 (ed. 6).

through sin, nevertheless recognizes this freedom of choice as still existing variously even in man's present state. It does this in *the Law*, not only in the fact that it contains commands and prohibitions, with promises to the obedient and threatenings to the disobedient, but also by its express witness that the choice between obedience and disobedience, between life and death, rests with man himself, Deut. xxx. 15, 16. In the dispensation of *redemption*, moreover, mention is made of a willingness and a seeking on man's part, be it nothing more in its true essence than a willing self-surrender to the Father's "drawing" to the Son, a non-resistance of divine grace, John vi. 44; Rom. ix. 16; as a necessary condition of its efficacy, *e.g.*, Matt. vii. 7, xi. 12; Luke xi. 1–13; Heb. iii. 8. The *in*efficacy also of God's offers of salvation is attributed to the unwillingness of man, Matt. xxiii. 37; John v. 40; Acts vii. 51. It may not be superfluous to observe, moreover, in opposition to the theory of a mechanical determination, that Holy Scripture variously recognizes man's freedom of choice in the outward sphere of life, but we need not stay to adduce proofs of this here.

The conclusions thus arrived at involve us in serious difficulties. These two conceptions of freedom seem mutually to exclude one another, so that if the first, which we may call REAL, as denoting the unity of the will with its true ideal—be predicated of man, the second, which may be designated FORMAL, must be denied him; and *vice versa*. And yet we feel obliged to maintain both views; the first, because it embodies the true self-dependence of our spirit, its independence of every foreign power; and the second, because our consciousness of guilt and our faith in God's holiness demand it. Without the first, we cannot understand the possibility of the perfecting of human nature in Christ or in ourselves; if we give up the second, we cannot explain our present condition and life. Herbart, for example, will have it, that "freedom must be only in good company,"* *i.e.*, in association only with what is good, and this may seem quite logical upon the principle of determinism, so far as he takes pains (in his way) to adopt this conception; but the problem before us

<small>These two views seem contradictory.</small>

<small>They must be reconciled.</small>

---

* *Zur Lehre von der Freiheit des menschl. Willens*, p. 41, 42.

FORMAL AND REAL FREEDOM.

is wholly unsolvable unless freedom be allowed also to choose bad company. Hence we find that both these views of freedom are usually recognized even in profound and important treatises upon the doctrine of human liberty, without the contradiction between them being solved or even attempted to be solved.* Even in Schelling's work, wherein the power of doing either good or evil is made the real and vital conception of freedom, true freedom is further on explained as identical with holy necessity; and yet the contradiction thus involved is left unexplained. Let us now inquire—how are these two apparently contrasted conceptions of freedom to be harmonized?

Views of formal freedom irreconcilable with real freedom. The *formal* conception of freedom has undeniably been explained frequently in such a manner as to exclude all possibility of reconciling it with what we have termed the *real* conception of it. The freedom of the will has been made to consist in the independence of its several acts,—which must be wholly uninfluenced by anything objective,—and in a perfectly spontaneous and absolutely primary movement of the will itself; and this can take place only when the willing Subject resolves upon the unrestrained exercise of his will, and becomes conscious of it. In this he is supposed to find his highest satisfaction, for " man's will is his heaven." For a being who is free, there is literally nothing which proclaims itself to consciousness as in and for itself

---

* Among modern writers, this remark applies, *e.g.*, to KANT in his *Religion innerhalb der Grenzen der blossen Vernunft*, compared with his *Grundlegung zur Metaphysik der Sitten*, and with his *Kritik der praktischen Vernunft;* and to DAUB in his "*Darstellung u. Beurtheilung der Hypothesen in Betreff der Willensfreiheit.*" Attempts at reconciliation may be found in BAADER, *e.g.*, a few hints in various parts of his *Fermenta Cognitionis*, and more fully in his lectures on Speculative Theology; in J. H. FICHTE, in his "*Sätzen zur Vorschule der Theologie;*" in FISCHER in his work "*Die Freiheit des menschl. Willens im Fortschritt ihrer Momente dargestellt*," (1833), in his *Metaphysik*, and especially in *Der Untersuchung über den spekulativen Begriff der Freiheit* (see Fichte's *Zeitschrift für Philosophie und spekulative Theologie*, vol. iii. part i.); in PASSAVANT in his treatise *Von der Freiheit des Willens und dem Entwickelungsgesetze des Menschen* (1835); in WEISSE in his *Abhandlung über die drei Grundfragen der gegenwärtigen Philosophie* (see Fichte's *Zeitschrift*, vol. i. part 2); in GOSCHEL's dissertation "*Erstes und Letzes*" (Bauer's *Zeitschrift für spekulative Theologie*, vol. i. part 1) in BILLROTH, in his posthumous *Vorlesungen übe Religionsphilosophie* (1837). It will appear, as we proceed, that the view developed in this chapter and the next chiefly coincides with that of Baader, Fichte, and Fischer.

VOL. II. B

good and necessary ; to begin with, all is indifferent and undetermined ;—free will must itself decide what it will prefer, and how much this is to be valued. Accordingly, it does not decide to choose anything because it is good, but the thing is good because it chooses it. It sets before itself definite aims so as to exercise its unbounded power in single acts, but the only quality attaching to these aims is, that the will appoints them. This free action of the will, being the exercise of its power of limitless self-determination, is its own absolute end.

It cannot be denied that this is the import of Archbishop King's theory in his treatise (before referred to), *De Origine Mali.** The above propositions are in substance to be found in his work, in the same or similar words ; this, for instance, is the oft-repeated affirmation of King —*non eliguntur res, quia placent, sed placent quia eliguntur.*

King's De Origine Mali.

But all objective moral truth seems thus to be lost in the void of irrational arbitrariness, for freewill uses its power in the choice of what we call evil as well as of what we call good ; and the subjective satisfaction to which this Eudaemonistic theory reduces everything must apparently be the same whichever choice be made.

The singular way in which King endeavours to avoid these inferences, without surrendering his principle of the absolute worth of a freedom indifferent as to the objects of its choice and choosing purely of its own accord, is worthy of remark, inasmuch as it anticipates in some respects Kant's theory as to the foundation of the moral law. King allows that God only can possess this

King's way out of the difficulty.

---

* We find this conception of freedom, as the strictest Indifferentism, coming up every now and then even in modern literature. Thus Bockshammer's doctrine of freedom inclines this way in some points, without, however, adhering to it or carrying it through. That freedom which involves the possibility of evil, it is said, must be man's highest good, and the independent development of his moral nature (independent in a strictly formal sense) is said to be the highest goal towards which creation strives. (See his treatise *Die Freiheit des menschl. Willens*, pp. 111, 137, 139.) Augustine controverts this doctrine very fully in his Antipelagian writings, especially in his *Opus imperf. c. Jul.*, and more concisely in his *Enchiridion*, § 105. Corresponding with this view of freedom we have Bockshammer's very strange opinion that if the possibility of relative badness (moral evil) were to be avoided, man would be nothing more than a thing absolutely bad, a machine destitute of all moral qualities, p. 139.

indifferent freedom, and even He only *in prima electione* (as King further limits it, illogically indeed, but unavoidably, if he is to allow any reason in the world's government); all subsequent decisions of will being determined by their necessary connection with the first. God bestows this freedom upon man also, but with certain limitations, to the end that man may have something *in quo sibi placeat* by way of indemnification on account of the constraints which material things impose on his mental and bodily power. Now as the freedom of the will appears in its most glorious form, and secures to man the highest satisfaction, if in the face of other impulses it manifests itself as the sole determining power, there must be LAWS which are contrasted with the impulses of nature.*

The contradiction in which King is thus involved is clear as daylight. For if the will be free so far only as there is no distinction as to value in the things from which it chooses apart from its choice, the moral law, being in itself good and regulating the will, so far as it is known, must destroy the freedom of the will, equally with any distinctions as to value among the objects of desire previous to choice. The principle logically allows indeed that the number and variety of possible objects for the will's choice may be limited; but it requires that so far as its choice extends all these objects must be of indifferently equal value. Starting from this conception of freedom as indifferentism in the objects of choice, the absolute standard of morality (as Baur rightly remarks†) can only be in the Subject himself. It is

Contradiction here.

* *De Origine Mali*, cap. v. sec. 1, especially p. 145 of the Bremer ed., 1704. Leibnitz gives a lengthened criticism of King's doctrine of freedom in one of the Appendices to the *Theodicée*. See also Sigwart, *Das Problem von der Freiheit u. der Unfreiheit des menschl. Willens, Tubinger Zeitschrift für Theologie*, 1839, part iii. p. 43, f.

† *Der Gegensatz des Katholicismus und Protestantismus*, p. 128, (2d Ed.) Among the Schoolmen, Duns Scotus and his followers made the essence of freedom, divine as well as human, to consist in the perfect arbitrariness of the act; see his *Commentaries* on the Sentences of Peter Lombard, lib. ii. dist. 25, qu. 1; and vol. i. p. 97, of this work. There is a general similarity between the theory of the Anglican bishop and that of Duns Scotus, especially in their conception of divine freedom. King's principle *res placent quia electae sunt*, corresponds with that of Scotus, *omne aliud a Deo ideo est bonum quia a Deo dilectum et non e contrario*. Both recognize, in addition to a divine will, a divine intellect which presents to the will an infinite number of objects, but does not

evident that there can be no transition from formal freedom, as thus defined, to that which we have designated real freedom.

Fundamental error of this theory. This conception of human freedom, which supposes it to imply Indifferentism in the things chosen, errs mainly in confounding the objective and subjective value of the possible objects of our will. The human will can indeed take that which is really the most degraded and the worst, to be, according to its own estimate, the noblest and the best, if only it contemns all that is truly good, and gives itself up as it feels inclined to desires which demand momentary gratification, and which often, as by a kind of fascination, are even bent upon what can only displease and disappoint. Thus there resides in it a power by its own perversion gradually to destroy even in consciousness the perception of truth. Discovering thus a *self-perversion* of the will, we already recognize that, prior to its decision, things are not indifferent and undefined, but that there exists an objective law of excellence to which the will ought to attach itself, and which it ought to make its own.* Freewill may now and then assert itself as a capricious unreasoning wilfulness, claiming immunity to be "*chimerique,*" as Leibnitz aptly expresses it,† but this must not be taken as the true conception of will.

Another form of this conception of freedom, technically described as arising from an *aequilibrium* of things, represents the will as receiving before its decision the solicitations of motives both on the side of good and on the

Libertas aequilibrii.

---

in the least determine its choice, for these objects are alike indifferent previous to choice. This Indifferentism in relation to human freedom was advocated by Molina and his followers, in opposition to the strict Augustinian method, and in Jesuitical morality bore its natural fruit in the dialectic longing, to undermine as much as possible the objectivity of the moral law, and to bring it within the range of subjective preference.

* While adopting a totally different theory of free will, Baur falls into the same confusion as King, when he asserts that every view which finds the ultimate ground of man's decision for good or evil in his power of self-determination, must lead to the conception of freedom as Indifferentism, and in the end to a merely subjective standard of morality. What he advances in justification of this assertion, in answer to A. Günther's acute criticisms (p. 177–180), by no means obviates these.

† *Theodicée,* p. 1, § 48. The passage is primarily directed against Molina's view of freedom.

side of evil, these being already determined as to their respective worth; but it maintains that, generally, in order to a free decision of will, these opposite motives must be equally balanced, like equal weights in a pair of scales, so that pure will, alone and of itself, may turn the balance. Now, as this view represents formal freedom thus described, to be the inalienable possession and distinguishing dignity of man, it must clearly be the task of will ever to keep itself in the balance between good and evil, or at least, after each decision, to return again to that *aequilibrium*. This doctrine of formal freedom, accordingly, cannot be reconciled with *real* freedom.

We need not pause here to prove at length that even if man were possessed of such a freedom he could exercise it only seldom, and by leave of circumstances, so that he would not be really free. If it be not resolvable into that other conception of freedom as Indifferentism, it could be realized only when at the same moment different motives influenced and urged the will with equal force to contradictory acts, so that the strength of the one would counteract and nullify that of the other.

This also untenable.

To this result is that abstract view of freedom driven which regards the will (though it is really active only when one with consciousness) as separated from all elements of sensation, perception, motive, and impulse, and yet as bound, if there be a preponderance of these on either side, to a decision in accordance therewith. And how can we possibly regard a freedom, the essence of which consists in maintaining an *aequilibrium* between holy and unholy impulses, and an independence alike of God's service and the servitude of sin, as man's highest honour, and a proof of his kinship and affinity with God ? If man possesses a faculty, one side of which is the ability to place himself in a negative relation to God's commanding will, such a power can contribute to the high position which raises him infinitely above all earthly existences known to us, not for its own sake, but only on account of its connection with another ability, the ability of attaining real freedom by making God's will his own.

As we are now endeavouring more correctly to define the

true conception of formal freedom, we may appropriately begin with considering the ordinary meaning of the language used regarding it. We describe that man as free who *can do what he wills.* That will therefore is free which is not hindered, whatever its purpose may be in its realization, but which can carry itself through. The will first readily seeks that its freedom in the sphere of the external, and yet it would maintain its independence of the external; it desires things as well as persons wholly to submit to it. But quite apart from any really moral estimate of this desire, experience and reflection soon teach any one susceptible of them, that there is another sphere still closer to him wherein he must maintain his freedom of will, namely, the sphere of his own inward being. He cannot conceal from himself the fact that the power of his will externally viewed is very limited, and that his success in making the circumstances and relations of the outer world correspond to his will, or in making it independent of them, depends very much upon his giving full effect to his will in the inward sphere. It is therefore a great matter to make the powers and activities of this inner sphere as subservient as possible to the will, so that in its self-determination, be it a decision concerning a particular act or a prevailing habit, all elements of the spiritual and psychical life may easily concentrate themselves thereto. In this sense, that will is denominated free which possesses this power over the inner sphere, so that no hindrance obtrudes itself on the perception of the person who wills.

The strength of the will is thus its freedom. Outwardly, this freedom manifests itself in the will being unobstructed and unfettered by external things and outward circumstances, in its power to choose its objects, so that its being determined thereby, is simply the reflex of the self-determination whereby it has intrusted its interests to them. It is evident that this freedom is capable of development and growth. Still it possesses no positively *moral* import; strength of will, the foundation of what we usually call character, may manifest itself in a perverted direction equally as in a just and true way. Indeed, it is often the sign of something better in a man, when his will or resolve encounters inner checks, preventing the full execution of his purpose; though strictly speaking, in such a case, the will is [divided against itself, and works in two different directions.

What man really desires and likes in this freedom, is obviously the highest possible self-assertion. The more the determining power of his will is hindered in its realization, by a power apparently foreign to him, the less does the man feel that inner self-assertion of the *ego*, without which he would not be a personal being. The more his will determines itself, both externally and internally, the more vivid will be his self-consciousness. But, if he more closely analyses this his self-consciousness, he must ere long be convinced that the decision of the question, whether such an independent self-assertion belongs to him, lies deeper still. In this question concerning freedom, the will has been hitherto regarded as already possessing some bias in its activity, and as already inwardly determined; the further question therefore arises, whether man in this self-determination of will is truly himself, *i.e.*, whether this self-determination of will be *the necessary consequence* of something present to him yet independent of him, or whether he has *the power of refraining from it*, or 'avoiding it. In this latter case only can he be regarded as the author of his own decisions and acts; while in the former case, he must look upon himself merely as the medium or instrument of an anterior cause, which appoints that whereby his will is necessarily determined. This is the very kernel of the question, wherein the contrast between formal and real freedom first obtains significance. That freedom of will, on the contrary, which consists merely in its power to realize its resolve as (so to speak) perfectly presupposed, seems, even though this realization may have to do only with the inner sphere of life, to be relatively external and remote from our investigation. It is freedom in its source, and not in the mere carrying out of the act of the will, with which we have immediately to do.

<small>Freedom is the assertion of self.</small>

Will, as we have already seen in the first chapter of the first book, is conscious self-determination, the self-determination of an *ego*. As there is no real exercise of will while self-consciousness still slumbers, so

<small>Will is conscious self-determination.</small>

there is no real self-consciousness without the exercise of will. *Self-consciousness* and *self-determination* appear together, as if by magic, in one and the same moment. When therefore modern philosophers, *e.g.*, Weisse in his work *Idee der Gottheit*, and elsewhere, attribute to the unconscious child, nay, even to the embryo in the womb, a power of will and of action through the will, they are certainly right in regarding the soul, or life, as active and productive even in its unconscious existence, and as effective, even according to its distinctive individuality, in the formation of its body. But this is not an action of *will*, but only a spontaneous impulse, a plastic power of nature in the soul, which, like any other impulse, is in its silent working subject to natural law.

Does the freedom then which makes man the responsible author of his actions consist in the bare fact that the will is *self-determination?* We cannot deny that inferior existences in nature possess a certain self-determination, so far at least as they are gifted with organic life. The plant develops itself from within, and has within itself, and not from without, the [positive source of its growth —*e.g.*, in putting forth leaves and blossoms; these are, to a certain extent, determinations which it gives itself. Nevertheless this development is associated with an invariableness of nature, and this self-determination resolves itself into submission to determinate law. Self-determination, however, in the true sense of the word, is to be found only in the sphere of spirit, for here only is there a real *self* or personality. But this self may be regarded as determinate being; indeed we can regard it in no other way at any given point of its existence. And if its self-determination is only the necessary action and consequence of this determinate being, we cannot trace therein any true freedom. There may still be recognized a continual realization of self, necessarily involving a self-alteration. We must take it for granted that the things external to the Subject, so varied and changeable, excite and impel continually to new self-determinations; and that the determinateness of self resulting therefrom is the combined product of those external excitements and of self-determination;—a product wherein the given determinateness of self now embodies itself.

Freedom is the predicate of will.

Is *consciousness*, then, to be regarded as that element of will which elevates self-determination to the rank of freedom? But the point in question is whether the consciousness of self-determination, if it be only consciousness, is not itself a mere self-delusion. Were it only the knowledge of becoming determined, could this mere knowledge transform necessity into freedom? Certainly not. On the contrary, the consciousness of this necessity, if it did not include the pledge of its removal, would only double its fettering power, by giving up to its dominion a new sphere of human nature, namely, self-consciousness. Conscious self-determination is only a matter of experience, a psychological fact; freedom is a conception of far higher import.

Self-consciousness not freedom.

Hence it follows that it is not a mere abstraction, but a well-grounded distinction, if we regard *freedom* not as something included in the idea of will, but as something which will may be destitute of, without ceasing to be *will*. We can easily understand how theories which resolve freedom into a speculative Determinism abide by the identity of the conceptions "will" and "freedom;" that which distinguishes freedom as something higher than a mere form of volition is not recognized in such systems of logical necessity.* But Holy Scripture, the Christian Church, and experience alike speak of an enslaved will, *servum arbitrium*. The will which cannot by its own energy withdraw itself from the prevailing power of sin, and when temptation comes cannot withstand it, is morally destitute not only of real, but even of formal freedom. If there be in such a person a volition which resists the prevailing power of sin, though it be only a *velleitas* which cannot realize itself, such as is described in Rom. vii. 14-24 he will feel the want of freedom as a heavy burden; just as the sick man feels pain so long as his bodily organism reacts against the prevailing power of the disease. If again that

Distinction between will and freedom.

Enslaved will.

---

* This we find in the theory developed by VATKE in his oft-quoted work "*Die menschliche Freiheit*," &c., in which he follows HEGEL, especially § 4–28 of the *Rechtsphilosophie*. As here in the Determinism of absolute logic, so also in SCHLEIERMACHER's Determinism of absolute causality, we have in substance the denial of freedom, and hence arises the assertion that a will which is not free, is inconceivable. See Schleiermacher's "*Abhandlung über die Erwählungslehre*," p. 83.

resisting volition disappears, and the will resigns itself wholly to the sway of selfishness, the man will no longer feel the slavery of sin, but though his volition assents to it, it is only on that account the more really present. The *voluntarium* remains, but the *liberum* is lost. It is a bold yet perfectly justifiable expression of Augustine's when he speaks of a "*servum propriae voluntatis arbitrium.*"

What properly constitutes formal freedom is the power of resolving and of acting otherwise. If the will ultimately possesses the power or ability of determining in a way different from that in which it does determine, the person who thus wills is free, and in his volition he is quite himself, his self-determination cannot be resolved into a mere *being determined*.

TRUE ESSENCE OF FREEDOM.

In the older metaphysics "contingency" was usually considered necessary to freedom of action, understanding thereby nothing more than that the agent must possess the power of acting differently. And so far as formal freedom may be predicated of single acts, it is certainly right thus to define freedom. But they who take freedom to be only the self-development of the individual, and his activity from within outwards, and who recognize it wherever one individual is not determined by another, will not allow anything like contingency in freedom. With them the negation of compulsion, of any external determining power, suffices to constitute freedom; the negation of inner necessity they do not consider at all requisite. Now the old word for contingency in German was "*Zufälligkeit,*" and here we have an ambiguity in our language which has often led to misunderstandings and false inferences in discussing the nature of freedom. In ordinary conversation, and in philosophical language too, *zufällig* ("fortuitous"), is now used to describe an occurrence which is beyond the range of rational sequence. It denotes the adventitious appearance of an unlooked-for and unmeaning element in the definite and advancing course of our life towards its goal. No one can prevent such an element, and if it be only the trivial unintentioned concurrence of unimportant circumstances it is not usually noticed. But if it gains ground,—if it exercises a powerful influence on human affairs,—it produces

Meaning of "Contingency" as applied to freedom.

Meaning of "fortuitousness."

an uncomfortable impression upon the man whose highest aim is to hold all the conditions of his development within his own power, threatening as it does to make all reasonable planning of our conduct a matter of indifference and utter uselessness, and to involve our future path in impenetrable darkness. But this groundlessness of "fortuitousness" cannot mean that the fortuitous event has no producing cause. In such a case "fortuitousness" would be an absurd notion, and would denote only a subjective ignorance of the cause. What the "fortuitous" seems to want is not an efficient cause, but a final cause; it has a teleological, *i.e.*, negatively teleological—reference; it violates the sequence of our intentions and plans, so far as this sequence is within our calculation. It is evident, therefore, that the conception is merely relative; what we take to be a fortuitous event may in the view of an all-seeing Intelligence be serviceable to some definite end.

Now can we fairly apply this conception of "fortuitous" to human action, and use the word to describe man's freedom or power of choosing otherwise? They alone do so who would depreciate the freedom of the will, and give it a bad name; for who could think much of an ability which could only manifest itself in random and objectless acts? There is nothing whatever in the conception of formal freedom to justify such a designation of it. The fact of there being several alternatives does not prevent the will from pursuing a definite end in the choice of one rather than another of these; indeed, we cannot imagine any free volition, either of positive or negative moral import which has not some such end in view. We must, therefore, distinguish between the *contingens* and the *fortuitum*—the ἐνδεχόμενον of Aristotle, from his συμβεβηκὸς —and "the power of being or doing otherwise," from "fortuitousness."

<small>Not the word for freedom.</small>

Now if the moral law as God's will to man is to be realized by him in a free obedience, the possibility of doing otherwise seems to be necessarily implied in this freedom to obey. This power of doing differently is described in relation to the unconditioned rule or law of the will as the *possibility of evil*. The very fact that there is such an unconditional rule for the will, obliges us to give the name of freedom exclusively to that which is in harmony therewith;

<small>Freedom implies the possibility of evil.</small>

yet the possibility of deviation from it—by which man puts himself at variance both with himself and with God—is included in this freedom, for only thus can harmony with the given rule be really free. But this possibility exists only in order that its realization may be continually prevented by the self-decision of man, and that thus it may be wholly done away with even as a possibility. Personal creatures must start from what is relatively undetermined, in order by self-determination and self-decision to put an end to this undeterminateness. The will would not be what, in virtue of its formal freedom it should be, viz., a power of true self-determination, if it could not assert itself in such a manner as to give with unfailing necessity a moral character to each of its acts. The starting-point is a freedom which does not yet involve an inner necessity, but the possibility, of something else; the goal is the freedom which is identical with necessity.

This investigation gives us a provisional insight into the close connection subsisting between the two conceptions of freedom—formal and real, but only a provisional one; the deeper foundation and completeness of it cannot be discovered till the nature of created personality and its relation to God become the topics of our inquiry. Real freedom—the clear decision of man for good which excludes the possibility of evil—could not be conceived of, at least not as freedom, not as the completest, self-assertion and self-realization of man, if it did not spring from formal freedom; this is its essential pre-supposition and condition. But formal freedom has in the sphere of morals no other destination save to pass over into real freedom; the former is the *means* to the realization of the latter as the *end*. If this be so, it is inaccurate to speak of two conceptions of freedom for both are different stages of the same; indeed the first is only a stage which is intended to pass on towards the full realization of freedom. When the will has fully and truly chosen, the power of acting otherwise may still be said to exist in a metaphysical sense; but morally, *i.e.*, with reference to the contrast of good and evil, it is entirely done away.

Formal freedom the means towards real freedom.

In the description here given of formal freedom, we have made use of the term "possibility" in a sense now usually set aside as wholly abstract, denoting thereby the sphere of the barely possible as distinct from that of the necessary or actual. Free self-determination presupposes possibilities which may or may not be realized. The conception of a possibility which stands in this indifferent relation to the actual is of great importance in connection with our theory of freedom.* If possibility be regarded simply as the germ of a determinate reality,—as a potentiality continually passing on to realization,—it is only necessity in disguise. If all the requisite conditions have been fulfilled—for no event springs from one condition merely, but from many—realization must ensue upon this possibility or potentiality, and nothing whatever in such circumstances can ensue but the reality thus defined. If, moreover, possibility be itself the commencement of reality, and in concrete union therewith, the well-known logical definition comes in, viz., that the union of possibility and actualization is necessity. But the freedom of the will necessarily presupposes a *pure* possibility, whose sphere extends beyond what is actually realized,—a sphere, therefore, which cannot include the positive ground or cause of the determinate realization. The will is free, and has power to decide for itself, because other determinations are possible to it besides those which it actually gives itself. This is not the bare logical possibility which denotes what is not contradictory in thought, neither is it that possibility which ever leads on to reality; it is a possibility for the realization of which there is a perfectly adequate condition, namely, the will,—a condition which has it in its power either to leave the possibility as it is, or to realize it in act. We readily grant that such a possibility—distinct from actuality, yet in itself real—cannot be transferred to other spheres, for it belongs so exclusively to free will, that as will is never found without it it has meaning only for the will, and therefore for the spirit, all whose activity is brought about through the will. Action alone constitutes the transition from this possibility to actuality, there is no other mode of connection. When this possibility

§ 4. MEANING OF POSSIBILITY.

---

* TRENDELENBURG makes an important distinction between the possibility which springs from the ability of the agent, and that which the end virtually determines. See "*Logische Untersuchungen,*" ii. 108. Here we have to do only with possibility of the first kind.

of not being, or of being otherwise, is predicated of the lower animals, where there can be no mention of freedom, the reference must still be to freedom,—to that free will which is the basis of their being, the creative freedom of God.

By ABILITY we understand (as the ordinary derivation of the German *Vermögen* from *Möglichkeit* shows) possibility placed in a Subject; or, more exactly, the pure possibility—without a shadow of necessity—of a determinate action, or of any particular mode of action, viewed as an attribute of the Subject. Thus understood, the term belongs in the strictest sense to the freedom of the will. But it is evident from this very definition that we must not attribute to this ability any impulse towards the realization of all that is contained in it, still less to the Subject of it the task of carrying into action all its possible tendencies, as they may be present to him. We must, therefore, distinguish between ability and natural bent or disposition. The latter denotes a positive tendency to certain acts, an impulse to carry certain desires into effect; and if in the development of the character these corresponding activities are not realized, this may be explained, apart from external hindrances, by the fact that natural disposition or mental talents may be, negatively at least, suppressed through the ability belonging to free will, which thus can prevent their development.

Meaning of "Ability."

Meaning of "disposition."

At this point of our inquiry a question may be answered which perplexes some, through their taking too narrow a view of the conception now under discussion; it is this,—Does CHOICE (*i.e.*, an act of choosing) belong to the essence of formal freedom?

Three things are to be distinguished among the requirements of formal freedom.* The first is the objective presence of plurality of possibilities for the self-determining will. The second is the consciousness of these various possibilities, either before, or in the act of deciding. Besides this mere consciousness, the third implies an actuating influence of these various possibilities upon the will; it is a wavering and hesitation between opposite

Elements of formal freedom.

---

* A fourth, which in this series should come first, viz., that the Subject willing, should have a glimmering, however illusory, of other possibilities, need not be considered here, seeing that it is only an illusory representation that is spoken of, though some think that this is sufficient to constitute freedom.

determinations, which generally precedes the good or evil decision. We have already seen that there can be no freedom without the first of these. But are we to regard the third, wherein the mere presentation of one and another possibility becomes a bias in different directions, and thus divides and perplexes the mind, as an integral part of formal freedom? What is there to warrant our so regarding it? An undecided vacillation and wavering of mind certainly is not anything done, it is not an act of will, but a state which is not free, a state in which the man is being determined, and which he must put an end to and negative by a free act of will. Free self-determination is, I say, the negation of this state of indecision. How can this undecided wavering between opposite impulses, which is to be removed by deciding, be considered as an element of the freedom of the will? What sort of freedom would that be, every exercise of which necessarily included a preceding dependence upon, and perplexity concerning the objects presented? If we refer the question to the sphere of morals, and suppose that such a wavering between good and evil previous to self-determination belongs to freedom, then an element of evil would necessarily pertain to freedom, and so far as this freedom was divinely ordained, God would be made the author of evil; for this wavering of the will would clearly witness to its having some inclination to evil. The representations derived from the analogy of the balance, which in early times Julian, and in modern days Wolf, made use of in order to illustrate the nature of this formal freedom, and to which Baur in combating this freedom would bind it,[*] should be altogether banished from the mind in considering the matter. Analogies from the sphere of mechanics are least of all suited adequately to illustrate mental phenomena, and it is evident from our investigation thus far concerning freedom, that this comparison of the balance is particularly inapt to illustrate the self-determining power of free will; strictly taken it leads, on the contrary, to Determinism.

The second requirement.   It might seem as if we did not need the second requirement—the consciousness of different possi-

---

[*] *Der Gegensatz des Katholicismus und Protestantismus*, p. 127, f., and elsewhere. See also Mr. J. S. Mill's *Examination of Sir W. Hamilton's Philosophy*, p. 519.—*Tr.*

bilities—in order to formal freedom; and that the objective presence of such possibilities is sufficient. No one would on this principle hesitate to attribute this freedom to an action, though rash resolve and enthusiastic devotion to any definite aim had excluded all consideration of other possibilities. Confining our thoughts to any one particular act, this is quite true; we supply by our knowledge the representation of another possibility which is not really present to the consciousness of the actor. But if this freedom is predicated of will, or of conscious self-determination, the objective ability of doing something else which it involves must, generally speaking, be recognized by the Subject himself,—though this need not necessarily occur in every particular act.

Some will recognize a free choice only where not merely a negative state of not being decided, but a definite state of indecision between conflicting alternatives precedes the decision or resolution of doubt. Thus viewed, freedom of choice must not be identified with formal freedom. The choosing or wavering by which free self-determination is said thus to be guaranteed would really be prejudicial to freedom. But the conception of choice is thus unjustifiably limited. Choice is to be found wherever volition, with the express consciousness of other possibilities, exists. Formal freedom may be identified with freedom of choice in this sense.

Freedom of choice.

We find something analogous to this freedom, a glimmering of it in the dark realm of impersonality, in the playful whims noticeable in the nobler specimens of the lower animals. When we notice these manifold impulses, varying according to the fancy and whim of the moment, we are impressed with the belief, that however mysterious and enigmatical the springs of animal life must be to us, they are not in these cases governed by any inner, any more than by any outward necessity. This power of volition, however, appears in the animal, only as a freakishness when the earnestness of its life momentarily ceases, and thus it bears the character of fortuitousness, and is nothing more than arbitrariness,—not will or freedom which belongs to man alone. In all that pertains to the natural determining of the animal, it obeys, and cannot help obeying, the blind force of

What is analogous to freedom in the lower animals.

instinct. When the object of desire, or the possibility of its satisfaction presents itself, instinct immediately arouses the creature's activity towards it. This irresistible power is not felt by the animal to be something foreign to it, a constraint put upon it, it is its own instinct,—that wherein its nature consists; it has no other inner nature save this instinct leading direct to its object, *i.e.*, it possesses no real *self*. In man, on the contrary, any such force of instinct rousing him to action in order to its satisfaction, is a restraint put upon him, for he is a man in virtue of an inner unity in the depths of his being, an independent centre which subordinates what forms the essence of the lower animals, into a *substratum* out of which he can form for *himself* the instrument of his manifestation, either in good or evil. This centre is the will, and wherever will is, all action must spring from *it*, 'instinct or impulse is no more the cause which produces it; like any other stimulus, it is subordinate to the decision of the will, and when in any case it leads to effort and to action, it does this only through the will. When, therefore, we meet with instances of the force of mere instinct and impulse in human life, *e.g.*, in the ungovernable eagerness with which rude men and savages, when impelled by hunger, will fall upon food when it is presented to them, they awaken in us an uncomfortable feeling of repulsiveness and disgust, which is still very different from our moral feeling of abhorrence at evil itself. It is the temporary obliteration of the line of demarcation between man and the brute, which arouses our feeling of disgust at such sights.

Free will is not a mere agility or quickness of movement; a gymnastic wherein activity and strength are frittered away to no purpose; it is an operating cause, a determining principle. If we would see the workings of this principle, we must look for them (as above remarked) in the inner sphere of life. The most direct and immediate product of will is the moral being of the person who wills, the form of his moral life, the fixed and prevailing tendency of his deposition, his character whether good or evil. Character would be reduced to a mere determinateness of nature and the true conception of it destroyed, had it not as its condition or determining principle the will of the Subject. In the next chapter we shall have to consider more minutely this inner world, and the way in which it springs out of freedom.

As to the causality of the will in the outer world and its power to influence it, it is obvious that it must be limited in a very determinate manner. Were it otherwise, the human will would be almighty, and could exist but in one Subject. The world is not a wholly undetermined material, which had to wait for this single will to give it definiteness and form; this will finds it—not indeed perfect, for it is susceptible of further determinateness,—yet already ordered and fixed in various ways; and thus the will, when it would go forth into the boundless and universal, meets with a thousand restrictions on every hand. If the human will is to accomplish anything in nature, the first condition of its action must be that it attach itself to nature's invariable laws as the rule of its activity. As long as it tries to be unconditionally free, it feels itself fettered on every hand; to enjoy its freedom it must submit to nature's laws.

The power of the will externally limited.

Insane as it would be to deny these limitations, it would be equally impossible to affirm that the human will has no power to realize itself in the outer world, and to determine it as it would not be determined if will were absent. Where in all the world would there be any real power of causation, if the will—having in itself this power, and being in its very nature causality and efficiency—could effect nothing? We must regard all finite causation as a mere pretence, and reduce all personal existence to the lifeless passivity of a huge world-mechanism, if we would destroy will, and deny to it the power of producing by its self-determination any change in the outward world; thus regarding it merely as the conductor of an impulse given it by other springs and wheels of the machine.

But not wholly negatived.

Seeing that the question as to the power of the will to effect anything externally has only a subordinate bearing upon the main topic of our inquiry, we need not here discuss the relation of freedom to, and its effects upon, the general order and course of nature. We may only remark further, that if the Creator has honoured finite spirit by making it the focus of the universe, wherein spirit and nature meet, we may be certain that nature with its

Will must not be subordinated to nature.

FORMAL AND REAL FREEDOM.

laws is ordered accordingly, so that it shall not destroy the free action of the will. At any rate, it is a very doubtful procedure, or a overweening submission of mind to nature, when, in order to preserve intact the order of nature in complete independence, the human mind subordinates itself to nature by denying its own freedom. We have already sunk into the depths of naturalism, when nature and its order are made more sure and unerring than mind in all its dignity and power over nature.

If this conception of freedom can hold its ground against the exceptions of Determinism and of the religious consciousness urging our dependence upon God, it supplies us with the necessary basis which we were seeking on which to rest the undeniable truth of the consciousness of guilt and of the certainty that sin cannot be derived from God. It involves both the power of the will of itself to make a new commencement, and to mould its determinations by its own decisions.

This view of freedom solves our problem.

The elements of the conception of freedom developed in this chapter are to be found in Augustine, though he does not sufficiently perceive their mutual relation, and is consequently inexact and wavering in distinguishing and connecting them. In his polemical works against the Pelagians, and in his letters written about the same time, he uses the expression "free will," *liberum arbitrium* in a threefold sense. First, he means by it freedom in general, a form of spontaneity essentially belonging to the human will as distinct from outward constraint, and from the natural power of animal instinct. This freedom of self-efficiency continues through all states and stages of human life; man possesses it in evil*—so far as this is a matter of will—as well as in good, before the fall, in the fall, after the fall, in redemption—in its beginning and its completeness;—it is in virtue of this, according to Augustine (we do not of course agree with him), that man can charge

§ 5. Augustinian Doctrine.

His first meaning of free will.

* Yet even here Augustine hesitates. In the *Retractationes*, lib. i. c. 15, he considers it safer to call the will of fallen and unredeemed man *cupiditas* rather than *voluntas*, an observation which warrants Möhler's reproof, which does not apply to the reformers, that, according to this representation, "at the fall a piece of human nature must have fallen out."

himself with guilt or acquire merit. But this freedom by no means prevents the power of the most perfect necessity resting upon man as to the essential character of his will and conduct, though this necessity must be carefully distinguished from constraint. In his earlier (*e.g.*, *De Arb. lib.*) as well as in his later works (*e.g.*, often in the *Opus imperf.*), Augustine describes this relation by the example of a general desire for happiness, which is not a matter of constraint, but a prompting of free will, and yet is a necessary feeling. In like manner the sins of the natural man are *voluntaria*, and yet in all his works he cannot do otherwise than sin; so, too, the holiness of the perfected is *voluntarium*, and yet in all the outgoings of his life he cannot be otherwise than holy. Augustine sets forth this view of freedom in the early chapter of his treatise, *De Gratia et Libero Arbitrio*, in the beginning of his work *Contra duas Pelagianorum Epistolas*, and in the first book of the *Opus imperf. contra Julianum*.

Then again, according to Augustine, free will is man's power to decide in the choice between good and evil. He assigns this power to the first man before his fall, without, however, adopting the Pelagian illustration of the *libra*, and their notion of an original inclination equally to both sides. The *liberum arbitrium* involves from the very outset, he allows, the possibility of evil, but this he explains thus:—As man in his higher nature (his soul) is created out of nothing, that spontaneity which is given to him, in order that he may willingly decide upon the good, may turn itself also to the negative of good, to evil.* But Augustine regards this moral alternative originally pertaining to man's free will as by no means a higher attribute, but a weakness and imperfection; and coupling this with his third acceptation of freedom, which we shall presently give, we have the recognition of the doctrine that from the beginning this alternative was destined to be destroyed by the free decision of the will for good and with the *adjutorium* of divine grace—without which,

Second explanation of free will.

---

* AUGUSTINE therefore, like SCHELLING, in his treatise on Freedom, includes the possibility of evil in the freedom of the creature only so far as it has its root in any respect independently of the absolutely holy God; Augustine, however, finds this root according to his negative view of evil, in that negative *nihil*, whereas Schelling finds it in the basis of the divine existence, operating and sending forth, of itself, a fulness of positive determinations.

according to Augustine, the prevalence of this decision would not have been possible. This freedom of will as to its positive side (*i.e.*, the power of the will to determine itself for good), was lost by the fall; what was left is the negative side only, the mere form of spontaneity in evil; and this, together with the freedom assigned to man by Augustine in the reception of irresistible grace, must be resolved into a merely subjective shadow without any effective causality.* Augustine develops this view of freedom chiefly in the sixth book of the *Opus imperf. c. Julianum,* and in the treatise *De correptione et gratia.*

Lastly, oftenest and most readily Augustine explains freedom, Augustine's according to the words of our Lord, "If the Son third view. shall make you free, ye shall be free indeed," as the decision of the redeemed for what is good and holy; which in this present life is still blended with a *posse peccare,* but in a state of perfection is one with a *non posse peccare,* with a *felix necessitas boni,* and thus is raised to the pattern and standard of God's freedom.†

CHAPTER II.

THE FREEDOM OF THE WILL IN MORAL DEVELOPMENT.

NEANDER considers that one of the fundamental principles of Pelagianism was its taking freedom to be "the ability to choose equally and at any moment between good and evil."‡ The emphasis here clearly rests upon the words "equally and at any moment." If we attentively consider what hindered that acute

§ 1. THE PELAGIAN VIEW OF FREEDOM.

---

* See NEANDER's *Church History*, vol. ii. 1302.

† These distinctions in AUGUSTINE's conception of freedom are not done justice to by WIGGERS in his *Versuch einer pragmatischen Darstellung des Augustinismus und Pelagianismus,* pp. 131-138, 178 ; nor in MARHEINEKE's *Ottomar,* pp. 131-173. The distinction between the first and the second view is more fully developed by RITTER in his *Geschichte der Christlichen Philosophie* vol. ii. p. 341-343.

‡ *Kirchengeschichte,* vol. ii. p. 1259.

and earnest inquirer, Julian of Eclanum, from obtaining a clear knowledge of man's present state and his relation to grace and redemption, we shall find that it was this *atomistic* view of the nature of free will. According to it free will is wholly indifferent to its own acts, and is ever ready at any moment of life to incline to one side or the other. This freedom as a perpetual *aequilibrium* or continual oscillation between good and evil is taken to be the true *primum mobile* in man, and does not lose its position till it attain its true goal of holy or unholy resolves; but while everything about it changes it remains unchangeable, a movable and yet immovable *possibilitas peccandi et non peccandi*, deciding everything yet never finally determined itself. Actions are thus regarded as isolated; there is no recognition of that law according to which certain moral states are produced by repeated acts, of that relative power which the will's decisions towards evil possess, to communicate a definite tendency and character to the will itself, prompting it under certain given circumstances and influences to decide in a certain way. Not a word is said about moral development in good or evil, in individuals or the race. We have already indicated the deficiencies of the Augustinian doctrine of freedom, and the most important of these will occupy our attention by and by, but it is decidedly superior to the Pelagian theory, in that it recognizes some impulse towards progress and some sources of development. Pelagius and Julian content themselves with a principle, which if more thoroughly examined in its nature and bearings would certainly have perplexed them in the maintenance of their doctrine of freedom,* but which, being adopted only reluctantly, and held only superficially, exerts no thorough influence,—I mean the principle of habits.†

What this atomistic theory implies, There are many theories concerning the freedom of the will now-a-days put forth very similar to this. It is supposed to be a power ever resident in man, and ever ready equally to choose good or evil, and to make holy or unholy resolves. According to this

---

* *Augustine* notices this clearly in his *Opus imperf. c. Julianum*, lib. iv. c. 103, and elsewhere. Concerning the Pelagian view of freedom see Jacobi, *Lehre des Pelagius*, p. 35.

† *Epist. ad. Demetr*, c. 20, *Opus imperf.*, lib. i. c. 69.

CHAP. II.] FREEDOM OF THE WILL IN MORAL DEVELOPMENT. 39

every man possesses the power at any moment, in virtue of the freedom of his will, to turn aside from sin. Any given person in any given case is said to do good or evil according to the unbiassed preference of his free will at the moment. The immediate consciousness of being able to choose otherwise, which, if it does not accompany every decision, might accompany it, is said to sanction and confirm this notion of freedom. Were the decision held in obeyance for a moment, and the person asked whether this were the only possible course, the consciousness of this ability to choose otherwise would be felt. Thus the facts of our consciousness of guilt and of repentance testify that the acts to which they refer might have been left undone.

Others have shown in various ways the strange and in some respects absurd consequences which this view of freedom involves. It will suffice for us here to enumerate the main objections.

All those endeavours to influence the mind and behaviour of others which form the groundwork of education in the family, of legislation (including punishment for transgression) in the state, of spiritual offices in the church, including religious discourses and homiletics, necessarily pre suppose the possibility of influencing the voluntary decisions of others. When these endeavours are directed to an individual case, or to men collectively, there must be some knowledge of their moral nature, their ways of thinking, their prevailing inclinations and dispositions; and the effort must be shaped and moulded accordingly. But if free will, upon which all morality depends, be regarded as a power essentially indifferent to all motives and determinations, and wholly unbiassed at every point, such endeavours are utterly useless, save as they act upon the understanding—bringing ideas before it and so securing the bare possibility of their being somehow regarded in the self-determining of the will. But there is not the least likelihood that they will effect anything definite; for the decision which has corresponded with them for ninety-nine times may (if the will be unbiassed by them) at the hundredth time fail to exert any influence. The advice to direct our moral influence upon others conformably to their characters is utterly useless; for according to the doctrine in question the

Its logical consequences.

individual's character can never affect the determination of his will, but the will in its decisions must be wholly independent of everything external to it.*

It is further clear that this doctrine of freedom contradicts a conception which life can never be robbed of for the sake of an abstraction, and whose reality is confirmed to us by daily experience,—I mean the conception of CHARACTER. "The tree is known by its fruits;" each of us acts according to his character, and in his acts his character is shown. Character, indeed, does not exclusively consist in a definite tendency of the will; it is also dependent upon the natural disposition and talents of the individual; natural idiosyncrasy and personal volition are internally blended, yet in such a manner that the latter is the governing principle. Will being thus the ruling principle, character is, as Fischer justly calls it, "the formed will," thus presupposing the will's susceptibility of education. But if there be in the will the present only, apart alike from the past and future, if it be essential to it to be wholly undetermined save in the actual deed, and if all the several decisions and acts of the man come forth disconnectedly from the empty void of a neutral freedom, it is in vain to speak of character; man's course of action leads hither and thither as if ruled by chance only; there is no distinctness about it, and it never exhibits any fixed and prevailing bias.

This theory excludes the idea of character.

Such a freedom, accordingly, is quite incompatible with any co-operation among men for a settled purpose. In order to united action there must be mutual confidence among those who combine, that they will act on given conditions conformably to the common end. But upon this theory it is quite uncertain how they will act; the most considerate—if, indeed, we can speak of considerate or inconsiderate in connection with this doctrine of freedom—may suddenly begin to act most capriciously, the end which they now pursue, they may the next moment forego; and the will in its unapproachable freedom may disregard any impulse whether from within or without. If everything depends upon this uncertain and indeterminate freedom which, in co-operation

And of society.

---

* "The doctrine of a motiveless volition would be only causalism." Sir W. HAMILTON, *Appendix to Discussions*, p. 597.—*Tr.*

with others, may just as easily choose the most worthless as the weightiest reasons, the most capricious and arbitrary impulses towards wild and momentary whims are quite as valuable as the wisest and most conformable conduct. It might easily be shown that the maintenance of anything like a society or commonwealth would be utterly impossible upon this view of freedom, for society necessarily presupposes our being able, in some degree at least, to calculate upon human action in given circumstances.

The interests of religion, moreover, are violated by this doctrine of freedom. The efficacy of divine grace, being conditional upon such an arbitrary will, loses all its certitude. We could not reasonably be surprised to find a man who to-day is a regenerate Christian, becoming a reckless villain to-morrow, or the angel before God's throne transformed in a moment into a devil, and *vice versa;* for on the principle of an indifferent freedom, divergence from a chosen path is quite as easy and likely as perseverance in it. This uncertainty, moreover,—making every thing doubtful,—must continue to all eternity; it could only be removed by the destruction of freedom of choice, which belongs not only to the nature of man, but to personal existences generally. Indeed, closely considered, all these conceptions—a state of holiness or of sin, regenerate and unregenerate, angel and devil, God's kingdom and the world's,—lose all their significance, for they imply conditions which depend not upon the determinateness of nature, but upon the permanent decision and prevailing tendency of will, which this theory of freedom denies. Every resolve of the will is said to be an absolute commencement, conditioned by nothing already done. According to this doctrine, moreover, it would be possible, in contradiction of Christ's statement in Matt. vi. 24, to serve two masters (if, indeed, any mention can be made of service), to keep up a continual wavering between good and evil; such a freedom, moreover, would be the very μετοχὴ and κοινωνία between righteousness and unrighteousness, light and darkness, the possibility of which St. Paul denies in 2 Cor. vi. 14.

It destroys the essence of religion,

It is evident, moreover, that on this principle the conception of redemption is explained away. According to it we cannot consistently speak of the need of redemption in any true sense. It would be in

And of Christian Redemption.

every one's power—we cannot say to redeem himself, for this would imply the bondage of the inner life—but to begin from any moment to do only what is holy and right. And all susceptibility of redemption would also vanish if this freedom were to be maintained, because redemption involves the beginning of a state wherein all elements for the development of evil in man are removed, and the good foundation of eternal holiness is laid.

It cannot be denied, indeed, that Determinism is in some respects preferable to this doctrine of freedom, because while it is not more prejudicial to the interests of morals and religion, it is much more in keeping with the interests of science and of practical life.

Determinism preferable to this doctrine;

We do not, however, mean such a Determinism as that, *e.g.*, of the *Système de la nature*, and of La Mettrie's *L'homme machine,* based upon the notion that human conduct is merely the product of external causes working upon the soul. This mechanical view of the world and of the will, which finds determinateness and passivity everywhere, and determining power nowhere, which regards all as a series of transmissions of one primary push or blow, has been once for all overthrown by the principle of "*organism,*" discovered by the more modern philosophy of nature (*Kant's "Kritik der Urtheilskraft"*). No one can any more entertain the notion of putting man on a level with the vegetable world below him.* The knowledge which excludes this coarse determinism is twofold. On the one hand, we recognize a complete whole, consisting of living and mutually dependent parts or members, each one of which is complete in itself, and —while a means in relation to the rest—is at the same time its own end. Above all others, the human individual must be thus regarded as a living member of this great whole. And, on the other hand, we discern a development proceeding from a central source, and everywhere traceable, in relation to which all external forces are not, properly speaking, causes, but only predisposing occasions and instruments of advance. If all

which adopts the principle of organism,

---

* This power which the principle of "organism" possesses in excluding such a doctrine of Determinism is recognized by DAUB in his "*Darstellung und Beurtheilung der Hypothesen in Betreff der Willensfreiheit,*" pp. 74–76—a treatise which does good service to the criticism of all save the highest forms of Determinism.

organic life contains a self-dependent principle, by virtue of which it does not suffer any external influence to operate directly within its own sphere, but first of all takes the external into the depths of its own thought, so that, being transformed and assimilated, it may spring forth anew,—much more must this hold good of spiritual life.

It is further to be observed that this self-dependent distinc-
<small>and of individual character.</small> tiveness manifest in organic nature in the various species, each with its own distinctive character (which cannot be explained as derived from others, nor perhaps from combination of others), appears in the sphere of personal existence as belonging to each individual, forming an element in our conception of personality which even the theories opposed to human freedom cannot ignore, without denying personality, and contradicting the plainest facts of experience. That a person's conduct, under any given circumstances, is not simply the result of the nature which he has in common with the whole species,—that two individuals in precisely the same circumstances, even when the very same representations enter their minds, will nevertheless act very differently,—these undeniable facts must be shown to be reconcilable with any theory of Determinism laying claim to thoroughness. In explaining any individual decision and its source, we must take into account, and indeed as a main factor in our reckoning, the distinctive character of the Subject—especially his determinate bias towards good or evil—and the particular tendencies in which the one or the other bias is apparent.

Recognizing all this, a more refined Determinism supports
<small>How this Determinism explains will.</small> itself on the principle that man when he decides is already decided, and does not act from a spontaneous freedom of choice, but according to his own distinctive individuality—which includes also his moral character, and the particular bias of his will. According to this, his conduct proceeds from himself, in virtue of that self-dependence which belongs to him as an individual; yet at the same time it springs, by strict necessity, from causes which at the moment of choice are beyond his control. Viewed apart from the ever present but ever subordinate influence of outward circumstances, his behaviour is the never-failing

product of the collective character of his inner life. If at the moment when he is called to any decision of the will his whole inner life, in its minutest outlines, were as in a picture unveiled to our view,—his notions of right and wrong, his principles and thoughts, the strength and idiosyncrasy of his affections and desires, his inclinations and prejudices, even the most secret and hardly known even to himself,—we should be able, provided of course that we possessed the requisite judging faculty, to predict with unerring certainty how in any case he would decide.

This is the kind of Determinism which Romang (following Schleiermacher) advocates in his work "*Ueber Willensfreiheit und Determinismus*," 1835, though he sometimes descends to the lower view; and with considerable tact he contrasts this refined and ennobled Determinism with a very crude and vulgar theory of human freedom. Sigwart's acute dissertation concerning the question of the freedom, or otherwise, of human volition,* assumes essentially the same standing-point, and he, too, ignoring the intellectual and ideal view of freedom, combats only the bare atomistic notion of it.

Advocated by Romang and Sigwart.

But if this Determinism is victorious against that doctrine of neutral freedom which we have been describing, can it equally hold its ground against a more refined conception of freedom, which is compatible with the

§ 2. DETERMINISM.

* *Tübinger Zeitschrift für Theologie*, 1839, 3rd part, pp. 1–222. The Dissertation has since been published separately. See also the chapter on "The Freedom of the Will" in Mr. J. S. MILL's *Examination of Sir W. Hamilton's Philosophy*, where this doctrine of Determinism or "invariability" is advocated in contrast only with the crude doctrine of Liberty which Müller here rejects. For instance, "Just so far as the will is supposed free, *that is, capable of acting against motives*, punishment is disappointed of its object, and deprived of its justification," p. 510. Again, "Suppose it true that the will of a malefactor, when he committed an offence, was free, *or in other words, that he acted badly, not because he was of a bad disposition, but for no reason in particular:* it is not easy to deduce from this the conclusion that it is just to punish him," p. 513. The true doctrine of free will Mr Mill seems himself to recognize when he says, "If he could not help acting as he did, that is, if *his will could not have helped it,* it would be unjust to punish him. . . . But if the criminal was in a state CAPABLE of being operated upon by the fear of punishment, no metaphysical objection, I believe, will make him feel his punishment unjust," p. 514.—*Tr.*

indisputable facts of prevailing moral natures, of distinctive dispositions and permanent varieties of character? Before answering this question, we must more closely examine a distinction of great importance in human nature, that, I mean, between the life of the self-conscious spirit and the basis of natural life on which it rests.

This *basis of nature* includes not only the corporeal part of our being, but our psychical life; nay, more, even in the sphere which we usually regard as spiritual in a narrower sense, we find it still in the shape of inborn talents and inclinations, which strive after the attainment of their ends with all the unconscious necessity and unerringness of natural impulse. Before personality awakes, when as yet we cannot speak of any moral volition, this basis of nature may be found; and when the *Ego* is evolved and begins to assert itself, it finds a natural life already in some degree developed, which co-determines its self-consciousness, and presents subject-matter and incitement for the will. This basis of nature, as such, is not only common to man, working alike in all; it may be divided and classified in the narrower spheres of race, and it individualizes itself in different persons. Each one is born not only with the nature common to man, but as this particular man, according to the distinctions of sex, with the impress of some particular race, belonging to a determinate nationality, embodying the type of a particular family in stronger or fainter outlines, distinguished from all other individuals alike by the physical and psychical nature peculiar to him, by certain talents and inclinations, and by his own distinctive organization, which, like an infinitely complicated web, cannot be found in exactly the same form in any one else. This basis of nature, accordingly, may more accurately be called the natural individuality of any one, which, as a living idiosyncrasy and a growing germ enclosing a fulness of distinctive energies and impulses, precedes all activity of consciousness and will. The man when he awakes to conscious self-determination finds himself already in various ways determined, and however great the determining power of his will, it is at least certain that he never can destroy this individual distinctiveness, nor neutralize its progressive development—not at any rate by a single act

[margin notes: Two parts of human nature; 1. The basis of nature. Natural individuality.]

at the outset. Thus the very basis which finite personality requires is at the same time its boundary.

Now if (as some maintain) man's only task be to develop and manifest his own natural individuality, the doctrine of strict naturalistic determinism might justly be embraced. The will would then be nothing more than the form in which what was already inwardly determined (developing itself like all organic life) realizes itself outwardly; —the necessary evolution of individuality, in order to leave its impress on some other being. But it is obvious, that we cannot in this sense speak of a natural *basis;* the basis is no longer basis simply, when it is made the all in all. This way of thinking recognizes nothing but nature, and, doubtless in a very intellectual manner, denies intellect altogether. A more enlightened determinism will recognize a moral and religious task assigned to man, over and above the mere manifestation of his natural individuality, and thus will allow the self-dependent significance of his will. The natural foundation of our higher self-consciousness does not in this case set itself up in opposition to the will, as if it were something already perfect, fully determined and inaccessible to the will's power, but only as a delineation in outline of a full human individuality. The will, instead of being the mere instrument of natural individuality, becomes the co-determining principle of its development, by the direction which it takes, and according to the energy with which it asserts its resolves. It cannot perhaps change the main outlines, but the full realization of the character delineated cannot be attained without it. Thus, the spirit as will, is in this respect, and within certain limits, lord even of the natural life.

Now, above this basis of nature, yet in intimate connection with it, stands man's highest development as a *moral* being. This sphere includes his relation to God in knowledge and action, and, springing therefrom, the relations in which he stands to the world, to mankind and nature. This development is essentially nothing more nor less than the development of the human will. Here it is that we must look for freedom; not in any one isolated act or decision, but in the process of moral growth, in the living movement of this development. It is, in the highest sense of the term, *self*-development, *i.e.*, development by free self-determination. Freedom is power *to become*—to form one's own character—out of self.

Character formed by will.
If we contemplate man at the moment when he decides upon any action of moral import, we must allow that he is even here to some extent already determined as to his moral nature, and it is very easy for Determinism to show that pure self-determination from what is wholly undetermined is not to be met with. But so far as the moral life is thus already determined, it refers us to a former self-determination as its cause. The powers to which the will consents, in turn act upon it; if it confirms the effects of their action upon the inner life, they begin to take possession of it, and inclination thus gradually becomes disposition. But upon the relation in which the will stands to this gradually formed disposition (for its self-movement and self-determining are by no means resolved into it)—whether it always surrenders itself to the power to which it is most inclined, or whether side by side with this inclination, there is in it an endeavour in a contrary direction,—upon this depends the ease or difficulty, the quickness or slowness, wherewith these or those dispositions of whatever kind take root in it, and obtain full sway. If therefore, in any given case, a person acts conformably with a settled disposition, we have only to look beyond the present act, and to review the course of his past moral development, in order to see that the act in question, though necessarily following from that disposition, must still be regarded as free. Character is certainly a principle or cause of single determinations of will, but viewed as to its origin, it is itself the *result* of determinations of will. Character is never innate, it is something gradually formed, and its formation depends upon the free decisions of the as yet unbiassed will, " The corrupt tree," says our Lord (Matt. vii. 19, 18), " bringeth forth bad fruit," " it cannot bring forth good fruit," and yet He regards man as responsible, alike for the commission of evil, and for the omission of good. For we are accountable not only for that which springs directly from our volition when it could determine otherwise, but for that also which is the necessary result of a state into which our free volition has brought us.

There are, indeed, many whose wills seem but very little determined and biassed in a moral point of view; it is difficult to trace in them progressive development in any particular direction, whether good or evil, and this circumstance is apt to perplex our judgment. But from the nature of the case, we must expect to find settled disposition manifesting itself differently in different persons. These very shades of difference are themselves owing to the will; nay, even moral indifferentism is itself a bias, having its gradual development like any other particular affection.

The phenomena of habit in other spheres of life afford an instructive parallel, illustrating by way of analogy and of contrast the manner in which the will develops itself into any permanent moral bias or settled character.

Even in reference to the body and things corporeal, by the frequent repetition of any particular movements or acts, springing naturally from the prompting of the will, there arises an impulse to repeat them from time to time, which the mind, as if mechanically and involuntarily, obeys. Thus the act becomes a habit. We are obliged to suppose, though we cannot actually see it, that even after the first time of doing it, a minimum tendency towards the act done, has been left behind, and this tendency grows in strength, and the gratification of it becomes more spontaneous, the more frequently the act is repeated. The act may be insignificant and objectless, there may be nothing prompting to it, no need of it, but the frequent repetition of it itself begets a kind of need. If, on the other hand, it does arise from some want, some prompting of the sensuous nature, habit gradually subordinates the reappearance of it, as a settled desire, to a certain rule. Habit strangely possesses a twofold and contrasted power; it lessens the pleasure of sensational enjoyment, and thus blunts the desire after it, and yet, in another sense, it reproduces and intensifies it.* This power of habit, unquestionably extends to acts of a directly mental and spiritual nature. Thus, for instance, in the case of one man, teaching becomes a habit, in another, verse-making, in a third (to name an instance in the moral sphere), almsgiving, and so on; in given circumstances, and conditions, the act is

The law of habit as to body,

as to mind.

* See Bishop Butler's *Analogy*, part i. chap. v.—*Tr.*

FREEDOM OF THE WILL IN MORAL DEVELOPMENT.

done as if spontaneously, without any determinate resolve or intervening act of will.

<small>Habits of thought.</small> This force of habit is to be found, not only in outward acts, but in the inward movements of mental life. When upon regularly returning occasions the mind falls into the same groove of thought—this association of ideas gradually becomes a habit, so that it recurs without the mind's being cognizant of it; yea, even when the mind is differently occupied, it will upon the given suggestion run through the same series of thoughts. Thus by mere repetition functions, which are naturally subordinate to free will acquire the power of acting independently of it; any special tendency or bias which the mind gives itself becomes a power within it, a power oftentimes so strong as to bear sway, not only involuntarily, but even in spite of the opposition of the will. These are facts which the atomistic theory of freedom, maintaining that all actions spring from an entirly unbiassed will, can never reconcile nor explain.

<small>Habit versus manners and character.</small> The power of habit is so apparent, so obvious, that it is not surprising to find some psychologists endeavouring to explain all moral conduct and phenomena of will, disposition, and character, good or evil, upon this principle. And certainly the law of habit possesses very great influence in confirming any course of behaviour, whether moral or immoral, and in explaining the formation of virtuous or vicious modes of life.* But does it suffice to explain the formation of disposition and of character? Men who are the votaries of habit are by no means men of marked or forcible character and determined will; on the contrary, they are usually men who allow themselves to be acted upon and to be tyrannized over by vague impressions and humours. The power of habit is, therefore, greatest in the case of children early in life, though it asserts itself through another cause in mature life ; and it is most manifest in those stages of intellectual cultivation wherein the moral and spiritual life has attained least development and independence. Habit, when counter-

<small>Habit a mechanical power.</small> acting the self-determination of the will, acts as a merely mechanical power, or force of nature stereotyping life ; it belongs to the sphere of

---

* HEGEL calls habit "the mechanism of self-consciousness," *i.e.*, of the feeling of one's own distinctive personality. *Encyklopädie*, § 410.

unconsciousness in and through which it prevails. Manners and customs denote those modes of action which, in themselves alterable, have become established. They express what is higher than habit; they are not unconscious or mechanical forces, but, while determining powers, are quite compatible with mental independence; we, therefore, speak not of the manners but only of the habits of animals. Habit is a power which lowers manners (*mores*) to mere naturalness. If we say of a man that he is led to a mode of action or behaviour which is of a moral import by mere *habit*, we imply that his conduct has lost its moral significance; but who could thus speak of his manner or mode of action when it springs from disposition or character?

Habit properly belongs to single acts which it moulds according to its own permanent rule. To attribute the settled bias of the will with all that this includes —the prevailing tenor of the man's mind and his settled convictions—to habit as its source, would be to explain what is most inward by what is relatively external. The power of habit may do much for man, but it cannot make him the child either of God or of the devil. If, for instance, we contemplate the power of sin as a prevailing tendency of the will, we find that it does not consist in that mere repetition of certain deeds which forms the essence of habits, but in a great variety and multiplicity of actions all springing from one perverted principle. Man makes this principle his own when, with clear self-consciousness and deliberation, he acts according to it; his adoption of it becomes more inward and fixed the oftener he does so; and thus in proportion as it finds a groundwork in the man's natural inclinations for the special tendencies in which it embodies itself, it attains dominion over the various departments of his life. How can such a development be ascribed to the mere monotonous law of habit? Man's sinful obduracy involving him in contempt of God and of His holy law is far more than a bad habit.

<small>Settled character not owing to habit.</small>

The freedom of the will thus appears in the progress of moral development; and this answers to the relation between formal and real freedom, as we discovered it in the preceding chapter. Man begins with formal freedom in order to attain to real freedom; the

<small>Formal and real freedom blended.</small>

CHAP. II.] FREEDOM OF THE WILL IN MORAL DEVELOPMENT. 51

reconciling of the two is brought about by gradual development. How could this development connect and harmonize the starting-point with the goal if there were in it no element of formal freedom?

All that is necessary is to guard against separating free will from its living union with the other activities of the spiritual life, and ascribing to it a merely outward relation to these. Thus to isolate it would involve us again in the dilemma of representing it as indifferent to all these elements, of denying their action upon it, or of allowing that it becomes determined in a slavish manner. But as the mind uses the body as its organ, brings all its members, muscles, and nerves into subjection to it, and pervades them with its determining power, so the feelings, inclinations, interests, convictions, and principles, which together make up our practical and spiritual life, are blended together into an inner body by free will; it is their real soul, their formative and motive principle, the spirit of the spirit, and its heart of hearts.

Will the centre of the soul.

That the will is this,—that it is inseparably one with all the other elements of personal life, yet as their innermost determining centre,—is confirmed by the usage of language. We speak of self-consciousnesss and reason as something which the *ego* "has," but we identify the *will* with the *ego*. No one would say "my will has decided this or that," though we say "my reason—my conscience—teaches me so and so."* The will is the very man himself, as Augustine says, *Voluntas est in omnibus; imo omnes nihil aliud quam voluntates sunt.*†

Language confirms this.

If we give due weight to this truth we shall have no difficulty in explaining the old and worn-out examples which ordinary Determinism is wont to urge in proof that the will is influenced in its decisions by certain representations which act as *motives* or principles, and that these lead to decision and action simply through the will as their instrument. That would be indeed a strange psychology

The union of motives and will.

---

* There are some customary modes of expression which may be adduced to the contrary, but in these will stands for a certain determinateness of will.

† *De Civ. Dei,* lib. xiv. c. 6. Here in the *nihil aliud quam* Augustine goes further in the assertion of the principle than we do.

which regarded *those* thoughts only as active and effective in the mind, in relation to which the will was only receptive, or to speak more correctly, only *passive*.* This would be in effect to deny the will altogether, for will is nothing if it have not in itself real causality. But really it is no less false to represent motives and will as powers of the inner life mutually excluding each other, so that then only when motives are not sufficiently strong to lead to a decision, will may come in and decide. If the freedom with which any decision is come to be in inverse ratio to the degree of its determination by motives, Determinism must ever win the day. It might easily be shown that such determining motives are present even when at the moment of decision we are unconscious of them. The will must not, however, be represented as something separate from and added to the motives, as if the motives accomplished one thing towards arriving at a decision, and the will another which was still wanting. However the adjustment be made, the notion of an external combination between will and motive is quite erroneous. Even supposing that freedom could be maintained on such a principle, it would follow that man decides freely, only when conflicting motives have produced some hesitation in him; and that his freedom is most clear and striking when he decides without motives or in spite of them. But every one must regard it as an unworthy thing to decide in important matters without or against motives, and therefore groundlessly and arbitrarily; and no one feels it to be a lack of freedom but rather the highest kind of freedom when he is led promptly and unhesitatingly to a decision by forcible and clearly perceived reasons. This indisputable fact ought to have put the advocates of determinism, of indifferentism, and of freedom *in aequilibrio* upon a better track. Are thoughts in themselves to be regarded as definite motive principles or impulses bearing on the will? The question is not whether they should be but whether they actually are. Experience answers NO, they are not themselves

The highest freedom.

Representations are not in themselves motives.

---

* See HERBART's remarks on Wolf's view, *Ueber d. Freiheit des Willens*, p. 35. Herbart (died 1841) was himself an espouser of Determinism, but of a determinism penetrated by moral earnestness and based upon a psychology quite different from that of Wolf, according to whom the will is nothing but a ball tossed to and fro by contrasted thoughts.

motives but they *become so* only when we blend with them the thought of our own interest and make it the subject matter of our enquiry.* But what we reckon as our interest—with the degree of strength attaching to it—depends upon our sphere of life, and ultimately and decisively upon our will in its inmost bias. We may, for instance, with tolerable certainty influence a man by thoughts and representations of the effect of his actions as tending to his bodily weal or woe; but this is owing to the self-perversion of his will whereby the subject matter of such representations has become his main interest. Again to order our behaviour according to moral principles—to resolve that we will obey our moral judgment—is an inward decision *prior to* our motives, springing from the inner centre of freedom, and preceding the influence of a settled and higher principle upon our decision. The principle of selfishness generates from itself a system of motives acting upon the will, each sustaining and confirming the preceding; it imparts to thoughts and things in themselves wholly meaningless and unimportant when measured by the principle of obedience toward God, the greatest importance in reference to the man himself. Motives are only the *media* through which the free volition acts, they are not the producing causes of the free volition; they are parts of that inward *body* which the will forms for itself out of the materials presented to it, in order therein to manifest itself. The will attracts to itself those thoughts and feelings which correspond to its central and germinating tendency, not by a definite resolve, but as if by magic and imperceptibly, and makes these the prevailing motives and determining principles of the inner life which co-operate with it towards the given act. As, therefore, the state of the mind and its changes are recognized in the expression and movement of the body, so do we judge of the essential character of the man's will, which he has derived only from himself, by the motive according to which he acts. His will is embodied in these motives; they are constituent parts of his will, but it is not in the least degree robbed of its freedom by them. The act of the will, moreover, is never, strictly speaking, dependent on the motives, though it may be owing to some bias or tendency inherent in the will itself.

<small>Will begets motive.</small>

* Herbart himself recognizes this, pp. 37, 53.

Romang, in order to reconcile the principle of freedom with the doctrine of determinism explains that principle thus: "we may call," he says, "a being free in so far as it acts *according to its distinctive determinateness or nature*, and from its inner and central essence."* Adopting this form of explanation we should say, "a being is free in so far as the inner centre of its life from which it acts *is conditioned by self-determination.*" From what has been said in the 2d part of Book I., it is clear that the doctrine of human responsibility can be maintained upon this conception of human freedom alone. The limits within which the forensic view of accountability must confine itself are not those of the moral and religious aspect of the question. The inquiry is made to end where it really begins when Romang,† Sigwart,‡ and before them Hume,§ suppose that the doctrine of accountability is satisfied by the recognition that the act in question is the deed of the given individual, that the deciding agent in the resolve is after all the man himself, his own nature, his distinctive character. In order to accountability we must have more than this; we must prove that this, his distinctive nature and character, springs from his own volition, that it is itself the product of freedom in moral development.

§ 3. MORAL DEVELOPMENT.
Determinism has often made use of the conception of development to aid its argument, and it may therefore seem strange that this conception should be used as a weapon against it. In all development

---

* *Ueber Willensfreiheit und Determinismus*, p. 73.
† As before, p. 73.
‡ As before, p. 138.
§ *Enquiry concerning Human Understanding*, § viii. Mr. J. S. MILL thus defines responsibility :—"What is meant by moral responsibility ? Responsibility means punishment. But the feeling of liability to punishment is of two kinds. It may mean expectation that if we act in a certain manner punishment will actually be inflicted upon us by our fellow-creatures or by a Supreme Power. Or it may mean, being conscious that we shall deserve that infliction. . . . It is not the belief that we shall be *made* accountable which can be deemed to require or presuppose the free-will hypothesis ; it is the belief that we ought so to be ; that we are justly accountable ; that guilt deserves punishment," p. 507. He adds further on : "It is well worth consideration whether the practical expectation of being thus called to account, has not a great deal to do with the internal feeling of being accountable ; a feeling, assuredly, which is seldom found existing in any strength in the absence of that practical

the present moment with all it contains proceeds with stern necessity from that preceding, and this again from its antecedent, and so on. The agent in such a development must be determined by his own past, collectively viewed as an antecedent, so that he does not possess at any moment of his life that freedom whose essence is self-determination of what is still undetermined, and ability to choose differently. In this rigid continuity there seems no break in the chain where such a freedom might come in. Allowing that it is still undecided how it may have been at the outset, and even granting that free self-development may have had its place there, still during the subsequent course of the development freedom would not be present or actual, but only something past.

Determinism, therefore, may more correctly be designated pre-determinism. Freedom is denied because man in every present moment is dependent upon a past which, though it be ever that of his own life, is not in the present moment at all in his power. The chain of development in which alone man as existing in time can realize his moral nature, must exclude the possibility of his realizing it as a free being. This, as is well known, is the form of Determinism (though not perhaps exactly in the way here presented) which Kant adopted, and which he regarded as insuperable in reference to man in his present state, and inexplicable by any empirical or argumentative treatment.*

Kant's view.

But if we examine this doctrine more closely we find that it is based upon quite a mistaken conception of development. If each moment be only the necessary consequence of the preceding, in which therefore it must already have been contained, how could it ever come to be something more—to be an advance on the preceding? Each successive step would be only a repetition of the preceding, indeed it could not be called a step in advance, for

Based on a wrong idea of development.

---

expectation." Thus does he evaporate human responsibility and the sense of guilt in order to reconcile it with his theory of Determinism. See Book I. part ii. of this work.—*Tr.*

* *Kritik der reinen Vernunft*, in der "*Auflösung der kosmologischen Ideen von der Totalität der Ableitung der Weltbegebenheiten aus ihren Ursachen.*" *Kritik der prakt. Vernunft* in der "*kritischen Beleuchtung der Analytik der reinen practischen Vernunft.*" See also his *Religion innerhalb der Grenzen der blossen Vernunft*, p. 58 (2nd ed.).

it would have no distinctive features marking it as different from the preceding; it would be the same step occurring at a different time, modified, perhaps, by the coincidence of other circumstances. Now it is clear that on such a theory the words "step" and "development" lose all their meaning. The successive stages of true development are never linked together according to the law of analysis, but they are united by the most living synthesis. It is not from the outset a perfected plan, which has only to be carried out in various external conditions; but this distinctive and perfected plan is *produced* by means of the development itself, which springs from an indwelling active and determining principle.

It is no less contradictory to the true conception of development to suppose that each successive step is altogether different and new, having no connection with the preceding, but a new commencement in itself. Unity amid manifoldness, and continuous identity binding all in one complete whole, would thus be lost. We should have a development without anything developing itself, and therefore not, properly speaking, a development of all; nothing but an arbitrary passing from one stage to another—a chaotic heap of isolated, groundless, and meaningless movements.

<small>Indifferentism inconsistent with true development.</small>

In every true development, therefore, there must be two tendencies indissolubly blended, namely, the CONSERVATIVE principle, maintaining the connection of the various parts of the development, its identity and permanence in the midst of change, and uniting its various stages in one harmonious whole; and the PROGRESSIVE principle, formative of what is new, producing at each stage not only what belongs to the preceding and springs out of it, but a new commencement, a distinctive element in the construction. This latter principle carries on the development through manifold changes, and conceals the hidden unity by a multiplicity of phases. While the former tendency endeavours to maintain the past in its closest connection with the present, the latter endeavours to elicit and unfold the living germ of the future out of the present. Each of these tendencies requires the other as its necessary complement. Each would put an end to the life of the development, and therefore to

<small>Two principles of development.</small>

itself—the one by torpidity, the other by destructiveness—were it to crush the other in order to rule supreme itself. The unqualified negation of the progressive principle is as destructive as is the reckless ignoring of the conserving tendency.

This fundamental law of all living development, this blending <small>Development in nature;</small> of permanence and change, of rest and movement, of being and becoming, may easily be illustrated in the sphere of organized nature. In the development of every organic being there works, on the one hand, the conserving tendency, which in each successive moment confirms and embodies the contents of the preceding. Upon this depends the permanent union of the several stages of the development. In virtue of this, the continuous threads of what has gone before are carried on and interwoven with what follows, and no stage can be understood without a knowledge of all that goes before. But, on the other hand, there works in the same development a progressive tendency, which endeavours to make each successive stage as independent as possible of what has gone before. From this tendency new and distinctive formations and phenomena arise, which cannot be regarded as a mere unfolding of preceding stages.

Now in nature this development is directly controlled by <small>necessarily controlled.</small> the particular type of each species. The progressive principle is obviously the one which determines and decides; for the conserving principle can conserve only what the progressive principle forms. This principle, therefore—the formative impulse of organized existence—or by whatever name this *qualitas occulta* be called, is recognized, in one form or other, by every scientific theory of nature. In it is embodied the distinctive type, the image of the whole, which is impressed upon each successive stage. Limitations and malformations may occur, for each living thing is not only subject to the law of its kind, but is under the dominion of other forces indifferent to the end and purpose of the organic individual. Still this distinctive type, regarded in its relation to the progressive power which is guided by it, realizes itself according to a law of strict necessity.

As to human development, we must bear in mind the <small>Development in man.</small> distinction we have pointed out between the natural and the moral being of man. Upon the formative impulse, which determines the development of his physical and psychical nature, there is impressed not only the type of his species in its peculiar sphere as to race, nationality, &c., but a distinguishing type marking this individual, which preserves its main features throughout the development, in spite of hindrances and limitations arising not only from the co-determining influence of other forces, but in man's case from the co-existent power of free personality. The progressive principle of man's moral development is the freedom of the will, the ability of the *ego* to determine itself from the indeterminate.

As to his psychical nature.

As to his moral nature.

Even to this the highest formative impulse, there is prescribed a normal type, the moral law, which contains the ideal of the morally perfect man. But this is not impressed in a determining way upon the formative principle, seeing it is free; and though this principle be under an obligation in its outward manifestations to coincide with its type, it may in its working not only partially but wholly separate itself from that type, and oppose it.

The will's relation to its moral type—the moral law.

Still, however, freedom is bound by the general law of development in its opposition to, as well as in its harmony with, its normal type. It cannot remain ineffective in relation to the free Subject; its self-determinings must lead to the determination of the *ego*. The progressive principle, whether it proceed in a normal or in a perverted direction, is not an unlimited movement, but it hands over what it produces to the conserving principle, which implants it in the inner life, and in the will itself.

The conserving element, the law of development.

The relation of these two kinds of law to the moral being of man is so remarkable, that we must pause a moment to contemplate it. If we compare them with each other, the first is the rule for man's nature as free; it possesses no necessity save moral obligation, it determines man's normal moral being and action, but not the abnormal. The other law, that of development, holds sway in man's moral being and action, abnormal as well as normal; it binds created personality as by a meta-

The moral law and the law of development.

CHAP. II.] FREEDOM OF THE WILL IN MORAL DEVELOPMENT. 59

physical necessity; it asserts itself, even though the will strives against it, as an insurmountable limit to its freedom. And yet in general the determining power of this law is not perceived by man as constraint. The former law (as we saw, Book i., pp. 31, 32), seeing that it involves obligation, must withdraw into the recesses of consciousness, because, on the one hand, according to its very nature it must allow the physical possibility of transgression, and yet, on the other hand, it cannot surrender its determining power. The latter law, on the contrary, the transcendental law of moral development, does not admit of such a possibility, it abides apart from consciousness, exercising its secret power upon human life. We do not discover it by an immediate feeling, but by closer consideration, and hence it is that only a few in any age have had any strong presentiment of its ruling power. In moral action man must not trouble himself about this law. While God has given the moral law for man to realize, He reserves to Himself the realization of that other general law as His own holy prerogative. Our moral development is subject to this law just as our physical development is to nature's law; but it is not a commandment for us.

This universal law of development, causes evil as well as good behaviour to give a bias to the will whence the several acts proceed, a bias perhaps at first very slight and imperceptible, yet growing stronger the oftener the will yields to it. Experience teaches that the service of good gives increased power in goodness, and this is still more true in the case of evil, as we shall see in the second chapter of the fourth book.

The degree of determinateness in this development. As in every development, the progressive principle must take the lead and begin, it follows that in the moral development of man this commencement must be made by the free self-determining of the will. And we have already seen, that this self-determining does not at once pass over into a continual determinateness. At every point of moral development (the first commencement excepted) the will is certainly (to use Herbart's expression) in some degree "characterized;" in this present life, however, it is never fully so. Were the will fully characterized according to the principles of God's will, man would be a saint. It characterizes itself more and more continually. These further determinations again, which the will gives itself, are not caused by the determinateness which it already has, for though this determinateness has great influence upon moral development, the inner progress of this development cannot be produced by it. They are the product of the will itself, so far as it is still relatively undetermined. Over and above those dispositions and characteristics, produced by its self-determining, the will still possesses a hidden sphere of incalculable freedom and independent action. The energy of this action is not wholly unlimited by the character formed, but still the new determinations proceeding from it form part of the course of moral development as co-operating and modifying powers. The will's power of moral self-determining is not easily exhausted, nor are the moral elements of life from the time when a man's character is generally formed, to be regarded merely as manifestations and acts of the character thus decided.

It follows that in all moral development, we must distinguish two elements, that of state, *habitus*, and that of act, *actus*. He who looks upon moral development merely as an aggregate of isolated deeds, which never go to form a settled moral state or character, or who imagines that this state is without any influence upon the subsequent conduct, destroys the idea of development altogether. But he too equally does so, who regards this settled moral state as the original one for the man, the *prius*, and every moral act, every moral decision, as its necessary outgo and effect. The fact is, that the state or character is of moral significance only so far as it has been produced by an act which is simply internal, which is the free inclination of the will in some particular direction, either to or from the principle of moral truth,—the reception of this principle into the innermost disposition or the shutting of the heart against it. By such internal decisions, wherein consciousness and the power of action concentre upon some single point, a permanent state or character is formed, the will has given to itself a determinate bias, and from this bias, when occasion offers, a series of acts or omissions proceeds.* The conserving

Distinction between state and act.

---

* AQUINAS, (*Summa, prima secundae,* qu. 51, art. 2, 3), following Aristotle instructively discusses the question how a *habitus* of the agent may ensue from his acts.

FREEDOM OF THE WILL IN MORAL DEVELOPMENT.

principle preponderates in this series if we view it in relation to its source, and as long as it is not interrupted or diverted by any new decision. Self-determination has to do with it only as a negative power, excluding any necessity in the outgo of the successive acts or omissions. In the progressive development of human life, however, the new relations and circumstances with which man comes in contact will rouse the will to new decisions, giving rise in time to new series of determinations.

Action is in this sense the producer, and character is the product; yet the latter in turn possesses a tendency to assert and to manifest itself in corresponding action. Our Lord's expression in Matt. xii. 33 combines both these factors. As the quality of the fruit depends upon the nature of the tree, so the good or evil acts of man depend upon the good or evil state of the heart, but this very state is itself again dependent upon the primary decisions of the will; ποιήσατε τὸ δένδρον καλόν—σαπρόν.*

Let us pause here for a moment in order to point out the phases which the consciousness of freedom in its relation to Determinism is wont to pass through. From the standing-point of natural consciousness, in the first place, free self-determination alone is manifest, necessity is hidden. Man trusts implicitly in the immediate feeling—which is present in his resolve to act, or which he can call up at any moment—that he can choose either the one thing or the other. The fact thus remains concealed from him that the determinateness of his inner life, the character already formed, exercises an influence upon every decision, and that his consciousness of freedom may arise merely for his not perceiving the determining causes. Then, secondly, from the standing-point of a more acute intellectualism, the matter is reversed, freedom is altogether hidden, and in tracing back each decision to its source determinism forces itself upon us at every point like a chain of brass in which not a single link is wanting. If freedom be not wholly surrendered to these questionings of the

The phases of our belief in freedom. The first.

The second.

---

* Ποιεῖν must here be taken in its strict sense, chiefly because if we translate it "*supposing* that the tree be good," &c., the argument ἐκ γὰρ τοῦ καρποῦ τὸ—δένδρον γινώσκεται loses its force.

intellect, it takes refuge behind the bulwark of faith as a presupposition which conscience and God's holiness oblige us to believe.* We can easily see how a determinism which ends thus may boast of being the only scientific way of thinking. This superiority is distinctly laid claim to by the latest advocates of determinism, Romang and Sigwart. But a doctrine which sacrifices the most important data of consciousness and particulars of experience—data which most strongly stimulate the mind to inquiry and discovery, and facts which it is the office of science to harmonize and embrace — in order to facilitate the construction of a pet scientific system, does not truly satisfy the requirements even of science itself. If any one says, " I cannot accept the idea of freedom, because it violates the circle of my scientific thought," all we can reply is that this circle is too narrow and needs widening. All this talk about Determinism, as if it were the only scientific view of the matter, is most astonishing, in the case, for instance, of Romang's "Doctrine of Natural Religion," where great pains are taken to maintain intact the highest truth of human life —man's responsibility—side by side with the deterministic theory, and the writer is thus involved in a series of contradictions which cannot be supposed necessary to any truly scientific view.

The third. The third phase can be no other than the view obtained from the standing-point that we have established, according to which, the determination of the present by means of the past is not denied, but is partly limited and partly traced back to a former self-determining. If this complex and modified doctrine of freedom can be maintained, freedom can assert its validity against its opponents. At the same time determinism is not absolutely excluded, but some truth is recognized therein, and Freedom attains its own full recognition and definiteness by blending Determinism with it.

All development in moral, as well as in merely organic life, has its epochs. These epochs generally occur when the progressive principle obtains a decided preponderance over

---

* See Sir W Hamilton's theory which assumes this phase. Notes to Reid, pp. 601, 602.—*Tr.*

that of conservation. New impulses of development continually break forth and suddenly alter and supplant established growths. When these epochs are very striking, they seem to form an entirely new commencement, and to break off all connection with the past. But soon it appears that a thousand fine yet firm threads, hidden deep within, maintain the connection unbroken amid the most sudden and greatest changes.

§ 4. EPOCHS OF MORAL DEVELOPMENT.

It is at these epochs especially, in moral development, that man's freedom of will evinces its greatest strength. In the sphere of merely organized life wherein development is bound directly and inseparably by nature's laws, these epochs are necessary in but one direction and towards the completion of the whole. But the case is different in the moral development of man. Within the range of his earthly life there is a hidden sphere of unaccountable movement on the part of free will, underlying the moral character already formed; and it is only by the recognition of this that we can speak of any epochs in moral development. Now as any such epoch, by exciting the inner spiritual life, may excite also this free self-determining to greater activity, it may become a turning-point or crisis. Two different paths present themselves, and the man must choose between them. Whatever direction he now gives to his moral life, this it will retain until perhaps a new crisis occurs.

Moral epochs may be turning-points.

There is indeed but one turning-point only, in the full sense of the word, in human development, now that it is perverted by sin. It is the decision between continuance in the old life and the commencement of a new one in regeneration. But this absolute turning-point cannot be considered here, because the possibility of it depends upon conditions which lie far above human freedom.

One great epoch— regeneration.

Still we cannot deny that epochs and turning-points in a subordinate and limited sense do occur before and apart from conscious and personal participation in the blessings of Redemption. They commonly take place at those periods of human life which may be called the epochs of man's natural development. The youth's entrance upon the age of manhood, for instance, may be one of these, perhaps the most important, according to Prodicus's

Subordinate epochs.

well-known allegory regarding Hercules. But the epochs of natural and moral development do not always coincide. Crises in physical and mental development, like important changes and disturbances in our outward life, may act as incitements and impulses to more thorough self-decision; but it depends upon the will whether it will heed them or not. In innumerable instances they leave not a trace behind, and epochs afterwards occur wholly independent of them when the man's inner life urges him to some definite resolve; and with clear consciousness he either confirms his past volition and effort, adopting it more firmly, or belies and rejects it in order to adopt some other course. The more mature and settled a man's moral life becomes, the less frequent will be such epochs, and the more dominant will the conserving principle become. His life in this case will be in the main nothing more than a carrying out in every relationship of principles inwardly established, and in maintaining these amid manifold temptations to let them go. But as in life there can be no outward growth without a corresponding strengthening of principles within, the maintenance of what is already attained does not exclude the attaining of something more.

Now, as moral development proceeds only by means of a progressive self-determining, which cannot be regarded as a mere product of determinations to which the will has already surrendered both itself and its moral life, we must maintain in opposition to the Deterministic view that the decisions of a man's will must ever be beforehand unknown and unknowable to his fellow-men, however exact their knowledge and correct their judgment.* Therefore, the very best adapted influences brought to bear upon a man which have in view these decisions, or the results of which are dependent upon them, can never secure a certain given result. We are not here speaking of influence brought to bear upon any company of persons in order to some outward act. Here, it may be true that a man who can clearly excite selfish interests will not fail in his influence upon the majority. But we have here in view those

Impossible to calculate the decisions of will.

---

* Kant, though by no means a Determinist, judges otherwise: see especially the *Kritik der prakt. Vernunft*, p. 144 (6th ed.) We shall examine by and by how this accords with his doctrine of causality and of ideal freedom.

CHAP. II.] FREEDOM OF THE WILL IN MORAL DEVELOPMENT. 65

decisions of will which essentially belong to the inner moral development of the individual. Experience teaches that here the relation of means to end must ever be beyond our calculation, and it teaches this in cases where the object of our influence is most dependent and plastic, namely, in the education of the young. There can hardly be named a more striking example of the pertinacity of self-deceptions that flatter self-conceit in the face of the clearest facts a thousand times repeated, and the incalculable power of arbitrariness to produce utterly groundless opinions, not to say perverted acts, than is presented in the vaunting assurance wherewith many teachers asserts that by their instruction, if it be only made use of, the youth's virtue will be secured as certainly as the finished work comes from the hands of the artificer.*

<small>In the case of youth;</small>

In like manner regarding developed character, we can never with perfect certainty predict what the decision will be in any particular case ;—not only because subjectively, our knowledge of the character and of the circumstances must be very imperfect ; but also because objectively, the character itself in its earthly growth is never so fixed and certain as to be insusceptible of new and different determinations from the inexhaustible source of free will.† Is it in the drama of art only, and not in that of life, that persons occasionally belie their character, and act differently from our calculations ? If we think of some one whose holy disposition is fully known to us, tempted externally to some nefarious action, we should without hesitation say that he could not be overcome by the snare. We may thus consider

<small>And of matured character.</small>

---

* Such rash hyperboles sound very strangely in FICHTE's "*Reden an die deutsche Nation,*" because his doctrine of freedom enables him to maintain that no man—that no finite being—can be so firmly settled in goodness that his morality is for ever sure (*System der Sittenlehre,* p. 254), and this should have led him to a very different conclusion.

† SCHILLER's WALLENSTEIN judges otherwise. He says—
 "Could we the deep recesses of man's heart unfold,
 Unerringly his will and acts might be foretold."
But this is only a part of that false assurance which proves his ruin. This uncertainty is most strikingly illustrated in the conduct of those capricious undecided persons, who allow themselves to be guided in their resolves by momentary occurrences ; and we usually say of such that we cannot reckon upon them. But the same thing is true in some degree in all earthly life, of the most confirmed villains, and of the noblest and best of men.

VOL. II. E

ourselves justified in such a conclusion in a negative form. Yet even in this case if we would state our assurance very definitely, we should feel the need of carefully guarding and limiting our judgment. For supposing that nothing was wanting to complete our knowledge of the individual, and that the web of his inner life, in its finest and most delicate threads, lay clear before us, could we venture to claim the power of predicting, with unerring certainty, in what manner, and with what degree of firmness the temptation would be rejected? And how would it be in the case of some other temptation to which his distinctive nature was more liable? But if we turn the negative judgment into an affirmative one, it becomes still more evident that our prediction can never be certain, but strictly taken, can only approximate to probability. Can we lay any claim to the power of calculating, with unerring certainty, what would be the result of an appeal to our friend in any given case to some act of self-denial? Who shall guarantee that at the very time when the appeal was made, some turning-point, arising from the depths of his free will, severing the threads in the web of character, and introducing new ones, may not occur in his moral development? Nay, that the very temptation in question, to good or evil, may not be the occasion of this? Thus every calculation, as it can only proceed from what has already taken place, must cease to be infallible. Some one may say that he knows for certain that his friend in a given case will act so and so, and in no other way, but this is trust in him, not a confidence of the understanding based upon a recognized necessity. Accordingly the Apostle Paul warns the regenerate Christian of that self-confidence which thinks there is no need for fear (1 Cor. x. 12), and he requires him to work out his own salvation with fear and trembling (Phil. ii. 12). During this earthly life, our subjective will never becomes perfectly one with its external ideal, with objective goodness; our assured hope, therefore, of persevering in goodness must ever have as its dark back-ground the conscious possibility that in the formal freedom of our will arbitrariness may again arise.

In closing this chapter, we may recapitulate the main heads of our conclusions concerning Determinism and Indifferentism. If freedom be the self-determining

Conclusion.

of the will from that which is undetermined, Determinism is found wanting; because in its most spiritual form, though it grants a self-determination of the will, it is only such a one as springs from a determinateness already present:—and Indifferentism is found wanting too, because, while it maintains indeterminateness, as presupposed in every act of will, it does not recognize an actual self-determining on the part of the will which, though it be a self-determining, yet begets determinateness of character.

CHAPTER III.

Transcendental and Empirical Freedom.

§ 1. Freedom traced back to its original source.

According to the results of the preceding chapter the conception of Freedom may be maintained, not only in opposition to that mechanical Determinism which recognizes only external limitations of action, but even in the face of that more refined Determinism which includes the distinctive character of the agent among the determining causes of the act, and which allows to that character the most decided influence upon the ensuing act of will. Freedom in living moral development has power to rise above even this range of view. Indeed, a correct perception of the nature of moral development has nothing to fear even from pre-determinism, which, according to Kant, is the most dangerous extreme of deterministic thought. Kant based this upon experience and understanding, together with his principles of fixed connection (or invariability) and immanence; but neither experience nor understanding will suffer us to regard moral development as if each present moment were nothing more than the necessary result of the preceding.

But have we now really obtained what we were in search of, namely, "a principle of such self-dependence that its causality can make a new commencement, and can also fix a boundary beyond which the origin of sin is not to be looked for" (p. 1)?

We have first a progressive development, wherein every moral element seems to be the combined result of free self-determination, and of dependence upon what has already been realized. We recognize an element of freedom in this development; indeed, we cannot understand it as it is, apart from freedom; but this freedom is limited at every point; it is a freedom distorted and interrupted in successive moments of time. Even those epochs of moral development, the importance of which we considered in the last chapter, are no exception to this general relativity of freedom; for, however much the elasticity of free will may be strengthened in them, and the power of the past overcome, they can be distinguished from other points in the development by a *more* or *less* relative independence only. In order to satisfy the requirement we have suggested, freedom must clearly have its source in the region of the Unconditioned.

As our present task is chiefly to find out the origin of sin in freedom, the question occurs whether sin against conscience, against the clear consciousness of duty, may not give us what we seek, namely, a pure commencement which will exclude the determining influence of former sin.* And yet we cannot but hesitate as to the

_{Is this to be found in conscience?}

---

* Sins against conscience are of two kinds—sins apart from conscience, and sins of unfaithfulness to conscience. In the latter, the supremacy of conscience is recognized and to a certain extent asserted, but the resisting bias of the will prevails. The former are sins which ignore the authority of conscience. A relative subjection of conscience gradually takes place in the man's consciousness through the revolt of the will from it, so that it remains silent concerning many sins at the moment when they are committed. But conscience is never wholly suppressed; and such transgressions may still be called sins against conscience, seeing that they must at the outset have overcome its warnings, though, by their frequent repetition conscience has been silenced. Only thus can they be said to have rejected or ignored the authority of conscience; in all other respects, however much they objectively violate the law, subjectively, they must be reckoned among sins which are not committed in violation of conscience; indeed, they belong to the class called sins of ignorance. Sins, accordingly, which are characterized by recklessness and obduracy may also be reckoned among sins against conscience, and this agrees with the conception of premeditated sins discussed in vol. i. p. 205, and the two divisions of sins here named correspond with the two there described. But we see here the relative justice of a strict phraseology, which applies the name sins against conscience to such sins only as have themselves been committed after a struggle against its dictates and warnings.

_{Sins against conscience twofold.}

absoluteness of this kind of sins, because the boundary between them and others is very uncertain, not only in the judgment of others but in the sinner's own consciousness. We are able, certainly, to know concerning some sins when we become conscious of them that they were not sins against conscience: concerning others we may know the contrary. But between these there are many transgressions of very doubtful character.

Could it really be otherwise? Is not clearness of consciousness, upon which this distinction rests, mani-
This only relative. festly a relative thing? Sinful lust is also cunning; it knows how to enwrap the soul before decision in a mistiness which conceals all definiteness of outline. We may be reminded that whenever a man hears the veto of conscience he is conscious at that very moment of an unconditional obligation which supersedes and silences all other considerations. Obligation is unquestionably objective and unconditioned; but the form it assumes in the consciousness of any one, the clearness with which he perceives it, the strength of the impression it makes upon him,—these are subjectively conditioned by his state of mind and character,—as has been already explained and illustrated in our investigation.

And does not experience show, that after the commission of a sin against conscience, other sins commonly follow of the same kind, some of which may be perfectly free, necessarily implying a succession of new commencements, but which, for most part are committed with inward upbraidings and strivings against them, so that the man feels the chains in which his own acts have bound him? Yet these are none the less sins against conscience. A sin against conscience, moreover, has no security against the effort of any given tendency to advance itself, neither against the power of habit; it is not, therefore, an act of pure self-determination;—it is not a simple determination of will wholly independent of past acts; it is a self-determining limited by some quota of determinateness.

Still there seems to be another resource which we must not pass over in silence, seeing that the aim is to
The notion of an aequilibrium as the basis of freedom. rescue a great spiritual faculty from serious complexity, and this is sufficient apology for expedients apparently far-fetched and even desperate. It is supposed that in each man's moral development there must be

a moment when there is a perfectly equal balance of opposite impulses, the strength of which in the individual is just the result of his past life at the time being. The determining influence of every thing up to this moment would be obviated by this counterpoise, and the man would be in a position demanding an unconditional self-decision, and thus a basis of freedom would be obtained for his future moral development. According to this hypothesis the life of a man awakened to moral consciousness would be divided into two periods, in the second of which he would be responsible, in the first not; in the second evil would have its source in freedom, in the first in some unknown source. But allowing the possibility of this, allowing that a momentary equipose, such as is supposed does occur once in the vicissitude of every life, what sort of freedom should we have left us? A freedom, which is at the same time an utter dependence upon outward circumstances, as we have already seen in the theory of freedom *in aequilibrio*. It is, moreover, an arbitrary assumption that the power of the past in a man's life shows itself merely in the determinate strength of his various impulses, and that the will itself has nothing to do with it.

If, then, even here, we can find no opening for free action wholly unconditioned,—if we cannot find the δός ποῦ στῶ of Archimedes, starting from which the principle of freedom might primarily determine the development,—then that constant reference to a past which contains in its bosom the germ of the present, sends us continually back from one stage to another, till we reach *the very beginning* of conscious moral development in the individual, near to which, if not in immediate coincidence, we find his first act of sin. However firmly we may feel compelled to reject that predeterminism which Kant held to be insuperable in the sphere of experience, we cannot hide from ourselves the fact that each successive moment is conditioned in some degree by that which has preceded it. If, therefore, there be any unconditioned freedom, any pure outgo of self-decision from the undecided in human life, it must be found at the commencement of the development. If we can find it here, the consciousness of guilt, which imputes every sin to the individual as accountable, finds an adequate

Is it to be found at the beginning of the development?

explanation. However much a sinful state which is now beyond our power may have to do with the sinful act, the sinful state itself takes its rise in the first act of sin. If in the course of development thenceforward there be only a limited freedom, a freedom blended with dependence, the element of bondage which we thus encounter resolves itself into freedom; for it springs from that primary act of free self-determination.

But even this explanation is denied us. If there were at the outset of our conscious life any such an individual fall, wherein the will emerged from a state of pure indeterminateness into a decision to commit sin, from which commencement, likewise, our development, hitherto normal, became perverted, this first dark deed casting its ghastly shadow over our whole life would surely leave an indelible mark upon our memory. But who can definitely say when and how he for the first time acted in opposition to his awakened moral consciousness? Our recollection certainly goes much farther back than is generally supposed, if our attention be early enough directed to this point; and many a one may remember when, for instance, the first thought of hatred, of envy, of vindictiveness, was kindled within him, and what a spirit of rebellion it stirred up in his heart when a child. But if we dig deeper in the mine of memory, we discover, previous to the earliest of these occurrences, other things, which prepared the way for them, and were of like character; and in trying to fix these, like agitations begin to appear in our recollection behind these again, which, when we would grasp them, are lost in the twilight of uncertainty. A pure commencement, a primary act of sinful decision, cannot in this manner be arrived at. We cannot discover such a commencement, simply because there is no such thing. However important the epoch of the awakening of moral consciousness, it had a past behind it which must have had some co-determining influence upon the child's conduct.

Impossible to find it even here.

The freedom, therefore, of the first decision to which a moral import can be attributed is not unconditioned; indeed, it is not even conditioned equally for all. Surely it is not a matter of indifference how the child has been trained up to

The first decision is variously conditioned.

this moment, whether it has been wont to obey the will of its parents, in which the moral law has hitherto been embodied, to govern its desires, to respect the established rules of its narrow sphere of life; or whether it has had no such training and discipline. Educational nurture cannot perhaps give principles, but it surely is no superfluous work to mould the material of that future moral development which is contingent on self-determination. It is evident, too, that in the ever-varying stream of time, the moment wherein the firstling of conscious sin is born, is very differently determined—as to circumstances, and their relation to the will's decision—in different persons. Different degrees of temptation, and the fact of the inner life being well braced when the temptation occurs, or being taken by surprise in some careless moment, have each a co-determining power, even for a man of riper years. A man, for instance, whose moral nature was not firm enough to resist a very strong temptation, might, with the greatest probability, be expected to resist a less powerful one. How, then, could an infant under age be raised above the modifying influences of these differences?

And here the question suggests itself, whether it be at all likely or conceivable that this most important decision as to the character of the moral life would be left to the weakness of childhood. We say the highest decision; for whatever changes may occur in the subsequent development through the efficacy of freedom, its general tenor and bent must have been given at the outset. Such an assumption is certainly very venturesome. We know well that in the awakening of the moral consciousness, a new principle appears, which cannot be accounted for by preceding stages. But this principle itself has different degrees of strength in man's inner life according to *its* development: who, then, can hold it to be a matter of indifference whether this decision be entrusted to the highest stage of this development, or to the lowest, to a stage in which the mind has no clear conception of the real import of its opposition to the demands of conscience? No one doubts that a lower degree of accountability attaches to the acts of a child than to the acts of a man; and is the decision of the will on the part of the child to be

Uncondi- tional freedom not to be expected here.

CHAP. III.] TRANSCENDENTAL AND EMPIRICAL FREEDOM. 73

exclusively that on which the whole weight of accountability is to rest?

Vain, therefore, is the attempt to find a spot in our present life wholly unconditioned by anything preceding it whereon to base the pure self-determining of our moral being, by an act of freedom. And yet some such primary act of self-decision, arising from a state of perfect indeterminateness is necessary, to explain and account for that share of freedom which we meet with in man's progressive moral development. Without some such pure commencement by self-determination, impossible though it be in man's temporal development, this narrow and limited freedom hovers beyond our grasp, as if in the air; in the paths of practical experience,—*i.e*, that method of thought which looks for the subjective condition of man's moral nature in the sphere of experience only,—Determinism can never be thoroughly overcome. If, therefore, we cannot find a beginning before the beginning, our convictions will hold fast to the witness of our moral consciousness that we are free in spite of all intellectual doubts, but it never can be seen how the conception of freedom can be scientifically maintained.

Nothing unconditioned in our present state.

Thus the course of our inquiry compels us TO LOOK BEYOND THE REGION OF THE TEMPORAL, IN ORDER TO FIND THE ORIGINAL SOURCE OF OUR FREEDOM. If the moral condition in which we find man, apart from redemption, depends upon himself, and is the result of his own self-determining, if the testimony of conscience, which imputes to us our transgressions, and the witness of religion that God is not the author of sin, but hates it, be true, human freedom must have its beginning in a sphere beyond the range of time, wherein alone pure and unconditioned self-determination is possible. In this region must we seek that power of original choice which precedes and conditions all sinful decision in time. It is a significant fact that a philosopher, even of Herbart's tendencies, to whom the flights of speculation were as foreign as the careful observation of psychological phenomena was congenial, felt himself obliged to put the origin of evil in man beyond the range of phenomena, and to refer it to a kind of intellectual or ideal world (though not, of course in the Kantian sense)

Conclusion arrived at.

Herbart's theory.

among "the inner conditions or qualities of simple essences, which are not temporal or transient, but permanent, and are susceptible only of a mutual limitation; when, for example, several contrasted qualities are combined in one and the same essence."*

The conclusion to which we thus are driven reveals to us the unfathomable depth of our consciousness of guilt, and the mystery of that inextinguishable melancholy and sadness, which lies hidden at the foundation of all human consciousness, being most profound in the noblest natures. The lower animals are light and joyous, content if their actual wants are supplied, secure and untroubled from without. But in the consciousness of man that dark cloud of moral evil casts its shadow even in his most joyous moments; and amid the sounds of heartiest joy there runs an unsilenced undertone of secret sadness. We might dwell long upon the fact, though here we can only passingly refer to it, that many strange and striking characteristics of art and mythology in ancient times and in the popular poetry and household songs of modern life, find their explanation here. That pain and sorrow, moreover, which some modern philosophers fancy they can perceive as the pervading and prevailing character of the life of the lower animals, if viewed as a universal thing, is hardly anything more than a reflex gloom which the sadness of human self-consciousness casts upon the animal world. Personality alone possesses this original source of uneasiness and anguish, and it alone can have it, because its existence can be traced back beyond the confines of time.

<small>This conclusion accords with consciousness.</small>

In this self-determining of personal beings beyond the confines of time, we have the strongest internal argument and warrant for the imperishableness of the existence distinctively belonging to them. Their being has not its source in time; how then can time carry it away? We by no means adopt the principle that "what originates in time perishes in time," as an axiom to be recognized as self-evident, though it has recently been postulated as a matter of course.† Beginning of existence in time involves the possibility but not the necessity of annihilation. That which once did

<small>Argument for immortality.</small>

---

* *Gespräche über das Böse*, pp. 161, 162.
† *E.g.*, by Romang, "*System der natürlichen Religionslehre*," pp. 584, 585.

not exist may possibly return to non-existence. Our religious consciousness, though obliged to allow the possibility of annihilation, could not let go its belief in the continuance of personal beings; it would consider this possibility to be one whose realization must ever be excluded by the positive will of divine love. But our conviction of personal immortality can be established on philosophical grounds and beyond the reach of doubt, only upon the recognition of the principle that the germ of personality has its origin beyond the boundary of time —in other words, when the guarantee of our immortality is found in the primary creative will of God, whereby alone created personality has its being.

The question whether Holy Scripture teaches the doctrine of eternal damnation, *i.e.*, of a damnation endlessly extended in time, or whether it suffers us to indulge the hope of a future restoration of all fallen beings to God's love, will come before us at a subsequent stage of our inquiry. However this may be, it is an essential element of Christian consciousness that man becomes partaker of blissful fellowship with God only through the redemption and grace which are in Christ Jesus. His consciousness that apart from this redemption he is given over to misery and condemnation from which he never throughout eternity could have rescued himself is only the negative correlative of the same faith.* This is not the melancholy sense of weakness and limitation attaching to man's phenomenal existence, but when he awakes to the consciousness of his desert of God's punishment, " it pierces to the dividing asunder of soul and spirit both joints and marrow " penetrating the very heart of the *ego*. But how eternal damnation is at all (morally) possible, how a created being can ever incur the desert of such a punishment, can be seen only when we recognize the transcendental significance of freedom, and therewith an original guilt lying beyond the limits of time.

<small>Everlasting perdition.</small>

It is only natural that many philosophers should refuse to admit the conception of freedom because it is a puzzle to them; but when theologians, who are sincerely devoted to Christian truth, fancy that they can fairly vindicate Protestant theology against Pelagianism by surrendering the conception

---

* KANT assents (upon his standing-point), to the verdict of this consciousness. See his *Religion inn. der Grenzen d. bl. Vernunft*, p. 95.

of freedom, they should beware lest they undermine what they would confirm.*

§ 2. THEORIES OF TRANSCENDENTAL FREEDOM.
The idea of a self-decision of the will previous to the birth of the soul into this world whereby the man's moral nature is biassed, has been adopted by many. We do not dwell upon the Platonic theory,† for it is difficult to decide how much of it is merely mythological and how much really belonged to Plato's philosophy. The same remark applies to PHILO's development of the Platonic doctrine. For when in the passage which mainly bears upon this subject,‡ he speaks of the air as the element of ascending or descending souls, it is not easy to reconcile this with what he says concerning the νοῦς of men as the ἀπόσπασμα of the divine soul or nature, and concerning heaven as its original abode. This idea is developed by Plotinus§ with greater philosophic discrimination: he explains the various mental differences among spirits by means of it. Still his doctrine of the general necessity of evil prevents his obtaining from this any explanation of the sense of guilt in moral consciousness. With this view the thought had already been adopted and developed within the Church by Origen, He did not, however, recognize the exact point where the

* This remark is specially applicable to the learned JONATHAN EDWARDS, in his well-known treatise on *The Freedom of the Will.—Tr.*

† Prominently stated in the *De Republica*, x. 617 (Bekker's ed., p. 3, vol. i. 508). Even Plotinus fails to harmonize Plato's views upon this subject; *Ennead* 4, book ii. cap. 1.

‡ In his work *De gigantibus*, Pfeiffer's ed., vol. ii. pp. 360–364. Concerning Philo's doctrine of the original fall of souls, see DAHNES *Jüdisch-Alexandrinische Religionsphilosophie*, part i. p. 306, and GFRÖRER's *Philo*, part i. pp. 371, 374. The theories of pre-existence in Jewish Rabbinical theology do not much concern us here. For while they have an advantage over Philo's Platonic view in that they are freed from the dualism of human corporeity (until we come to the Cabbalists who usually fall back upon this), they do not like Philo consider the moral bearing of the doctrine, as explaining the moral impurity of the soul in this its earthly life. The chief quotations from the Rabbins, bearing upon pre-existence may be found in *Eisenmenger*, part i. p. 467; part ii. pp. 8, 9; with which may be compared FLUGGE's "*Geschichte des Glaubens an Unsterblichkeit*," &c., vol. i. pp. 45–74. The allusion to pre-existence in the Book of Wisdom (viii. 19, 20), seems to imply contrasted constitutions of pre-existent souls, and a corresponding contrast in their bodies.

§ See *Ennead*, iv., book ii. cap. 1–6, and the acute remarks concerning Plotinus's doctrine of imputation and freedom by VOGT, "*Neoplatonismus und Christenthum*," p. 74, 87, 91, 92.

difficulty lies; he looked for it where it does not exist, namely, in the fact of the existence of a material world, and in the multiformity of created beings. Origen again neglects to free his doctrine of pre-existence from the conditions of time, describing it as a life in time preceding man's earthly life; and yet he attributes to it too much. He is not content with describing it as a perfectly holy and blessed life, he considers that spirits in this primary state were partakers of the divine essence.* But apart from these misty notions concerning emanations, the difficulty of conceiving of a fall in this spirit-world is, by his theory, enhanced to an impossibility.

The church in its doctrinal development, was naturally very slow to adopt this idea, because it was so closely connected with notions which in their origin and nature were manifestly foreign to Christianity. They who inclined to the strict Augustinian doctrine, laid stress upon the moral depravity and guilt of the individual as connected with the fall of our first parents, while they who inclined to Pelagianism, endeavoured to establish freedom as the principle of individual responsibility in the present life. The supposition of a pre-existence of spirits, conditioning this life by a primary decision of will, was a dreamy fancy of some few theologians such as Scotus Erigena,† and of small isolated sects such as the Cathari. The full import of that idea was unperceived since then until recently, when the conception of freedom began to be more thoroughly examined, and the diffi-

The teaching of the Church on this.

---

* ORIGEN's view may be found in his work, περὶ ἀρχῶν ii. cap. 9, 6; comp. cap. i. 1; i. c. 8, 2 and 4; iv. 36 (in the summary) See also the interesting parallel between Origen's view and that of Philo, concerning the original state and fall of souls, in Thomasius' *Origen*, p. 154, 160, 290.

† SCOTUS, indeed, held that man fell from his ideal being in his mortal and sensuous life *in primo homine*. But as he did not consider the narrative of the fall in Genesis as literal history (*De divis. naturae*, lib. iv. c. 15), and as he held that it was originally ordained of God for man to multiply, though not by ordinary generation (lib. iv. c. 12), the doctrine of a primitive ideal state as pertaining to individual spirits—*ex prima conditione*—seems to be implied (though Scotus nowhere expressly asserts it), if the transition he speaks of from ideal into sensational being have any real meaning. The corresponding expressions, however, of Echart the Mystic (see Martensen, pp. 27, 126) cannot be regarded in the same light. What Echart means is not a spiritual existence, and conduct preceding and conditioning this earthly life, but a transcendental union of the mystical and speculative thinker with the Absolute, by means of intellectual intuition.

culty of explaining the consciousness of guilt arising therefrom in man's life in time began to be recognized.

It was in this way that KANT adopted it. We cannot fail to perceive how desirable it is in this as in other subjects that our philosophical theology should affiliate itself with Kant, because, notwithstanding the untenableness of his conclusions, we must not forget how much there is practically to be learned from his energetic spirit. When the harvest time of philosophic theology shall come, in some distant and final epoch, it will be perceived that Kant's contributions thereto, notwithstanding the fettering formalism of his ethical system, have borne far more wholesome and more abiding fruit than what has appeared against Kant by those who follow Spinoza. It will then be seen that the practical consequences of his philosophy have been far more important in behalf of Christianity than Kant himself, much less his followers, have supposed;—in behalf of Christianity as it really is, I mean, unmodified, "unrectified" by an allegorical interpretation, whether moral or speculative. His practical philosophy, in its subjective tendencies, when fully developed, lead indeed at first to an enlightenment somewhat negative in its character. But in its principles, and in its objective spirit, it stands far above the shallow and superficial notions which have been put forth in its name against religion.*

Kant's moral standing point.

The *Kritik der reinen* (*i.e.*, theoretical) *Vernunft*, led to the negative conclusion that reason cannot know "things in themselves." It is certain, that beyond the connection of things which it recognizes, there is such a realm of "things in themselves," forming the determining basis of these connections; but the nature of this kingdom, the way and manner in which these connections are caused, proves to be wholly undiscoverable. The possession of "synthetic *a priori* judgments," is allowed to the reason in opposition to mere Empiricism and Scepticism, but these synthetic judgments *a priori* with their logical basis— the pure conceptions or categories of the understanding—are only allowed to be "regulative principles" for every possible fact of experience. They are of use "immanently," but not

Reason knows only a world of phenomena.

---

* Dr PAUL's work, entitled "*Kant's Lehre vom Radicalen Bösen. Ein Vergleich mit der Lehre der Kirche*" (1865), has done good service in proving this.

"transcendentally," that is, in reference only to things within the range of experience, and not beyond this to the super-sensuous "intelligible" world. But as there is no experience possible to us, save within the boundaries of space and time, and as space and time do not belong to things in themselves, but are only subjective forms attaching to our sensuous intuition, we cannot attribute any objective reality to this our world of experience, but must regard it as a series of representations, somehow arising from things in themselves, and, conformable to law, *i.e.*, as a world of PHENOMENA.

Now, in this world of phenomena, of which we in our empirical existence form a part, the necessary connection of cause and effect holds sway as the unavoidable condition of any possible experience; and this does not leave the smallest room for freedom, for the power of commencing a new series of changes. This "necessity of causal connection," excluding freedom from the empirical sphere, is not so much the determination of volitions by inwardly sufficient grounds, but rather that law of the phenomenal world involved in its dependence upon time, which obliges us to look for an adequate cause for every event in something else "preceding it in the order of time." This something else may be a settled state of the acting Subject, but, nevertheless, it is evident that the acting subject at the moment of action has not the power of choice, the decision does not rest with him, therefore he is not free.

<small>In which cause and effect hold sway.</small>

But it is a fact, ratified to us by our Reason, and which immediately necessitates its own recognition, that we are conscious of an Unconditional Law enjoined for our conduct. The peculiarity of this law, is that purely of itself, and in virtue of its very form as unconditioned and universal, it determines the will, *i.e.*, the maxim or regulative principle, according to which the will decides itself, apart from all the impulses arising from the phenomenal world. But if this law determined our rule of action "materially," *i.e.*, by reference to any objects, we could not be thus conscious of it as unconditional. For such objects must have been given to us empirically, and therefore in the world of sense, and everything pertaining to sense is conditioned. We have therefore, in the consciousness of this practical law, an irrefragable proof that

<small>Practical Law of duty.</small>

we belong not only to a world of sense, but to an *intelligible world*, beyond the limits of time and space, though we are not in a position to make any theoretic assertions as to what it is. But if we cannot avoid recognizing such an unconditioned law of obligation, we much attribute to ourselves a will independent of the natural law of phenomena, and of the conditions of time *i.e.*, FREEDOM. If phenomena were "things in themselves," this freedom would be inconceivable, because our acts would in this case be virtually determined by the very mechanism of nature. But as things as they appear as pheno-

Proving the existence of an ideal world.

mena are only our perceptions of them, and yet have their basis in the Intelligible, there is no contradiction in supposing that an act, which viewed as a phenomenon, is subject to the law of necessity o nature, may, at the same time, have its origin—apart from any causal connection in time—in the Intelligible, in the pure empirically undeterminded WILL, *i.e.*, may be free.*

We have already seen (vol. i. p. 338), that Kant, if he

This leads to "radical evil."

thus abides by this doctrine of an intelligible commencement, as the basis of freedom and responsibility in reference to moral conduct, which is *conformable* to Law, must certainly attribute the same origin to moral conduct, which is *contrary to Law*. Thus fearfully does the intelligible world mock the thinker who, with a lofty consciousness of human dignity, would wring from it its mysteries. Piercing into the depths, he breaks through the crust of the phenomenal world, in order to discover pure self-ruled will; and behold, he finds RADICAL EVIL!

In this intelligible or ideal freedom, we have unquestionably

Intelligible freedom a basis of obligation.

a foundation for the moral imputation of evil different from any that can be afforded by a concrete and empirical conception of it. Not only does our conscience hold us responsible for our

* This exposition is, in the main, taken from the chapters in the *Kritik der reinen Vernunft*, entitled "Concerning the grounds for dividing all topics into Phenomena and Noumena," chiefly in the section entitled "Solution of cosmological ideas concerning the universal derivation of events from their causes;" also from the chapter in the *Kritik der praktischen Vernunft*, entitled "Concerning the principles of pure practical Reason;" also from Kant's "Critical Inquiry into the Analytic of pure practical Reason;" and from the section in his "*Grundlegung zur Metaphysik der Sitten*," entitled "Concerning the concept of Freedom as the key to the Autonomy of the Will."

immoral acts, but where we would exculpate ourselves, on the ground that these acts are to be attributed to a perverted bias of our nature, which has become a second nature to us, conscience sweeps away these pleas, by holding us accountable for this perverted bias itself. And if we would still defend ourselves, by urging that this perverted bias has been present in us, as far back as our recollection is able to trace our development, and that its origin is lost in that dark region of our being, where, to say the least, we cannot distinguish what in us was self-determined, and what was extraneously determined, conscience continues in spite of all still to hold us accountable for this bias with all its consequences. Now, intelligible freedom furnishes us with the key to this, with the proof that this testimony of conscience, strange as it is, is true and just. The essential features, moreover, of this freedom, as discovered by Kant, admonish us beforehand that by it alone shall we be able to avoid the conclusion to which even those necessitarian systems which do not deny the existence of God logically lead us, namely, that the determinations of the human will—evil as well as good—must be traced back to God—to God either as the real Actor therein, or as the unconditioned Creator of an utterly dependent creature who thus acts.*

It was the sign of a great genius, when Kant, after he had given up man's spirit as a captive to the world of sense (in his *Kritik der reinen Vernunft*), still held fast to the indestructible consciousness of a thoroughly authentic and practical truth in the midst of the ruins of all higher knowledge. That "perseverance in his course, despite of consequences," of which he boasts in his *Kritik der praktischen Vernunft* (p. 154), must have convinced him that if his criticism really had power to destroy all theoretical knowledge of the super-sensuous, no fact of consciousness whatever (and his recognition of an unconditioned practical Law is based upon a fact of consciousness) could hold its ground; every such fact being inseparably connected with theoretical judgments. We may estimate the strength of his

Kant's nobility of mind.

---

* It must, however, be confessed that the manner in which Kant himself applies the concept of intelligible freedom to the solution of this problem (*Kritik der prakt. Vernunft*, pp. 148, 149, 6th ed.) is very unsatisfactory, and does not even touch the real kernel of the difficulty.

moral consciousness, which would not for an instant entertain a doubt concerning that practical truth, by the logical force of the argument which should have driven him to a negative conclusion even in this sphere.

While, however, we must pay this tribute to Kant's noble spirit, and to his earnest love of truth, we need not refrain from the calm investigation of the question, whether his view of transcendental freedom, in his more minute definition of it be really tenable.

Here is a freedom in an intelligible or ideal sphere, quite beyond the range of our concrete being and consciousness, yea, separated therefrom by an immeasurable gulf. Not only are the two realms perfectly distinct, but their principles are contradictory; freedom reigns in the sphere of the Intelligible, but in that of the concrete, the stern necessity of nature is supreme. If this be the relation to each other of the two worlds, we have really no right to predicate intelligible freedom of one concrete phenomenon or act, any more than of another; and it must be regarded as a mere assertion on Kant's part, when he says that "every human action done according to some maxim which has reference to the moral Law, proceeds directly from intelligible freedom." For the fact of our consciousness regarding the moral law,— whether to act in unison with or against it,—demands, upon Kant's principles (like every other fact or event in the inner or outer life), an "immanent" explanation, *i.e.*, an explanation according to the empirical connection of cause and effect. If there be a blank here, it cannot really be in the fact itself but must be owing to our unskilfulness, or to the unavoidable limitedness of our capacities to discover the true explanation. Let us call to mind the way in which Kant led us to the discovery of this intelligible freedom. The transition from the world of Sense into the world of Intellect is not made to consist in the consciousness of self-determination in any act nor in the self-imputation of our conduct generally, to which Conscience obliges us, but in the consciousness that we are determined by a practical Law of unconditional authority.[*]

<small>Kant's dualism between the intelligible and the concrete world.</small>

---

[*] This transition or outgo is explained in Kant's *Grundlegung zur Metaphysic der Sitten*, as effected in a different way. "This freedom of the will," we read

Now from this may be inferred (if we grant Kant all that he demands) *a universal principle of intelligible self-determination* for the life in time of personal beings; no critical philosophy, conscious of its proper limits, would take upon itself to determine any thing further.* To attribute an intelligible origin to *every particular act,* because it happens to be accompanied with that consciousness of a practical Law, would be to exclude the prevailing character, the basis of disposition (to which not only each particular act, but that very consciousness itself is referable) from that origin. But how could the *Kritik der praktischen Vernunft* be in the least degree justified in this negative judgment? When Kant thus confines the claims of the moral law to the maxim or principle which bears upon "each particular act," this is no logical inference from his scientific principles, but is owing simply to an atomistic or isolating tendency in his own ethical views. He does not fail to perceive, however, that the impossibility of determining the moral value or otherwise of human actions, logically follows from the remoteness of the Intelligible and its freedom. "The moral quality of actions, their good or ill desert," he remarks in his *Kritik der reinen Vernunft,*" is wholly concealed from us, even as it relates to us. Our self-imputations of guilt can only have reference to our empirical character."†

[Sidenote: Kant not justified in this.]

Apart from this abstract separation of the two spheres, it is further evident that the empirical or concrete moral life—the moral character of the man as phenomenon—is to be regarded as more than a manifestation of his intelligible or true being.‡

[Sidenote: This dualism makes concrete life a shadow.]

p. 124, "practically (*i.e.,* in idea) to underlie, as a condition, all its spontaneous acts, is *necessary* to a reasonable being, who is conscious of his power of causality through Reason,—*i.e.,* of a Will as distinct from desire." If this is not mere tautology, we must take this consciousness "of a causality through reason, therefore of a will," to mean the consciousness of the practical Law of Reason, which determines the will.

* See the *Grundlegung zur Metaph. der Sitten,* p. 125, 126.

† *Ibid.* p. 429. It is equally impossible, according to Kant's principles, to refer our self-imputation to man's empirical character, and it contradicts what Kant himself teaches a little further on, p. 432. According to his principles, there could be no place for self-imputation or accountability in the world of experience as such.

‡ In his *Kritik der reinen Vernunft,* p. 430, Kant calls the empirical character "the sensuous or concrete" of the ideal character.

But how can pure freedom be manifest in what is its direct opposite—in the stern "mechanism of nature?" The phenomenon is said to have its foundation in the intelligible, so that "a difference in the intelligible or ideal character of any man causes a corresponding difference in his empirical character." But the phenomenon is much rather the complete *disguising* of the noumenon, nay, even its flat contradiction In fact, the intelligible existence conditioning our life in time can be manifested in concrete moral character only when this life is more than a mere manifestation of it, when it has the power to carry out what is originally established in that ideal existence by free self-determination. If, on the contrary according to the representation which Kant and others give of transcendental freedom, all is adjusted behind the scene of this earthly life, the so-called manifestation resolves itself into an unreal and vain show.

Now, if provisionally, and without attempting fully to explain the relationship, we compare this transcendental freedom with the conclusions arrived at in the last chapter concerning the nature of moral development, we find that the principle discovered by Kant manifests itself in our present life much more clearly and strongly in its reality as freedom than he will allow. And this actual entrance of the intelligible into our empirical life, and the weighty import thus attaching to the latter, so strongly impresses Kant himself, that he not only endeavours in his "*Kritik der Urtheilskraft*" to construct a bridge over the chasm between the supersensuous and the phenomenal, but in his *Kritik der "reinen,"* and *der praktischen Vernunft*, he sometimes quite forgets that there is such a chasm, and speaks of intelligible self-determination in morals as if it were homogeneous with empirical causality and its effects. Hence it is that Kant often speaks of man's intelligible character as his "way of thinking" (*modus cogitandi*), in distinction from his "way of feeling" (*modus sentiendi*), *i.e.*, his empirical character. In like manner, Kant, in his "*Kritik der reinen Vernunft*," p. 429, distinguishes between the part which "freedom" and which "nature" has in a man's actions,— "nature" denoting the innocent defect or accidental tempera-

Inconsistencies in Kant's views.

* *Grundlegung*, &c., p. 432.

ment,*—a way of speaking which would destroy the conception alike of nature and of freedom, if judged of by Kant's real principles. To this we must add what we have already referred to, his deriving evil from an *inability* in man fully to manifest himself according to his intelligible nature in his empirical life; for if empirical causality have this power of limiting intelligible causality both must be essentially homogeneous. Whatever the worth of Kant's view may otherwise be, these are only isolated inconsistencies arising from a just sense of a living union between the two spheres. Kant always returns to his real standing-point, according to which the intelligible and empirical are absolutely contrasted, the one including all freedom and independent existence, the other being only necessity of nature and dependent manifestation.

What we have said suffices to show wherein the main error of Kant's view consists. It is the proud disdain with which he regards our empirical being and consciousness as developed in time; and this has prevailed in the idealism of our philosophy ever since Kant, and through Kant's influence. The empirical is unjustly degraded when the data of its consciousness and its essential cognitions are wholly separated from God and His revelations, and are chained down to a world of sense which is nothing but appearance and vain show. Does man's being, apart from the eternally Intelligible, consist of nothing more than a sensuousness analogous to that of beasts? has it no other form than that of an animate mechanism of nature? Does experience arise only from the connection of sensational perception with the formal operations of the understanding? Is there not an experience possessing the highest and most directly spiritual significance? The *Kritik der reinen Vernunft* will not allow this, it excludes any such a conception of experience; and yet Kant uses the word "fact of reason" to denote man's unavoidable consciousness of the unconditional and authoritative moral law, and thus he scarcely disguises the truth that even with him a fact of inner experience must be the basis of transition into his intelligible world.

Kant's main error.

* In the "*Kritik der Urtheilskraft*," Introduction, p. 18, the two conceptions, "nature" and "freedom," are said ever to restrict the respective spheres of their working in the world of sense!

Now if this transition were really accomplished so as to enable man to gain possession of the intelligible world, he might easily brook the degradation of his empirical world, nay, even its forfeiture,—its dissolution into a merely subjective though still necessary conception. But even this appropriation is denied him; he does not get beyond the mere " obligation and command in its practical bearing;" if reality be denied to the sphere of nature with its mechanism and in the world of sense, "freedom also is only an idea of the reason whose objective reality is itself doubtful."*

His exclusive idealism.

Yet how strange is the issue of this philosophy! It opens man's eyes to the nothingness of this world of Experience, and at the same time tells him that he is bound to this nothingness with chains which cannot be broken. Beyond, in the heavenly region of the Intelligible, it assures him that truth resides, but, at the same time, that he can never reach that region. Thus he stands wavering between heaven and earth, attracted or repulsed by each in turn, and conscious only of his own cognitions and their subjectivity.

Unsatisfactory results.

But Kant takes a very decided step in advance in his *Religion innerhalb der Grenzen der blossen Vernunft*. Rightly feeling that it is practically insufficient merely to postulate the intelligible "in its practical bearing," he lays down some further definitions concerning the action of transcendental freedom, upon which our empirical moral nature is to be based. But of what avail will this be to us ? According to Kant's principles, it is utterly impossible for freedom (belonging, as it does, to the intelligible sphere) to be determined by anything in the phenomenal world.† If, therefore, man's free will has given to itself any determinateness beyond the bounds of time, no event of any kind in time can effect any change in it. Now, man has perverted the

---

* *Grundlegung zur Metaphysik der Sitten*, p. 114.

† See *e.g. Kritik der pr. Vernunft*, p. 142 :—"In the existence of the Subject, apart from the limitations of time, nothing precedes the decision of his will ; but every act, and indeed every determination of his being, changes in conformity with his inner spirit ;—yea, the whole course of his existence as a sensuous being is (in the consciousness of his ideal existence) to be looked upon merely as the consequence, and never as the determining ground, of his causality as noumenon."

principles of his conduct by an intelligible or ideal act, by subordinating the principle of obedience to the moral law to that of self-love; and herein radical evil consists.* If this be so, it is utterly impossible for him to become free from this perversion at any point of time whatever. He could not even do this, if we could conceive of his utterly losing the subjective notion of time; for the removal of one intelligible or ideal act by another following it, contradicts our conception of the ideal altogether; and the perversion of principles produced by freedom must continue for ever.†

Notwithstanding this, Kant still maintains the possibility of man's restoration, even in this his empirical existence, and by his own endeavours.‡ But he has done nothing whatever,—I will not say, to make this assumption conceivable,—but to free it from the obvious contradictions with which it is beset. Man must adopt reverence for the moral law, "as in itself a sufficient motive to determine his volition" § (if he does this at all during his present life), not by any gradual reform, but "by a revolution in his mind, by a kind of regeneration or new creation." But we look in vain for a principle which will accomplish this wonderful transformation; for that transcendental freedom, whose self-decision has moulded man's existence in time and his empirical character, has already "adopted" the perverted principle.

The possibility of restoration.

Kant appeals to the fact that Duty requires this revolution in man's way of thinking, and that he must be capable of it, according to the well-known *dictum*, "I ought, therefore I can."|| But this argument will convince no one who remembers Kant's previous conclusions. The radical depravity of mind which springs from

Kant's argument for this possibility.

---

* *Religion inn. der Grenzen d. bl. Vernunft*, pp. 26, 27.

† Predicates which contradict one another may be applicable to the same subject in the same relations; but this is possible in virtue of *time*. If intelligible existence be necessarily free from time, this possibility is removed. Two decisions, therefore, which contradict each other, cannot be attributed to man in his intelligible character; though it is conceivable that in his intelligible existence one thing may be predicated of him, so far as he depends upon the principle which infinitely conditions him; and another, so far as he depends upon his own decision; but it is the *difference of relation* which makes this possible.

‡ *Religion*, &c. p. 48.   § *Ibid.* p. 52, 54. || *Ibid.* p. 49, 54, 60.

perverted principles is not an *inability* arising from the weakness of our nature, but an *unwillingness*, perfectly free, and having reference to man as noumenon; necessary to man's empirical moral life and conduct, only because it has been decided upon by a decision of the intelligible will. Kant had already *once* for all concluded, from the conviction of obligation and responsibility which he found so deep-seated in human nature, that evil has its origin (notwithstanding that deep-seated conviction) not in inability, but in an intelligible act of freedom. And he could not, therefore, a *second* time use the axiom, "I ought (to avoid evil), therefore I can," which lies at the basis of that reasoning, in order to prove the opposite —the possibility of overcoming that radical evil. If to the man in the thraldom of sin the "can" derived from the moral ideal asserts itself as an "ought,"—if it says to him in the name of the law of practical reason, "Thou oughtest to be holy in every moment of thy life, therefore thou canst be so from this moment onward,"—he might reply, "I ought, perhaps, to be able, but I cannot."

Kant more distinctly describes his views concerning this ability as follows :—"Evil as a natural bias cannot be *destroyed* by human power; this can be brought about only by good maxims, and cannot therefore be accomplished if the highest subjective basis of all maxims be presupposed as depraved;* yet it may be *overcome*, because it is met with

* Why did not Kant in this case argue, "I ought, therefore, I can," seeing that the claims of the moral law demand the entire avoidance of evil? Upon the standing-point of the *Kritik der reinen Vernunft* we may reply, Because, if in consequence of such a "can" perfect holiness were realized in any human life, the phenomenal would be put on a par with the supersensuous, and empirical reality would be one with the Ideal; and thus Kant's entire theory of knowledge, which is based throughout upon the distinctness of these two spheres, would be overthrown. We need not take the question objectively; it is enough that, according to this theory of knowledge, the spirit of man is deficient in a faculty whereby to recognize such a similarity, and to express it in a judgment, which being theoretical, would depend upon the nature of a given object in experience. If such a man existed he would be judged not only by others but in his own consciousness as if there were an "ought" still present and binding, distinct from his moral being. If, therefore, there be necessarily in human consciousness an "ought" which surpasses the "can," then the axiom "I ought, therefore I can," is wholly done away with. If this axiom be maintained, the theory of knowledge contained in the *Kritik der reinen Vernunft* must be given up. For as the consciousness of the moral law actually forms the transition from the phenomenal to the Intelligible world, the axiom, "I ought, therefore

in man as a free agent."* This, and similar assertions, may have been congenial to Pelagian tendencies then in vogue, but they can never be consistently developed from the principles of Kant's system. According to these the one extra-temporal act of freedom is an unalterable predetermination for the whole course of time,† the idle dream of self-redemption and regeneration by one's own power, fares no better than "that well-intentioned expectation of moralists, from Seneca to Rousseau," that the world would continually advance from worse to better. ‡ Man thus remains irretrievably lost in the abyss of radical evil. Kant, himself, virtually admits this in the places already quoted, and frequently in his *Religionslehre* the bias towards evil is, according to him, utterly indestructible in human nature. But apart from his notion of ideal freedom he is forced to this conclusion by another part of his system, his dualism between the ideal and the real, the abstract and the concrete, which allows, not the *perfect* removal of evil from the empirical existence of man, but only a so-called "infinite approximation thereto." This inevitable issue of Kantian thought, comfortless as it is, will not suprise any one who perceives that with so thorough an apprehension of sin nothing but the Redemption provided in Christianity can secure the hope of real holiness and bliss.

It is easy to see that our moral life, as it actually is, contradicts this theory of intelligible freedom. Viewed fairly, and as it really is, it presents to us (as we saw in the preceding chapter) neither that absolute freedom which Kant's Practical Reason postulates and requires, nor that total want of freedom or necessity of nature which his Theoretic Reason would discover, but in

Our actual moral life contradicts this ideal freedom.

I can," if taken in its full meaning, returns endowed with the authority of the Intelligible into the temporal or empirical world. But such a return is inadmissible upon Kant's theory.

* *Kritik der reinen Vernunft*, p. 35.

† By predetermination Kant understands simply that every single act, viewed empirically or as an occurrence, owes its existence to conditions beyond the bounds of time; conditions which, at the moment when the act is done, are beyond the control of the agent. But from his conclusions concerning the relation of the abstract or ideal to the concrete or phenomenal there ensues quite another and more powerful predeterminism. The volition beyond the bounds of time in the region of the ideal, is for all volition in time, an invincible Fate.

‡ As before, p. 5.

fact a CONDITIONAL and LIMITED FREEDOM. We have seen that in this present life this freedom asserts itself in its self-movement as a progressive principle of moral development. But the Kantian conception of freedom is no more compatible with this than is the doctrine of a causal connection of every thing in time. Neither is it in harmony with the conservative aspect of man's moral development, which traces a connected series in its progress; it contradicts this just as the empirical notion of indeterminism contradicts it. Every act of will—so far as it can be fairly regarded as moral and imputable to the Subject—comes forth, according to Kant, from the abyss of transcendental freedom without any connection with what has preceded it, and without any bearing on the future moral life. Kant expresses this very clearly when he says, " Every evil act, when we trace its origin in Reason, must be contemplated as if the man had fallen into it direct from a state of innocence."*

It is hardly necessary for us here to prove at length that our consciousness of guilt, if strictly analysed, while it confirms the germ of Kant's thought, by no means sanctions its development. It by no means confines itself to the abstract fact of a transgression of the known moral Law, without making any further distinction. We need not here repeat what has been so ably said on this (from the standing-point of an intelligent Determinism) by Herbart, in his *Pyschologie*, and Romang in his treatise upon "The Freedom of the Will and Determinism," against the doctrine that imputation presupposes absolute freedom in every act of will as such. We shall here only venture to add two observations.

In some parts of his writings, Kant lays great stress upon the fact that we hold a man responsible for his transgression, and therefore judge his act to be free; even when empirically considered, it is the necessary result of circumstances over which he has no control, —bad education, for instance, evil bias of temperament, bad company, and so forth:—and he considers this a strong confirmation of his theory of transcendental freedom.† But would our unprejudiced moral sense judge after this fashion ? We certainly may hold the man responsible for an evil act com-

Degrees of guilt.

---

* *Rel innerh. der Grenzen der blossen Vernunft*, pp. 42, 43. *Kritik der reinen Vernunft*, p. 432.

† *Kritik der reinen Vernunft*, p. 432. *Kr. der prakt. V.* p. 145.

mitted under such circumstances; but we by no means allow that this act is the necessary result of these circumstances. We consider that his self-determination acts as a limiting force upon these circumstances, that the decision to yield to, or resist the temptation, really depends upon the bias of his will, and that this in turn is contingent upon his self-determination, either at this or at former moments of his life. But as we allow that circumstances, independent of choice, have a co-determining influence, we recognize (so far as these are present) degrees of responsibility and imputation. When the will has resisted the temptation, but owing to the circumstances referred to, the temptation has been so strong, that an extraordinary power of resistance would have been necessary to overcome it, our verdict as to the man's guilt is somewhat mitigated. If, on the contrary, we find that these circumstances were all in favour of the evil-doer's resistance of the temptation, we find the guilt of the act enhanced. How little does our moral judgment thus, uncorrupted by any one-sided scholastic doctrine of guilt, coincide with the Kantian abstraction! It may sometimes seem indeed to confirm it, because all the outward circumstances contributing to the moral development of the sinner, are never, strictly speaking, fully known to us; often we are quite ignorant of them, and when a decision is required of us, we have to confine it to the isolated act. The confession of the sinner himself may sometimes reveal to us the genesis of his transgression, but it cannot unfold that bearing of past circumstances upon his act, because he is himself but partially acquainted with them, and is still less capable of instituting a just comparison between his own circumstances and those of others. But even if we have to restrict our judgment to the act in itself, our moral judgment by no means regards it, according to the Kantian idea of freedom, as a bare fact of a violation of a moral command present to consciousness at the time; it recognizes in the act itself different degrees of criminality, arising partly from the objective importance attaching to the duties neglected, or sin committed, and partly from the subjective clearness of the consciousness of the opposite duty.

Christianity ratifies and confirms these facts of our moral judgment. It first of all does justice to the abstract view, because it presupposes a moral sense in all mankind, and holds each one answerable for every transgression of the moral law. This principle runs throughout the New Testament, and it would be superfluous to quote particular passages. The Apostle Paul recognizes this inextinguishable spark, even in the darkened consciousness of the heathen, and on the ground of it he holds them responsible, Rom i. 32, ii. 9-16. Can these declarations of Holy Scripture be interpreted as referring to an act of transcendental freedom, which, according to the Kantian view makes all human sins alike in guilt? The Doctrine of Christianity certainly is, that all sins are equally sins, because all spring from the same perverted principle, and herein lies the main distinction between good and evil. But Christianity recognizes within this essential sameness the greatest differences in the degrees of guilt. It speaks of a sin, which as distinct from all other sins, will never be forgiven, Matt. xii. 21, 22; and of another which a brother is not to pray for, 1 John v. 18. These special sins are not certainly that Radical Evil, which is said to be universal, and beyond the range of time; they are particular acts of persons committed in time. They are, moreover, developments in time, whereby the man enhances the power of sin in himself, so that Divine grace is withdrawn, and he is given over to a reprobate mind,—Rom. i. 24, and other passages. Christianity, moreover, recognizes degrees of guilt, contingent upon the strength of the sinner's consciousness of the full import of his sinful act, and upon the perception he has of the obligation of the moral standard. He who knows not this Law as his Lord's will, and transgresses it, is worthy of punishment, because his conscience must recognize its general obligation apart from this; but a double punishment is merited by him who does also thus know it as his Lord's will, Luke xii. 47. "To whom much is given, of him shall be much required;" the enormity of the guilt increases with the clearness of the moral consciousness. The appearance, therefore, of Christ, in history, involed a $\kappa\rho\iota\sigma\iota\varsigma$. Sodom and Tyre and Sidon incurred God's judgments on account of their sins; but those Galilean cities incur it in far higher degree which rejected the Son of God. For if what had been done in them had been done in Sodom and Tyre and Sidon they would have repented, Matt. xi. 21, 24. Not only, therefore, are there degrees of guilt, but these depend upon circumstances, arising from time and lying within its range. Here, too, mention is made, not of man's estimate only, but of God's; and how can we reconcile with this a view according to which all guilt and imputation depend upon the decisions of transcendental freedom, and all that occurs in time, is the logical consequence of those decisions?

There are two truths, ignorance of which rendered it impossible for Kant to take a right view of the relation between man's ideal or abstract being and his empirical life in time.

On the one hand, Kant—and not Kant alone, but all of a spiritualistic tendency who regard time and space as limits foreign to the nature of Spirit, a tendency to be found alike among philosophers and theologians—Kant mistook the truth that every derived and conditioned being requires time and space in order to the full realization of its existence.

<small>Finite existence requires time and space.</small>

Concrete spirit cannot be itself, it cannot have the component parts of its being, as if instanter, because it does not exist of itself, because its existence has a dependent beginning; it must, therefore "become" in order to be what it is according to the conception of it. The form or condition of its being, as well as of its development, is TIME. Created spirit, further, as conditioned, cannot begin to exist without excluding from itself another conditioned being (spiritual as well as *material*, for spirits are in their nature more impenetrable than bodies, only that they can overcome their impenetrability by love as the *communicativum sui*, whereas bodies cannot), and separating itself from it. This essential limitation must have a definite expression, and this it obtains in a CORPOREITY conformable to spirit. If finite spirit loses the power to imprint its immanent or inherent limitation distinctly on this externality objective to it, it lacks also the power to operate, and to manifest itself to other beings of its kind. Time and space, accordingly, distinguish or separate created being as individual; and as conditions of experimental knowledge* wherein the spirit takes

---

* TRENDELENBURG has ably shown that while the *Kritik der reinen Vernunft* has demonstrated that time and space are the subjective *a priori* conditions of our perception and experience, it has by no means proved that they are merely subjective, that they are not also forms of " things in themselves."

up into itself the fulness of separate being, they again unite what is separated.

We have no right to regard the determinate form which time and space—our gradual development and our corporeity—have for our perception and consciousness as the only possible one universally and for ever established; yet we are justified in regarding the entrance into the "now" and the "here" as an advance in the being of the individual spirit, whereby it attains the full determinateness of its own existence. Philosophy looks for man's state of humiliation and his state of exaltation in wrong places when it seeks the former within the limits of time and space, and the latter in the negation of these limits, and in the so-called pure spirituality of the Spirit's existence. As the true master in any art shows himself in limitation, so God has not disdained to assign an existence within the limits of time and space to things of the very highest moment; and this is the second truth which Kant failed to perceive. It is not usually God's method to display His great thoughts ostentatiously. He rather conceals them, quenching their beams from bold presumptuous eyes, and hiding His higher works beneath a plain and simple form. When the true artist unveils an inner infinity of beauty and of grace within the narrow space of the human frame, from whom does he learn this but from the Creator, the Master Artist? Time, which the critical and idealistic philosopher so much despises, has been so highly esteemed by God as to perfect in it, and at a definite point of time (Gal. iv. 4), the Incarnation of His Son, and to accomplish in it the Redemption of the human race. The Word of the righteousness which is of faith is not far from thee that thou shouldest ascend up into heaven or descend into the deep; it is nigh thee, within the limits of thy earthly being (Rom. x. 6–8), and during time the possession of life eternal is offered thee (John vi. 47).

Time and space not a limit, but an advance.

§ 3. DEVELOPMENT OF KANT'S PHILOSOPHY.
Schmid.

The view of freedom and of its relation to evil, which Kant developed, has been surrendered in its most essential points by his immediate adherents and followers. C. CH. ERL. SCHMID would not entertain the notion of a positive basis of evil, nor of a self-determination of freedom towards evil in the sphere of the

Intelligible; he derived evil, on the contrary, from a limitation of our moral freedom,* a limitation, however, original, and therefore to be attributed to the intelligible substratum of our empirical character. FICHTE contented himself with an explanation of evil not differing essentially from that which derives it from sense, and upon a principle which, so far as he took pains to define it, resolved it as necessarily as does sensationalism into mere limitation and negation; he took the source of evil to be merely the *vis inertiae* of nature.† SCHELLING was the first to take up the thread of the investigation where Kant had left it, in a work which is unquestionably the most important contribution to modern speculation regarding freedom and evil, and which in profundity and exhaustless wealth of thought, in nobleness and power of exposition, has seldom been equalled in philosophic literature, I mean his "*Philosophischen Untersuchungen über das Wesen der menschlichen Freiheit und die damit zusammenhangenden Gegenstände.*‡ It is obvious, that as Schelling's Dissertation does not treat of human freedom and the origin of evil in an isolated way, we must view the conclusions it arrives at in their connection with the principles it develops.

<small>Fichte.</small>

<small>Schelling.</small>

<small>Schelling's theory; two principles in God.</small> In order to explain freedom, the treatise begins with the contrast between two equally eternal principles, darkness and light, the real and the

---

* *Versuch einer Moralphilosophie*, pp. 335, 336, 379, (2d ed.).|

† *System der Sittenlehre*, pp. 262, 263. The otherwise unimportant work of A. C. CHRIST. HEYDENREICH, entitled "*Freiheit u. Determinismus und ihre Vereinigung*, 1793, keeps more closely to the primary import of Radical Evil. Yet, this ultimately destroys the Kantian thought, for it takes Radical Evil to be part of God's plan of nature, according to which "the pupil of providence must begin with evil in order that his personal birth, and the authoritative majesty of his good spirit, may gain strength by conflict therewith, and by these active endeavours to pass from darkness to light, may merit Divine rewards," (pp. 130, 131), *i.e.*, man's task is to make good what God has purposely made evil.

‡ *Sämmtliche Werke*, part i. vol. vii. pp. 331-416 ; compare also his *Denkmal der Schrift Jakobi's*, &c., in vol. viii. pp. 19-126, and his *Briefe an Eschenmayer* pp. 161-189. An exposition of the doctrine of Satan as an "ambiguous principle," an exposition in perfect keeping with his doctrine of "potences" (see vol. vi. pp. 231-278), is to be found in Schelling's *Vorlesungen über die Philosophie der Offenbarung*, (part ii. vols. iii. iv.) ; but any later inquiries concerning man's freedom in connection with evil, which may have greatly modified the views put forth in the above-named dissertations, are not there given.

ideal, the particularizing and universalizing, Self and Intellect. The union of these two principles is the condition of all life; idealism needs a living realism as its basis. Both principles therefore are in God, for we must distinguish God as *existing*, and the *basis* of his existence which He has in Himself as *causa sui*, yet, which as an essence, is distinct from Him the self-existent, "*nature in God.*"* God is a *personal Being*, only in so far as the ideal principle in Him and a basis independent of this are blended together into one absolute existence.† While the absolute indifference of the Ungrounded (that which is without cause) precedes this twofoldness of principles, absolute identity of spirit rises far above this; but above spirit again, is the originally Ungrounded, inasmuch as it is now glorified as LOVE which is all in all.‡

In nature these two principles are blended only in a certain degree, but in personality they become perfectly one.§ In God, their identity is indissoluble, but in man it is and must be separable, for were it indissoluble in him as it is in God, man would not be distinct from God, and God could not reveal Himself as Spirit and Love.‖ The distinction between the two principles does not yet, however, amount to the antithesis of good and evil; the principle of independent existence, abiding at the foundation, or as a potentiality merely, is rather itself an element of actual good, it is its necessary basis.¶ Evil begins to appear in a positive perversion of principles,—independent existence forcibly separating itself from the principle of intelligence, and assuming the pre-eminence.** The possibility of such a perversion is involved in the separableness of the two principles in personal beings, whereas in nature they are bound together as if by a law of necessity.††

These blended in man.

Evil the perversion of these.

We pause for a moment in our account of Schelling's theory, to notice the fact that evil is in these statements represented as the positive antithesis of good, a principle of disturbance and division inimical to all order and harmonious connection. It

Derivation of evil from ideas explains only its possibility.

---

* *Sämmtliche Werke*, p. 358; *Denkmal Jakobi's* pp. 69, 71, 72; *Briefe an Eschen.* p. 164.   † *Ibid.*, pp. 394, f., 399, f.; *Denkmal Jakobi's*, pp. 79, 80.
‡ *Ibid.* pp. 406-408. See note B at the end of this chapter.
§ *Ibid.* p. 375.   ‖ *Ibid.* pp. 359, 377.   ¶ *Ibid.* pp. 360, 361, 375.
** *Ibid.* pp. 362, 363, 389, 390, 399.   †† *Ibid.* p. 375.

is directly recognized here, that any derivation of evil from ideas, can go no further than to demonstrate its *possibility;* the realization of it is never reached in this manner; it can only be discovered by experience. Indeed, as Schelling himself expressly recognizes,* evil is not only the loosing of the bond between the two principles,—if it were only this, we might imagine some teleological necessity for evil, *e.g.*, that man must become conscious of each of these principles in its distinctive nature, in order perfectly to harmonize them,—but it is the perversion of their true order and adjustment; and this perversion would no longer be a perversion, if it were a condition of their perfect adjustment.

Now Schelling in many places describes the relation of evil to good in this sense, not only when he is speaking of the possibility of evil, but when he is treating of it as a realized fact. Thus he argues that "in order to man's becoming conscious of the two principles, it was necessary that there should be some solicitation to evil."† In like manner he says concerning the will of "the basis" principle,—"though it has no desire to violate love, it may often seem to have;"‡ so that we dare not attribute to this will, whereby the revelation of love itself is conditioned, "any real or intentional opposition to love," in virtue of which it would become an evil will. That activity of "the basis" principle, which constitutes the independent and distinctive will of man, is necessary in order to good only so far as it remains in "the basis," and is subject to the other, "the ideal" principle; § and thus the endeavour of "the basis" in created beings "to actualize itself for itself alone must ever be in vain." ǁ Accordingly it is said of man that "he has in himself the springs of self-movement both to good and evil,"¶ a statement which would be meaningless if man must necessarily incline exclusively to good or exclusively to evil, or successively to both. That this is not meant is clear from an expression in p. 439 ;—"as man

marginal note: This clear from Schelling's statements.

---

* *Sämmtliche Werke*, part i. vol. vii. p. 365.   † *Ibid.* p. 374.   ‡ *Ibid.* p. 375.

§ *Ibid.*, pp. 365, 399. Speaking of disease, which he calls "the true prefigurement and type of evil," Schelling says, "It arises from the effort of something whose life and freedom is given it only to abide in its place a part of the whole, to live and act for itself alone."

ǁ *Ibid.* p. 378.   ¶ *Ibid.* p. 374.

in his independent existence is Spirit, he must be free in respect of both principles." Accordingly Schelling says further on, "as man would be dead to all distinctiveness o character if he remained in the centre, it is necessary for him to endeavour to come forth towards the circumference;"* ye this implies that man must be strongly solicited to evil, though not necessitated thereto. Evil is, accordingly, described a man's own choice and guilt.

But still a different aspect of the subject is now and then *The notion of* presented amid all these thoughts, which would *the necessity* lead us to a different conclusion. If, as Schelling *of evil* *traceable in* says, "good consists in the subjugation of man' *Schelling.* self-dependence, in its being reduced from activit to potentiality,"† it follows that this self-dependence must firs put forth its activity in an abnormal "centrifugal" directio before it can by self-restraint become good. But this puttin forth of its activity is itself evil. And, accordingly, Schelling' *Dissertation* maintains that evil was necessary to the mani festation of God, that every essence becomes manifest by mean of its opposite, love in hatred, unity in discord.‡ The will c Love must meet with something that opposes it, in order tha it may realize itself;§ in the realm of spirit there must be principle of darkness, the spirit of evil, *i.e.*, "the dividin asunder of light and darkness"‖—by the separation of th second principle from the first. The mystery which sin woul profane must be made manifest; for that inner bond betwee the dependence of things and the divine essence, which is a it were before all existence, and is therefore awful, reveal itself only in the contrast of sin.¶

We believed, and certainly for good reasons ventured t *Naturalistic* assume, that this decree in the divine order of lif *tendency the* and its development, might admit of the possibilit *cause of this.* of evil only as the point of coincidence, which ev in its beginning might find in the principle of self-dependenc so that its realization might remain a matter of will or contir gency, but could have no foundation in rationality, or i designed and causal necessity. In that view the ethica principle is maintained, as, indeed, it should be in any inquir

* *Sämmtliche Werke*, part i. vol. vii. p. 381.
† *Ibid.* p. 400; *Briefe an Eschenmayer*, p. 174, f.
‡ *Ibid.* p. 374.   § *Ibid.* p. 375.   ‖ *Ibid.* p. 377.   ¶ *Ibid.* p. 39

concerning evil; but the spirit of a naturalistic philosophy pervades this latter view. Here the realization of evil is made a divine necessity. Evil is converted into a cosmical force, or "potence" active as the inciter of all powers both in nature and in man;* —nay, the very conception of good and evil in man is made contingent upon the knowledge of this general evil.† Here we have really the naturalistic idea of the identity of Spirit and nature, according to which the former proceeds from the latter simply by quantitative differences and gradations. The appearance of Spirit—when man was made —was not the entrance of any new principle into the sphere of created life, as is expressly represented in Genesis (i. 26, ii. 7), its principles are only those which were in nature before, but their manifestation is more perfect. Nature glorifies itself into spirit, or Spirit raises itself out of nature, by an ever-increasing separation, and by the higher and more intimate combination of those principles in their operations.

Generally speaking, it would hardly be for the interest of Theology to act upon the earnest warnings of some distinguished men, *e.g.*, Steffens, Baader, and Rothe, and to ally and blend itself with speculative and naturalistic science, in order, as it is said, to renew her youth; and we cannot believe that the clearest understanding of evil can be attained anywhere save in that sphere where alone there is evil properly so called,‡ namely, in the sphere of the spirit and of freedom. "Foreshadowings," or "types" of evil may be found in nature, but these can be explained only by a right understanding of moral evil. Here it is that the problem must be solved, if ever it be solved at all.

The religious view the only true one.

Besides these two views of the relation between the irrational and the intellectual or ideal principle, there appears in Schelling's writings a third idea, which is essentially dualistic. The contrast between "the basis" and "the ideal" principles now assumes the form of a serious conflict between the independent forces, wherein the one seeks to destroy the other. The "basis" principle acts against freedom, and "anticipating the coming light (in history), rouses all powers out of their state of indecision, and provokes

Third and dualistic view of Schelling.

---

* *Sämmtliche Werke*, part i. vol. vii. p. 372. † *Ibid.* p. 381.
‡ This is recognized in Schelling's Dissertation itself, p. 377.

them to opposition."* But the ideal principle asserts itself on the other side with an equally decided hostility; there seems to be a contradiction between the universal will and man's individual will, and the union of both seems difficult if not impossible. For that centre of universal will in which man was created is "a consuming fire"† for every particular will, and therefore for the principle of self-dependence, for the will and action of "the basis" principle, whereby man becomes a distinct being. Mention is, in like manner, made of an "independent and isolated action of the *basis* principle" from which creations must have proceeded, which, however, had not strength to continue; ‡ and at p. 410 it is said generally that "all beings of nature have existence in the *basis* principle alone," whereas, according to other statements—and we may add, according to Schelling's doctrine of Identity—we must suppose that both principles are blended in every being.

Can this strong leaning towards Dualistic conclusions in Schelling's theory surprise us? That theory presents to us two equally eternal and relatively independent, nay, even conflicting principles, and an original Unity raised far above these,—the only guarantee for the triumph of the intellectnal principle and the overthrow of the basis principle, so far as this guarantee cannot be derived from experience—namely, "absolute Indifference," "the primary Basis," or "the Ungrounded," of which nothing can be predicated save that it is "predicateless."§ If "the basis" principle be full of presage, like a night abounding in mysterious forms, enclosing in its darkness a gleam of glimmering light, the Ungrounded must be the original night in which all outlines and determinations vanish, and such a state of indifference cannot secure for us the desired guarantee. As it is wholly indifferent to any contrast of good and evil, there is no reason why (so far as activity can in any sense be ascribed to it) it should give pre-eminence to the ideal principle rather than the basis principle. The fact that Schelling's *Dissertation* calls this ungrounded original by the name of LOVE does not explain this. For however independent of time this elevation of it to love may be, the *Dissertation* represents it as the

Marginal note: This not to be wondered at.

---

* *Sämmtliche Werke*, part i. vol. vii. pp. 379, 381 ; compare pp. 399, 400.
† *Ibid.* p. 381. ‡ *Ibid.* p. 378. § *Ibid.* p. 406.

result of a process. But herein is the very difficulty—how can any process whatever spring from this "Ungrounded," which is "nothing but the negation of all contrasts," and in which we can neither conceive of an impulse to become anything, nor of a will to create anything? And how can this ungrounded essence certify to us that the eternal result of the process will be love? The Dissertation seems to obviate this latter difficulty, and indeed the former too, by describing this result as the aim of the Ungrounded;—"The Ungrounded divides itself into two beginnings equally eternal (which could not be in it at the same time or as one) in order that these may become one by love, *i.e.*, it divides itself in order that there may be life and love and personal existence."* But in order to set before it this aim of love, the Ungrounded must be more than the mere " Ungrounded " or "predicateless Essence," it must be a conscious and loving Essence, and its evolution as Spirit and personality cannot be the after result of a process set on foot by the adoption of such an aim.

Thus this doctrine overleaps its own bounds, and leads us to *data* which coincide with Christianity, namely, to the recognition of an absolute Personality raised far above the process of this world, yet operating upon it so as to determine it and lead it on to its goal. We have thus also attained a Unity strong enough to subdue the conflicting contrasts rampant in the world; whereas, if these contrasts be traced back even to this Divine being, "the Ungrounded" is much too abstract an essence to ward off the Dualism involved in the supposed separation of those two principles in God Himself.

As to the conception of human freedom, which is the theme of the *Dissertation,* it is based upon the dualistic element which we have traced in Schelling's views. The Idealistic conception of freedom being recognized in its truth, yet being described as inadequate for the solution of the problem because it is general and formal, "the power to do good and evil"† is set forth as the real and living conception of freedom. But here again the difficulty arises, how could power to do evil ever spring from God, who is the most perfect Being and purely good? If freedom be an ability to do evil it must have its

Real freedom according to these principles.

* *Sämmtliche Werke,* part i. vol. vii. p. 408.   † *Ibid.* p. 352.

origin somewhere apart from Him. This it is which obliges the *Dissertation* to pass from the conception of freedom to the setting up of those two principles, one of which is described as "that in God which is not Himself, but is 'the basis' of His existence."* Man, therefore, as he derives his origin from that "basis" which, while inseparable from God is not God Himself, "possesses in himself a principle independent of God,"† and in virtue of this he may possess a freedom which essentially includes the ability to do evil; and at the same time evil can be regarded as something positive "when a germ of freedom is recognized in the independent basis of nature."‡

While a *real* freedom is here maintained,§ a *formal* freedom is likewise defined. Possessing this, man has also an original will, the will of the "basis" principle, by which he moulds himself. ‖ He possesses no existence as a spiritual essence before or independent of his will.¶ His several actions, therefore, issue with inviolable necessity from his determinate nature, yet this inner necessity is itself his freedom; for "the nature of man is essentially his own deed."**

<small>Schelling's formal freedom.</small>

But is that difficulty which has so often met us—the difficulty involved in the relation of evil in the creature to the all-appointing will of God—that knot in which all difficulties centre,—really solved by this? Evil, as such, can have its origin in the creature alone; but its realization implies the stirring of the dark basis of nature, its separation from the ideal principle, its acting in the creature for itself alone, and its reacting against unity and order.†† "Evil," says Schelling, "is nothing more than the primary *basis* of existence endeavouring to realize itself in created being."‡‡ Now, in order to preserve God's own freedom, and to avoid Dualism, this independent action of the *basis* principle must

<small>Relation of evil thus explained to God's will.</small>

<small>Doctrine of sufferance.</small>

---

* *Sämmtliche Werke*, part i. vol. vii. pp. 357, 358.
† *Ibid.* pp. 362, 363 ; comp. 354.
‡ *Ibid.* p. 371.
§ It is hardly necessary to remind the reader, that the expression "real freedom," is not here used in the same sense as that given it in the first chapter of this part of our work. Schelling's view of freedom, as here given, is quite distinct from ours.
‖ *Ibid.* p. 385.   ¶ *Ibid.* p. 388.   ** *Ibid.* p. 385.
†† *Ibid.* pp. 374, 375, 380, 381.   ‡‡ *Ibid.* p. 378.

involve a letting of it work on God's part, who is spirit and love, and this is taken to be "the only conceivable idea of permission."* But this permitted working of the "basis" principle is clearly the point wherein those very difficulties centre, which Schelling himself sums up in a few bold outlines in the beginning of his work—difficulties which beset the attempt to reconcile the fact of evil with the principles of theism. How can God permit the basis principle in created being to endeavour to realize itself, if this endeavour involves or leads to evil, and to a will opposed to God?

Is this question already met by the argument that there must be a basis of existence distinct from God the self-existent? This argument brings us only to the necessity of the basis principle "in its unity with the self-existing God," and in so far only as it is what its very name imports, "the basis," the foundation or *substratum* of the ideal principle;— the necessity of a basis which leaves this its true position and becomes a self-operating and dominant principle, is by no means proved. If the argument did hold good for the perversion of the basis principle, then, notwithstanding the above protestation made by Schelling, evil must be a universal principle, conditioning even God's existence,—a conclusion which would directly contradict the avowed anti-dualistic aim of the Dissertation. If, therefore, we cannot affirm regarding this elevation of the basis to be the dominant principle, that God must or could have positively willed it, however conditionally, —as the condition, that is, of his existence,—the idea of permission retains its strict and literal sense, namely, "not hindering an activity proceeding from another cause which he who permits it might have hindered." But there is no reason why this idea of permission may not be applied to a principle arising solely within the sphere of created being, by whose independent working evil is produced; for the absolute dependence of the creature, which might be urged as an objection against this, would clearly be done away with by the supposed permission. If, on the contrary, the divine permission of evil be ultimately resolved into a positive act of will, in order that God, by means of the contrast thus produced, may have a real existence as love, we come face to face with the impossi-

* *Sämmtliche Werke*, part i. vol. vii. p. 375.

bility (already demonstrated in this work) of deriving evil from the divine will without destroying the true conception either of evil or of God's will.

While this doctrine of "the basis" principle, therefore, does not furnish any means of solving the universal difficulty save what are equally furnished, though in a different manner, by Theism itself, it involves another and special difficulty regarding human freedom in evil as the foundation of accountability. According to Schelling's doctrine, man possesses the power of doing evil so far only as his freedom springs from a basis distinct from God Himself; and he is stirred to the actual willing of evil by the solicitations of the basis principle, and is striving against unity. In so far as the divine permission for this striving to realise itself in created beings may be understood literally as a divine self-restraint, provision is certainly made for a relative independence of God in the basis principle and its workings, and for a relative independence in man when he chooses evil; but how can freedom and accountability be based upon this, when man is free from that determining power, only in so far as another eternal and universal principle takes possession of him, rousing his independence, and giving it supremacy? Man's will is thus swallowed up in the movements and conflicts of general cosmical forces, alternately retiring and advancing, which leave no room for independent action on the part of created being.

Another difficulty.

It is easy to prove, that according to Schelling's development of formal freedom, man must have in himself the springs of self-movement alike to good and to evil, that as spirit he is independent of both principles, and that when he chooses evil as the perversion of the true relation between the two principles this is his own act, a resolve come to from a state of original indecision. Granted;—but if we keep to this the will cannot be conditioned by two contrasted principles. In this case the definition of freedom given in the *Dissertation,* "the power of doing good or evil," cannot be the primary, but only the derived conception of it.* For to assign a double principle

Schelling's formal freedom does not remove this.

---

* This inference is confirmed by the statement in p. 403 that evil will come to an end at some future time, so that freedom must then at least cease to be the power of doing evil.

to creature freedom is altogether different from attributing to it the necessity of deciding between two equal possibilities presented to it, the one good and the other evil.

In short, the conceptions of formal and real freedom, according to the terminology of Schelling's *Dissertation*, do not harmonize. This is clear from the fact that man's transition from a state of indecision to one of resolve for good, is pronounced impossible, without some general basis of temptation to evil which shall elicit the self-assertion and the contrast; so that "when the will of the love principle arises, it may meet with some resistance, wherein it can realize itself."* If we understand this rightly, it sacrifices "formal" freedom to "real,"—to a real freedom which is not, properly speaking, freedom at all, but only an absorption of our moral consciousness and volition in a general cosmical process. No doctrine of freedom which supports itself by a dualistic element can satisfy the expectations which it awakens, even in the moral interests of freedom.

Schelling's formal and real freedom clash.

Let us now see how Schelling defines this formal aspect of the conception of freedom.

As to ideal freedom and its relation to moral life in time, the penetrating eye of Schelling cannot fail to have perceived the contradictions in which the Kantian theory is involved. Of the conflicting methods adopted by Kant in prosecuting the inquiry, Schelling chose the one which fell in with his principles, and carried it through; and thus inconsistency was avoided. Kant had already avowed that "sensuous life, on account of our intelligible consciousness of its existence (*i.e.*, freedom), possesses the absolute unity of a phenomenon which must be judged according to the absolute spontaneity of freedom."† He called the empirical character not of single acts, but of man, "the outline ($\sigma\chi\eta\mu\alpha$) in sense, of ideal character."‡ If this is to be taken literally, it implies, not that the single decisions of the will which contradict each other variously, even in the same subject, may be directly referred to intelligible or ideal freedom,—though Kant commonly does this,—but that man's moral life as a whole is

Schelling's limitation of Kant's theory.

---

* *Sämmtliche Werke*, part i. vol. vii. p. 374, 375.
† *Kritik der prakt. Vern.* p. 144. ‡ *Kritik der reinen Vern.* p. 430.

to be regarded as a reflection in time of an intelligible and primary choice; that it is produced, as it were, by the refraction and dividing of the single beam of light as it passes into the element of time. Now, starting from this point, Schelling apprehends the act of self-decision determining man's life in time,—an act which does not precede life in the order of time, but imperceptibly runs throughout it,—to be "an act in its nature (according to the nature of the case?) eternal."* Man, whose character seems fixed and determined during his life here, "has given to himself in his first creation a definite form," namely (as we are immediately told), "that of independence and selfishness; and as he has been from eternity, so is he born. As he acts here, so has he acted in the beginning of the creation and from eternity."†

Thus Schelling expressly maintains the strict predetermining of all moral character and conduct in time by an intelligible or ideal self-decision. This Kant had concealed from himself, though it was the logical consequence of his theory of freedom; but as the freedom of the will would thus be utterly destroyed, it was necessary somehow to save it. Kant, according to his usual plan, abides by the theory of a double source, empirical and intelligible, of particular acts. The one, which is wholly necessitating, but pertaining only to the phenomenal world, he discovers in those temporal causes to which he attributes the outward and present character of the agent. The other, the true one, whereby man has his conduct perfectly under his own control, he takes to be transcendental freedom. Schelling admits that each act proceeds from the heart of man according to the law of identity, and with absolute necessity; for he understands this necessity literally, and in no way attributes to man the power of acting otherwise. But he holds this inner necessity to be itself freedom; for "the nature of the man is his own deed,"‡ having its source in that eternal self-decision.

<small>He carries necessity further than Kant.</small>

<small>Maintaining it to be freedom.</small>

It is clear that the reasons which hindered our adoption of the Kantian theory of ideal freedom, instead of being obviated, are really intensified, by this logical development of them. According to this, we must expect the manifestation of moral

* Schelling, as before, pp. 385, 386.   † *Ibid.* p. 387.   ‡ *Ibid.* pp. 385, 386.

character in time according to a law of inviolable necessity, which, on the face of it, is objectionable, and on closer examination is found to be contrary to the facts of moral development and to our moral judgment.

There is one point in particular wherein Schelling's more thorough carrying out of Kant's principle increases the difficulty, or rather shows it in its fullness. Kant having recognized a Radical Evil derived from intelligible freedom, was guilty of the logical inconsistency of requiring the conquest of this evil on man's part as he exists in time, and of asserting man's ability to effect this, without allowing as the basis of this ability a self-decision on the part of his intelligible freedom. But it is evident that if such a conquest on man's part, such a change from evil to good, be possible, it must already be contained in that transcendental deed which predetermines man's empirical life; for if not, the highest act of freedom—which should, on Kant's principle, take place before and above time,—is accomplished within the limits of time. Schelling, therefore, holds that "the original act through which man is what he is, already includes his allowing, or at least his not positively preventing, the influence of the spirit of good leading him to turn to what is good." *

The question as to a moral change.

How are we to understand this statement? Man's surrender to evil in that transcendental act may readily be supposed to have been only partial, a limited surrender, qualified, peradventure, by a susceptibility on man's part of conversion with the help of God. The life accordingly in which this conversion took place would be divided into two successive periods, the first, that wherein the affirmation of evil in the original transcendental act was realized, and the second, that wherein evil is qualified, and the help of God (conditioned in part by the strength of evil) obtained, in order to a transformation of the moral life. But would this view be compatible with the relation between the ideal and the temporal? The original transcendental act is supposed to determine man's empirical life throughout,—the life embodying exactly what the original act contains. What place is there, then, even with God's help, for a determination

Contradiction in Schelling's view here.

* Schelling, as before, p. 389.

of character essentially different? That original act "not only precedes life in the order of time, but imperceptibly runs throughout time as an act in its nature eternal." If every moment of temporal life stands in the same relation to that original act, how can life be divided into two periods, in one of which it is realized and in the other negatived? If on these principles such a "transmutation" in life be possible, we must ascribe to the transcendental act itself a twofold import; on the one hand, decision for the perversion of the two great principles, so that self-assertion may prevail; and on the other hand, decision for the right adjustment, that self-assertion may be subdued. But this is not merely a twofold import, it is a complete contradiction, which, as we have just proved, violates the conception of that transcendental act altogether. Besides, even if the original decision beyond the limits of time were of this kind, we should expect its manifestation in time to be, not man's moral renewal after a life spent in the service of self, but a continual and ineffectual struggle between conflicting tendencies.

Schelling, according to the principles of his system, and in conformity with the idealistic view, extends the influence of man's ideal freedom further. Considering its relation to man alone, apart from nature, not only does his moral being depend upon that ideal act, but his entire empirical being, his present existence, is throughout regarded as resulting from it. This outward existence is not a mere appearance (as Kant held) presented under the subjective forms of space and time, beneath which the unknown world of "things in themselves" lies; Schelling holds that it is seen in its reality, and the destructive contradiction in which, according to Kant, "the reality underlying outward apearances stands in relation to freedom"* is thus removed. For this whole sphere of life is included in the realm of freedom, and man's ideal freedom—his eternal self-decision—is regarded as the creative principle of his present state. Hence Schelling maintains not only that this free act precedes consciousness as well as existence, but that "it constitutes consciousness, and never, therefore, can be presented to consciousness."† Even man's bodily form, certainly that of the

The transcendental act made to include the whole life.

* *Kritik d. reinen Vern.* p. 418. † Schelling's *Dissertation*, as before, p. 386.

individual in its nature and circumstances, is determined by this eternal act.* How can there be any doubt that man's inner idiosyncrasy has the same foundation? This is not expressly stated in the *Dissertation*, but it is said generally "man's nature is his own act;"† "his nature and life are determined by the ideal act."‡

Conscience contradicts this notion.

It is a frequently recurring phenomenon in the history of the human mind, that when a new principle is discovered, and before its appropriate limitations are known, it is triumphantly applied to spheres and made to solve problems to which it is wholly inapplicable. It is thus that we explain the earnestness with which Schelling and some of his clever followers apply the idea of transcendental freedom unveiled by Idealism, to explain all the restraints and hindrances of our empirical life. But by extending it thus widely to all the strange and enigmatical phenomena of our moral life upon which it seemed to throw any light, its firmest basis, the sense of accountability in conscience, was imperceptibly let go. No one holds himself responsible for his natural bodily defects, or the inborn inequalities of mental organization; but his conscience accuses him of whatever contradicts the claims of morality in his life, without previously asking whether he have an inborn bias thereto or not. Many

Facts are against it.

facts of experience, moreover, directly contradict the extension of that transcendental act to other spheres of life. If, for instance, the man's bodily nature in its form and circumstances be determined by that act, how can we explain the fact that man's corporeal nature is often strikingly at variance with his mental character? How are we to explain the fact, for instance, that Socrates himself was in his corporeal nature a contradiction of his own observation, "in a fair body a fair soul must reside," taking this in its logically converse form? It is no argument to say that strength of mind and nobleness of disposition can give, even to the most contradictory and plainest of features, a beautiful expression; and on the other hand, that the most beautiful countenance will betray to the acute observer a base soul and vacant mind by its repulsive lineaments; for the question still remains

* Schelling's *Dissertations* as before, p. 387.   † *Ibid.* p. 385.
‡ *Ibid.* p. 389.

whence comes the original contradiction which is thus, to a certain extent, overcome, but not completely obviated? And as to mental idiosyncrasy, even if we put temporal development out of the question, and contemplate any original talent and natural bent of disposition, it cannot be denied that this is determined as a rule by national and family types of character, by peculiarities of parentage, &c.,—influences which cannot be resolved into the intelligible self-determination of the person thus determined. This view, accordingly, violating as it does the idea of creation, and resolving the most positive deed into a mere permission to happen, obviously contradicts also the conception of generation. Once more, if to this attempt to explain man's temporal existence in all its limitations by that eternal act of self, we add the statement above quoted, that the "transmutation" of man during his life here is likewise traceable in its distinctiveness to that act, how can we explain the fact that at the same time with his moral conversion there is not also a corresponding change in his mental idiosyncrasy and bodily form.

How plainly are the advocates of this view admonished by these facts, in their bearing upon their own principles, to distinguish between the sphere of freedom and that of necessity in human life!

Finally, we must glance at a problem very difficult in itself, which seems to be quite inexplicable on the view here taken of transcendental freedom. If man's empirical existence and consciousness in time be only the logical result of a perverted free act beyond the limits of time,—of an original fall,— must not the ideal or intelligible existence, which is freedom itself, be necessarily more perfect then the empirical? Must not this latter be an inferior existence—an existence sunk in bondage? Certainly. How then are we to regard the future life of man? Schelling's *Dissertation* does not explain this, not even when treating of the question—whether evil ever comes to an end, and how? It confines itself to general statements and modes of expression which cannot be taken literally; yet it is clear, from a few incidental remarks, that the doctrine of personal immortality is recognized. Indeed, nothing less than this is conceivable upon the principle of an

The doctrine of immortality in its bearing on Schelling's theory.

intelligible or ideal existence of the individual determining himself in that original act. Now, if evil is to come to an end—whether or not for all personal beings we need not here consider—the limitation of being arising from it must be removed by a restoration of the nature freed from sin to an existence beyond the bounds of time. But it is a self-contradictory notion that a being should pass from a temporal to an eternal existence—that it should at any moment change its temporal mode of existence for an eternal one—in such a manner as during time to begin to exist eternally.

<small>Contradiction here.</small>

It will no doubt be objected that if there be a contradiction here, it is to be found at another point in our own view, since we, too, recognize a self-decision out of time in a nature existing in time, and must therefore assume a transition on the part of free beings, if not from temporal to eternal existence, yet from extra-temporal existence into time. But there is no contradiction in supposing that the non-temporal existence of a being should be followed by its entrance into time. The existence in time of a conditioned being is quite a different, and, as we shall see by and by, more real state, and 'negatives and supplants the non-temporal. By its commencement in time it makes the non-temporal its presupposition and its past; the non-temporal gives it a determinateness which it has not in itself, but it does this by means and for the sake of the temporal life and consciousness; for in itself it is just as little past as it is present or future. But if, on the contrary, the temporal existence of a being is made the presupposition of its extra-temporal existence, so that the former must cease in order that the latter may begin, we have in this case an extra-temporal existence commencing at a given point of time, which therefore—while required according to the very conception of it to be independent of time—would be entirely dependent upon time.

<small>Objection examined.</small>

Still, perhaps, we have only to go one step further to find the contradiction obviated by considering that the existence independent of time, while following upon human life in time, also precedes this, according to the true conception of it. In order to imagine this, no one must crudely and absurdly suppose that life in time divides and

<small>Attempt at a solution.</small>

disturbs the unity of the extra-temporal, separating it into two distinct parts, as if it ceased with the commencement of the life in time, and began again at its termination. We are to view the matter thus: This extra-temporal existence penetrates and modifies temporal life, but is undisturbed by it, and ever maintains its independence;* so that the natures which partake of it, when their temporal life is completed, "shuffle off this mortal coil," in order thenceforward, as before their temporal life or apart from it, to exist eternally.

If this view of the relationship be maintained, our temporal life can have no conceivable end in reference to that higher truth of our being, our intelligible and transcendental existence; otherwise, on this standing-point, we could not avoid the contradictory ideas of a determination of extra-temporal existence by life in time, and even an interruption thereof at two distinct points, the commencement of independence in temporal life, and the result as the issue of temporal life. But if life in time be objectless in reference to intellectual and ideal existence, it is not, as it would logically be, according to other inferences from Schelling's doctrine, a diminished or reduced existence, but would sink, as with Kant, into an unsubstantial and shadowy existence, a passing phantom or shadow, which in some incomprehensible way the only true Being casts. And yet what substance there must be in this shadow, including as it does the consciousness of phenomena and self-consciousness on the part of the ideal being, a consciousness which entirely veils its true existence,—this, forsooth, can be fathomed only by speculation,—and which reflects nothing but the shadow. With such a representation of the temporal life of man, the true Incarnation of the Logos would be utterly irreconcilable; if man's earthly life be dissipated into a mere phantom, a Docetic view of that doctrine must be resorted to.

Logical results.

While we distinctly recognize the fundamental ideas of transcendental freedom and intelligible or ideal evil as the true keys to solve the riddle of the self-imputation of evil in conscience and in judgment, and of the Divine forgiveness and

---

* This must be the meaning of what is said, pp. 385, 386: "The act whereby man's life in time is determined does not precede this life in the order of time, but imperceptibly penetrates it, as in its nature an eternal act."

punishment, and as the abiding fruits of Idealism, especially in Schelling's profound development of it, we are at the same time compelled by the argument here developed to reject the more determinate application of these fundamental ideas in his Dissertation upon freedom.*

CHAPTER IV.

Freedom as the Possibility of Sin.

§ 1. The true idea of God.

Sensualistic, materialistic, and atheistic modes of thought in general have the undoubted advantage of being able to deal with the problem of evil much more easily than can Christian theism. From such proud standing-points mountains and valleys are usually lost sight of, and the eye wanders carelessly over a perfectly uninterrupted prospect of waste and level plains. The giant problem, therefore, of evil, is as if it were not. But it well-nigh overwhelms with its greatness the minds of those who recognize and adore a God in Himself perfect, of Himself eternally conscious, as the absolute principle of all finite existence. In the preceding chapter it was observed that the greatest difficulty concerning the existence of evil is *its relation to God*; and as our task now is to explain human freedom, so far as it includes the possibility of sin, in its divine origin, we must, in the investigation of this chapter, begin with considering *the true idea of God*.

God a personal being.

In our day, the adversaries of religion seem more generally than ever at one with those who regard Christianity as alone adequate for the salvation of mankind, in the conviction that religion cannot be what it

* Steffens, in his *Christliche Religionsphilosophie*, vol. ii. (see the sections "on the origin of Sin," and "Concerning evil in Nature," p. 1–100), avows his belief in an ideal fall of the human soul. But his exposition there is so indistinct and involves itself in such manifest contradictions, that it is hardly possible to say what his view really is. Rückert, in his *Theologie*, vol. i. p. 227, and Paul, in his work entitled *Kant's Lehre vom radicalen Bösen* (1865), may also be named as espousers of this doctrine of an ideal and original fall.

essentially is without the consciousness of God as a PERSONAL BEING, self-conscious, and self-determining.* Of what avail to piety is a God too high, too abstract, and unreal to be personal? Religion is fellowship with God; but there can be no fellowship with an Absolute that is not *I* in Himself, nor *Thou* for our prayers; with such an Absolute, Love—which in the very conception of it presupposes personality alike in the subject of it and in its object—loses all its meaning, and instead of childlike trust and willing submission, blended with the sure hope of a perfect solution of all problems, we have self-enthrallment to a stern fatalism, and to a necessary chain of causes and effects; or self-absorption in the unfathomable basis of all things, the anticipation as if of a future annihilation, to which consciousness thinks itself destined.

That theology also which fancied it could build up a system of Christian Doctrine apart from divine Personality was obliged after all to allow that this conception is inseparable from practical religion. Schleiermacher, while he speaks of "serious imperfections in the idea of a personality of the highest nature," considers that the highest piety must "by an unavoidable necessity," adopt this idea, in order to interpret to itself or others its directly religious feelings, or when the heart is engaged in converse with the Highest.† Here we have essentially that subjective Dualism which holds that in order to interpret his religious feelings a man must for his own use adopt representations which he allows to be logically inadmissible.‡ But we refer to these statements simply because of the admission they contain that religion is hardly conceivable without belief in a Personal God.

Schleiermacher admits this as a belief.

Even in the sphere of language there is an august sanctity attaching to the very name of GOD, the violation of which leads to serious confusion. The name of God belongs originally and distinctively to the

The very Name of God.

---

* STRAUSS, for example, in his *Dogmatik*, begins his discussion concerning the Personality of God with the recognition of this.

† "*Reden über die Religion*," 3rd Ed. p. 199.

‡ We cannot allow that the conditions of Schleiermacher's logic concerning the difference between philosophic and religious apprehensions of God at all do away with this contradiction. See as before, § 228, p. 168 in particular, and Appendix E, li. lii. p. 528.

sphere of Religion, and whoever dares to use it must do so, not in a sense totally different from or contrary to that in which Religion uses it, but with the clear and reverent recognition that it denotes Personality. If he would express a wholly different conception, he must choose another word.

But we by no means wish to imply that the conception of a personal God is unattainable by philosophy. On the contrary, we are convinced that a purely philosophic investigation, pursuing an independent course, will be necessarily led to this conception, and can never without it arrive at a conclusion which will be a secure resting-place for its ever restless questionings.* Never can philosophy satisfactorily explain finite reality, especially in its highest form as finite Spirit, while it refuses to acknowledge a personal principle as its original source. It cannot entertain the notion of an essence above personality, without, when it comes to define it, degrading it into an essence really below personality.

Philosophy admits it.

But personality does not exclusively belong to God. What, then, is divine personality as distinct from human personality? In other words, *in what sense is Divine personality absolute?* The answer to this question will show whether (as J. G. Fichte and several disciples of Hegel, especially Strauss,† have in our day affirmed), Christian Theology is obliged to surrender the possibility of an Absolute Personality on account of the supposed contradiction between the conceptions "absolute" and "personal."

Divine Personality Absolute.

The conception of personality certainly implies that the personal being distinguishes himself in himself, and this not merely in a logically formal sense (in that the subject in self-consciousness posits itself as

Personality implies self-determination.

---

* SCHELLING, in his *Denkmal Jacobi's*, p. 54, says that a thoroughly rational perception of the existence of a Personal Being as the Author and Ruler of the world will be the ultimate fruit of thorough and comprehensive speculation. Though the forms of philosophy now in vogue tend so little in this direction, Schelling's prophecy is advancing towards its fulfilment.

† *Christl. Glaubenslehre, passim.* To these names may be added that of the learned Mr MANSEL in this country, who, while denying the conceivableness of an Absolute Personality, yet recognizes what he takes to be rationally inconceivable, as an object of Faith. "To speak," he says, "of an absolute and infinite Person is simply to use language which, however true it may be in a superhuman sense, denotes an object *inconceivable under the conditions of human thought.*"—*Limits of Religious Thought*, Lect. iii.—*Tr.*

object), but really. Completeness and definiteness, plurality and difference, are by self-consciousness given to the unity of the *ego*, and are regarded as its determination. By this concentration the separableness of the various elements and conditions of life is lost sight of, so that personal beings are capable in themselves of a unity wholly different from that of impersonal existence (and consequently of an infinitely deeper discord). But this unity cannot be without a plurality or manifoldness, which is at the same time regarded as one.

If we apply this to God, we find that it clearly contradicts a notion which first arose in the Patristic developments of Christian Doctrine, and which prevails in ancient and modern Theology. Fearing lest, if any distinction were allowed to exist in God, we should have to regard His nature as made up of component parts, many maintained the *simplicitas essentiae divinae* in so abstract a sense, as to exclude all real distinctions in the divine Essence, and to attribute those which we make to our own subjectivity. But if we deny any distinction of attributes in the Divine Nature, we must, on our own principles (as Strauss fairly argues),* admit that we cannot have any real knowledge of God; and thus we should be logically driven to the conclusion that the Divine nature is wholly unknowable. Aiming at God's highest exaltation, this view virtually robs God of that reality without which it is even obliged to confess we cannot really think of Him. It is manifest—so manifest that we need not stay to prove it—that this negative result, equally with the assumption of an absolute knowledge of God, contradicts both Holy Scripture (especially in its teaching concerning the manifestation of God in Christ) and unbiassed Christian consciousness. It is equally clear to what a strange and degraded position theology is reduced by such a renunciation of any knowledge of its object matter. It is marvellous how such an acute and powerful thinker as Schleiermacher could have shared the fear we have named of the divine essence being reduced to a conglomeration of attributes; for, not to speak of higher ranges of existence, we find that even

Patristic doctrine of simplicitas.

Erroneous.

* *Christl. Glaubenslehre*, § 35 (vol. i. pp. 540, 541). See also BAUR *Die Christliche Lehre von der Dreieinigkeit und Menschwerdung Gottes in ihrer geschichtlichen Entwickelung*, vol. iii. pp. 332, 333.

the lowest organic unity (which essentially includes a manifoldness) is raised above the category of merely mechanical juxtaposition.

This foregone conclusion as to the incompatibility of any real distinctions in God with the simplicity of His nature, is so deeply rooted in modern theology, that many, when mention is made of a plurality and totality of attributes in God, can only understand it as meant in a Pantheistic sense. Far rather may we say that Pantheism will ever arise in its strength out of ˙Theism, as long as Theism abides by the doctrine that the Divine essence obtains a determinate and self-distinguishing existence only by passing into the vorld. The strength of Pantheism lies in the necessity of an advance from abstract to concrete Unity, through plurality and difference; its real overthrow is secured by the acknowledgment that "God has LIFE IN HIMSELF" (John v. 26), that as there cannot be life without manifoldness in unity, God has, in Himself, the *fulness* of being — "unsearchable riches" of positive attributes — and that, consequently, He has no need of the world in order to be eternally the Living One.

Adopted in modern theology.

Without the recognition of these truths, the conception of the Divine Personality, which may be described as the specific characteristic of Theism as distinct from Pantheism, cannot be maintained. Were God mere abstract Essence, excluding from itself all actual ˙distinctions, as the view we have named would take Him to be,—thus supplementing Pantheism, which finds real distinctions possible in God only by the apotheosis of the world—there would be in God no self-determination by Will. For will is self-determination by action, action at first purely internal; but where no distinctions are allowed, nothing can be determined or defined. In this case the divine will cannot be regarded as a power of outward causation proceeding from within ; for if God cannot determine Himself, He cannot by self-determination produce anything else. How, upon this principle, can any mention be made of any divine Will, as distinct from divine knowledge or self-consciousness ? And what has this self-consciousness to be conscious of, if God be bare existence ($\dot{α}πλῶς\ ἕν$), without any distinction of attributes ?

Personality implies self-determination.

What could God be conscious of, save of His self-consciousness? His Personality would be reduced to the bare formula "*ego* = *ego*."

<small>Apology for the older Theology.</small> When we find the older theologians embarrassed in the attempt to reduce all definiteness in the conception of God to a merely abstract idea of identity, we must make allowances for them* by the recollection that the destructive consequences of such a process were as hidden from them as they are patent to us. They might easily have been deceived as to the inner contradiction between this idea and their own consciousness, for they held that God's essence, while simple unity, and excluding all real differences, was complete in itself and distinct from the world, so they called the world in its relation to God, the *fundamentum in re* for those divine attributes which were not distinguishable in God Himself. They thought they could secure the definiteness of their conception of God as a being possessed of intelligence and will, by holding fast the distinction between Him and the world. But it can never be seen how God can distinguish Himself from the world, if He does not distinguish Himself in Himself, not only hypostatically, but essentially. If God be in Himself bare essence without attributes, He attains determinateness of being only in the world; but how in this case could God know Himself as distinct from the world, and therefore as a Being to this extent at least determined?

<small>Notion of the negative absolute.</small> The impossibility of this is now fully recognised, even when, by the principle of immanence, the Absolute is apprehended as the Identity wherein all differences vanish. But here also the bare negativity of this notion of the Absolute clearly appears. For this conception is arrived at only by doing away with all determinations in their distinction one from another, *i.e.*, in their definiteness, and regarding all as identical. Such an Absolute really contains nothing but the destruction of all determinations established in the world—in other words it contains nothing whatever;

---

* It is curious to find Mr MANSEL, in the last edition of the work already named, quoting the very passages in the works of the early theologians in which this notion of God is set forth, as confirmations of the confessedly irrational conception of God which he by faith accepts.—*Tr.*

every determination, every attribute, would be brought down into the world, being (according to this notion) not the Absolute itself, but merely its realization by self-limitation. This negative absolute, which is at the same time the basis of all things, the βύθός of the Gnostics, the σῖγή of the transcendental Deity, who can be known only by negations, as the Pseudo-Dionysius calls Him, the eternal Nothing of the philosophic Mystics, is merely the ability of the human mind to withdraw itself from each and every determinateness, in order in turn to derive all determinateness in thought from this limitless Abstraction. It can be the Cause of all things only in so far as it is the abyss in which all things are lost.

It must be allowed that such a notion of the Absolute is utterly incompatible with the knowledge of God as a person, or indeed with any knowledge of God whatever. It is, therefore, a clever artifice of the Dogmatism of Strauss to urge on all explanations of the Christian doctrine concerning God in its historical development, while they are endeavouring, as far as possible, to avoid the extreme of anthropomorphism, to the abyss of the Negative-Absolute. Certainly, it is not very difficult for a clever logician to make this the apparently necessary result (if utter resultlessness can be called a result) to which the successive stages of the argument, connecting several gradations of thought, conduct us. But as this Absolute obtains reality only as a process accomplishing itself through the finite, and therefore only as it destroys itself as the Absolute (*i.e.*, only as it is again abstracted from the abstraction with which the speculation began), it is admitted, in the very conception of it, that it is not the real but an *unreal* absolute. THE ABSOLUTE WHICH REALLY EXISTS IS GOD. If the category of reality be maintained only in relation to the world, as for instance, in the propositions, "God is the truth of the world," "the world is the realization of God," all attempts to avoid Pantheism are unavailing. In order really to exist as the absolute One, God must possess in Himself, and independently of any relation to the world, the fulness of positive determinations—a fulness self-sufficing on account of its inner infinitude; a πέλαγος τῆς οὐσίας, as Gregory of Nazianzen finely styles God in one of his Christmas Sermons.

Irreconcilable with Divine personality.

Now, besides the tendency to apprehend his own existence by self-consciousness, in virtue of which he is a personal being, there is in man a tendency to distinguish the existence of a *non-ego*, another being separate from himself. Though we are not justified in making the existence of the *non-ego* a necessary condition of man's apprehending his own *ego*, yet we cannot conceive how he could be *conscious* of himself without distinguishing himself from some other being. If Spirit in another individual Being did not furnish the condition of his original awakening, *i.e.*, that reaction of the *non-ego* which elicits the flash of self-apprehension— nature would answer that purpose. Man's *self-determination*, moreover, as well as his self-consciousness, involves a necessary reference to another being; but in an opposite direction. Self-consciousness is the self-withdrawment of the *ego* from the non-ego; but self-determination is the self-extension of the *ego* to the *non-ego*, in order to have and to hold itself *in* it as well as apart from it.

Human personality implies a non-ego.

We must not be beguiled into the belief that we may transfer these determinations to the case of God's Personality without necessarily destroying His Absoluteness. If God needs another being in order to be what in His own nature He already is, *i.e.*, personal, He is not absolute but conditioned; and the more literally we understand that other being, the more evident does this become.* If, again, that other being be something developing itself in time, then God in the realization of His personality must be conditioned as to time, and must therefore be liable to a gradual " becoming " or growth into existence. But he who regards the idea of the absolute as real (if he objects to separate the Diety from that idea), will not certain y

Consequences of transferring this to God.

---

* If, indeed, this other being is immediately withdrawn again,—*e.g.*, by the supposition that God at once regarded it as Himself, and appropriated it as part of his own essence,—the violation of the idea of the Absolute would be avoided, yet only by the identification of the essence of the world with that of God,—*i.e.*, only by the annulling of that idea. A God who must lose Himself in nature and then come back to Himself in spirit is anything but absolute. See the thorough refutation of this notion of the Absolute by means of the true idea of the Absolute, in DORNER, *Entwickelungsgeschichte der Lehre von der Person Christi*, ii. pp. 1096–1133.

allow God's nature to be confounded with or involved in a gradual "becoming" or development, which implies that the being so developed is at every point deficient in what essentially belongs to Him. Now, if it be still more determinately maintained that the existence of finite spirit, as a *Thou* corresponding to the divine *I*, is the condition of the divine personality, we cannot avoid the logical conclusion that there must have been a time when God was not yet personal. For whether finite spirit be looked for on earth only or in the stars, it is unanimously recognized by all who make this the condition of divine personality, that finite spirit necessarily presupposes nature,—nature not merely in idea, but in empirical reality. But then it inevitably follows that somewhere in the past the existence of finite spirit, and therefore of a personal God, was still future.*

This dependence of God's personality upon what is finite cannot be harmonized with His absoluteness by the further supposition that this finite is produced by God Himself, and that He ordains to realize His personality by means of another being. The issue, utterly incompatible with Theism, would still be, that God, not perhaps in His substantial essence, but certainly in His existence as a Person,—has finite being for His temporal, or, at least, only conceivable *Antecedents*. If it be fully granted, as Fischer himself seems to do,† that finite persons, whose very existence is dependent upon God, possess this conditioning relation to His personality, only in so far as they are not utterly dependent, but are self-determining, the violation of the Divine absoluteness is still more apparent. For in this case God is conditioned by Beings whom, in proportion

---

* STRAUSS's doctrine regarding God is involved in this contradiction. For though he denies the divine personality, he holds that it is contained in the conception of the Absolute " to personify itself into the Infinite," (*Dogm.*, vol. i. 524)—that is in finite spirit. But as finite spirit must have nature not only for its ideal but for its real presupposition, as actually preceding it in the order of time, there must have been a time when the Absolute had not yet personified itself in finite spirit, and did not correspond with its true conception. And hence indeed it is clear that it could not have fulfilled the true conception of itself as the Absolute after its personification, because this was preceded by a defect in the Absolute; and thus such a notion of the Absolute is self-destructive. From what we say above it is clearly in vain to call to our aid the supposition of intelligent inhabitants of other worlds, (*Dogm.* i. 673).

† *Die speculative Dogm. von Strauss, geprüft*, part i. p. 40.

as they condition Him, He cannot wholly determine. To this it must be added that these other Beings, by distinguishing Himself from whom God begins to exist as Personal, though produced by God Himself, can fulfil this purpose only by coming into collision with Him somehow, or being somehow thrust upon Him. To imagine that God ordained the existence of finite beings, with this end in view—to be the negative condition of His self-consciousness—would be to involve ourselves in a seemingly profound, but really absurd circle; for none but a personal Essence can purpose or plan. Before this purposing, prior to it in thought, if not in time, God must have possessed that personality, in order to realize which He is said to have created finite spirit; He could not, therefore, have had any such purpose in view.

God would not be really unconditioned if His nature were not perfectly complete in itself. But His nature is thus perfect only when the distinctions, without which He would not be a living unity, are immanent or inherent in Him in an eternal and perfectly independent manner. God's personality can be regarded as absolute, only when He has the conditions requisite for the realization of it, not in another being, but *wholly in Himself.**

God as a Person must be complete in Himself.

But how can it be possible for God's self-consciousness and self-determination to exist without His distinguishing Himself from some other being?

Why God's personality need not imply a non-ego.

Let us examine more closely why it is that human personality cannot be conceived of without

* The conception of the Trinity, moreover, we may remark in passing, cannot warrant this conditioning of God's personality; provided, at least, that the fundamental doctrine of identity of substance be maintained side by side with the hypostatical distinctions;—and it is in virtue of that doctrine alone that this idea of the hypostatical distinctions can be harmonized with Monotheism. If Father, Son, and Holy Ghost be only conditions or elements whereby the Divine self-consciousness and unity are realized, they are not, strictly speaking, hypostases at all. If the Son or Logos be regarded as the other Being, in contrast with whom the primary Being is eternally to realize the consciousness of Himself, the identity of substance between Father and Son must be given up; and it would be difficult to see how the eternal self-consciousness of this other being (the Logos) would in this supposition be derived. It is easy to see that the Trinity of the Divine Being is closely connected with the true idea of His personality; but the connection is very different from that which is here supposed.

this self-distinguishing from another, *i.e.*, a *non-ego*. The
<small>Case of human personality.</small> relation of personality to the categories, Relative and Absolute, depends upon the elements which are included in self-consciousness. If these are raised above Relativity altogether, the personality is absolute. Hence, even if the human race were regarded (according to a fantastic and realistic method already referred to) as one personal essence complete in itself, this personality would be unavoidably relative; because the elements of its self-consciousness would, if they had no other reference, necessarily be referred to God as the original and distinct source of its nature and existence. But the essential relativity of human personality is already manifest in the fact that it is only that of the individual as distinct from the race. The elements of this self-consciousness never constitute a complete and independent *all*, but only a particular part, belonging to something else and limited, a portion of finite existence. To deny this, and to claim absoluteness for individual personality, would be an utterly untenable extreme of monadic atomism.* It logically follows, therefore, that the portion of human nature and life which constitutes the distinct being of any individual, cannot be included in the central *ego* of self-consciousness, without excluding something else, a *non-ego*.

But the causes of this excluding function of self-conscious-
<small>God's personality all inclusive.</small> ness in man are not to be found in God. The elements of God's self-consciousness constitute an infinity of determinations—a totality, *cujus centrum* (to use an expression attributed to the Hermes Trismegistus, and often used by the Mystics of the Middle Ages, yet defended by such a theologian as Jno. Gerhard against Scaliger†) *ubique circumferentia nusquam*. To suppose the determinateness thus predicated of God to be incompatible with His infiniteness, would be to make infinity syno-

---

* FRAUENSTADT (born 1813), more than any other modern writer, approaches this extreme in his work *Die Freiheit des Menschen und die Persönlichkeit Gottes*, in the *Studien und Kritiken*, and in his criticism of Schelling's Lectures. In order to preserve human freedom, he denies creation; but the way in which he makes substance, according to Spinoza's idea of it, the basis of freedom and personality, would, if logically carried out, oblige him to deny the production, by birth, of personal being.

† *Loci theol.* tom. 1, loc. 2; *De Natura et attr. Dei*, cap. v. 91.

nymous with *in*determinateness, to identify the *indefinitum* (ἀόριστον) and the *infinitum*. Spinoza's celebrated axiom, *determinatio est negatio*, is based upon this confusion, if, that is, it be taken literally ; and thus it is taken in Spinoza's system, though not expressly affirmed. It seems very strange at first sight, though, upon consideration, easy to be understood, that Spinoza's philosophy, while excluding all determinations from its Absolute—*i.e.*, pure substance—because negations are not to be attributed to it, yet cannot free its Absolute from complete negativity.

If this were really so, if God could be infinite only by being utterly undetermined and predicateless essence, we should have to follow the Platonic warning, "Call not God the infinite essence, for existence contradicts the infinite." If in this case we will not take refuge in the asylum of the utter unknowableness of God,* nothing is left us but the dilemma—either pantheistically to consider the finite determinations of earthly being as constituent parts of God himself, or elements in His being, or to attribute finiteness of God, and existence in time and space as distinct from the world, just as K. V. Th. Voigt† most

The absolute is not the undetermined.

---

* As Sir W. HAMILTON (*Discussions*, art. 1) and Mr MANSEL do. Sir W. Hamilton's words are, "The last and highest consecration of all true religion must be an altar '*to the unknown and unknowable God.*'"—*Tr.*

† "*Ueber Freiheit und Nothwendigkeit aus dem Standpunkt christlich-theistischer Weltansicht,*" 1828, §§ 27, 28. It is surprising to see how this author boasts concerning this notion of a finite God existing in time, and in virtue of His "visibility" (p. 67) existing also in space. "It is only thus," he says, "that the idea of God obtains any true definiteness and conceivableness ; " and yet he cannot save this notion of his from the most obvious absurdities, except by leaving it involved in cloudy indefiniteness. To say nothing of space being attributed to God, and of essential existence in time necessarily involving a gradual development of God, we would seriously ask the advocates of this doctrine whether an essence existing in time could be even conceived of as original and unconditioned ? If its existence in time had a commencement, as it did not exist before that commencement, it could not have created itself, but must have been created by something else. If, again, its existence in time was beginningless, however far we go back, every moment of its existence is conditioned by preceding moments. It is impossible to resolve this conditioned into an absolutely self-conditioned by any *regressus in infinitum*. But if conditioned essence cannot be conceived of as self-conditioned, it must be regarded as conditioned by something else ;—unless, indeed, it be utterly inconceivable. Thus, it is evident, that though this doctrine means to speak of God, it unintentionally speaks of the world instead of God.

zealously and acutely does, after the manner of the Socinian theologians and K. Vorstius. But in reality there is no contradiction between determinateness and infinity. Infinity not only implies determinateness, but positively requires it; it demands a fulness of determinations in no way limited from without by any other being, not from within by one another. As these determinations of the divine nature are distinguished from each other, an element of negation and of finiteness is certainly implied in relation to God;—and this is the necessary presupposition for God's creating a finite world, wherein distinctions become diversities among natures mutually excluding one another.* But as these determinations (to retain the abstract expression) are blended in the most perfect unity excluding all outward separation, the element of finiteness in them is eternally absorbed in the divine infinitude. God would not really be infinite if He were destitute of all determinateness; for in this case the Infinite would have its outward antithesis and its essential limit in determinate being. God is the Infinite, because the fulness of His nature, unlimited from without and undisturbed in itself, is perfect harmony, —a harmony wherein any one element does not contradict but confirms the rest. The world, even were it boundless in extent as to time and space, would still, viewed as a whole, be in character or quality finite, because there is a separateness among the beings who compose it, in virtue of which each exists only as it excludes others from the sphere of its existence; consequently, the inner unity of God is specifically higher than that of the world.

<small>Infinity demands determinateness.</small>

The fact, therefore, that our self-consciousness as *ego* is conditioned by the exclusion of something else as a *non-ego*, does not hold true of all personality, but only of personality within certain limits and relations, only of man's personality and self-consciousness according to his individual character. God, in virtue of the infinite fulness of his Being, does not require

<small>God's self-consciousness complete in itself.</small>

* In so far as this diversity holds true of the relation between the substance of the world and the substance of God,—for the essence of the world is not the essence of God,—we may by means of it understand how the so-called categories of reflection, as well as of causality, suffice to furnish us with true knowledge in this sphere.

another being, a *non-ego*, by the exclusion or removal of which He becomes manifest to himself as *ego*. He is the *ego*, the I AM, eternally and unconditionally.* When, therefore, Jacob Böhme on the contrary asserts that "nothing can be revealed to itself without contrariety or diversity; for it would have nothing to oppose it, it would ever proceed from itself and never return to itself; but if it never returned to itself, as to that from which it proceeded, it would know nothing of its original state: and thus even God requires a *contrarium*, so that His hidden Will may reveal itself:"† and when Schelling considers that "a negative and repelling power, opposing the affirming and extending power, is the necessary condition of all self-consciousness,"‡ we do not dispute the truth and profundity of these views in reference to created being, but to apply them directly to God, seems to us an unwarrantable extension of the analogy between the divine and the human. God's personality is, for this very reason, absolute, because the contents of the divine self-consciousness *form an infinite and wholly self-sufficing totality*.

But we could not see how these contents could be perfectly manifest to the self-consciousness of God, how God himself could be pure light and clearness,— the Father of lights (James i. 17),—if He were conscious of them, and of His own essence, as something *independent* of His self-determination, as preceding his will in virtue of an eternal necessity. Man can never thoroughly penetrate with his consciousness the obscurity in which the beginning of his being is hidden, because he does not exist of himself alone;—according to the words, *ea tantum scimus, quae facimus.* In like manner, the personality of God would be based on a reality which He could not penetrate, the light of eternal self-consciousness would not shine into the innermost depth, and the Spirit could not "search the deep things of God" (1 Cor. ii. 10) if His determinate essence or

<small>God's essence does not precede his freedom.</small>

---

* Here we are quite in accord with ROTHE's *Ethics* (vol. i. pp. 87, 88), for we do not believe it at all difficult for theistic speculation understanding its principal and true motive to overcome the stumbling-block connected with the divine personality.

† "The way to Christ," book 7 "Of Divine Contemplation," chap. i.

‡ In his Dissertation upon Freedom and the *Denkmal Jacobi's*.

substance preceded self-determination in Him as its cause. Indeed, while we regard God in this partial and realistic way, as " necessary essence " or " original Being," our idea of God is involved in insoluble self-contradiction. For whatever is beyond and apart from God's freedom is clearly something given (a datum discovered by His self-consciousness as already existing), and it cannot lose this character by God's merely formal self-affirmation as the perfect One. Now, if the essence of God were for Him something given,—something already present,— the question " From whence is it given ? " could not be evaded ; God's essence must in this case have its origin in something apart from Him, and thus the true conception of God would be entirely swept away.

If the attribute of independence, *independentia,—i.e.*, the Unconditioned,—as it is usually predicated of God, is to convey any conceivable thought, we must resolve this negative view, which our older theologians, Quenstadt, Baumgarten, and others, so closely held to, into the positive statement that " God is the self-conditioning and self-causing Being " (*ens a se ipso*, or *aseitas*, as the schoolmen expressed it, αὐτοουσία as the later Greek Fathers designated it). Thus the definition of God as *causa sui* receives another and more positive import than that in which Spinoza uses it. According to him, as is well known, it simply denotes that the essence of the *Substantia* necessarily implies its existence. "*Ipsius essentia*," says Spinoza, "*involvit necessario existentiam, sive ad ejus naturam pertinet existere.*" But this necessarily existing substance is not endowed with any vitality or freedom. Now the *true* import of the *causa sui* is that God's essence is solely His own act.* The distinction of cause and effect, of determining and being determined, which we find in the sphere of the finite, is in

<small>Positive meaning of "unconditioned."</small>

---

* This seems to be expressed by the *voluntas necessaria* of our older theologians, by which they meant God's will directed to and bearing upon His own essence, in distinction from the *voluntas libera*,—*i.e.*, His will going forth to something else. Still, the designation *necessaria* applied to the *voluntas* indicates a difference between their view and that given above. The will, which must be wholly determined by God's essence, can be nothing more than God's affirmation of Himself in His eternal self-consciousness ; and this can be called a will only by a very inexact application of the term, for nothing is determined by it.

God completely done away. In Him determining power is to be regarded as the very kernel or centre of the conception of causality. But how can an essence be *causa sui*, save as it generates itself by conscious self-determination? For if we are to imagine this eternal self-creation to be only a kind of unconscious impulse or continual desire after self-realization, it would imply a state originally passive and already determined, —a state which could not for a moment be conceived of as primary or original, but for which we should have to seek a determining principle in some other primary essence.

Here then we have a special application and extension of the cosmological argument for the existence of God. This argument, in its simplest form, infers (as is well known) the existence of a primary essence, who is both *causa sui* and the First Cause of all things, from the law of causation concerning finite existences; the idea of an endless *regressus* of causes being self-contradictory. But the question at once suggests itself, Why must this primary essence necessarily be a Person, *i.e.*, God, as distinct from the world? Why may we not suppose it to be the world itself, not of course 'the sum total of finite existence, but the immanent principle or impersonal basis of the world? It is clear that the argument thus far does not raise us above Spinozism, for Spinoza regarded Substance as the immanent cause of all things, which are its *modificationes*.* Even the greater accuracy which Leibnitz gives to the proof—by inferring from the contingency of the world and the possibility of its non-existence, a necessary essence having in itself the ground of its own existence—does not really help us. For the contingency of the world's existence is a truth self-evident only in the case of each several thing in the world, and why might not this "necessary essence" be just the essence of the world itself, manifesting itself in the totality of individual existence, "unfolding itself," "renouncing in order to find itself," or by whatever phrases pantheistic modes of thought may describe the relation?

The cosmological argument.

---

* *Ethic* i. prop. xviii. *Deus est omnium rerum causa immanens, on vero transiens.* Prop. xxiii., *Omnis modus, qui et necessario sequi debuit vel ex absoluta natura alicujus attributi Dei, vel ex aliquo modificato modificatione, quae et necessario et infinita existit.*

CHAP. IV.]   FREEDOM AS THE POSSIBILITY OF SIN.   129

The cosmological proof does not avail much in behalf of Theism, until we perceive that no real thought can be attached to the expression *causa sui*, unless it be taken in a real and positive sense, and in harmony with the explanation just given, viz., that all determinations of God's essence have for their principle and basis His absolute will. The cosmological proof leads us on through the whole range of causes which are themselves in turn effects, upwards to the recognition of an all-conditioning First Cause, or essence, which is *causa sui*. And taking this expression in the manner just explained, we must regard this First Cause as a self-determining intelligence, *i.e.*, an absolute Personality, a Being self-existent and distinguishing Himself from the world.

Its true import.

This view of the absolute self-dependence of God is not new to Christian theology. Even Lactantius gives expression to it in one passage when he says, *ipse ante omnia ex se ipso est procreatus;* * and in another more accurately thus—*ex se ipso est, ideo talis est qualem esse se voluit.*† In like manner Jerome says, *Deus ipse sui origo est suaeque causa substantiae.*‡

Confirmations of this view.

From the foregoing investigation it appears that God's personality differs from man's, not only in the nature of the contents included in his self-consciousness, but also in the *principle* out of which the contents spring. In the sphere of relative personality freedom is only the *co*-determining cause of the distinctive nature which marks out the individual as himself, and as no one else. God's personality is absolute, inasmuch as freedom is the *unconditioned* principle of His nature, so that He is what He is wholly by self-determination. The uncaused and primary beginning of all existence is FREEDOM, or Action. "There is ultimately, in the last and highest instance, no existence whatever but Will. Will is primary being." ‖

Freedom the principle of God's nature.

Adhering strictly to this conclusion, we must assert that all

---

* *Div. Instit.* lib. i. cap. 7. LACTANTIUS quotes approvingly the formula of Seneca (badly constructed as it is in two particulars), *Deus ipse se fecit.*
† *Ibid.* lib. ii. c. 8.
‡ *Epist. ad Eph.* 3. (Opp. ed. Martianay, tom. iv. part i. page 356).
‖ *Schelling's Sämmtliche Werke*, part i. vol. vii. 350.

truths, even those which we call necessary, and the denial of which would violate all consecutive thought— the fundamental truths of mathematics and metaphysics—have their ultimate basis in the absolute self-determination of God as the original source of all reality. Descartes was right in not deducing these truths from a necessity independent of God's will, but he was wrong in supposing the divine essence to be something anterior to God's will, and then in representing this will as deciding itself with perfect indifference towards the divine essence, and establishing (for example) the laws of mathematics.* According to this view, the world-governing will of God is alienated from God's essence and eternal Reason, and becomes a mere arbitrariness which ignores and violates the truth of the divine nature and reason. Mathematical truths are beyond a doubt a revelation of the eternal order and harmony of the Divine nature, a reflection thereof in the sphere of the Finite, in existence, in time, and space. But the perfect harmony of God's nature does not arise from a necessity bearing sway over Him; it springs from His own Freedom.†

God's will the basis of truth.

Weisse, a clever philosopher of our day, in an effort to recognize and understand Divine freedom, opposes our doctrine of the absolute originality of Will, and (following Leibnitz) assigns to Will a region of pure thought, a metaphysical necessity of Reason, as its formal principle. He believes that only thus can a purely metaphysi-

Weisse's theory.

---

* See in particular the *Responsio sexta* to the objections against his *Meditationes*, No. 6.

† These statements, which remain unaltered as in the first edition of this work, if taken in their fair and literal sense, can be interpreted only as affirming this,—the divine nature in its ultimate basis is not determined being, but Will or self-determination. If it were determined being, God's nature would be ever a given object for his eternal self-consciousness, just as our nature is relatively for our self-consciousness; and this would involve the contradiction pointed out above. Thus in God the possibility of another, a different standard, is neither affirmed nor denied; this is a perfectly meaningless representation, utterly impossible to us, whose very being and intellect have their ultimate source in God's absolute and primary Will. Accordingly Professor ZELLER, who is an espouser of the system of logical necessity, might have spared his unfair deductions from our view, *e.g.*, "three times three might have been ten if God had only willed it so," &c., (*Theolog. Jahrbücher*, 1847, p. 210); such fatal strictures do not affect our argument, but only a caricature of it drawn by himself. See also p. 141 of this volume.

Objections of Zeller.

cal basis be given to the philosophy of the Real. He defines this necessary principle more accurately as "the negative presupposition of divine freedom, a region of the non-existent, an unrealized realm of mere possibilities, by the election or annulling of which divine freedom—including a power of not doing or of doing otherwise—realizes itself."* But we cannot see how God's absolute freedom is preserved by this mode of representation. For if God not only may but must choose or annul those possibilities which lie within this sphere of "the metaphysical necessity of Reason," in order to realize His freedom, freedom must, to begin with, have something independent of it,—though it be something never to be realized,—something over against it, or rather as its *prius*, by which it is conditioned as by an eternal fate. In a certain sense we too must certainly allow that human reason, or, to use a better term, spirit, recognizes the *prius* of divinity or Deity,—the primary principle which in thought precedes the determinations of the divine nature,—but not in the sense in which Weisse takes it. Taking it in Weisse's sense—apart from the impossibility of forming an idea of such an independent world of absolute forms—we can neither reconcile such a world with God's absoluteness nor with the acknowledged fact that the world is wholly conditioned by God. Weisse rightly regards the conflict between freedom and necessity to be the main problem of philosophy in its immediate future. But if necessity, in whatever form, be regarded as absolutely first in order, freedom must ever be absorbed in it; for a necessity, essentially bound by the law of identity, can never produce the free but always the necessary alone; whereas freedom, in the very conception of it, includes all possibilities, even that of positing something contrary to tself—of ordaining even an unerring necessity.

Objection.
The objection that, in rejecting this metaphysical basis, arbitrariness or chance is made the principle of all existence, does not really lie against our view, but

* As far as I know, WEISSE first put forth this thought in his *Metaphysik*, in hap. i. of the Introduction; afterwards he gives it in his Review of Romang's work on Freedom and Determinism, (*Heidelberger Jahrb.*, 1836, Nos. 62-64); and often since then, but most fully in his *Sendschreiben an Fichte über das Philosophische Problem der Gegenwart*. We may also compare what Weisse says in his *Philosophischen Dogmatik*, vol. i. §§ 460-477, concerning God's will and freedom.

only against an unskilful and incomplete representation of it. Arbitrariness is a severance of will from the law of rational sequence ; it therefore presupposes such a law as already present; whereas we hold that all rational sequence has its root in the primary divine Will. Chance, also, as we have already seen (p. 27), is a negative, and, indeed, a teleologically negative conception ; it excludes all design in reference to determinate events ; we can speak of chance only when an indifferent event occurs which has no bearing whatever upon any definite aim in the sphere of being ; but we cannot speak of chance where the first beginnings of all aims and designs are decreed. In this profound source of all existence, those notions of chance and arbitrariness which are urged against absolute and unconditioned freedom as the principle of the divine nature have no meaning whatever ; they are utterly inapplicable.

God Himself chooses and decides upon all the determinations and laws of His own being; and we must therefore conceive of Him, originally and primarily, as "Undetermined existence," yet as possessing an unlimited power of self-determination. This statement is certainly exposed to the objection that God is thus conceived originally as *Nothing* ; and utterly predicateless being might certainly be thus designated, were it not at the same time the limitless power of self-determination. But our statement means clearly that God, in the original basis of His existence, is *nothing but* WILL and FREEDOM. This original Will is eternally the source of an infinite fulness of being in God Himself, for it wills only Life and Love. If it had not willed these, if it were viewed in itself alone, and not as the source of an infinite fulness in God Himself, it would be merely the silent depth of that Negative Absolute wherein all determinations and distinctions vanish—or rather never appear; —wherein there is neither light nor darkness, neither thought nor being, neither understanding nor will, neither *I* nor *Thou*, neither self-realization nor love.

Primary idea of God.

In these investigations we have gone beyond the task which we marked out for ourselves. It was to prove the *possibility* only of Absolute Personality, the compatibility of the Absolute with the Personal. We have discovered the impossibility of representing the Absolute

Summary of the argument.

in the true import of the term as "the neuter or impersonal God" as (Jacobi with clever wit designates this impersonal essence), and the *necessity* of recognizing in it the SELF-CONSCIOUS GOD determining Himself by FREEDOM. It is easy to see how the proof of the *possibility* can hardly be separated from that of the *necessity*. For, in demonstrating the possibility, the conception of the absolute must be analysed, and its determinations must of themselves appear,—determinations which not only admit of, but demand PERSONALITY. These determinations present themselves when we advance from the notion of a merely negative Absolute to that of a positive and actually existing Absolute. If this advance be just and necessary, this latter conception of the Absolute is really higher than the former, and we are no longer obliged to distinguish between the Absolute and God. That is the method which Schelling adopted in his Dissertation on Freedom, and in his Treatise against Jacobi, in order to harmonize the idea of a personal God with that of the Absolute,* and thus to make Religion and Philosophy at one with each other. But a personal God, who is not Himself the Original Being, but is conditioned by a primary cause in any sense independent of Himself,—as the basis of His own being and of finite existence, —cannot be the object of perfect and undivided surrender on the part of the human heart, and of its unhesitating confidence that He will bring all beings dependent on Him to their completion. If God, as He is in Himself, be not *the Alpha*, we cannot be certain that He will be *the Omega*. The "τὰ πάντα ἐξ αὐτοῦ" is the guarantee for the "τὰ πάντα εἰς αὐτόν."

§ 2. GOD'S FREEDOM THE PRINCIPLE OF OTHER EXISTENCE.

The developed conception of Personality as of a Being complete in Himself implies that the Person has self-determination of will as the principle of His external working. If God be a Person, another being cannot spring from Him in virtue of any compulsory necessity of His nature, but only by His free will. Hence the well-known saying, "as He *thinks* so it is," is false,

* SCHELLING expresses himself clearly on this point in his *Denkmal Jacobi's*—*Werke*, part i. vol. viii. pp. 81, 82; and in his *Brief an Eschenmayer*, p. 189, f. Compare his statements concerning the principles of Pantheism and Monotheism (*Werke*, part ii. vol. ii. Lecture 1–4).

or at least very misleading; for Holy Scripture says this, much rather of God's Word as the effective outgo of His Will. "He commandeth and it stands fast."* God thinks of the world eternally, but the necessity of a beginningless world and of time as eternal *a parte ante*, by no means follows from this. He thinks of and wills both the world and time in their inseparable connection *as having a beginning*. Further, if God's personality is absolute, no necessity can oblige him to decree the existence of another being. In order to derive the existence of the world from God we have neither the "mathematical necessity" of Spinoza as he strongly expresses it in the first book of his Ethics,† nor the "logical necessity" of modern philosophers, according to which God had fully to realize Himself in or through the world; but only THE FREEDOM OF LOVE, of the Will, which in producing another being, makes this its aim, that the created being may share the blessings of existence and (so far as he is susceptible of it) the highest and most perfect good in fellowship with God.

The conception of CREATION essentially includes the production of another Being by an act of will, by conscious self-determination; the power to create, therefore, can be attributed only to a Personal essence. Further, in creation it is implied that the act is distinctively an *absolute* conditioning, *i.e.*, that it is not limited by anything external to the Creator, but is an unconditioned act, complete in itself; and to establish this principle was the design of the old formula, "Creation out of nothing." The doctors of the Church never added to this the absurd represen-

<small>Creation out of nothing.</small>

---

* Strauss's *Dogmatik*, i. 564, takes exception to the latter clause of the saying of Thomas Aquinas, " *necesse est, quod sua scientia sit causa rerum, secundum quod habet voluntatem conjunctam,*" (Summa p. i. qu. 14, art. 8); but we rather recognize a *confused* perception of the essence of Christian Theism in the main sentence, and the *true* thought in the subordinate clause. Schleiermacher also (*Glaubenslehre*, vol. i. p. 437, comp. p. 222) represents thinking and producing in God as one.

† *Propos.* 17, *Schol. Ego me satis clare ostendisse puto a summa Dei potentia sive infinita natura infinita infinitis modis, hoc est, omnia necessario effluxisse vel semper eadem necessitate sequi, eodem modo ac ex natura trianguli ab aeterno et in aeternum sequitur ejus tres angulos aequari duobus rectis.* If there be any truth in the comparison it is incorrect to speak of a logical sequence of things from divine power as *effluxisse*; no one can look upon the fact that the three angles being equal to two right angles as something derived from the triangle.

tation of the world's gradually coming into existence out of nothing, as if *nothing* might be looked upon as the cause of the world's existence. It is incongruous, therefore, to seek to refute this notion by the old canon *ex nihilo nihil fit;* but it is equally incongruous to decry as Pantheism the use of this canon altogether in this question concerning creation.* The true conception of creation has no objection to make against the maxim *ex nihilo nihil fit;* according to it the cause of the world's existence is the Will of God, and in it, as the unlimited and infinitely powerful principle of all reality, the *nihil* has no place. If, therefore, creation is an unconditioned conditioning, absolute Personality alone can create. Now, that which alone can determine God, who is perfectly self-sufficient, to create a being different from Himself is LOVE. Accordingly, creation is nothing less than the free self-communication of God, who might exist in Himself alone, but wills not to do so, in order that other beings may exist and may have eternal life in fellowship with Him.

And yet this freedom seems at once to resolve itself again into necessity, when we remember that love itself is a fundamental determination or attribute of the divine nature. Now, if the world be the necessary object of this love would not its existence follow by a logical necessity from the very nature of God?

Does this imply necessity?

The distinction drawn by Leibnitz between metaphysical and moral necessity is undoubtedly true and suggestive. The latter is really a higher necessity than the former,—much more elaborated and spiritualized,—superior chiefly because it has in it the element of *design*, which is foreign to the metaphysical necessity. But we have now to do not with the determinate character, but simply with the existence or non-existence of the world; and if it be granted that God's love cannot realize itself save in relation to the world, the connection between the condition and consequent is as firm in the light of moral necessity as of the merely metaphysical.

Attempts to solve this difficulty.

Nor is the difficulty removed by the fact already established that every attribute of the divine nature—and therefore love

---

* HEGEL often does this; *e.g., Encykl.* § 88; *Logik—Werke*, vol. iii. p. 80; though without express reference to creation.

—springs from the divine self-determination. Assuredly God is love because He wills to be love. But what right have we to suppose that He could not be love at all without giving up His freedom? Absolute freedom requires not only that an Essence should not be dependent on another, but that the *existence* of another should not of necessity follow from it. Nay more; the independence implied in absolute freedom is not unfettered if it have to realize itself by means of another being however dependent. If God, on account of his love, could not exist without the world, then absolute freedom, which is the source of His determinate nature and attributes, must have nullified itself in producing love; for it would then follow from God's nature that He *must* stand in a necessary relation to another being. He would not then be complete in Himself, self-subsisting and needing nothing— $\Theta\epsilon\grave{o}\varsigma\ a\mathring{v}\tau o\tau\epsilon\lambda\grave{\eta}\varsigma\ \mathring{a}\pi\rho o\sigma\delta\epsilon\acute{\eta}\varsigma$.

We can solve this problem only by means of the idea of the Divine Trinity. Its inmost significance is that God has in Himself the eternal and wholly adequate object of His love independent of all relation to the world, John xvii. 24, "Thou lovedst Me before the foundation of the world," see also v. 5. This requires alike the unity of the Essence, and the distinctness of the Persons. For without the distinction of Persons, without an *I* and a *Thou*, there could be no love. Again, without the unity of Essence, there would follow from the love of God a necessary relation to an essence distinct from God. Both are therefore implied in what is said of the Logos in the beginning of St John's Gospel; the distinction of Persons by the $\mathring{\eta}v\ \pi\rho\grave{o}\varsigma\ \tau\grave{o}v\ \theta\epsilon\acute{o}v$; the unity of Essence by the $\theta\epsilon\grave{o}\varsigma\ \mathring{\eta}v$. But as it is the Logos through whom the immanent love of God eternally realizes itself, He also is the Mediator of outgoing love, *i.e.*, of that activity and self-manifestation of God towards other beings, whereby the world is created, sustained, and carried on to its completion.

The doctrine of the Trinity solves it.

Indeed, without the Logos, without that eternal distinction of Persons, in virtue of which God, as essentially Love, is complete in Himself, we cannot conceive how divine love could reveal itself as divine, and therefore perfect, in and through the world. For He only is capable of an absolutely perfect love to another being,

Perfect love must not need its object.

who is wholly self-dependent and self-sufficient in relation to that other being. Where these are wanting, love is more or less blended with need, and therefore is not wholly free from selfish relations, which ever kindle desires and passions. That wholly disinterested love, which is perfect freedom, and which is at the same time as true and *reliable* as the most unerring necessity, is possible only where there is no need or want. The perfection to which human love can attain, is in its nature relative, though perfect of its kind. For though it is conceivable that at some future time the sense of need in the individual will cease, when it has fulfilled its purposes as an impulse to union, a temptation to selfish isolation in the community, and a school for triumphing love, still man as a created being, can never lose his need of God. If God had need of the world, of a being different from Himself, in order to be (according to His nature) love, this love, would not be absolutely perfect. It is only because He is wholly self-sufficient, in virtue of the distinction of Persons in the unity of Essence, that His love can be pure self-communication and condescending self-sacrifice, as it reveals itself to us in Jesus Christ. A Godhead suffering want and needing help may be welcomed by a romantic and mediæval imagination, in order to afford scope for the religious play of its fancy, so full of mystery and interest ; but the earnest truthfulness of Protestantism will never mistake such cloudy imagery for reality.

From this it follows that there is no necessity for the world *Contingentia* in relation to God, and that even upon the prin*mundi.* ciple of God's love, the saying is a false one, " God would not be God if there were no world." It seems very religious to say, " as it is in the nature of goodness and love to communicate themselves to others, God cannot be without the world." And then, in the place of this love, there is easily set up a spurious, strange, and metaphysical abstraction, which does not presuppose, nay, which even does away with the Personality of God, namely, " the immanent and logical process between the infinite and the finite.* Contingency, therefore,

* MARTENSEN'S *Meister Eckart,* pp. 70, 71 ; this is said with the honest belief that thus the divine personality and love may be fully maintained. [In his *Christian Dogmatics* (§ 59), Martensen expresses himself more guardedly. He says, "In a certain sense, we may say that God created the world in order to satisfy a want in Himself ; but the idea of God's love requires us to understand

as opposed to necessity, provided that it does not imply in its object the absence of reasons or aims, but only the possibility of non-existence, may be predicated of the world's existence, and in this sense Theism has ever adopted the expression *Contingentia mundi*. What else does Holy Scripture teach? The key note of the Old Testament is throughout, that the world has need of God, not that God needs the world; that the world is the product of God's freest will, and depends for its being on the breath of His mouth; that mankind as a race, and the chosen people in their midst, owe whatever greatness and glory they possess to His free will, His promise and His covenant; that to Him alone is the glory due. And this fundamental view of the relation of the world to God, which certainly does not imply any necessity in its existence, so far from being contradicted in the New Testament, is really presupposed there. And yet there is something inapposite in describing the world's existence as a "contingency," for "the contingent," according to the definition already given, is more than the mere possibility of not being, and is the antithesis not of "the necessary," but of "the intentional." We should therefore speak of contingency only in reference to intelligent beings who can purpose and plan. If this be the true meaning of the word, contingency as well as necessity is by freedom excluded from the Divine love as the source of the world's existence. Love has certainly purposes and aims in the creation of the world—its knowledge is wisdom. But as perfect love, its aims are eternal, not centering in itself, but in the being whose existence it wills. To apply the conception of "design" or "purpose" in its usual acceptation to this relation of the world to God, would therefore lead to erroneous results, if we did not give due prominence to the distinctive character of the design as originating in love. God does not will to receive anything Himself by His external workings, as if He needed any thing for the realization of His nature; the being whom He thus creates, receives all that is in any way compat-

this want as quite as truly a *superfluity*. For this lack in God is not as in the God of Pantheism, a blind hunger and thirst after existence, but is identical with the inexhaustible riches of that liberty which cannot but will to reveal itself. From this point of view, it will be clear in what sense we reject the proposition, and in what sense we accept it, "Without the world God is not God."—*Clark's Foreign Theol. Library*, 4th series, vol. xii. p. 114].—*Tr.*

ible with its true character and the limitations inseparable from it.

<small>Created existence must be personal.</small>
This will of Divine Love, that there shall be existences distinct from God, as perfect as the idea of derived being will allow, may be described more accurately, as the will that there shall be Beings like to God, and capable of fellowship with Him in love and knowledge. This necessarily implies the highest possible independence in the Being created. Existence, without self-dependence, is so far removed from a being who can perfectly mould and determine Himself, that though it may, by its absolute dependence, reveal to others God's eternal power and thought, it can in no way be like Him. A being which cannot know itself, cannot know God; if it does not possess itself, it cannot surrender itself to God. Real being and life in God includes just as much the consciousness of some degree of independence in relation to God, as the consciousness that the difference of nature which makes this relative independence possible, is by no means a separating barrier. If, therefore, there be beings in the sphere of created existence who are capable of existence in God, they must not only have their being like objects in nature from God, but must have being also in themselves, and of themselves. Thus St Paul (Acts xvii. 28) says that man has his being in God; and as the connection shows, he represents this as a distinguishing honour, resulting from the fact that " we are also His offspring." As God wills the highest unity, He creates the highest distinctiveness or individuality (see vol. i. p. 114). It is only by virtue of these essential elements of personality that likeness of God and fellowship with Him are possible in a created being. If, therefore, Divine Love wills to give the most glorious existence which any being besides God can possess, it ordains creature personality. Thus God's creative will aims at PERSONALITY, and His distinctive purpose in the world's creation is that personality may realize its true nature.

<small>Freedom necessary to created personality.</small>
In order that personality in the sphere of created existence may be the image and reflection of the Divine Personality, and may be as if the eye and heart of the world, God must also will that there shall be beings external to Him, who can determine

themselves from the undetermined, and thus far mould themselves as *causa sui*. The real proof of this is contained in what we have already said; in explanation, however, we may add the following. Without a self-determining which is really *self-causative*, the other element in the idea of personality (*i.e.* self-consciousness) necessarily loses its meaning. It is an imperfect and unreal representation, if we endeavour in thought to engraft self-consciousness upon animal life, apart from self-determination. Man could not really distinguish himself from all that he is not,—his consciousness would ever be unsettled and transitory,—if he had not in himself a principle of free movement, if he did not possess the power voluntarily to determine himself from himself, and thus to limit, in some degree his becoming passively determined from without. If there were a being already wholly determined before and irrespective of its self-determination, so that all included in consciousness as self-determination were only the necessary result of his being thus determined, we should, in such a case, have a self-determining indeed, but one utterly powerless to realize itself in independent action, or even to move from its appointed place. Causative self-determination is not really possessed unless not only the conduct, but the very nature itself, *is somehow conditioned* BY ORIGINAL SELF-DETERMINATION. And this is FREEDOM. An essence or nature is free when, starting from a state of original indeterminateness, it attains determinateness by self-decision.

This conception, as it is one of the most significant and profound, is also one of the most difficult in the whole system of Christian Theism.

To make the freedom of man the *unconditional principle of all determinations* in his nature, and to regard the sum of its determinations as his self-determination, would contradict the true conception of derived being. The distinction between absolute and relative personality would, on such a supposition, be destroyed, and the determinateness of human nature to which experience testifies the barriers (I mean) which limit it, would be perfectly inexplicable. Moreover, as human personality is realized only in the individual, it would be impossible to explain, on this supposition, how individuals ever attained that common

Human freedom relative,

character which essentially unites them as one species. It is clear that this could not be accounted for by a reference to those natural circumstances, conditioning the temporal origin of the individual, for according to this view, those natural conditions must themselves be regarded as the product of self-determination.

The self-formation of conditioned Being is possible only upon the basis of certain fundamental determinations of its nature within the limits ordained for it by God.

And conditioned.

Herein consists the difference between God and man;—in man self-conditioning is already conditioned, in God it is unconditioned. In God there is absolute freedom; in man there can only be a freedom limited by necessity; and this fettering barrier can be removed only by man's recognizing himself through love as one with God, and in this love affirming himself just as he is determined of God: God's appointment concerning him he thus makes his own. Human freedom cannot have the whole of human nature as the sphere of its immediate and creative principle, but only *one* department of it; that, namely, in which the capability of love resides, by whose power the established barriers are made to be no longer barriers.

This department is man's MORAL nature. What man is as a moral being in his natural state, apart from what he may become through redemption, has its origin in the unconditioned, *i.e.*, in his self-determination.

Pertaining to the sphere of morals.

The human spirit, therefore, is concerned in the question of the freedom; the will so far only as it has to do with morals, with the antithesis of good and evil.

Moral freedom.

As an isolated phenomenon, a volition or act morally indifferent, seems to occur in the same manner as one which bears a moral import, *i.e.*, as an act of choice involving the ability to do otherwise. But a careful observation of our own experience testifies that we look for freedom in such a volition or act, so far only as we surmise or presuppose therein something of a moral character, of a hidden moral import. Had we nothing but that immediate consciousness of being able to choose otherwise, which accompanies the movement of the will towards a decision of whatever kind, we should certainly have no firm ground in this to conclude that we possess freedom in the true sense of the word, as a self-determining, which does not resolve itself again into a being determined. The reasons which justify, yea more, oblige us to this conclusion are essentially of a moral kind. These moral considerations justify our belief in that universal (metaphysical) freedom, the *possibility* of which only can be metaphysically proved. *Metaphysical freedom* is necessary, because of moral freedom. Freedom in its particular manifestations must extend beyond the moral sphere, into all spheres of action, so that the principle of the Moral in freedom may be able to realize itself in life and act.

But even in the sphere of Morals human freedom is not without a presupposition or condition, to which it must have some relation, though in its self-decision it is not determined or bound thereby. Wherever we look for the first decision of human freedom, it always has one antecedent, viz., God, and His Will that man's will may ever by freedom continue in fellowship with Him. Thus the freedom of this primary decision resolves itself into a choice between fellowship with God and departure from Him; into the choice whether man will hold to the original source of his being, or will break away therefrom so as to be wholly self-dependent. The only literally original and utterly unconditioned volition is that of God as the producing cause of certain determinations of His own nature; such volition belongs exclusively to God. But God has given to man an image or reflection of his own absolute freedom, having endowed him with the power of conditioning himself as a moral being by choosing between different and equally possible courses.

<small>Something conditioning moral freedom.</small>

Lest we should expose ourselves to the reproach of hastily adopting a conclusion of such great importance in our inquiry, let us examine this point still more minutely.

The possibility of evil in and for itself by no means essentially belongs to the idea of freedom. To predicate the possibility of God's falling away from His own nature, which is love and goodness, because He is absolutely free, would be not only meaningless, but absurd. Certainly He is perfect love, simply

<small>God's freedom does not include the possibility of evil.</small>

because He wills to be so ; and we can understand and know that He is so, not by any notion of metaphysical necessity, but only because of His self-revelation in actual being. But in Himself He wills what is perfect, and nothing else, eternally and unchangeably, and his deeds and workings must therefore correspond to His perfection. It is an inviolable necessity that the divine attributes of goodness and wisdom, holiness and righteousness, should embody themselves in His works, but this necessity is a positive one, based upon freedom and self-determination. As for a metaphysical necessity, from which what are commonly called the moral attributes of God are derived, and which forbids God, the eternally self-determining One, to be mere physical essence, there is not, there cannot be any such thing. Apart from the revelation of God in history, our own existence, the nature and volition of our spirit—the idea, inseparable from our self-consciousness, of a higher perfection, such as the divine perfection must be—these all witness to us that God is a moral being, *i.e.*, that He is love. While, therefore, we certainly recognize in the depths of that absolute self-determination, wherein God's determinate nature is based, the possibility of its not willing itself to be love, but to be a nature shut up in itself,—the possibility of His forbidding any distinction of person between Him and beings external to Him by an act of His self-determination,— this possibility is wholly destroyed by the eternal reality of what He actually has willed.

But it is different with the self-determination of man. He cannot primarily and independently ordain for himself moral good, nor does he possess it necessarily as his own. He can be good only by maintaining a certain relationship to One who is distinct from him, and who conditions his existence—*i.e.*, to God. Now, seeing that man has not moral good as his own essence, there is, in virtue of his self-determination, together with the possibility and the obligation of good, *the possibility also of evil*, and of a fall from God.

<small>Human freedom does.</small>

According to man's true nature indeed, God is not a stranger to him, nor is His holy will a merely external law. It is man's appointed destiny to make his will perfectly one with God's, so that all further possibility of separation may be removed; and it is only by fulfilling this his destiny that he can be perfectly at one with himself, and with his true ideal, as well as perfectly free. But seeing that the realization of this destiny depends upon his self-determination, man as man, and prior to any self-determination—man in his pure "naturalness," as Hegel calls it (which is different from his *present* "naturalness" or state by nature)—cannot thus be one with God; and herein lies the incipient possibility of evil, of a fall.

But if the *possibility* only of a fall be implied, it is evident that man does not begin with an original separation from God and from his own ideal. Such a beginning is impossible; but it is equally impossible that what man is before any self-decision can have any conditioning force that was not ordained by the divine will. Before the primary self-decision there can be nothing but, on the one hand, an undecidedness of personal beings; on the other hand, their existence through God, and in virtue of this (seeing that no separating decision has intervened) their dependence on their eternal Original; a dependence, however, which has no moral import, for it has not yet been affirmed by any self-decision. We cannot, therefore, speak of an original "neutrality" between fellowship with God and departure from Him, nor of a hesitation or wavering between the love of God and selfishness;—as for the first idea, it is a mere abstraction; and as for the second, it implies a power of evil in man, a sin before sin. And yet in his original state man is morally undetermined, a being not yet decided; in virtue of his personality he must be so.

What man's "not yet being decided" implies.

If God, in order to exclude this undecidedness, and the possibility of a perverted decision implied therein, had not willed the existence of *personal* beings, the world would have been, not an insolvable riddle,—for this would have implied that the hidden meaning of the riddle had been preserved somewhere,—but utter darkness and silence, hidden from itself, as its Creator would have been hidden from it. But God having willed personality as the centre of the world, He must have allowed it a morally undecided commencement.

We have already recognized that the power of free self-

CHAP. IV.] FREEDOM AS THE POSSIBILITY OF SIN. 145

determining is the highest *independence* of which the creature is capable; but this independence is by no means to be regarded as a germ or beginning of *evil*—of *selfishness*. It is rather the necessary condition of moral good in the creature; of love to God, and of everything holy and perfect which this includes. This independence, indeed, is not immediately oneness with the man's true nature; it regards this as a decision still before it; but it is not at variance with it;—the state of not yet being at one with goodness, must be distinguished from actual disunion or variance. And if this state involves the possibility of separation and variance,—the possibility of the man making self and not God the centre of his volition and effort,—such a transition, from natural and sinless independence to selfishness as the source of all sin, can be accomplished only by a *change* and *self-perversion* of the will, and not by any mere hindrance or pause in the development. A clever analyst of human nature, Passavant, describes "the process of development in a free being in three stages,"—thus, "I *will*," "*I will*," I will GOD'S WILL";* for he adds, the pause at the second stage, and the "*I* will" ensuing upon this, is evil. But the fact is, this "*I* will" is by no means a mere pause or dwelling upon the second "*I will*"; it is to be distinguished from this (to use the phraseology here chosen, if, indeed, such an expression be allowable) as a distinct "moment" or stage, even as this is distinct from the first "I *will*." That independence which has its appropriate place in normal development finds its expression in the first moment "I *will*"; and herein, according to the true conception of the will, the second stage "*I will*" is already contained. If, therefore, the natural and guiltless self-assertion be expressed by "*I will*," the alternative presents itself either to proceed to the third stage "I will GOD'S WILL," or to turn aside to the other "*I* will," wherein the will of the creature unnaturally makes *self* its centre.

Thus, side by side with that decision of man for good, which he arrives at only by a free and deliberate blending of his will with a will previously distinct from his, there exists as a

Side note: No germ of evil implied in this.

Side note: Passavant's analysis.

---

* "*On the Freedom of the Will and the laws of human Development*," Preface, p. v.

negative condition the possibility of evil; inasmuch as while he is called to perfect fellowship with God, he *may* turn away and separate himself from God.* We thus see how erroneous it is, when the freedom according to which man can do evil as well as good is spoken of (after the manner of Hegel in his *Rechtsphilosophie*) as something *contracted* in human nature, as something in itself *bad*,† in contrast with freedom when it has become one with its ideal. The realization of evil certainly involves the deepest degradation of man; but this deep degradation arises from man's originally high and dignified position. It is the immeasurable energy and profundity of independence in personality which includes in itself the power of the *ego* to make *self* the centre of its world. Even in the degeneracy of freedom realizing itself in perverted action, there still shines a gleam of its essential splendour. And though it be an exaggeration to speak of man in his fallen state as a fallen demigod, this is nearer the truth, than to make him, as Materialism does, a demi-animal, a being who, in spite of all his efforts to raise himself above the sphere of the mere animal, ever pitiably falls back again below the level of his half-brother the brute.

Now God's causative power, which produces a freedom and self-determining external to Himself, is truly an act of creation; for it is a consciously free and in itself unconditioned *conditioning* of another being. But it implies, at the same time, a self-restraining of God's will in its causative activity; a voluntary permission granted to this other being to choose his own character as a moral being by self-determination. This is the nature of the causality, the only one of its kind, whereby the freedom of the creature is produced;—an act of producing, whose highest unconditionateness consists in its not conditioning its product a single degree further than is absolutely necessary in order to give it existence.

---

* Even BASIL justly said in his 'Ομιλία, "ὅτι οὐκ ἔστιν αἴτιος τῶν κακῶν ὁ θεός"—ὁ μεμφόμενος τὸν ποιητὴν ὡς μὴ φυσικῶς κατασκευάσαντα ἡμᾶς ἀναμαρτήτους οὐδὲν ἕτερον ἢ τὴν ἄλογον φύσιν τῆς λογικῆς προτιμᾷ καὶ τὴν ἀκίνητον καὶ ἀνόρμητον τῆς προαιρετικῆς καὶ ἐμπράκτου.—*Opp.* ed. Garnier. tom. ii. p. 79.

† *E.g.* MARHEINEKE in his *Rescension der Möhlerschen Symbolik*, pp. 31, 32 of the separate reprint.

CHAP. IV.] FREEDOM AS THE POSSIBILITY OF SIN. 147

We have already proved, in an earlier part of our inquiry (pp. 67–75), that an act of free self-decision, which originally fixes the bias and character of our moral being, must be *extra*-temporal.

§ 3. PRIMARY SELF-DECISION EXTRA-TEMPORAL.

All SELF-CONSCIOUSNESS indeed seems to be a victory over time. It is so not only objectively, in that it makes what is far above time its subject-matter, but subjectively also. Those creatures only are given over wholly to the dominion of time who live merely in the present, without any capability of associating therewith the past or the future—without recollection of the one or presentiment concerning the other. Even in the nobler of the lower animals we find a faculty both of memory and of foresight, for without these they would be utterly insusceptible of domestication and training. But this susceptibility is not only very limited, it is also of a kind wholly dependent upon instinct and external causes. It is not until self-consciousness dawns in man that the marvellous power appears, of bringing to view in the present by a free intelligent act, what is no more, and what is not yet. The forgotten, which leaves not a trace behind, but has sunk into the dark past of individual life, may by recollection be brought again into the light of consciousness; and the unknown future, which as yet has no existence, may by reason and calculation be foreseen. Thus with surpassing power the mind of man bids defiance to time, and combines in one what time separates and keeps asunder.

Man's power over time.

And yet, though the mind can break through one and another barrier, and can gain one and another advantage over time, it cannot help feeling that even in these partial victories it is subject to time's more general laws. It can never clearly and thoroughly discern its own future; indeed, it cannot determine with perfect certainty concerning a single moment of it. But it becomes still more sensible of the unconquerable power of time when it finds that it cannot retain its own possessions, that memory can by no means command the entire past nor marshal with readiness all its parts. It would that no act, no experience were in vain, that every present should be a stage of memory for the future, thus forming one clear and connected development; but it is driven on, as if in the dark, and not knowing whither, in the

Yet fettered thereby.

conflict of various impulses counteracting one another. Thus endeavouring in vain to keep fast hold of that which vanishes with time, it becomes conscious of the power of time as a barrier; whereas the mere animal is wholly unconscious of time, in whose power it stands.

So far for the relation of our self-consciousness to time. Let us now consider the manner in which created personality is in its very being affected by time. Personality, as we have seen, while conditioned as to its existence, is in its nature imperishable. Is personality, then, a victorious power subduing time to itself? We must reply in the affirmative if mere continuance, the endless extension of bare existence, be a conquest of time. Contemplating the sphere which experience enables us to survey—our earthly and temporal existence—we experience this important limitation;—the prime of our individual life, when it reveals its full power and freshness, is only a passing moment. What Goethe somewhere says of corporeal beauty, that the beautiful is most beautiful only for a moment, is true of human power and activity generally. Before its bloom is fully opened it is still an imperfect bloom, a moment after, it has already begun to fade. This moment is the true *present* of our earthly life previously it was future, afterwards it is past; why cannot we command the past and the future that they be as the present ? Time cannot rob us of existence, but it is our earthly limit, in that it hurries on and sweeps away the constituent parts of our earthly life in continual becoming and passing away, in alternate growth and decay.

<small>Relation of personality to time.</small>

But when what at present limits us shall be taken away will *time* itself also, as the measure of existence disappear? If we imagine those limitations removed, we find that we still possess a life of imperishable duration in time : a life which grows not old, but continually abides in unweakened power and never failing fulness; and a consciousness which loses nothing it has once possessed, and which can call up from the mine of memory the most distant past with unfettered freedom. Such an existence, we perceive, must subjectively afford the purest satisfaction, for it is fixed yet variable, simple yet manifold, becoming yet remaining, active yet at rest, susceptible of the highest

<small>Personality by continuance conquers time.</small>

bliss, and a clear reflection of God's image. Time would then have become only the immanent form wherein life was carried on in perfect freedom, but life would still be *life in time*. Thus what we now feel to be the limiting power of time—the powerlessness of our spirit to maintain its energy and freshness, the disgust we feel in having to lose what we had already attained, the pain of making progress over ruins,—all this is only the special form of our present life in time; time itself is the simple measure of the advance of our being in its self-development. The power which continually hurries us on, and which we feel as a constraint foreign to us and imposed upon us, is not *time in itself* and its uninterrupted succession,* nor is it change of itself—the vicissitudes of our circumstances; it is the fact that this constant succession and change tyrannizes over us; it is not for us the free outgo of self, but a stern necessity of nature hurrying us on.

And yet if we turn our thoughts to God, that which for us seems the *necessary form* of our existence, must be regarded as a *limitation* if referred to Him, a limitation incompatible with His perfection.

Time would be a limitation for God.

Where there is any succession in time it is impossible for the *ego* to possess the past and the future in the same moment with the present. Certainly, notwithstanding the inconceivable swiftness of time, which is really nothing but the impossibility of putting limits to its subdivision (the " infinite divisibility " of time, as it is commonly called—but this is a misappropriation of the word " infinite "), we can imagine a being existing in time yet possessing the power of considering at once every state answering to its nature, and of maintaining every conformable activity as long as he pleased—calm and undisturbed amid time's restless motion. We could also imagine a capability in such a Being to penetrate with clearest consciousness any moment of its past that it might

---

* Nor is it the endlessness of this succession, as some might suppose; according to JACOBI's well-known account of the awful impression which the idea of endless duration made upon him when a child (*Briefe über Spinoza*, p. 328). This impression is produced by an arbitrary abstraction of time from all its contents, by a representation of all duration, "independently of all religious ideas," as a mere empty form; just as the horror which the thought of annihilation produced in Jacobi, arose from the representation of time as filled with rich and pleasant contents.

recall. Still it would hold true concerning even such a Being that the full realization of its existence would be in the present only ; past and future would still be in the background, as no longer real or not yet realized. And even if every moment of its existence to which it turned its thoughts were fully clear to view, it would recognize it,—and, therefore, its own being in reference thereto,—as something already past or still future *i.e.*, it would regard it differently and less perfectly than the present. For were this distinction of past and present quite non-existent, the temporal form of consciousness would already have become eternal. With duration there must necessarily be change. The past as well as the future is ever a *minus* in comparison of the present. A certain separation of moments or parts— an approach and a withdrawal— are essentially contained in the conception of time. Conditioned Beings have existence in time necessarily assigned to them because at the very outset of their existence there is a separation between their production by the divine will, and their continuation by means of their own activity. That alone is perfect Being and consciousness,—perfect not only according to the capacity of a limited existence, but absolutely,—which contains within itself an infinite yet undivided fulness of attributes without any separation of elements, which spreads itself throughout an Infinite, yet concentres itself in the inmost present,—a present which has not a past and future distinct from itself like that of temporal beings, but which includes past and future absolutely within itself. This brings us to the conception of ETERNITY.

The popular idea of eternity as a limitless extension of

Popular notion of eternity.
duration, hardly requires any detailed refutation It is manifest that a succession of moments which does not involve a becoming, or a transition from one stage to another, is utter nonsense. No one can demonstrate that development and change are compatible with God's absoluteness or (which is just the converse), that empirical existence can be conceived of without development and change. Scripture itself contains phraseology which contradicts this mistaken notion of eternity ; for instance where an eternal Being is described as the absolutely present one, John iii. 13, " The Son of Man who is in heaven ; " viii

58, "Before Abraham was I AM," and i. 18. The Kantian theory, that time and space are the subjective and *a priori* conditions of our knowledge, contains the truth that all visible representation unavoidably paints its objects on the tablet of time and space; but to bind speculation down to this visible representation, as Jacobi does in one of the maxims of his philosophy, is virtually to deny Speculation altogether.*

While the true idea of God in its development rejects the popular notion of eternity as inadequate, care must be taken lest we fall into the other extreme, the negative view. According to this we arrive at the idea of God's eternity simply by negativing all limitations of time; and this is really no better than if we fancied that we freed God's will from the limits of space by reducing it to the idea of the geometric point. In considering God's nature as *non*-temporal, we are far short of recognizing it as exalted above time and as really eternal.† If this negative view be assented to as a sufficient explanation of what is most positive, the consequence will be, that the idea of the divine Being as the Eternal will be emptied of all its fulness, emptied even of what conditioned being possesses under the conditions of time,—and will be reduced to a pure and indefinite abstraction.‡

<small>Negative idea of eternity.</small>

---

* The Christian's faith and hope, moreover, will never allow itself to be deprived of their object, because that object is incapable of visible representation, according to the present type of our knowledge and experience; and he who would banish such elements from Christian consciousness as abstractions, will do well to consider how he will escape the philosophy which makes empirical existence the Absolute,—a philosophy which itself admits its fundamental opposition to Christianity. That maxim harmonizes with Jacobi's confession that as to his feelings he was a Christian, but according to his understanding a heathen; a contradiction which his philosophy characteristically obviates simply by denying the testimony of feeling.

† It is, therefore, an abuse of language to call mathematical and metaphysical truths eternal.

‡ STRAUSS, *Dogmatik*, vol. i., 562, argues that eternity is irreconcilable with God's personality,—"We cannot but think that a self-consciousness ever the same would be no more real, than would a sound ever one and the same be audible." Here we find both mistakes regarding eternity;—"self-consciousness ever the same," implies an eternity of limitless duration, "the single sound which could not be heard," implies the merely negative idea of eternity.—Mr Mansel in like manner says, "The only human conception of personality is that of limitation."—*Bampton Lectures*, lect. iv.—*Tr.*

152 THE POSSIBILITY OF SIN. [BOOK III. PART I.

The divine eternity in the concrete conception of it, can be apprehended only in its union with God's absolute self-realization. Viewed in this light, it evidently does not exclude, but, on the contrary, includes an infinite fulness. God has in Himself the commencement or perennial spring of his Being, and the commencement is by no means a fulness, it is undetermined simpleness; but seeing that He is the Eternal, He may without the need of time realize Himself as an infinite fulness. Now time, as we are conscious of it, embraces an inexhaustible fulness of determinations, and so does eternity in the consciousness of God ; but not imperfectly as with us,—for with us determinations are separate, and sometimes exclude each other, so that when one occupies the present, all others are thrown into the past or future,—but perfectly, because in *an undivided and inseparable unity*.

<small>Positive idea of eternity.</small>

God could not bestow this positive eternity of existence upon any other Being;—a Being thus endowed would itself be God, while necessarily distinct from and dependent on God,—a notion which is self-contradictory. But as He wills personality external to Himself, God wills also the self-grounding or self-decision of personal Beings. This self-conditioning, as we have already seen, is possible only apart from time. If, therefore, the divine Will that there shall be Personality in the sphere of created existence includes the resolve that this Personality shall have an extra-temporal commencement of its being, this extra-temporality must be something different from eternity. We cannot suppose that this background of our moral development, this extra-temporal self-decision, consists of two successive elements, first, a volition of the undetermined, and secondly, a volition of the determined. This background, so far as we have to do with it, is nothing but a self-determining of the undetermined. The non-temporal Being, seeing that it must be distinct from eternal Being, cannot as such possess the power of self-development. In order to this, every Being whose existence is dependent, requires the transition into time and its successive development, so as gradually to add link to link in the chain of self-realization. But in this very

<small>Distinction between created personality and God.</small>

negativity and indeterminateness pertaining to extra-temporal Being, there lies the possibility of that self-conditioning commencement,—that primary self-decision on the part of personal natures, without which the characteristic of unconditioned, which must lie at the root of freedom even in *created* beings, can never be maintained. For the very reason that this existence is as yet, so to speak, only half real in comparison with earthly and temporal life, it is the appropriate sphere for the strongest decisions of freedom. The settled reality of temporal life, the fixed natural laws by which it moves, the close connection of the successive stages of its development, these—while they are the conditions of man's determinate life in its growth to complete and matured individuality—limit his freedom and confine it within a narrow range. The very fact that created personality does not at the outset possess full reality, secures to it the power of giving to itself a fundamental bias whereby it will, and in turn must, forego the unlimited power of self-determining in order to attain full and determinate reality.

<small>Self-decision in the sphere of (negative) timelessness.</small>

Almost all thinkers, from Empedocles to Kant (and Schelling himself in part), who have indistinctly surmised or clearly recognized that our temporal life is conditioned by an extra-temporal act of self-decision, have been misled by one unwarrantable supposition in defining this truth. I refer to their belief that the sphere of the non-temporal is to be regarded as a *higher* sphere, an *ideal existence*, wherein the soul possesses the highest advantages, shares the undisturbed apprehension of eternal ideas, and lives a life of perfect bliss; a sphere wherein, as "the thing in itself," *ens per se*, it knows God and all truth.*
The transition, accordingly, from this original existence to life in time, from the ideal into the empirical (if the discovery of this transition was not given up altogether), was regarded as a

<small>Relation of this sphere to temporal life.</small>

---

* KANT's Lectures on Metaphysics certainly lead to a narrower view, though as they were published long after his death (1821), and with little care, from a college manuscript, they can hardly be considered as authorities for the Kantian doctrine. At p. 232, "Concerning the state of the soul before birth," it is stated, that "it had been without consciousness of itself or of the world;" and it was only Kant's spiritualistic contempt of nature and corporeity which led him to regard this "purely spiritual life of the soul" as a higher state of existence.

fall and an apostacy. We need not here repeat what we have already said in other parts of this inquiry to prove the impossibility of deriving our existence in time and space from evil as its cause. But as to the origin of Personal beings in the sphere of the ideal, it cannot mean anything more than the fact that the necessary condition of their full existence as personal beings is thereby secured. This silent timeless realm of shades is, as it were, the womb wherein all personal beings lie concealed in embryo. Here are the simple undetermined rudiments of our being which precede its concrete realization. We must not, therefore, look here for the fulness of Godlike life, but only for the power of deciding either for free union with God by submission to His will, or for the assertion of self-dependence. However this primary decision took

Necessary transition into temporal development. place, it was the transition of these "intelligible" or ideal existences into space and time, corporeity and development, and we are not justified in regarding the present form of our corporeity and of our development, wherein growth is at the same time decay, as the only one possible. Man's perfect life after the Resurrection—wherein he will discern the height and depth of the eternal and the temporal, of God and the world,—wherein the limiting powers of innate slowness (*vis inertiae*) and of outward hindrances, and above all the disturbing power of evil, will be perfectly overcome,—incomparably excels our present existence in the fulness of its realization ; and so our present existence itself surpasses the extra-temporal and hidden germ of our being at its commencement.

These considerations enable us to explain how it is that we

Does consciousness inform us of this ideal act? do not possess *any consciousness* of this intelligible or ideal existence conditioning our life in time nor of this primary decision. Let us consider what it really is that we are deficient in. As our earlier investigations have partially shown, and as our subsequent inquiries concerning original sin will more fully demonstrate, we find in our moral consciousness undeniable facts which are utterly inexplicable save upon the supposition of a self-determining, preceding this our life in time. These truths assert themselves in unbiassed and thoroughly earnest consciousness as distinctly as if man were actually conscious of such an original act conditioning his moral state in time. Thus this intelligible self-determination is by no means so foreign to our consciousness that it has no presentiment of it; on the contrary, it is reflected there in a very definite manner. Not, however, immediately; there is not, nor can there be an empirical consciousness of that extra-temporal act as such; it can be known only by Speculation.

To this question Schelling replies, " that free act cannot Schelling's appear in consciousness, because, as it precedes reply. and determinates the nature, it precedes consciousness itself."* There is no doubt that our consciousness in its present form is conditioned by that act, and therefore that the act cannot be within the range of consciousness as a given fact. But another reason why it cannot be known in consciousness is, because the non-temporal beings in whom it takes place have not yet attained the *full reality* of personal existence. The actual and earthly relations in which they find their appropriate place are not present at this point of their existence, and the freedom of their self-determination necessarily precedes these relations. Nor do these
Negations
pertaining personal essences distinguish themselves from each
to ideal   other;—not that in the sphere of their primary
existence.
existence, and in the deciding of their nature, they are really indistinguishable,—but they do not yet distinguish themselves, each from each, for as yet they have no mutual relations, nor can they until they enter upon corporeity and the actual relationships of the world. If they had such a relation, their existence would not be purely spiritual, but would express the limits pertaining to them as individual beings—*i.e.*, it would be concrete or material—in contradiction to what is presupposed. But they can hardly be conscious of their own nature before they exist in the distinctiveness of each individual, save as they perceive in God, in the infinite fulness of His nature, those elements which, according to God's creative will, are reflected in man. They recognize themselves, *i.e.*, humanity in its general features, in *the mirror of God*. Hence in their temporal life two facts appear;—on the one hand they possess an intuitive and immediate knowledge of God; and, on the other hand, their knowledge of God is

* *Werke*, Part i. vol. vii. 286.

moulded and formed by means of the conception of man ; (and hence Atheism finds a pretext for reducing the idea of God in the human spirit to a magnified conception of man, and thus for reducing religion to a psychological misconception). Every real awakening of the God-consciousness, as it forms a necessary element of the inner life, every elevation of the soul to God, is a resort to its original and extra-temporal state, wherein God was the object of its ideal knowledge. But as in this original state the soul finds itself in God, yet not without the consciousness of its independent existence as distinct from God, it discerns an unconditional OUGHT, an obligation to remain ever in fellowship with Him in whom it has its being.

It is interesting to compare here the manner in which Leibnitz in his *Theodicée* endeavours to establish the principle that man is to regard himself and not God as the primary cause of sin. Upon this subject Leibnitz says,* " Man is himself the source of the evil which is in him ; what he is he was in idea. God, actuated by the indispensable reasons of His wisdom, has decreed that man shall pass into existence such as he is." And in the striking allegory with which the *Theodicée* closes, Pallas convinces the high priest of Dodona how " her Father had not made Sextus wicked ; he had been so from all eternity, and he had been always free." Sextus, indeed, must be an essential part of " the best world," and Jupiter therefore had given him existence, and " had allowed him to pass from the region of the possible (in the divine understanding) to that of the actual," because His wisdom could not refuse existence to the world of which he forms a part.† According to this, Leibnitz attributes in one sense *much more* and in another *much less* than we to the extra-temporal existence of personal beings, as it precedes and conditions their life in time. Much more ;— for according to him, man in the whole range of his temporal life is already entirely perfected in that region of eternal ideas, and this involves the monstrous notion that the evil conduct

Theory of Leibnitz.

* *Theodicée*, iii. § 151 : "L'homme est luy même la source de ses maux, tel qu'il est, il étoit dans les idées. Dieu, mû par des raisons indispensables de la sagesse, a decerné qu'il passât à l'existence tel qu'il est."
† *Theodicée*, iii. § 416.

and nature of the man are included in the idea which he has to realize in time. Much less ;—for this extra-temporal existence of man, which determines his actual life, is only in the Divine Understanding, which Leibnitz expressly distinguishes " as the source of essences " from the Divine Will " as the source of existences."* Hence it does not appear how Leibnitz can fairly argue from this merely ideal pre-existence that man is the source of his own evil, that he who is evil here has been, *by his own choice*, evil from eternity. According to the doctrine of Leibnitz, man is what he is by an eternal necessity of the Divine Understanding ; and the causation of evil is removed from the Divine Will so far only as God's will is dualistically represented as distinct from His understanding.

§ 4. NON-TEMPORAL SELF-DECISION PERTAINS ONLY TO PERSONAL BEINGS.

Personal Beings alone have the source of their existence in free self-determination. Our conception of freedom cannot be more degraded and narrowed than by extending it to existences in nature. We may indeed say with Schelling, that " everything actual, even nature, has its source in activity, life, and freedom," † *i.e.*, Divine freedom, and as created by God. Personal beings alone have one ground of their existence in *their own act ;* it is freedom in this its non-temporal basis that constitutes the difference between Spirit and Nature, for everything pertaining to this distinction depends upon it. An intelligent Theism not only forbids the naturalistic degradation of man to the level of other existences in nature, it also has to guard against that fantastic exaltation of natural existences to man's level, which would regard them—such at least as have life and sensation—as weakened personalities, and as sharers in immortality. Nothing can be more incompatible with Theism than are those crude theories of natural philosophy wherein Spirit and Nature, the moral and physical, are cloudily confused. As to the self-limitation of any created being by a primary and non-temporal act of its own, we must not lose sight of the reasons which led us to

* *Theodicée*, p. i. § 7 : " Son entendement est la source des *essences*, et sa volonté est l'origine des *existences*."
† *Werke*, as before, p. 351.

acknowledge it. They did not lie in the supposed need of some principle other than God's discriminating understanding to explain the manifoldness of finite being, and the shades of difference between *perfect* and *imperfect* creatures. We can-not but respect the lofty earnestness of ORIGEN when he found himself compelled to trace the differences of created beings back to primary and perverted moral differences; but, objectively viewed, his was a speculative theory of the world, which could only apprehend these differences as arbitrary disturbances of an original sameness, and which considered an infinite series of creatures, only numerically different, to be the highest creation of God. It was a theory very inadequate, and erroneously derived from mere abstractions; yet it found its corrective in the unbiassed Christian consciousness, and scientifically in Augustine's better understanding of the divine plan.* The presence of *moral evil*, and the irrefragable *self-accusation* of conscience, are the two facts of experience which compel us to look beyond the sphere of experience to an extra-temporal commencement; and we find neither of these in the inferior ranges of created being, but only in man.

Origen's theory.

Bearing in mind this qualitative and essential distinction, it cannot be affirmed that Nature ever produces personality. Nature, certainly, is ever striving upwards towards man in its progressive process of development, and this is profoundly set forth in the account of the creation in the book of Genesis. But what it endeavours to bring forth is not *personality* conscious of itself and God, self-determining and therefore capable of union with God; in this respect, it does not present a single approximation or analogy in the dark realm of its perishable forms. What it aims at is *individuality,* so that the being formed may not merely be an exemplar of the species, but may have a distinctive individuality of its own. This individualizing process advances at every stage of its development, it presents ever more manifold and characteristic forms, ever richer and more

Nature in its relation to Personality.

---

* In his treatises *De Ordine, De libero arbitrio,* in the *Civitas Dei* (lib. xi. c. 16, 23), and elsewhere. See the *Summa* of AQUINAS, upon the questions, *Utrum sint plures ideae,* i. qu. 15. art. 2, and *Utrum inequalitas rerum sit a Deo,* i. qu. 47, art. 2, where Origen's view is refuted.

striking differences of genus, species, race, and so forth. But it does not after all attain to individuality properly so called; its individual productions are still, even at the highest stage, wholly determined, and are bound by the general character of the sphere to which they belong; the life of individual existences is wholly spent in fulfilling the natural design of the species of which they are only single manifestations or specimens. Nature cannot solve its problem in its own sphere; the potentiality it aims at in its dark strivings, can be found only in the entrance of a far higher principle. The *ego* alone, including self-determination and self-consciousness, is the infinitely profound centre, round which the elements of individuality and idiosyncrasy gather, and wherein they form a complete and independent whole. It is impossible to ignore the fact, that Nature finds its inherent teleology, its final goal, in man; yet man, who solves the riddle of nature, is not nature's highest product, nor its loveliest blosoming. Man rather anticipates nature, not only ideally, as if he were its final end, but *really* in virtue of the extra-temporal origin of every *ego*. In temporal development, nature prepares for personality a basis of natural life; and as it thus becomes a part of personal existence in its concrete and conditioned form, we can understand how blind unconscious existence has its being through the Will of *that* God, who, because He is love, must reveal Himself in his creation. Schelling calls nature in its relation to man "the Old Testament;" and the comparison is just, in the sense that the Messianic prophecies of the old covenant were fulfilled, yet at the same time, infinitely surpassed in the Incarnation of the Son of God. As the Old Testament was a preparation and training for the New (παιδαγωγὸς εἰς Χριστόν),—but not its principle, as if the New were only the product and fruit of the Old,—the like holds true of nature in relation to man. Valentinus the Gnostic, shows a true insight into this relation when he says after his manner, "the angels of the Demiurge were thrown into consternation when they recognized in its image, in man, a principle given him by Wisdom far higher than any included in the kingdom of the Demiurge."

The initial possibility of a fall from God, which we have recognized as a negative condition of the freedom of created beings, was not intended to continue, but was to be wholly done away. The Fathers, the Schoolmen, and the earlier Protestant theologians, apply the axiom πᾶν κτιστὸν τρεπτόν, without hesitation, to the will and moral being of man;* and so far as our experience goes, they are right both as to the commencement and the growth of man's moral life. But we cannot adopt the axiom without qualification; the τρεπτὸν must become ἄτρεπτον when the goal of sanctification is attained, though the spirit does not cease to be κτίσμα. The removal of the possibility of evil cannot take place mechanically by an interposition in the life of the personal being, which would make him merely passive. Such a notion is forbidden alike by the principle of organic life and by that of personality, and would contradict all that our investigation thus far has taught us concerning the true import of freedom. If the possibility of evil be removed, it must be by the voluntary co-operation of the being in whom it is. As it is objectively connected with the freedom of his self-determination, this possibility must also become subjective in order to its removal by a decided and persistent refusal of its realization. From the οὐ γνῶναι τὴν ἁμαρτίαν, which the Apostle Paul attributes to the relative innocence of unconscious childhood, before the awakening of the inner discord (Rom. vii. 7), man is to pass by the deliberate rejection of evil to the μὴ γνῶναι ἁμαρτίαν (2 Cor. v. 21), by which the perfect holiness of Christ is negatively described. This can take place only by the possibility of evil implied in freedom becoming the subject of consciousness.

§ 5. THE POSSIBILITY OF EVIL PUT AN END TO.

It must first become the subject of consciousness.

How, then, can this possibility become the subject of consciousness? As the possibility of evil is from the outset

---

* They affirm this partly in connection with the view of Origen and Augustine, that evil of a privation is an effort after nonentity terrestrial existences are susceptible of this effort, because they were created out of nothing. GREGORY OF NYSSA cleverly expresses this in the *Orat. catech. magna*, c. vi. ; Τῆς ἀρετῆς καὶ τῆς κακίας οὐχ ὡς δύο τινῶν καθ' ὑπόστασιν φαινομένων ἡ ἀντιδιαστολὴ θεωρεῖται· ἀλλ' ὥσπερ ἀντιδιαιρεῖται τῷ ὄντι τὸ μὴ ὄν . . . κατὰ τὸν αὐτὸν τρόπον καὶ ἡ κακία τῷ τῆς ἀρετῆς ἀντικαθέστηκε λόγῳ, οὐ καθ' ἑαυτήν τις οὖσα ἀλλὰ τῇ ἀπουσίᾳ νοουμένη τοῦ κρείττονος. . . , Ἐπειδὴ τοίνυν ἡ ἄκτιστος φύσις τῆς κινήσεως τῆς κατὰ τροπὴν καὶ μεταβολὴν καὶ ἀλλοίωσιν ἐστιν ἀνεπίδεκτος, πᾶν δὲ διὰ κτίσεως ὑποστὰν συγγενῶς πρὸς τὴν ἀλλοίωσιν ἔχει· διότι καὶ αὐτὴ τῆς κτίσεως ἡ ὑπόστασις ἀπὸ ἀλλοιώσεως ἤρξατο, τοῦ μὴ ὄντος εἰς τὸ εἶναι θείᾳ δυνάμει μετατεθέντος. Compare c. xxi.

CHAP. IV.] FREEDOM AS THE POSSIBILITY OF SIN. 161

connected with the independent principle of movement in the personal being, he must possess a *rule* or standard determining the action of this principle of movement, and forbidding the realization of that possibility. There is such a rule guiding the action of the powers of nature,—viz., *nature's law*. Now this realizes itself directly; the powers, whose operations it controls, are bound to it by a physical necessity, and so far as it goes, deviation from it, on the part of the subject powers, is impossible. If this seems to be otherwise, it is because the law of nature seems indistinct or indeterminate,* now too wide, and now too narrow. Deviations from particular laws of nature may often be met with,—*e.g.*, a stone when thrown will rise, contrary to the law of Gravity,—but these are owing to the counter-working of another law of nature, so that the simultaneous action of both, and the result, wherein each will be in part negatived and in part confirmed, is still subject to an unalterable law. Now, if the rule of the will were as immediately realized as in nature's law, and the physical possibility of an act contradicting it excluded, it would be itself a law of nature, and the action governed by it would be only blind impulse or natural activity. But this action is that of an independent and self-conscious principle of movement, *i.e.*, of free will. In order, therefore, to give the will room to determine itself of itself, and yet according to its absolute rule, this rule must, so to speak, *withdraw* as the law of the will; the MUST spiritualizes itself into the OUGHT,—the physical necessity into the moral.

How can this possibility enter consciousness?

But where does the law withdraw to? Where, save into the depths of the being whose volition it rules? In nature the outgo of power determines to blind obedience; but in this higher sphere the law accommodates itself to the freedom of the will, and assumes the form of an obligation of unconditional authority in consciousness, and makes itself felt, even when the conduct does not correspond with it. Were it otherwise, did the law of the will necessarily lead to corresponding action, we should no more have an immediate consciousness of

---

* An indistinctness of this kind we have in the notion, lately advanced and applied to Miracles, of the elasticity of nature's laws. Of the moral law it may in a sense be said that it is elastic; this we shall presently see; but the law of nature differs from the moral law in this, that it is not elastic.

VOL. II. L

it than of the laws, for example, which govern the organic movements of our physical life. Necessity in this case would be indissolubly one with realization; for we are wholly bound and borne along by the laws of our physical constitution, and they cannot become the objects of our immediate consciousness; they are discovered only by reflection. Again, if the powers of nature could in their operation violate the laws which bind them, even as the will can violate its laws, then must there be in the sphere of nature some inner consciousness into which those laws withdraw;—how otherwise could they be laws? How could they assert themselves as such?

The moral necessity, notwithstanding the difference in the sphere of its authority, may possibly equal the physical in the certainty of the coincidence between action and the law, but this can be brought about only by free will. If the harmony be complete, the function of the *law* will terminate. Its contents will have become subjective, fully and unalterably pervading the life, and it will no longer appear in consciousness as an objective law;—the distinction between it and the Will will be at an end. In the consciousness, therefore, of a Law for the will, we have a witness on the one hand of our *moral imperfection,* and on the other of our *formal freedom,* in virtue of which our obedience depends upon our own decision, in so far as the possibility of disobedience is possessed by us. Consequently, with the consciousness of this law of the Will, the consciousness of the possibility of evil must necessarily co-exist. The source of all moral obligation lies in the consciousness of absolute authority as the prerogative of God, a consciousness which we must attribute to the extra-temporal existence of personal beings.

<small>Consciousness of this possibility.</small>

Thus arguing on the ground of necessity, not indeed metaphysical,* but moral, we have arrived at the conclusion that evil must be possible to personal creatures, and that they must be conscious of this possibility. As to the realization of this possibility, it is a plain matter of fact of which ex-

<small>§ 6. SUPPOSED NECESSITY FOR THE FACT AS WELL AS THE POSSIBILITY OF EVIL.</small>

---

* This, too, is BILLROTH's opinion (*Vorlesungen über Religionsphil.* p. 93); and with his view of freedom and the relation of evil thereto, we, in many important points, agree.

perience must inform us. It cannot be inferred by any necessity from the data preceding it, although inasmuch as it is a fact, it can be better understood when viewed in connection with those data.*

But the logic of the Hegelian system will not suffer us to stop here. Vatke† maintains that,—granting the knowledge of evil and the possibility of the *ego* making it the subject matter of the will (or as we put it, the possibility of evil, and the *ego's* knowledge of this possibility), to be the necessary conditions of active freedom towards good,—it is a mere deficiency of logical acuteness not to perceive as the unavoidable consequence, the actual entrance of evil as necessarily conditioning moral consciousness. This doctrine is established thus :—"As sin is essentially a determinateness of the subjective will, it cannot be recognized unless it actually exists in the will; we can therefore be conscious of it as possible only as it thus actually exists ; and so far this knowledge of the possibility includes that of the actuality of sin."‡

Vatke's argument.

We have not here to do with the relation between the realization of sin in individual life as the race now is, and the first consciousness of its possibility. The question concerns the relation of this first consciousness to an original state of purity, and a fall therefrom. It follows, from the very nature of morality, and holds good of moral evil as well as of moral good, that the realization of sin must begin, not in a state, but in an act. If we picture to ourselves (as far as we can here, before our minuter inquiries concerning the manner of sin's realization) a primary act of evil, we find it to

Point of distinction between the possibility and the realization of evil.

---

* See the Dialogues between Julian and Augustine, concerning necessity and possibility in connection with the origin of sin, *Op. imperf.* lib. v. c. 45-64, in which Augustine fails, through not duly distinguishing between the import of these terms in the sphere of nature and in the sphere of will respectively, quite as much as Julian does through an abstract separation of the two spheres (he attributes *necessitas* exclusively to nature, and *possibilitas* to will; but he knows nothing of a *possibilitas*, which through the will becomes a *necessitas* for the will).

† *Die menschliche Freiheit in ihrem Verhältniss zur Sünde und zur göttlichen Gnade*, 272.

‡ *Ibid.* See also pp. 132, 143.

be an essential feature of such an act that something presented to the mind is realized. Therefore, in the case of evil, a presentation of that which ought not to be, must (according to our conceptions) precede the act. Further, as the primitive state of the personal being can be done away only by self-decision, the commencement of sinning must necessarily be conscious sin. When sin has obtained predominance, it often produces a state of unconscious intoxication, and thus ensnares the man into wanton wickedness and crime. But to begin with, a man cannot unconsciously be intoxicated with sin; if he could, sin would not be a perversion of will, but a mere aberration of consciousness. If it be thus with the commencement of sinning, that presentation of what ought not to be done, is necessarily a presentation of it as *such*—as what should not be done. Yet, as others have justly remarked, such a thought of evil is by no means an evil thought; consequently, there is as yet no commencement of the realization of evil in the man. Now, if we go a step further, and say that this which ought not to be, must present itself as *possible to him* —for how could he otherwise undertake to realize it?*—we denote the exact point where the Subject can withdraw from the wrong decision. The possibility of sinning is present to him, and is a matter of consciousness, in so far as it has proved itself possible,† and yet it does not become a reality. This point is not only possible; it forms the necessary presupposition of all primary realization of evil, and is therefore of universal import. The narrative in the book of Genesis of man's first disobedience sets forth most clearly the truth that the consciousness of the forbidding law,—and therefore the consciousness of a possible act which ought not to be done,— preceded the entrance of sin. This is clear not only from Gen. ii. 17, but still more plainly from Gen. iii. 3. The same is affirmed concerning the commencement of actual sin in us in Rom. vii. 7–9. Even in the present disturbed course of our moral development we find this to be the case, though, of course, only in a modified way. Or shall we say that certain particular sins would not be possible to us, and would not be

---

* See ULRICI, *Ueber Princip und Methode der Hegelschen Philosophie*, p. 178.

† This we can say with Vatke, though, as is evident from the connection, in a very different sense.

recognized in consciousness as possible, unless we somehow intermeddled with them?—that we could only succeed in rejecting them by somehow appropriating them? It must, therefore, undoubtedly be granted that the consciousness of the nature of evil cannot at the outset have its full depth, that it is capable of a progressive growth, and that *in our case* the experience of the reality of sin essentially contributes to this growth.*

But he who will not admit that this possibility of evil may be known without necessarily passing into act,— in other words, that it is a possibility which the will has perfectly in its power,—must upon his principles exclude the idea of possibility altogether. A possibility which *must* realize itself, is not a possibility, but a *necessity*. But if evil springs from man and his temporal development at all by way of necessity, there will be an inevitable contradiction between this "must" (as the affirmation of evil) and the "ought" (as the negation of evil),—a contradiction which would hinder our seriously maintaining the authority of the "ought." Marheineke, therefore, who, in his *System der theologischen Moral*, adopts Vatke's view concerning the doctrine of evil, gives us the following counsel:— "As regards practical life, the doctrine of the necessity of evil must be very carefully handled; and, considering the practically pernicious conclusions which may be deduced from it, it must be limited to what religion teaches, viz., that God permits evil."† But seeing that permission, in the proper acceptation of the word, does not make its object necessary, but only possible, the theologian is, according to this admonition, to retain in his convictions the necessity of evil, but to teach the opposite—its mere possibility—to the people: for them the affirmation of the necessity of evil is "to be limited" to the denial of that necessity!

Carrying out his principles, Vatke is obliged to predicate of Christ at least a *minimum* of evil. "Every one must have this experience (of actual sin) in the depths of his own self-consciousness, be it only in

---

* The reader may compare the inquiry in Book i. chap. i., which is closely connected with this investigation, viz., as to the question whether sin precedes the consciousness of the law, or *vice versa*. † P. 149.

sinful thoughts, because it is a *moral* experience."* "If, we contemplate an ideal human development, we find that evil makes its appearance in the will only so far as it is needed for moral self-consciousness, and to awaken conscience; afterwards it remains a mere possibility, which is never realized."† If, according to this, "the ideal" must once at least submit to temptation, in order thenceforward to overcome it, and never again to fall, we really know not which is most to be wondered at,—this notion of a moral ideal, or the absence (thus evinced) of any adequate insight into the significance of the first step in' sin. The *minimum* here tends directly to a *maximum:* indeed, when compared with perfect purity, it is a fall of unfathomable depth.‡ And if this single appearance of sin in the will left behind it any effects influencing the subsequent development,—as we would all the more probably expect, for the moral consciousness of such a man is said to have its inherent awakening therein,∥—Christ needed a redemption for Himself, and would have had to take His place in humility among sinners who needed cleansing. Now, seeing that He did not do this, that He presents Himself, on the contrary, as the Saviour of men, that He demands of them unconditional surrender to Himself, and connects the most bounteous promises with this surrender, Christ must, according to the theory put forth by Vatke, have thus incurred the guilt of a further sin,—a sin which (if our development of the nature of sin, and of pride in particular, in Book i., be not wholly false) must be regarded as the greatest and most damnable that man can be guilty of.

It is, on the contrary, clear, from the principles which we have developed, that Christ may have been perfectly pure and free from sin, and yet have possessed that consciousness of the possibility of sinning without which temptation would have been to him perfectly meaningless,§ without which indeed his

<small>The theological formula describing Christ's holiness.</small>

---

* See the Review above referred to, *Hallische Jahrbücher*, 1840, p. 1134.

† "*Die menschliche Freiheit*," &c. p. 291.

‡ On the moral significance of such a *minimum* of sin, which the theologians of the Kantian and Rationalistic school thought it necessary to attribute to Christ, see Daub's remarks in his *Judas Ischarioth*, part ii. p. 233.

∥ Compare vol. i. p. 403.

§ They who represent the presence of evil as a condition of the "ought" of goodness, will do well to consider the fact that Christ repels the temptations suggested to Him with the counter-assertion of the absolutely commanding will, with the "*thou shalt!*" "*thou shalt not!*" of the Divine law.

development would not have been truly human. The three expressions by which the older theologians negatively describe the various aspects of Christ's holiness, "*peccare non potuit, potuit non peccare, non peccavit,*" are each of them correct. The truth of the last is primary and general, it is a simple matter of fact. The second, whose contrary clearly is *potuit peccare*, is (if the third be granted) a correct expression in reference to the *commencement* and progressive development of Christ's earthly life. The first denotes the *completion* of this life, the result of His development, as conditioned by self-determination. It is of the greatest and most real importance that Christ, as the author of the Epistle to the Hebrews says (ii. 10, v. 8, 9), in order to attain that perfection whereby He could be "the author of eternal salvation," had to learn the highest obedience—the "not as I will, but as Thou wilt"— through the severest sufferings.*

§ 7. Can we thoroughly understand evil?

In determining how far the derivation of evil may be traced back by means of our speculative and religious knowledge, the question occurs, whether the origin of sin be fully conceivable or inconceivable?† This question really brings us back to another, viz., whether in our inquiry thus far concerning the freedom of the will, we have discovered an *adequate* reason or condition for the origin of evil. If evil were a consequence of freedom, if it proceeded from it by an inherent necessity, then as we have recognized this freedom to be the essential condition of the absolute world-plan, the existence of evil would certainly be perfectly understood.

* See NEANDER's *Leben Jesu*, p. 119 (4th ed.); ULLMANN's "Sinlessness of Jesus," p. 63, 64; DORNER on "The Sinless Perfection of Jesus;" KEIM, *Der geschichtliche Christus.*" Concerning the *formulae* quoted, see ULLMANN "The Sinlessness of Jesus," pp. 32, 33 (7th ed.), and the remarks concerning them in the Dogmatic Works of LIEBNER, MARTENSEN, THOMASIUS, SCHENKEL, and PHILIPPI.

† The words conceivable and inconceivable are not here used in their ordinary English sense, but denote what we can or cannot fully understand and logically explain. "Inconceivable" here means neither what is impossible to think of nor what is impossible to be, but what we cannot adequately explain. Mr Mansel thus limits his use of the word in his *Bampton Lectures* (ed. 5, p. xi.); but it is clear from his argument that he uses the word in a far wider sense, as equivalent with the expression "to be conscious of." "We cannot *be conscious of* the Infinite" (p. 86;) "*A consciousness* of the Infinite as such thus necessarily involves a self-contradiction" (p. 49).—*Tr.*

In the sphere of nature we are allowed to regard power as the ground or principle of its manifestations, and, strictly speaking, to regard the various phenomena of nature as resulting from power by way of physical necessity. Accordingly, if the operating power, the law inherent therein, be known, the phenomenon is thoroughly understood. In virtue of the limitedness of every finite power of nature, a case may occur when the corresponding phenomenon does not follow from its operation. Yet this does not detract from the physical necessity involved in the connection of the phenomenon with that determinate power. The power still contains the essential tendency towards the production of the phenomenon, and it actually realizes it when the external conditions requisite are given, provided that no other stronger power hinders the effect by its counteracting force.*

Does evil follow from Freedom as effects in nature from causes?

If evil followed according to the same necessary sequence from the freedom of the will in created beings, remembering that this freedom has its origin in the creative will of God, we should be obliged (according to Schleiermacher's argument in his *Glaubenslehre*)† to say, that so far as evil springs from the creature's freedom, God is its author. But we cannot even give expression to such a notion without contradicting ourselves and virtually destroying the supposed freedom. Freedom, in its formal sense, and in this sense we now speak of it, necessarily includes the power of doing otherwise, and therefore implies self-determination from the undetermined. If this is so, nothing whatever determinate—neither good nor evil—can follow by way of logical sequence from freedom; but whatever it be, in

Formal freedom excludes the necessary sequence of evil.

---

* Hegel calls this "the formal principle," Logic, ii., p. 90 (*Werke*, 1st ed.), while he ridicules the endeavour to explain phenomena in this way, with a scorn which, though it does not affect the category of "cause" or "reason," is applicable to an unskilful use of it in the natural sciences. As to the true import of the category, "principle" or "reason," it is to be observed, in reply to the charge of tautology, that power, regarded as the principle of its outward manifestation, is never exerted merely in one phenomenon and its constant repetition, but stands related as a general thing to a variety of phenomena. Were we to apply the categories of universal, particular, individual, to the relation between the freedom of the will and moral conduct, this would naturally lead to determinism.

† Vol. i. §§ 81, 82, 83; compare also his *Dissertation upon the Doctrine of Election*, p. 95.

CHAP. IV.] FREEDOM AS THE POSSIBILITY OF SIN. 169

determinate will or deed, it results from freedom's own self-decision.

Relation of free will to the determining reasons.

Being thus a power of self-determination, free will paralyses the determining influences of all those powers external to it which may answer to the causes or conditions co-operating to the production of certain phenomena in the sphere of nature, and thus self-determination proves itself to be in itself a *power*. The unfailing chain of condition and consequent linked together by a necessity of nature comes to a sudden break here, and a new principle with an independent causality forms the beginning of a new development. What free Being is, we learn by its self-manifestation in action, which is again a matter of experience. The efficient causes of the natural world are here spiritualized into *impulses* and *motives*, by means of which free will, as the primary and effective cause of action, arrives at its decision. What the motives are which appear in preponderating activity in any decision depends again upon the tendency which the will has given to itself by preceding self-decisions, and ultimately by its original decision.*

Freedom as possibility of evil.

Formal freedom thus certainly implies the *possibility* of evil, but no more than this. This possibility cannot fairly be exaggerated into a settled bias or tendency because the possibility of good is equally implied, and an "equal bias" towards two diametrically opposite courses is a self-contradictory notion, and would be no bias at all.† The words of St James (iii. 11) are applicable to such a supposition μήτι ἡ πηγὴ ἐκ τῆς αὐτῆς ὀπῆς βρύει τὸ γλυκὺ καὶ τὸ πικξόν; The Pelagian conception of freedom falls into this confusion, in so far as it represents freedom to be a root or spring both of good and of evil implanted in man by God;‡ a view which, if logically carried out, would lead to a pantheistic denial of the distinction between good and evil.

---

* For an explanation of the categories "cause," "reason," see note B at the end of this chapter.

† Compare what we have already said, p. 30 of this vol., as to the meaning of natural bias or talent, and its relation to power or ability.

‡ AUGUSTINE, in his treatise *De gratia Christi contra Pelagium et Caelestium*, c. 19, quotes the following explanation from Pelagius' work *De libero arbitrio* "*habemus possibilitatem utriusque partis a Deo insitam velut quandam, ut ita dicam, radicem fructiferam atque foecundam, quae ex voluntate hominis diversa*

170   THE POSSIBILITY OF SIN.   [BOOK III. PART I.

While therefore it is self-contradictory to regard the freedom of the will as an innate bias towards good and evil, and thus, as the positive ground or principle of both, it seems that we must still look upon it as *equally related to good and evil*, so far as it involves the possibility of both. This certainly would be the case if freedom were adequately described as formal freedom. But *real* freedom, which is the end and goal of formal freedom, that to which it must be raised by self-determination, is inseparably connected with good only. The will therefore is not (as is this merely formal freedom) made the sport of vague chance, but its own ideal, which realizes itself in *real* freedom, accompanies it as an "ought." Evil therefore does not spring from formal freedom in exactly the same manner as good; it does not take the direction designed for formal freedom, and marked out for it by the accompanying consciousness of moral obligation. It springs from formal freedom only by a violation of this design.

Freedom not equally related to good and evil.

Freedom becomes *arbitrariness* when in self-movement it violates or sunders its connection with its true end or design. Arbitrariness is not strictly speaking perverted will, it is the capricious self-movement of the will unaffected by any end, and wholly indifferent to the moral character of its determinations, and this in a sphere of action which, objectively viewed, is morally undetermined and indifferent. But this self-alienation of the will from its

Transition of freedom into arbitrariness.

gignat et pariat (the two adjectives and verbs here clearly attribute to freedom the production of evil as well as good as its determination), *et quae possit ad proprii cultoris arbitrium vel nitere flore virtutum vel sentibus horrere vitiorum.* Compare the acute remarks of JACOBI in his "*Doctrine of Pelagius,*" pp. 35, 36. We must not, however, lay too much stress on this Definition of Pelagius, for it is counterbalanced by other elements in his system of thought, and still more by Julian, who generally takes a wider and more correct view of the connection and bearings of these conceptions. Julian not only indirectly rejects the designation "*fructus libertatis*" as appropriate to the *mala voluntas* (see Augustine, *Opus imperf. Contra Julianum,* lib. vi. c. 11), but directly and acutely combats that view of the relation of freedom to good and evil acts of will, *Opus imperf.,* lib. v. c. 56; though his view of the act of will as isolated is no less superficial and erroneous. Among modern treatises upon the Doctrine of Sin, KERN's Dissertation regards freedom as the "principle of sin" in the sense above denoted, and at once infers from this that evil retains its place as part of what God has "ordained by means of freedom."—*Tübinger Zeitschrift für Theologie,* 1832, part iii. p. 110.

FREEDOM AS THE POSSIBILITY OF SIN.

true *end,* is, in a sphere where all is determined by the absolute end, thus far a self-perversion. Arbitrariness is here really an evil will, though at first viewed only negatively as a departure from the truly rational sequence of action, a self-separation from that order of the will which arises naturally from its highest aim, its true end. In violating this connection, volition forms for itself, out of disfigured and perverted elements, a connection of its own, a world of efforts, impulses, motives, wherein all is based on the principle of *limitless independence,* and is therefore squandered and deprived of any harmonizing aim.

We thus see how the category of "condition" (*ratio*) is ele-
Groundlessness of evil. vated and spiritualized in this higher and moral sphere, and how causelessness may, in a certain sense, be predicated of evil. The true principle or *ratio* of action, lies in its end or aim. If this is taken up into the will, the corresponding mode of action follows by way of moral necessity therefrom. Every morally good decision of the will is, in this teleological sense, well grounded, because the immediate end is conformable with the absolute end, and is the realization of that perfect harmony between the world and God, the world and self, whereof the will, perfectly sanctified and in union with God, is the chief element. If the question be as to the *wherefore* of the will's perverted decision, this may always be found in a variety of motives, were it only the desire to satisfy mere arbitrariness. But an objective and truly adequate cause is always wanting, because the decision does not correspond with the absolute end. We may describe ̦ the difference thus: moral good, viewed as the attribute of created personality, is the ideal of the eternally Divine understanding; evil, on the contrary, ̦is no ideal, no part of an ideal, it is a contradiction between the ideal and the factual reality.*

The recognition of this fact, that the possibility of evil as
Hence the saying, "evil springs from the misuse of free will." well as of good, lies in the freedom of the will, and that this possibility can only realize itself by an arbitrary separation from the true and legitimate self-development and exercise of freedom, is em-

* It is certainly one of the worst consequences of the system of Leibnitz (next at least to the want of freedom in that system), that he is obliged in the *Theodicée* to assign to the individual man, just as he is—with all the moral imperfections which pertain to his empirical life—a place in the region of eternal ideas.

bodied in the formula often adopted by the Schoolmen and the elder Protestant theologians who follow Origen and Augustine, "Evil has its origin in, *the abuse of free will*." Still we can hardly call this formula a happy one, for if free will itself can misuse every thing else in man, if it be the highest and most spiritual of all, and if it possesses the power of choice regarding the right or wrong use of all other powers, what is there in us which in turn misuses this free will ? The very conception of it implies that it can only misuse itself, though this expression is also inadmissible.

Let us now recur to the question suggested above as to the full conceivableness or the inconceivableness of evil. Kant concludes his "*Grundlegung zur Metaphysik der Sitten*" with these words:— " Thus though we cannot comprehend the practical and unconditional necessity of the moral imperative, we can fully conceive that it is *inconceivable,* and this is all that can fairly be demanded of a philosophy which aims at principles within the limits of human reason." If the critical philosopher could say this of his categorical imperative, need Theology be ashamed, if in reference to evil it must content itself with "the conception of its inconceivableness ?" From our present investigation, however, it is clear that we are by no means obliged to grant the unlimited inconceivableness of evil.

<small>Kant's view.</small>

All conceivableness or full understanding of a thing, depends upon logical consecutiveness of thought. It might therefore seem, as if we must regard moral good as *inconceivable,* freedom being logically inexplicable on merely natural principles. Thus Kant finds good and evil equally inconceivable on account of their common origin in transcendental freedom.* But though a principle essentially new and inexplicable by means of any temporal and empirical antecedents begins to operate in freedom, so far as freedom produces moral good a higher connection is authenticated in this principle, physical necessity is elevated into a moral necessity corresponding with and confirmed by the order of nature. As that higher, that moral order precedes the exercise of freedom, moral good cannot appear inconceivable to the spirit conscious of God's purpose concerning it; it must

<small>Conceivableness of moral good.</small>

* *Religion innerhalb der Grenzen der blossen Vernunft,* p. 71.

appear perfectly clear and perspicuous, implied in the divine order and self-evident. Granting that the conceivableness of any particular moral good cannot logically be inferred from its connection with any necessity of nature, being realized by freedom only, we have in the place of this its most perfect conceivableness as inferred from its connection with a far higher order pertaining to man as his true element. It is only when man quite forgets his true nature, and makes himself at home in sin, as if it were the normal element of his being, that moral good can become unintelligible and foreign to him. Deeds of moral heroism and of self-denying love awaken in us astonishment and wonder, simply because we all are tainted with sin.* But as this wonder is really admiration, we have in it a proof that we clearly understand the connection and harmony of such acts with an acknowledged principle.

Evil, moreover, is not an unintelligible thing, seeing that we allow the *possibility* of it to be a necessity; and as has been explained in our inquiries in Book i., we see that it consists in a great variety of impulses, having an inner centre of logical connection in one principle, which in its very nature puts those who are ruled by it at variance with each other and themselves. Yet, notwithstanding all this, the real point in question, the *realization* of evil, cannot be fully understood. We must acknowledge that evil is in its nature inconceivable, *i.e.*, incomprehensible, seeing that it is realized by arbitrariness, and arbitrariness is a violation of rational reason and true sequence. It is that which has being only by usurpation, and in the face of the exclusive claims of moral good. We can understand the connection of its particular manifestations with its principle, but this principle itself is a perversion, it is that which ought not to be. We know that as action or behaviour, it is brought about by means of motives of various kinds, but these motives, when viewed in the light of the divine necessity of moral good, are proved to be shadowy and false, a sphere of unreality which nevertheless exists, and wherein even that

{How far evil is intelligible: how far not.}

* When Christ expressed wonder at the faith of the centurion (Matt. viii. 10), this wonder arose, as the words themselves show, from the contrast between the centurion's faith and the unbelief which he usually met with in those about him.

perverted principle obtains realization in a world created by God. Evil is the inscrutable mystery of the world;* it ever remains, in its inmost depth, impenetrable darkness.

This inconceivableness holds true of *every sinful act*. Any sin may seem to us quite conceivable and easily understood; but this is, properly speaking, a merely subjective and *a posteriori* view; it arises from the fact that we find sin in ourselves and others as a co-determining element of human life. If we more closely analyse the way in which we endeavour to explain the occurrence of a sinful act in human life, an act of one's own for the sake of excusing it, we shall find that we take for granted the all-pervading influence of that sinful element, the strength of perverted motive and the presence of selfish maxims; and thus we only explain sin by sin. Sin in itself still remains incomprehensible, and this incomprehensibleness will of course present itself most clearly when the sin is, in the strict sense of the word, a *first sin*, or a *commencement* of sin, wherein the pure will becomes impure by self-determination. The truth of the old saying, that "Satan is the ape or counterfeit of God," is thus illustrated. It denotes the usurpation on the part of evil to be, like God, *causa sui*, to make its commencement from itself alone, and to have only itself as its presupposition.

<small>Particular acts of sin.</small>

He, therefore, who finds the origin of evil in a *fall*, cannot be greatly perplexed when it is still urged against him that the transition from a state of purity to one of sin is *inexplicable*. This inexplicableness is already contained in the very conception of evil. The incomprehensibleness of its origin arises, not so much from the limitedness of our *subjective knowledge*, as from the *nature of evil* itself. Hence it does not dwindle and disappear with the increase of our knowledge; and at no future stage of our development and growth in learning do we pass from this

<small>Objective significance of this unintelligibleness of evil.</small>

---

* I agree with RITTER (p. 23) when he says that we cannot call evil a *miracle*, but that, properly speaking, it is the direct opposite of a miracle. The miracle, as a miracle, is God's work apart from the world; evil, as evil, is the work of the world apart from God. The miracle is the secret of God, evil is the secret of the world. The miracle, in fact, takes place only on account of evil; God displays His holy secret power that the world may forsake its unholy secret and turn believingly to Him.

CHAP. IV.]   FREEDOM AS THE POSSIBILITY OF SIN.   175

incomprehensibleness to an insight into the higher necessity of evil. On the contrary, the purer and more perfect our moral and religious knowledge becomes, the more attentively we listen to the solemn voice of our inmost consciousness and to the holy word of divine revelation,—the more thoroughly do we perceive evil to be contrary to nature and to reason, and therefore unaccountable and groundless. If in the noblest moments of our life, when we experience the closest communion with God, we contemplate evil and its powerful working among men, this conviction as to its real nature thoroughly penetrates us, and we understand it better then than at other times, because we most vividly see it in its perversity, its arbitrariness, and feel how inconceivable it is. We can conceive of the most perfect perception of evil, that of God, to be only the most thorough recognition of its utter arbitrariness and its violation of all rational connection; though the divine perception of evil differs infinitely from ours, in so far as God not only knows evil in the world as something utterly alien to Himself, while we find ourselves involved in it, but beholds from eternity the victory of his kingdom over it as complete.

This incomprehensibility attaching to the nature of evil is fully exhibited* in its reality by Daub in his "*Judas Ischarioth.*" Through a mistake and error in his inferences, he regarded evil as a *miracle*,˙ classifying with it (as Manichaeism once did) all phenomena of nature which have no moral significance. Yet we cannot consider that it was any improvement in his views when in later years (as Rosenkranz informs us in his "*Erinnerungen a Daub*") he regarded the incomprehensibleness of evil as absorbed in the logical category of negativity. What is thus made intelligible or conceivable is not evil itself, but something quite different—a necessity, according to which evil is explained away. It is clear from Daub's " Examination of Hypotheses concerning the Freedom of the Will," published in 1834, that Rosencranz was rightly informed. In this work,

Daub's view of evil as a miracle.

* Exhibited, that is, as regards the origin of evil in the midst of conditioned good in God's guiltless and pure creation ; for DAUB considers that the origin of absolute evil, as the arch-enemy of all existence, is fully conceivable. See part ii., comparing pp. 94, 108, f. with p. 245, where he more fully develops these views, without, however, harmonizing them with those presented in the earlier part of his work.

though he does not even attempt to explain evil, he yet speaks o it as "a reproach to philosophy to allow it to be regarded as i any way incomprehensible."* Is it then to be considered a honour for philosophy to deny† evil as such, *i.e.*, as arbitrari ness, opposition to God, condradiction of nature and reason If this be an honour, then philosophy need no longer blush t thank Eve, "an animal capable of understanding and reason that we are no longer sheep grazing in the pasture."‡

* *Judas Ischarioth*, p. 147.
† See DAUB'S condemnation of any such denial of evil in his *Judas Ischarioth* ii. p. 109.
‡ *Vorlesungen über die philosophische Anthropologie*, p. 232. See also Daub' lectures, since published, *über das System der Theol. Moral*, part ii. 2, p. 22 (1843), where he calls the Fall "the animal becoming man." This revoltin incarnation from below is set forth in an Appendix to his Ethics, where there i a lengthy dissertation on the doctrine of sin and the nature of evil. But thoug it contains much that is clear and profound in estimating the various theorie concerning the origin of evil, the development of the doctrine itself is so over laid with lengthy discussions of formal definitions that it is not easy to get a the true gist of the argument. As to Daub's own view concerning the origin o evil, he professes to adopt the Hegelian theory, but without in the leas harmonizing it with the "doctrine of sin" according to Scripture and universa moral consciousness, though he places this side by side with it.

NOTE A.

ROTHE, in his *Ethics*, vol ii. 185, f., strongly objects to our view of evil as incomprehensible ; he considers that "if sin, even in its com
Rothe's mencement, be regarded as an act of sheer unaccountabl polemic arbitrariness, it cannot be condemned as sin, for it would in against our this case be no longer sin, but folly and madness, and therefor partaking of the irresponsibility of insanity." "If, on the con trary, with the necessity of sin we maintain some knowledge of it as included in every conception of it, the unconditional condemnation of it will be full established.' Concerning these statements we are obliged to affirm that the are not true unless they be reversed. Sin is, if Rothe will have the word, "folly and madness ;" and why should we not thus call it if the imaginary satisfaction which man seeks in it really cuts him off from the source of hi truest life, and ruinously sets him at variance with his own higher nature ? T look for rational order and necessity in sin is not only vain, but implies a serious misconception of its nature. If sin were a necessity, fulfilling itself in its realization by means of the human will, if it were a part of the divine order in the world's development, we cannot see how man could be held guilty before

God on account of it, because God's ordainments cannot contradict each other. If "madness" be taken in its strictly physical sense, in which sense alone it does away with responsibility, the term is of course inapplicable here, for we have no reason to suppose that in sin the connection between the sensational consciousness and the legitimate working of the formal understanding is severed. Sin as arbitrariness breaks away from that true and normal course of life which is alone in harmony with man's nature and destiny; but it sets up at the same moment another series of causes and effects, reasons and inferences, taking its rise in an unlimited and self-asserting independence.

"Of what use," asks Rothe, "are scientific inquiries concerning evil, if in its nature it be wholly incomprehensible?" My respected friend has already answered this question himself by the great interest he has taken in these inquiries concerning sin. For it cannot certainly be maintained that my investigations, when treating of this particular question, are inconsistent with this incomprehensibleness of sin in its ultimate source, in the sense in which I maintain it. And yet the question asked by Rothe certainly shows great difference of opinion between us, an essential difference in our theories of knowledge, a difference which is referred to in the Introduction to this work, pp. 11–16. Rothe will see that I am far from excluding all that does not form part of a necessary process in the world's development from among the proper topics of scientific inquiry, or of explaining it as "folly and madness."

Note B.

As the sense in which I use the categories "ground" and "cause" (*Grund, Ursache*) in this chapter and elsewhere, differs somewhat from that attached to them in the logic and metaphysics of various schools of philosophy, and as I do not know of any exposition of them which I could unhesitatingly refer the reader to, I shall endeavour, as briefly as possible, to give a statement of my view.

The conceptions "cause" and "effect" (*Ursache* and *Wirkung*) are generally used to describe the relation of the *will* to its *acts*. Now, it is evident that the manner in which the cause produces its effect is different in the sphere of spirit and freedom, from what it is in the sphere of nature. First, the causality which we find in nature appears in the sphere of spirit to be of a higher and more spiritual kind. It is no longer bound down to the strict law of identity as in nature, but the relation of the effect to the cause is a living and progressive one. Spirit as free will is able to produce something really different from itself, which, though dependent on the will for its existence, possesses, nevertheless, a certain self-dependence as distinct from it. This is in its fullest sense true of absolute spirit, and in a limited sense of finite spirit.

Must we in virtue of this distinction exclude the categories of cause and effect from the sphere of freedom and spirit altogether? Kant has done so in his *Kritik der reinen Vernunft*, and the most prominent modern systems of philosophy do so too. Kant recognises in the connection of cause and effect nothing but a strict necessity of nature, and subordinates everything that exists in time thereto, and then endeavours to save freedom by his so-called " idealizing of time," removing it to a sphere wherein causality has no place. But this way of treating the question seems to us to be nothing more than a *petitio principii*. He only will venture, on these grounds at least, to exclude causality from the realm of will, who adopts as his own the conclusions of Kant's *Kritik*.

The Hegelian polemic against the use of the categories cause and effect in the sphere of spirit, sets up in their stead, and as superior to them, a "reciprocity" or "reciprocal working" (like Kant in his *Kritik*).

This extension of a one-sided continually progressive causation to a causation which is reciprocal, and which has a reacting as well as an advancing power, is certainly a step in the right direction. Indeed, we must claim for this view a wider significance than the Hegelian logic itself attaches to it ; for we recognize that the Absolute Essence, having His absoluteness wholly in Himself, enters in His operations, which are the outgo of His love, into reciprocal working with created personality. And yet we cannot find in this anything which really transcends the category of causation, because this reciprocal working is itself a particular form of causation. It seems still more strange when this logic, by means of causation and reciprocal working, elevates and evaporates substantiality into *thought*,—this elevation forming the transition from objective to subjective logic (see *Encykl.* §§ 155–159). We have here to do with *real* conditioning and producing,—scientifically speaking, with our knowledge or conception of these,— and if we have found the true conception of causal relationship in the realm of Spirit, how can it be that this clear conception of the fact goes back or evaporates itself into thought as such ? This is a transition which Hegel himself find difficult, and which every one save his disciples must find perfectly absurd Yet this transition is said (*Encykl.* § 159) to be 'sufficient to solve necesssit itself, because thought is *freedom*. Yet we cannot deny that this transition i the very kernel of this system of logical pantheism which resolves the univers into a scheme wherein "thought" posits all given reality, merely in order t absorb all into itself again.

If this is what it leads to, every system of theistic philosophy will do well t pause before adopting this Hegelian evaporating of causation ; and so much th more as such a method will find it difficult to resist the temptation of resortin (like Strauss, for example) to Spinoza's doctrine of *substantiality*. We mus regard it not only as allowable, but as incumbent upon philosophic theology, t hold fast the idea of causation in God's relations to the world and in the will relation to its acts, until at least metaphysics have something better to offer Causation, indeed, in spiritual things is different from causation in the spher of nature ; it is something far higher. Besides the difference here specifie there is the consideration that in the sphere of the will causation forms part of the design—the final cause—which is present in the consciousness of the Subjec willing ; for will alone can set before it purposes. But the true idea of caus tion, as something determining and being determined, is by no means excluded for the design or purpose is not really and immediately determining in its influ ence, but becomes so by taking the causative powers into its service.

Now if the effect ensues from its cause according to a general law, and th union of cause and effect seems *necessary*, the cause becomes the principl (*Grund*, the *real* ground, as distinct from the *scientific* ground) of the effect, an the effect becomes the logical consequence (*Folge*) of the cause. If, on the cor trary, the cause produces the effect, not by way of necessity, but so that it migh not have produced it, or might have produced something else, in this case th cause is *free will*, and the effects are not logical consequences, but *acts*. Th view seems to be sanctioned by the general usage of our language, which take the word *Folge*, "necessary consequence," to imply a *necessary antecedent*, an the corresponding word *Grund*, "condition," or "principle," to imply a neces sary consequent or product; whereas this is by no means the case with the word *Wirkung*, "effect," which answers to *Ursache*, "cause." We can see this distinction clearly in the sphere of the spiritual alone, because, according to the above determinations, all *Wirkungen* or effects in nature are *Folgen* "consequents." If any one says, "Your evil acts are the *Folgen* (necessary consequences) of your perverted disposition," the meaning is obviously that the said evil acts necessarily appear with the given evil disposition; and propriety of language would forbid our using the word *Wirkung* ("effect") instead of *Folge*, because the necessity of the connection which we wish to intimate would not thus be expressed. Such acts considered in themselves are independent of freedom of choice, and yet remembering that they are the acts of a free *Ego*, this *ego* may be called, according to Ritter's expression (*Ueber das Böse*, pp. 15, 18), "the transcendental *Grund*—ground or condition "—(yet even here "transcendental cause" (*Ursache*) or "originator" would be better) "of its acts," in the sense that it is the subject to which these acts are to be referred as predicates; that while in their succession in time each is conditioned by the preceding, they must collectively be attributed exclusively to the *Ego* as their author.

In some particulars these conclusions coincide with Jacobi's view of these categories (*Von. den göttl. Dingen*, p. 213, f. (1811); see also *Die Briefe über Spinoza*, p. 414, 2d ed.; *Idealismus und Realismus*, p. 93, f. Among more modern works on Metaphysics we may name in particular J. H. FICHTE'S investigation concerning these ideas in his *Ontologie* (*über Gegensatz Wendepunkt und Ziel, heut. Phil.*, part 3); in his Dissertation, *Ueber Grund und Folge* §§ 131-161, and *Ueber Kausalität und Dependez*, §§ 235-267), compare also his treatise, *Ueber die Bedingungen eines spekulativen Theismus*, p. 12.

[The following extract from WILLM's *Histoire de la Philosophie Allemande* will serve to explain Schelling's use of the term *Ungrund* in his theory of the nature of God, which MULLER refers to pp. 96, 100. WILLM says :—" Applying to the Divine nature itself the law of causality, Schelling represents God as springing, so to speak, from something which is not God in act, but God in potentiality only. Beyond existence, and that which is the immediate basis (*fondement der Grund*) of it, he imagines a principle more elevated, more abstract, which he calls the primitive foundation (*fondement primitif, der Urgrund*) or that which is without cause or without basis (*sans fond, der Ungrund*), an essence absolutely pure, one and identical, which is absolute indifference. Such is the supreme principle, a principle similar to the 'absolute unity' of Neoplatonists, or to *Zeruane Akerene* of Parsism, from which Schelling professes definitely to deduce God and all differences. But all in this principle being absolutely one, there is nothing in it which could be the motive of a division or *diremptio* as Hegel would say. We may say, with the Neoplatonists, that Unity necessarily produces, that it has in itself the power of movement; but how could it produce duality, which is something other than itself? To say that the absolute 'thirsts to exist' is a metaphor which explains nothing; and to affirm that the absolute divides itself into two principles equally eternal, is to cut the knot and not to solve it." Vol. iii. pp. 327, 328.—*Tr.*]

PART II.

HUMAN FREEDOM COMPATIBLE WITH GOD'S INFINITE WILL AND KNOWLEDGE.

CHAPTER I.

THE RELATION OF HUMAN FREEDOM TO THE DIVINE OMNIPOTENCE.

§ 1. STATEMENT OF THE QUESTION. The freedom of the Will as man's ability of himself to make a commencement, to manifest himself as a moral being, is, to use the expression of a great philosopher, "a faculty in its principle unconditioned." The arguments of the preceding Part, especially the fourth chapter, will have convinced any one who does not reject the fundamental principles of our inquiry, that such a faculty may be possessed by a being whose existence is dependent. But it is a question still undecided, how such a self-dependent causality of the human will can co-exist with the *omnipotence* of God.

Proposed solutions. This problem is not solved by the simple observation that it is the Divine omnipotence which confers upon man this power of conditioning himself; for this is just the question, whether God's omnipotence can still be omnipotence, if it allows such an independence apart from it.

If, on the other hand, it be said, "in our consciousness human freedom seems to be an unconditioned power and a pure self-determining, but in the Divine apprehension, it necessarily springs by way of natural sequence from the being whom God creates;"—this would be no harmonizing of human freedom with the Divine omnipotence, but only a denial of human freedom.

The device, again, of preserving man's freedom by making him part of the Divine nature,—leaving to him, indeed, the power of self-decision, yet in such a way that the exercise of this power is, at the same time, an act of God in us,—this is likewise excluded, because this power of self-decision includes the possibility of evil, and no conceivable gain could compensate for such a sacrifice of God's holiness, a holiness which is really love, affirming itself and forbidding its opposite.

In order to solve the problem, we must first of all more accurately examine the true import of the omnipotence of God.

What is the omnipotence of God?

Omnipotence is limitless power. The power of a Being is unlimited when it is not necessarily conditioned in its operations by anything external to it, when therefore it can realize anything to which it has an inclination or will. When we predicate this attribute of God, it is clear that we cannot conceive of any will in Him which contradicts His nature; and accordingly evil itself, and everything logically contradictory to His nature, is excluded from the sphere of His almighty working. God's omnipotence, therefore, implies the commonly stated truth, that "He can do what he will." But we must further ask, Does not the limitlessness of God's omnipotence require that he shall realize all the possibilities which it may embrace ? In other words, that God wills and works all that he can,—that "power," "will," and "working," are in Him identical.

Schleiermacher answers these questions in the affirmative,* and Strauss adopts his decision.† "For," says Schleiermacher, "if there be anything possible to God which He cannot realize, we must suppose a self-limitation of the divine omnipotence; but this can never be allowed, no reasoning could make it conceivable to us." ‡

Schleiermacher's view.

We need not have recourse with Schleiermacher to the unity and sameness of *natural* sequence in order to see that this view of the divine omnipotence is quite irreconcilable with the idea of human freedom which we have developed. Freedom presupposes a sphere of the possible, wherein the will

* *Glaubenslehre*, § 54, 2 (vol. i. p. 309, Ed. 2). So also ROMANG, *System der natürlichen Religionslehre*, pp. 252, 253.
† *Christl. Glaubenslehre*, vol. i. § 38, p. 587.   ‡ As before, p. 311.

determines itself; but, according to this notion, this sphere must be already occupied by an omnipotence which realizes every possibility, and the freedom of man's volition and act can only express the particular manner in which divine omnipotence works in this sphere. We must reject this view of the divine omnipotence, moreover, because we regard even *evil* as the effect of freedom, and God's very nature excludes evil from the divine causation. It is clear also from our development of the idea of freedom that we cannot possibly attribute what is evil in man's acts and being to his freedom, unless the realization of good in his inner and outward life be also regarded as the outgo of his freedom.

If we imagine a limitless power working like the forces of nature, it must certainly effect everything towards which it feels an impulse. For in this department possibility and reality cannot properly be distinguished, the forces of nature are realized and spent in their very working; they are only a spontaneous effort tending outwards, they have no independent centre, no power of resting in themselves and of self-reservation. Now, if limitless power be the cause of determinate existence in virtue of a necessity inherent in it, and if this determinate existence is also necessarily operative, giving rise therefore to other causalities, these last can only be the instruments of limitless power, possessing perhaps a certain independence in their relations to each other, but in relation to it entirely determined; being in fact nothing more then the definite forms which the working of that limitless power assumes in its self-development. The forces which this causality produces become in turn necessarily operative causes like itself; but, apart from the different range of their working, they differ from it also by the fact of their being produced; and they necessarily accomplish nothing save what is given them by the first and universal Cause. In this sphere the canon holds true without reserve, *causa causae est causa causati*.

Exercise a power in nature.

It cannot be denied that Schleiermacher's view of the divine omnipotence, as a causality conditioning all finite beings and events, has in its main features been argued out in this way. Schleiermacher, accordingly, expressly adopts the formula of Abelard; *id tantum facere potest Deus, quod quandoque facit*, a formula which Abelard uses in a different connection, but which, if taken by itself, leads to that mathematical necessity whereby (as Spinoza holds) all things logically follow from God's supreme power, *i.e.*, from His infinite nature. By this view, however, God's omnipotence is inevitably degraded to a level with the forces of nature.

Schleier-
macher's
argument.
 This, indeed, is by no means what Schleiermacher aims at in his explanation of omnipotence. He calls omnipotence an "*eternal*" and "timeless" working, and he describes omniscience as "the perfect spiritualizing of the divine omnipotence."* But he holds that eternity when predicated of omnipotence can only be a negative conception, seeing that any thing positive in it already belongs to the conception of omnipotence. And as to omniscience being "the spiritualizing of omnipotence," Schleiermacher is obliged to qualify this by saying that "the main design of this conception is to enable us to regard the divine causality as a living energy, rather than definitely to assert a similarity between God and what we designate spirit."† Far be it from us to make light of the truth that God is the Living One (ὁ ζῶν πατήρ, John vi. 57; θεὸς ὁ ζῶν, Acts xiv. 15; 2 Cor. iii. 3, vi. 16, and elsewhere); indeed, we find this life not only in God's external causality, but in the inexhaustible fulness of His own Being. But life is an attribute which, in a limited degree, belongs to nature, and to every organic being in nature; and if a being be nothing more than living, its position is below that of man. Schleiermacher, therefore, has himself virtually retracted what he had before advanced beyond the bare naturalistic view of the divine omniscience.

The fact is, a theology which will not adopt the idea of divine Personality, has no alternative save to surrender the idea of the divine omnipotence as inconceivable, unless, indeed, as a negative expression, or to degrade it from its similarity with the moving and effective power of the human spirit to a

---

* *Glaubenslehre*, § 55, 1 (vol. i. p. 320).

† *Ibid*, p. 294. "If the expression *omniscience* is intended mainly to affirm that the omnipotent must not be regarded as a lifeless power, the same object would be gained by the expression 'perfect life.'" But does not the idea of perfect causality already of itself exclude the notion of a so-called lifeless power? If so, this addition of omniscience to omnipotence is a mere tautology.

similarity with nature. The attempt to raise it above personality really sinks it below personality.

<small>Personality linked with power.</small> It is in the sphere of Personality that power attains its real self-mastery, and is elevated into *ability* in the true sense of this word (see p. 29). It does not certainly rest with man to decide whether he will or will not exercise his power of self-determination in relation to any other Being. Personality in him is relative only and limited, and independently of his will another Being already exists, obliging him to put himself in some relation to Him. But he does possess the power of choosing how and in what directions he will exercise his activity. There are no forces in him compelling the will with an irresistible necessity to realize them (if there were, their realization would be brought about independently of the will); but the will is lord over its own action.

If we regard omnipotence as the limitless power of a personal Being, and therefore of a personal Will in relation to other beings, then supposing that God decrees that other beings shall exist, His nature will, to a certain extent, *reflect* itself in these beings. Otherwise the world would be wholly separate from God, its nature would be quite foreign to His, and there could be no conceivable fellowship between the creature and the Creator. God could not reveal Himself to us; and it would be absurd to entertain the least thought of God, if our spirits were not in themselves a revelation of God. But a necessity to realize all that is possible to omnipotence can never be predicated of the Almighty EGO. Such a necessity is, in a word, a determinism appropriate indeed for an agency in nature, but not for an acting will.*

<small>Omnipotence not the creation of everything possible.</small> Granting, then, that God could create much that He does not choose to create, we have in this power of choice no "self-limitation," as Schleiermacher terms it, unless we imagine at the same time some inner impulse in God urging Him on to

---

* It is evident from this that we distinguish (in God's external operations) between *potentia* and *actus*. RITTER (p. 42) objects to this distinction, because if we allow it we can only affirm that God possesses the ability of being almighty;—but this involves the *petitio principii*, that omnipotence means the realization of everything possible. The last chapter of Part i. of this Book has shown the sense in which I recognize a distinction between *actus* and *potentia*

realize all that is possible to Him. Such an impulse towards realization, if it exist, must be counteracted by an opposing force if anything possible to God is not to be realized. And yet, if in analysing this we keep the idea of a divine Will and of a conscious self-determination in our thoughts, we shall find that God would really be sensible of a limitation were He conscious of any necessity obliging Him to realize everything which He possessed the power of producing. The truth of the matter is, that if we allow such a necessity we cannot speak of a will at all as the active principle of all realization; the so-called volition would be nothing more than the passing of determinations already present into outward existence.

As to human personality, seeing that in itself, and still more in the individual, it is a limited one, freedom being conditioned by dependence, this necessity of realizing the possible is only relatively denied. In God as the ABSOLUTE PERSON it is *entirely done away*. A true conception of the absoluteness of God, which is possible to us only when the absolute essence is regarded as an absolute Person, will suffice to answer those dialectic questions which would embarrass the doctrine of freedom as inconsistent with the divine omnipotence. But it may be asked, is it not in any case better and more in keeping with our ideas of perfection, that all existences which God could possibly create should actually be produced by Him? Is there not a moral if not a metaphysical necessity that God should prefer the more perfect to the less perfect, and therefore excluding the possibility of any other procedure? We reply, if God is in Himself the perfect One, self-caused, and self-sufficient, it is a contradiction to suppose that a higher perfection could ensue from the production of any other being. Whatever be the design of the world in its creation, development, and consummation,

<small>Argument from perfection.</small>

<small>God is infinite perfection in Himself.</small>

<small>in God, without thereby attributing to Him a gradual becoming or development. This work cannot fairly be charged with surrendering the conclusions of the old metaphysicians, simply because of the outcry raised against them by modern philosophers; still I candidly confess that I regard the maxim concerning the identity of *potentia* and *actus* in God (on the distinction of which Spinoza rightly insisted, *Ethic.* p. i. prop. 33, schol. 2) as one of the metaphysical "old bottles" which will not contain the "new wine" of a living and clear idea of God, such as is sought after in all the nobler tendencies of our day.</small>

it certainly cannot be this. And for this very reason it is possible that in the world's development the greatest disorder and discord should appear in undeniable reality, without in the least destroying or (what amounts in this case to the same thing) lessening the divine perfections. We have already seen that this idea of the Absolute does not allow of any transition from God to the world, save that of *free love*. This free love is the highest principle directing the exercise of God's omnipotence. It is an old canon that the Divine attributes should not be separated from each other, and we are not therefore to regard human freedom in the light of God's omnipotence alone as an abstract thought, but only in the light of God's omnipotence when blended with His love.

But does not God's love demand with still stronger necessity the existence of the world, seeing that otherwise it would have no object? And must not God, in virtue of His ungrudging love, realize all that is possible, so that what could not be indirectly derived from the reality already created might result directly from the exercise of love? As to the first of these questions, it has already been answered (pp. 134–139), and as to the second, it is surely a very partial and external conception of God's love to make its greatness and its glory consist in a necessity of bringing every possibility to reality. Love is essentially will; personal beings alone are capable of love. But love, as such, cannot consist in realizing everything that is possible to the subject of it. Will is the self-limitation of an *Ego*, but this task assigned to love would be an unlimited one. The *possible* as such is, on account of this its unlimitedness, not the *subject matter*, but simply the *presupposition* of free will. And this is true alike of divine and human love.

<small>Argument from God's love.</small>

When in maintenance of divine freedom the older theologians held that what is possible to God *must* transcend the sum total of what He has at all times realized by His will, they involved themselves in a contradiction which Spinoza* long ago pointed out. Statements of this kind imply a possibility which never can be realized, and, therefore, what is not, strictly speaking, a possibility at all. The claims of divine freedom are best served by our giving

<small>Error of older theologians.</small>

---

* *Ethic.*, p. i. prop. xvii. schol. (Opp. Ed. Bruder, vol. i. p. 202).

neither an affirmative nor a negative answer to the question whether all that is possible to God's almighty will is realized. In order correctly to answer the question, either affirmatively or negatively, we must examine God's revelations in the actual development of the world, and the full determinateness of His will as therein revealed. The revelation of God in Christ must be included; for it chiefly informs us concerning the determinations of God's will; and it declares that the creative and sustaining love of God has for its final aim the existence of beings capable of perfect communion with Him. In this aim we behold the ungrudging bountifulness of God's love communicating itself in a fulness, and yet with a determinateness, infinitely surpassing all such vague notions as "the realization of everything within the range of God's power," and so forth. We cannot but perceive that this aim corresponds to the divine nature, and that a higher is inconceivable. But if it is God's will that there shall be beings capable of holding fellowship with Him, He wills also (as we have seen in the first part of this third book) that these beings shall turn to Him freely, with a freedom which does not exclude the possibility of the opposite, and which is therefore unconditioned in its self-decision.

Christianity the highest achievement of omnipotence.

From the standing-point which we assume, the question we have thus answered is distinct from that which inquires whether the world in its most comprehensive sense—*i.e.*, the universe—is to be regarded as an exhaustive self-revelation (or more correctly, when speaking of such views, self-unfolding) of the divine nature. This question we must answer decidedly in the negative, not only on account of the constitution of the world as far as our experimental knowledge of it goes, but on account of the essential relations of the ideas "God" and the "world" to each other. The finite can never by any enhancement or extension become equal to the infinite or its adequate exponent. If it be contradictory to suppose such an equality, the limitation of the divine omnipotence, which our conclusion that God could not create such a world seems formally to involve, vanishes at once. And yet God does fully reveal Himself, not, indeed, by causing all the determinations of His nature

Is the universe an exhaustive self-revelation of God?

to reflect themselves in determinations of the world, but by vouchsafing to personal beings in His universe when they attain perfection the perfect vision of Himself (Matt. v. 8; 1 Cor. 13, 12; 1 John iii. 2). Romang apparently makes a like distinction (in his *System der natürlichen Religionslehre*, p. 256) when he affirms, on the one hand, that the entire causality of the divine nature is embodied in the world, and when, on the other hand, he hesitates to assert that the entire depth and fulness of the divine nature is fully revealed in the world. We must ever bear in mind in discussing such questions that God is infinitely more than an "absolute principle" of the world, containing in itself in undivided and eternal unity what is separated and subject to temporal development. We must remember that He is in Himself the infinite One, and therefore has in Himself the determinate and distinctive fulness of being. This truth, as well as the recognition of God's personality, which is akin thereto, is variously asserted by Romang (*e.g.*, at p. 255), and yet we find the opposite idea stated with equal distinctness, when (at p. 257) he says, "God's nature must go forth, and be spent in His volition and acts," and when (p. 146) he avers, "An abstract and absolute Being not having the finite in himself (?) would be empty and void of contents; the infinite receives its determinateness and its contents in the finite only; for the finite alone is determined." According to this, the infinite is the undetermined. As too much honour is here given to the finite, the honour due to it and to the Creator is taken away when the author thinks (*e.g.*, p. 142) that he must sacrifice all independence on the part of the finite in its relation to God, in order to maintain the divine infinity. Had Romang held to the sentiment first expressed, he would have apprehended that true relation between God and the world, whereby the divine freedom, and the freedom of the beings who form the centre and heart of the world, would be alike maintained.

§ 2. SELF-LIMITATION OF GOD'S WILL. There is then no self-limitation of the divine will either in the existence of a finite world, or in the fact that all which is possible to the divine Omnipotence is not realized. But this self-limitation is necessarily implied in the gift of freedom to personal beings.

Yet, as freedom ever exists in the world by the almighty will of God, it is clear that this self-limitation is not a limitation of the divine power itself,—if it were, it would involve a contradiction, because in this case God's power would not be omnipotence,—but simply a limitation of its exercise and realization in the sphere set apart by God for the exercise of created freedom.

God's will in itself consists of this : as He is Himself good, so nothing but good shall be done by the personal beings whom He creates. Starting from this view of the divine will, and bearing in mind its holy earnestness, we should expect that God would produce good, and nothing but good, by means of His creatures. But moral good implies free self-determination on the part of the creature who realizes it ; and this is most clearly manifest when we trace it back to its innermost ground, which is love to God. God's will, therefore, which in other cases produces what it affirms, limits itself in this sphere so as to be a *requirement* only, and reveals itself as such to the consciousness of the creature. It limits itself out of love, which is the spring of all true self-limitation and self-denial ; and herein we have the principle which Schleiermacher missed, the principle of God's self-limitation. In order that good might be fully realized by his creatures, perfect Love,—wherein holiness and bliss are inseparably one, and wherein Spinoza's saying, *beatudo non virtutis praemium sed ipsa virtus*, fulfils itself in a higher sense than he imagined,—creates by God's creative will a principle of such independence, that it may, if it will, even decide against Him. From this love there springs that sphere of existence which cannot indeed be separated from the action of the divine will (if it could, it would have only a shadowy existence, and no mention could be made of God's self-limitation in relation to it), but in which this will does not work in a purely determining manner.

True principle of this self-limitation.

Thus we arrive at the conception of a *conditioned—i.e.* self-conditioning—will of God. Let us examine it more closely.

God's will is self-discriminating because it wills conditioned existence, *i.e.*, the universe, as one indeed, yet not as an abstract, but as a concrete unity, as a whole or aggregate wherein plurality is oneness. The

God's will self-conditioned.

fact that the various elements making up this whole are related to each other, one being made the presupposition of another does not involve any conditionality of the divine will.* Contemplating the sphere of nature only, while the various existences therein determine and are determined, and therefore mutually determine one another, we yet regard this as a sphere of pure determinateness on God's part, as one of absolute dependence which the causative will of God unconditionally pervades. Now, in the sphere of created spirit, God wills only what is good; but He wills—in conformity both with the idea of Spirit and of moral good—that this good shall be the offspring of free will in the creature; He wills its realization according to a certain law, as proceeding from the freedom of the will,—a freedom of the will which, as formal, necessarily includes the possibility of realizing the opposite. All that is really implied in the idea of a conditioned will of God is included in this one point.

It was maintained by some of the older Lutheran theologians, and still more definitely by the Arminians,† in combating the Calvinistic doctrine of predestination, that the true conception of a conditioned will of God includes the necessity of attributing to Him a will which cannot realize itself,‡ because the condition on which its realization depends is not included,—*voluntas Dei* INEFFICAX. This we cannot admit. The idea of a conditioned divine will certainly does imply that God suspends the immediate relation between His will and its effect in those departments wherein His will is conditioned. But the notion that we must attribute to God an ineffective will, and thus violate his omnipotence, disappears if we only adhere to the truth that

<small>Inaccurate language of theologians.</small>

---

* It is thus that Schleiermacher understands the idea of God's will being conditioned (*Glaubenslehre*, p. 314), because, of course, he could not understand it in its true and strict sense on account of the principles of his dogmatic system. In this sense even the advocates of the doctrine of unconditional predestination among the older theologians of the Reformed church admitted *decreta Dei conditionata*, *e.g.*, PET. VAN. MASTRICHT in his *Theologia theoretico practica*, in a passage quoted by BAUMGARTEN (*Unters. theol. Streitigkeiten*, vol. i. 128 ; compare HOTTINGER, *Fato doctrinae de praedestinatione et gratia Dei exercit*, i. § 51.

† See *e.g.*, EPISCOPIUS *Institutiones theol.* lib. iv. sect. 2, cap. 21 (Opp. ed. Amstelaed, 1650, p. 308) ; LIMBORCH's *Theologia Christiana*, lib. iii. c. ix. § 11.

‡ This must certainly be the meaning of the *voluntas inefficax*. For if we suppose that this will is ineffective, because and in so far as it wills not to be effective, it would not so far be actual will.

the element of universality in the divine will, concerning the realization of moral good generally, and the element of speciality concerning the realization of moral good by means of our free self-determination, are not really different elements, but are inseparably one and the same.

Here we have before us the conditioned will of God in its original form, as a will which requires moral good from man, but will not receive it unless it comes from man's free will. We find the same conditioned will in the sphere of Redemption. The will of God, according to which a part of the human race actually obtains the blessing of redemption onwards until the final judgment, is a conditional will;—though this has significance only for those who hold that in the fulfilment of this condition there is no irresistible operation of grace. The element of universality is the salvation of the whole race,—that it is not God's will that any one should be excluded therefrom;—the element of speciality is that man shall become partaker of salvation by a living and personal faith in Christ. The first of these two elements is not a mere abstraction of our understanding, not a mere "velleity" or indolent movement towards willing, which vanishes without producing any effect, because it lacks earnestness and power; for it is clear that such a mere velleity cannot be attributed to God. It is a positive element in the divine will exerting itself to a definite result; and this result is twofold; in the sphere of created spirit it is the consciousness of the divine law dwelling in the spirit of man, and in the sphere of redemption it is the accomplishment of an adequate scheme for the salvation of mankind through Christ, and the presentation of this scheme to all, either in this life or in some unknown manner in a future state. But we cannot regard this element in God's will as an actual and perfect will of God without involving the Christian doctrine in inextricable perplexity.

God's conditioned will in redemption.

Even Chrysostom, as well as the Scholastic and older Lutheran theologians who adopted his view, distinguished between *voluntas antecedens* and *consequens*,* (προηγουμένη, ἑπομένη) in the sphere of

This recognized by Chrysostom.

---

* See GERHARD, tom. ii. *De Elect. et Reprob.* cap. i.. §§ 78, 79; QUENSTEDT, p. iii. c. 1, sect. 1, th. 5, 6; HOLLAZ, *Examen. theol.* p. iii. sect. 1, cap. 1, qu. 5.

demption, in order thus to establish the universality of God's will of mercy for mankind, and the consequent universality of the provisions of redemption, and of its offers. He should have applied the same principle to the sphere of morals generally.* We have already recognized the truth which lies in this distinction, but thus expressed it is defective—not only in its seeming relation to time (*antecedens, consequens*) which however, is easily removed—but in representing what is only an element in God's will as a totality—as a distinct and complete act of will—and thereby leading, if strictly taken, to a violation of God's omnipotence. In a merely popular treatment of the subject, indeed, we pass over this conditioning of God's will, and view what remains as a perfect will, apart from free self-limitation. But in a scientific inquiry, if the true import of the universal element be not entirely surrendered, we must bear in mind this self-conditioning of His will on God's part, else we shall have a seemingly ineffective will of God, a will without the power of realizing itself.

3. SELF-LIMITATION OF DIVINE WILL VINDICATED.

The self-limitation of the divine will is strongly objected to by the prevailing systems of modern theology.† It is said not only to be unrecognized by our pious self-consciousness, which is a consciousness of our dependence on God, but also to be contradictory to the true idea of God.

* LEIBNITZ assigns this wider reference to the *voluntas antecedens ;—Theodicée*, part i. §§ 22, 23 ; *Causa Dei* [*asserta, &c.* § 23 ;—indeed, a still wider reference, for he not only relates it to, but connects it with, human freedom generally (see vol. i. of this work, p. 276)—as BILFINGER (*De origine et permissione mali*, §§ 226–240), following Leibnitz among the philosophers, and BAUMGARTEN (*Evangel. Glaubenslehre*, vol. i. 415), among the theologians of that day. BUDDEUS (*Instit. Theol. Dogmat.*, lib. ii. c. ii. § 29), quotes from PHOTIUS a remarkable Platonic expression, which certainly contains the idea of a *voluntas antecedens* in its wider sense.

† SCHLEIERMACHER thus objects ; but this is in keeping with his doctrine concerning religion and his idea of God ; see especially his first Letter to Dr Lücke concerning his *Glaubenslehre* (*Studien u. Kritiken*, 1829, p. 270). The real cause of this strong protest may be found by comparing §§ 216–227 of Schleiermacher's *Dialektik*, and the corresponding sections in the Appendix C. and E. If the most adequate conception of God be that of a bare unity, excluding all contrasts—*i.e.*, according to Schleiermacher, all distinctions—as the transcendental cause of all volition and thought, it must certainly seem an ἄτοπον that a Godhead thus stripped of all reality should "practise acts of self-

Now, as to pious consciousness, it is undoubtedly the consciousness of redemption from sin ordained of God through Christ. But Schleiermacher describes it as something very different. "In so far," he says, "as sin is real, it may be regarded as ordered of God, as that which makes ‚redemption necessary, because without it redemption could not have been ordered of God."* Such a theory as this could be adopted only by those whose religious consciousness has been thoroughly impregnated with Schleiermacher's artificial view of the relation of God to sin. To one still unbiassed the matter is regarded in a very different manner. As certainly as the law condemning sin and the redemption destroying sin were ordained of God, so certain is it also that sin could not have been ordained of God. But seeing that sin is something real—and if it were not, what reality would there be in redemption?—our religious consciousness must recognize a reality which does not spring from the will of God, but from the creature's will in its independent action, yet which is the negative presupposition of the highest counsels of divine love. If our pious consciousness in understanding its own deliverances is sufficiently on its guard against Dualism, it cannot avoid the recognition of a divine will whereby God reserves to His creatures the power of deciding somewhat which He has left undecided, and therefore the recognition of a free act of self-limitation on the part of the divine will. The same inference may easily be deduced from our belief in a righteous judgment of God, and in the divine government of men and of the destinies of nations.

No one can think that pious trust in the power of God will be in the least impaired (at least as far as Christian piety is

limitation" in order to allow scope for the free self-determination of the human will.

Among recent writers VATKE (pp. 375) and RITTER (pp. 38–40) have declared themselves opposed to the idea of a divine self-limitation, as stated in the first edition of this work. In reply to Ritter's affirmation so axiomatically stated, "no one can negative himself, least of all God," I observe 1. That if Ritter converts the idea of self-limitation into that of self-negation, he must allow me to adhere to the idea of self-limitation, and then to ask him to prove the assertion that no one can *limit* himself ; 2. That I regard it as an inadmissible limitation of God if the power of self-limitation is to be attributed less to Him than to any other being.

* *Glaubenslehre*, §§ 81–83, (vol. i., pp. 493–497.)

concerned) by the recognition of this divine self-limitation, because such a trust does not exist where there is personal opposition to God's will—and this is the possibility with which we have here to do—but only where there is a self-renouncing union with God. It holds true, of course, in the Christian life, that whatever influence the arbitrariness of others may have upon him whose will is surrendered to God's, it is not merely put to the account of a law of nature indifferent to the salvation of this particular man, but is to be looked upon as part of a divine plan for his moral training (Rom. viii. 29).

Schleiermacher's appeal to the demands of our religious consciousness regarding this question is contradicted by a truth often affirmed in the *Glaubenslehre* itself. Pious self-consciousness, as Schleiermacher himself admits (in a passage already quoted in this volume, p. 114), needs, above all things, a *personal God*, and a living intercourse between Him and the spirit of man; and thus it finds God represented in the revelation of Christ. Now, scientific theology, the more closely it attaches itself to that consciousness, as Schleiermacher thinks it should, the less will it be disposed to sacrifice the possibility of a divine self-limitation, arising from God's free personality, to a conception of God which denies not only that possibility, but even divine personality itself, by identifying God's working, willing, knowing, being, and power, and reducing all these attributes to an abstract unity and bare causality.*

The idea of a personal God contradicts Schleiermacher.

* It is still more strange that a theological view, diametrically opposed to Pantheism, and maintaining absolute Personality as the very kernel of our knowledge of God, should allow itself to be misled by the false notion of the profundity of abstract unity to throw overboard all the distinctions above named as incompatible with the idea of the Absolute, and yet at the same time to make other distinctions in God which are really far more serious. *E.g.*, the divine ideas that are said to constitute the elements of God's self-consciousness are represented as "flowing from the depths of His Being, revealing themselves in finite reality, and when their finite forms vanish, being again absorbed in the divine Being or consciousness;"—BRUCH's *Lehre von den göttlichen Eigenschaften*, pp. 154-156; see the author's beautiful confession in the Preface, pp. iv., v. If this highly esteemed theologian would consider how he would maintain that *self-dependence* in God which certainly belongs to His personality, if the divine ideas—without which God would have no personality—necessarily realize themselves in a world "absolutely distinct" from God, he, too, would see the significance and importance of the distinctions we insist upon.

CHAP. I.] FREEDOM COMPATIBLE WITH GOD'S OMNIPOTENCE. 195

If the question were viewed objectively, it might unhesitatingly be granted that any limitation imposed from without, and thus contradicting the idea of the Absolute (as denoting a Being wholly self-dependent and self-contained), would certainly destroy the true idea of God. But how can this be affirmed of a self-limitation on the part of the will of God in relation to a sphere of being whose limits are fixed by God himself, and where there is no interference with the divine absoluteness? Instead of prescribing for God certain bounds based upon *a priori* reasoning, as to the manner in which He must will and determine, it becomes us rather to learn the actual facts of the case in all their reality and importance, asking first *how* His will has determined itself, and then examining the *wherefore* of this determinateness, and its connection with other truths already known. And seeing that these facts, conscience I mean, and the religious consciousness of God's holiness, together with the saving revelation of God in Christ as based upon these, reveal to us in human nature a principle of such self-dependence as can be explained away neither as man's being passively determined by God (according to the doctrine of absolute dependence) nor as God's own self-determination (according to the doctrine of absolute immanence), shall we venture still to maintain that God *could not* will such a self-dependence external to Himself, because forsooth of His omnipotence?

To deny this self-limitation is really to fetter omnipotence.

Altogether apart from the divine love, we would have to conclude that an almighty will so utterly destitute of the power of limiting itself in its operations actually interfered with its own illimitable power of causation. In this case, God's will would be hindered by its very omnipotence, hindered too in bringing His creation to its highest reality, to that which is likest to Himself, hindered from creating self-determining personality.* With all its limitlessness it would still need to be freed from its own omnipotence, if this omnipotence did not allow it to

Omnipotence itself implies the power of self-limitation.

---

* NITZSCH in his protestant reply to Möhler's *Symbolik*, rightly designates it an error of the Reformers, "when they describe God's permissive power as a *minus* of power, for in reality it constitutes a *plus*."—*Theol. Studien und Kritiken*, 1834, part i. p. 55.

give space to a freedom external to itself. The omnipotence of God is essentially spiritual, and for this very reason it cannot be a mere force of nature working of necessity; it is self-contained, and can limit its operations with perfect freedom. It is, moreover, the characteristic of true strength to be tolerant, and readily to allow others to retain their freedom, seeing that it has nothing to fear from them. And shall the Almighty forbid his noblest creatures to be free, because He would then be no longer the only worker? Must it be regarded as an inconceivable thing that He should condescend to admit them to a relatively independent co-operation? In a far nobler spirit is that rule ordained which does not at the outset exclude the possibility of transgression, but which has in it the means of overcoming any faiiure in its realization. Suppose that any State possessed the power of binding all its citizens by force, so that any violation of the laws would be impossible; were it to exercise this power, it would at once cease to be a State, and would be reduced to a mere machine. And would not the same hold true of the world as created by God—this universal State of personal beings?

But in the Christian doctrine concerning the nature of God, love and not omnipotence is the central attribute.

Love limits omnipotence.

God's power submits to every limitation which the holy will of Love puts upon its working. Or, to express the same truth more accurately, Power, viewed simply in itself, possesses no moving or determining principle; God does not give existence to the world merely in order to show forth His infinite power and His absolute causality, but Love is the moving principle of power, because it decides upon the end to the accomplishment of which divine power is to be exerted. But as God has from eternity beheld this end—the perfection of the personal beings whom He has created, in communion with Himself—as already attained, and has therefore eternally considered free self-determination external to Himself as unalterably identified with His will, He regards that self-limitation of His will, real as is its import, yet as if already removed. We have, moreover, already learned that man's volition, notwithstanding his self-perversion, is ever sustained by God's all-embracing and co-working providence.

CHAP. I.]   FREEDOM COMPATIBLE WITH GOD'S OMNIPOTENCE.   197

But we cannot ignore the fact, that when we think we have solved this problem, a new difficulty springs out of this very solution. If God has not seemingly merely, but actually limited the action of His will in the world, by endowing His creatures with free self-determination, wherein consists the certainty that the end He has in view will be finally attained? Why is it not possible that all the beings who turn away from God should persevere in their apostacy?

§ 4. Is THE FINAL TRIUMPH OF EVIL POSSIBLE?

It might perhaps aid us were we to confine this question to the moral condition of the human race in this world. What in itself is an act of will, seems in virtue of an extra-temporal and primary choice to be from the outset a settled moral character. And on the basis of this determinateness we might imagine the appointment of means having prevailing power over man's natural disposition, so as to lead it with certainty on to the appointed goal. But this would only be to evade the difficulty. We perceive the true force of it when we consider the self-limitation of God's will in its relation to that extra-temporal source of our self-decision itself.

We are not disposed to give up the principles we have established on account of any logical consequences which may be deduced from them, and we therefore grant the obvious possibility of all created wills turning away from God. Considering the primary indeterminateness of created will, it can in no case be secured against a fall, apart from its own decision. But is it also possible that all fallen beings shall persist for ever in their apostacy. We cannot shut our eyes to the fact that the will is capable of an incalculable self-degradation in wickedness. And as God does not by His omnipotence prevent a fall, so neither does He rescue any after their fall by a mere exercise of power. Thus viewed, the supposed possibility cannot be excluded. But (as we have already seen in contrasting the true idea of evil with Dualism) evil has in it a twofold contradiction. It possesses a tendency to destroy the nature in which it resides,—that nature which is, notwithstanding, its necessary basis,—so that, if it succeeded in its efforts, it would destroy itself at the same moment. Again, in order to obtain and secure its existence in a divinely

The work of saving love may attach itself to the contradictions of evil.

ordered world, evil must attach itself to certain elements which have their appointed place in the realization of good, and must therefore labour against itself in its very efforts to realize itself. In this contradiction, though it never allows rest or satisfaction to beings given up to evil, there is nothing obliging these beings to forsake evil, and turn to good. As they are in their nature free, they can persevere in leading an existence the most contradictory. If this is possible to man during his earthly life, why should it be impossible to him in a future state? The inner contradictions of evil, when truly felt, may well set a man at variance with the sin which has dominion over him; but they have by no means the power to turn him to what is good. But still there lies in these contradictions a negative basis on which the saving action of God's love and grace can begin its work, and we may be sure this love will know how to use it. These contradictions are ultimately traceable to the fact that evil can never attain substantial reality, however it may strive after it,—that it can continue and spread only in a being who is ever God's creature;—and hence we discern the secret of the limitation put upon the development of evil, and the guarantee that, though it may hinder the complete realization of God's great world-aim, it cannot ultimately thwart it.

Herein we find the true answer to that more general question whether God can have an end which He never attains;—a question to which Töllner gives an affirmative reply in an acute Dissertation,* which, however, does not go to the bottom of the problem.

<small>Can God have an end which He never attains?</small>

God has beyond doubt established forces in the world which seem to our religious consciousness to be limited not by arbitrary caprice, but by a relative necessity, because they have been subjected by Him to the condition of historical development. Töllner lays much stress upon the case of the command given to our first parents. But in a general way we must allow that the law, taken by itself, does not attain that for which it was designed, viz., to lead man to righteousness. We are forced to the same conclusion when we consider the development of mankind since the appearing of Jesus Christ,

* *Vermischte Aufsätze*, Zweite Sammlung, pp. 1-32.

and the means divinely appointed for bringing home the truths of Christ's redemption to mankind. When in harmony with the offers of the gospel, salvation by Christ is preached to any people, or to any individual, are we not warranted in saying that the offer is made with the end in view that it may be accepted? And if, as in innumerable cases, the message of mercy be rejected, is God's purpose really frustrated? The omnipotence of the divine will, while it is by no means the all-determining centre of Christian Theology, is still an essential element, and the violation of it has a blighting influence upon all the blessings which the Christian religion promises and secures to man. But to ascribe to God a vain endeavour, a volition which surpasses His ability to fulfil it,—and what more distinctly deserves to be called a divine volition than the determining principle of all productive Will, fixing its aims?— is clearly to violate His omnipotence, and would, moreover, oblige us to separate God's omnipotence from His omniscience. Not even man (and still less God) can set for himself aims which he is perfectly certain that he can never fulfil.*

We must certainly ever guard against the error of elevating that element in God's will from which His law or ordainments generally spring, into a determinate act of divine predestination. We must also be careful not to reckon those higher determinations which our moral consciousness must attribute to certain natures, conditions, circumstances, and tendencies, as *positive aims* in the consciousness of God. Apart from us, as the apostle warns us (Rom. xi. 24), God may have His secret thoughts over and above those which He makes known to us; thoughts which shall not, peradventure, be fully revealed until His kingdom is far more widely developed, and perhaps not in their fulness even then † Thus, for example, before Christianity appeared, the purpose of the law must have appeared to the human consciousness as having in itself a determinate end and purpose; but when faith came, it was

<small>We know not God's ultimate purposes.</small>

* The examples by which TÖLLNER endeavours to establish the contrary are so meagre that we need not discuss them here.

† LUTHER, in his work *De servo arbitrio* (p. 96, Ed. of Seb. Schmid), ably says, "*Multa facit Deus, quae verbo suo non ostendit nobis, multa quoque vult, quae verbo suo non ostendit sese velle;*" but we cannot by any means adopt the further thought that the *velle* and the *ostendere* contradict each other.

manifest that in the circumstances of the human race at the time, its true object was to be παιδαγωγὸς εἰς Χριστόν. In like manner, as the redeeming work of Christ has for its purpose and aim that all who receive it in faith may become partakers of eternal life, the offer of it to this or that individual is designed distinctively to bring to light the bitter enmity of his heart against God; and what John the Baptist says concerning the mission of the Messiah, that "he will throughly purge his floor," and separate the chaff from the wheat (Matt. iii. 10);—what the aged Simeon said concerning His being "set both for the fall and for the rising again of many in Israel, that the thoughts of many hearts may be revealed" (Luke ii. 34, 35);—what Christ says Himself, "For judgment am I come into the world, that they who see not might see, and that they who see might be made blind" (John ix. 39), and concerning His double function, as the rock of salvation and the stone of stumbling (Matt. xxi. 42, 43, compare Rom. ix. 33; 1 Peter ii. 7, 8; 2 Cor. ii. 15, 16); and concerning the power of His Church in virtue of their faith in Him, the living Son of God, not only to loose, but also to bind in such a manner that it shall be bound in heaven (Matt. xvi. 19);—all this must be maintained in its strictest and fullest meaning.

In our present state, however, and before the close of the present development of the human race, there must ever be more or less uncertainty in our perception of the purposes of God, in particulars at least, and so far as these have not been declared to us by God's revelation of Himself in Christ. We feel that we are standing upon sure ground when we abide by the highest and all-embracing design of history—that divine kingdom which in its completeness will be nothing less than the perfect fellowship of man with God. As we recognize this to be beyond all doubt the great end and design of God Himself, we are equally certain that it will be attained, because if God had not eternally contemplated it as attained, man would never have existed.

One design certain: man's fellowship with God.

It is clear from what we have now learned concerning the self-limitation of the divine will, that we cannot regard the

CHAP. I.] FREEDOM COMPATIBLE WITH GOD'S OMNIPOTENCE. 201

idea of divine "permissiveness" as a mere resort of popular phraseology'; it must !be vindicated upon scientific principles as a fit description of the relation between divine and human activity. This idea corresponds by no means exactly as the compliment of the idea of divine self-limitation,—as if whenever the divine will ceased to be a producing will it became merely a permissive will. Some modern theologians, *e.g.*, Bretschneider,* thus explain the idea of permissiveness, but language is quite against them, for when that is done which God commands but does not Himself accomplish, we cannot surely say that He merely "permits" it. Permission on God's part is clearly contrasted, not with the divine causation, but with the divine *command.* When God, by a fiat of His will, creates what is highest in His creation, the sphere of spirit determining itself by means of freedom—an act of His will which is at once the greatest and most glorious revelation of His majesty, and the freest self-limitation—His will in its relation to this sphere, when it exists, ceases to be a causative, and becomes a commanding will. God's will becomes a commanding will when it ordains that a certain event shall be brought about, not by itself, but by another's will.† Now if this other Will be endowed with freedom and self-determination, and if the self-limitation of the divine will, refusing itself to realize what corresponds to it, be real, we have with the commanding will the obvious possibility of its violation.

§ 5. DIVINE PERMISSION OF EVIL.

Now, to the realization of this possibility on the part of man's free will, God's will stands related not as *compelling,* for the very existence of this free will is based upon its self-determination, still less as *allowing* it, for in this case it could not command the contrary, *i.e.*, obedience, but as *suffering* it, as passively *permitting* it. Though it has power to hinder the entrance of evil—for a sufferance or permitting of evil implies this power—it will not hinder it, because this could not be done without excluding that from the creation on which its highest perfection depends.

In this permissiveness the divine will not only negatively tolerates evil, but while it suffers it, it assigns to it certain

* "*Handbuch der Dogmatik,*" § 55 (vol. i. 413, 414 : 3d Ed.)
† Nature may be subject to laws, but not to commands.

limits, not to its internal growth—for it can in this respect grow to a fearful enormity—but to its workings in the world, which are continually counteracted and destroyed by the prevailing progress of the world's development as ordained of God. The idea of divine sufferance certainly implies that God does not prevent actual disturbances and hindrances which retard the realization of His world-aim; for this world-aim is to be attained by the instrumentality of free beings; but any disorder which would frustrate the attainment of His purpose, God does not permit. On the other hand God's punishment exactly corresponds to His sufferance of evil, provided that the evil in question be not removed again by forgiveness; so that the created spirit cannot rebel against the commanding will of God without immediately falling again under its sway as a punishing will.

God limits evil.

If these conclusions concerning the idea of divine sufferance of evil be regarded in the light of other principles already developed in our inquiry, there will be no need to confute the arguments urged chiefly by Schleiermacher* against them. Those arguments are based upon assumptions regarding the nature of God and His relation to the world, the untenableness of which we have already sufficiently shown. We agree perfectly in Schleiermacher's remark that "whatever God only suffers or permits must have its ultimate source elsewhere."† But so far is this from infringing upon God's omnipotence, that the contrary judgment—the notion that a mere permission on God's part is inconceivable—would negative the omnipotence of His will. When Schleiermacher argues, that if this doctrine be adopted, what in God is sufferance is predetermination in the Devil, and that what is predetermination in God is sufferance on the Devil's part, we can only regard this as an inappropriate and unmeaning jeer.‡

Arguments against permissiveness.

Schleiermacher's strong aversion to the idea of the divine

---

* *Glaubenslehre*, § 81, 4, (vol. i. 497), and especially the Dissertation on the Doctrine of Election, pp. 70-72.

† The elder Lutheran Theologians distinctly recognize this; *e.g.*, QUENSTEDT, p. ii. c. ii. sect. 2, qu. 5, object. διάλ. 11 :—"*Ubi nuda est permissio, ibi locum non habet causalitas.*"

‡ Still less appropriate is it when SIGWART (as before, p. 131) by an artificial argumentation, endeavours to infer from the idea of permission, that evil is in the world by the divine will. Nothing can really be inferred from that idea

permission of evil need not be thought strange; it arises naturally from the bias of his entire system. But when theologians who reject the doctrine of unconditional predetermination alike in the form in which Calvin, and in which Schleiermacher presented it, and who take exception to the manifestly contradictory or artificially complicated formulæ, by means of which those thinkers guard themselves against making God the author of evil—when such theologians who do not with Schleiermacher identify in one God's working, willing, power, and being, tell us that they cannot adopt the idea of the divine permission of evil and its more general principle, viz., the self-limitation of the divine will for the sake of created freedom, we cannot help regarding it as the indication of some deficiency in their perception alike of the principles and the consequences of their dogmatic convictions.

CHAPTER II.

THE RELATION OF HUMAN FREEDOM TO THE DIVINE OMNISCIENCE.

§ 1. THE FACT OF GOD'S FOREKNOWLEDGE.

IN endeavouring to explain, in the last chapter, how God eternally contemplates the self-limitation of His will in behalf of human freedom, as already removed, we made use of the assertion, without stopping to prove it, that God knows from eternity the self-decisions of the human will. In turning our attention now to the famous question, whether the freedom of these decisions is reconcilable with divine foreknowledge, we shall not stay to prove the truth of that proposition, but shall regard it as self-evident, and shall, in our investigations, take for granted that it is recognized. Socinus and his followers denied God's unerring knowledge of the future free actions of men,—because God's knowledge, though omniscience, has to do only with what

but the tautological proposition that evil exists in the world by the will of God so far as He suffers it to exist. The full answer to that argumentation of Sigwart may be found in Hollaz (as before, p. 495, note 2 : ed. 1750).

is knowable, but the future free acts of men are not knowable, save as *contingens*. They should have had courage to affirm, further, that God has devised for the human race neither a decree of salvation nor any plan of development, *i.e.*, that He does not concern Himself in the matter; for this far better becomes Him than to suffer any plans of His to be thwarted by unknown and utterly incalculable decisions of the human will, without ever being sure whether His purposes can in any case be carried out from the altered decisions.

It is equally clear that Divine foreknowledge of free actions is perfectly certain and unerring, so that these actions, as discerned of God, can never fail of their accomplishment, not vary even a hair's-breadth. Were God's knowledge in this respect only conjecture, though clothed with the highest degree of probability, it would still be liable amid millions upon millions of cases, now and then to prove faulty, and God would have to correct a mistake. On the other hand, it does not make any difference in the solution of this question whether or not we exclude what seems trifling and unimportant in human action, from among the objects of divine foreknowledge. The problem pre-eminently concerns those decisions of the human will upon which man's eternal salvation or ruin depends.

<small>Statement of the problem.</small>

How is it that the freedom of the will in these decisions is not interfered with by the foreknowledge of God? Being free, these decisions might have been different; yet remembering the unerringness of God's foreknowledge, they could not have been other than they are. Is not this an obvious contradiction?

<small>Apparent contradiction.</small>

Great importance is attached by theologians, ancient and modern, to *analogies* found in the sphere of human life. No one imagines that the freedom of his future acts is converted into necessity by his foreknowledge of them; why then should we attribute this influence to God's foreknowledge? But (we ask, in reply) does man possess any reliable foreknowledge of his free acts? The certainty which we may have as to how we shall decide in any particular case, without feeling our freedom encroached upon, cannot be used as an argument. We can never be certain that our foreknowledge in those cases is not itself a part of our

<small>Analogous cases in human life.</small>

foredetermination. As to the decisions of the will in the case of others, moreover, we must leave out of our account prophesies springing from Divine enlightenment; for these are not properly analogies from the sphere simply of human life. The behaviour of a man may be foretold by a consideration of his character and circumstances, only in so far as freedom properly so called—*i.e.*, the power of acting otherwise—is not really possessed by him. Nothing in this analogy remains, therefore, save instances of foreknowledge, by immediate intuition, springing from a power of divination possessed by some. But even here the fact of a perfectly certain prognostication of future events, or rather *actions*,— (the second sight of the Scotch and the like, are only the prognostications of certain *events* about to happen to another), —cannot be regarded as sufficiently established to warrant any inferences from them concerning the question before us. We have, therefore, no adequate analogy in the sphere of human knowledge.

Inadequate as arguments.

Yet the approximations to a perfect foreknowledge of the voluntary decisions of another, which we find among intimate friends and associates, afford a favourable expectation that human freedom may be reconcilable with Divine omniscience. We do not consider ourselves to have been a whit less free in any act, because we afterwards find that a friend had predicted our conduct with certainty. Or is this unshaken consciousness of our freedom to be explained as arising from the fact, that however necessary our decision may be as the result of our moral character, this very character itself is recognized as based upon our freedom? Be it so; yet it still holds that we never regard the foreknowledge of another to be in the least degree an operative cause of our decision.

Yet in some degree confirmatory.

Others adopt the opposite line of argument in the solution of this problem, and endeavour to harmonize human freedom with Divine foreknowledge, by laying stress upon the great difference between God's knowledge of what we call future, and our own. They admit that the freedom of human action would be destroyed if God literally knew *beforehand* what it would be. But God's knowledge is not like man's, subject to the condi-

2. PROPOSED SOLUTION OF THE PROBLEM.

tions of time and sequence, it is wholly extra-temporal; there is in God neither a remembrance of what is past, nor a looking forward to the future; and all that occurs in time—whether past, present, or future—is eternally known to Him as a complete and ever present whole. If, instead of *fore-knowledge* (*praescientia*), we attribute to God "the vision of what is ever present," the difficulty of reconciling Divine omniscience with human freedom disappears.

God's foreknowledge eternal.

This solution of our problem has been so often and so decidedly urged from the time of Augustine,* and Boethius,† down to the latest of our theologians, who treat of the Divine attributes,‡ that we shall do well to examine it more closely, to see whether it really furnishes what it promises.

The question is, first of all, whether it necessarily follows from the eternity of the divine knowledge that *time* and its continual transition from past to present, and from present to future, must be excluded from the perception of God.

Is time to be excluded from God's knowledge?

We have here to do only with such events in time as spring from freedom, and are known to us by experience. The most perfect knowledge that we can have of things of this kind—apart from our immediate consciousness of the facts of our inner life—is ocular demonstration. Our perception thus of what occurs in time is limited in a twofold way. For one thing it embraces only a small fragment of what happens in time; and for another, our knowledge of this small portion is only gradually obtained, and, therefore, becomes by degrees more and more obscure, till at

Perception of facts in time.

---

* *De Civitate Dei*, lib. xi. cap. 21 ; *De div. Quaestionibus ad Simplic.*, lib. ii. qu. 2, § 2. Outside the pale of Christianity we find the same thought, though expressed less clearly in Philo, *Quod Deus sit immutabilis:* ὥστε οὐδὲν παρὰ θεῷ μέλλον—και γὰρ οὐ χρόνος—αἰὼν ὁ βίος ἐστὶν αὐτῶν (αὐτοῦ). ἐν αἰῶνι δὲ οὔτε παρελήλυθεν οὐδὲν οὔτε μέλλει, ἀλλὰ μόνον ὑφέστηκεν (*Opera*, ed. Pfeiffer, vol. ii. p. 402.

† *De Consolatione Philosophiae*, lib. v. pros. 3–6.

‡ Bruch, p. 166. Strauss also lays great stress on this expedient. He thinks that all the pains taken to reconcile divine foreknowledge with human freedom might have been obviated, if the divine knowledge had never been divided into *reminiscentia visio* and *praescientia*. *Chr. Glaubensl.*, vol. i. 570. For the history of the question, see Daehne *De praescientia divinae cum libertate humana concordia*, 1830. A series of quotations from the Fathers and the Schoolmen, bearing upon this subject, will be found in Petavius *Dogmata theol.* tom. i. *De Deo Deique proprietatibus*, lib. iv. c. 4–7 ; compare tom. iii. lib. iv. c. 11.

last it fades away. A third, and the chief limit to this knowledge obtained by sight is, that we can never discern the present act of another thoroughly and in its internal accomplishment—but this is not a limit resulting from time.

Now God's knowledge embraces all time; every moment is present to Him without any waxing or waning. If God had to attain some knowledge which He had not before, or if the knowledge He possesses could in the least degree fade away, His consciousness would be reduced to a mere process of becoming and passing away and its absoluteness would be utterly destroyed.

But does it follow from this that in the divine knowledge there is no such thing as a succession of moments, no distinction of past, present, and future. In answering this question we must distinguish things which are often confounded. Past, present, future, are not as they are erroneously called, the "dimensions" of time, just as space has its three dimensions, without which it cannot rightly be conceived. Time has properly but one "dimension," it is, represented in our minds simply as a movement from any one point onwards, in one and the same direction, just as space is represented by a movement in three different directions; it is I say, if we regard it simply as time, and apart from its contents, nothing but a succession of single moments wherein the past is not to be distinguished as objectively different from the present or future. The distinctions of past, present, and future—taking these expressions in a purely formal sense,* as they are generally used, are wholly relative, changing every moment, and wholly subjective. What is "present" with us now will be "past" next moment, what is "future" now will immediately be present. These distinctions belong only to the consciousness of one who lives in time, whose existence is a "becoming," and who must conceive of time as an equable succession of moments backwards and forwards from the single point wherein he happens to be.† These distinctions, accordingly, do not exist in the consciousness of a Being raised far above temporal limitations.

<small>Time as a limit of man's knowledge.</small>

---

* In a more real sense we may say, for instance, concerning the natural course of human life, that the period of its waxing is future, that of its waning past, and its full completeness present.

† We can no more attribute two dimensions to time than we can to a straight line which is length without breadth.

But does the same hold good of the more general idea of time as a succession of moments? Criticism so regards it, and makes time merely the subjective form of human imagination, without any reality of its own. But he who assumes this standing-point of Criticism must not conceal from himself the fact that he will have logically to admit a great deal more. He must admit that every free decision of the will passes by a *salto mortale* into the region of the ideal. He must also grant that we can know nothing either of our own nature or of the nature of things, to say nothing of God's; because we cannot conceive of ourselves nor of anything external to us without the things conceived of being, alas! transmuted into a form from which it is utterly impossible to decide what they really are as "things in themselves." And yet so long as those who assume this standing point retain a practical faith in the objective existence of God,—*i.e.*, so long as the Kantian standing point has not been left for that of Fichte, will they not feel obliged to assume that God, in so far as we attribute to Him a perfect discernment of the human mind in its intellectual activity, and therefore, a perfect discernment of that form of man's thought, in virtue of which every thing is temporal, must recognize herein, as in a mirror, the sum of human action as a succession in time?

Time a part of God's knowledge.

Time, on the contrary, is not merely the subjective condition of our perception and experience, but *the objective form of conditioned existence* as such. If, therefore, succession of moments in time be something real, it is easy to see what the inference must be from the assertion that time does not exist in the divine knowledge, *i.e.*, is not an object of divine perception. It means nothing less than this, that God does not know the world as it really is.

Are we to be shocked at such an inference? May it not be the very perfection of divine knowledge that it recognizes the world merely in its universal ideal, and *sub ratione eternitatis?* If so, the conceptions of genus and species, and all those metaphysical and general notions which are independent of time, would, indeed, be contained in the divine understanding; but this understanding would have no relation whatever to individual reality, which

If not, God knows not the world.

CHAP. II.] RELATION OF FREEDOM TO DIVINE OMNISCIENCE. 209

cannot exist—which cannot even be conceived of—apart from time. Whatever the reality of finite being, as a world complete in itself, may add to these general conceptions, the divine knowledge would have nothing but these conceptions for its object matter. It is thus evident that God would be raised far above the knowledge of objects distinct from Himself, and that He would know the world only inasmuch as He knows Himself; nay, that His knowledge of the world, and His self-consciousness would be one and the same.

But it would certainly follow that if the reality of the world did not exist in the divine cognition, it could not exist by means of the divine will. But if the actual existence of the world in time and space cannot be derived from a creative act of God, whence can it have had its origin? This view, as it rejects any approach to dualism, has hardly any alternative but to explain the temporal reality of things as a mere phenomenon of finite consciousness, *i.e.*, to resort essentially to the Kantian standing point, in contradiction to its presupposition that time is something real. But if the principle that God views things only as existing beyond the range of time, be seriously maintained, this so-called phenomenon becomes a mere phantom. For things are really what God knows them to be, and human representations, so far as they differ from divine perceptions, are nothing but deceptions.

<small>Neither created the world.</small>

It would not alter the case, further, were we to adopt the idea of *a fall from the ideal* as the source of this lower region of temporal existence. For if this fall and its consequences be unknown to God, if God still recognizes only the unfallen ideal, this fall itself is a mere phantom, and so far from helping to explain anything, is itself, and as a datum of consciousness, utterly inexplicable.

More correct by far is it to say that God has willed those ideas, which together constitute the ideal world of the divine understanding, as *principles of development for an actual world in time and space;* and that there are such ideas in the divine understanding only so far as God eternally wills the existence of a world.

These ideas are principles of actual development in a *teleological* sense, and not as effective causes; for they contain

the *goals* and ends of all those developments; and thei
beginnings in our present existence, disturbed a
Relation of
divine ideas it is by a fall before time began, are far removec
to temporal from their final completeness. But if this world o
development.
time and space exists by the creative will of God
it must be objectively present to the divine mind. As God'
knowledge, moreover, is in itself eternal, it does not exclud
the recognition of succession in time as a mode of existence
On the contrary, it includes and penetrates it, without bein
in any way limited by it.* As space itself, together witl
everything existing in space, is included in the divine con
sciousness, so is time itself, as well as everything developed i
time, in like manner included. What is past to us does no
pass away from Him, and what is future to us is not yet t
come to Him. He sees every event in its proper place in th
order of time, in its close connection with what has precedec
it and what follows; separate from which it would no longe
be what it is, but something wholly different and indefinite.†

Supposing, now, that God's knowledge of man's action
Eternal makes them necessary, when otherwise they woul
knowledge be free, does not this apply to God's *eterna*
tantamount
to foreknow- knowledge of them, as a complete whole, quite a
ledge. much as to God's *fore*knowledge of what is futur

* VATKE argues differently, thus (p. 479) :—"The knowledge of whateve
exists within the limits of time "—and this knowledge Vatke also attributes t
God—"is a knowledge of what is limited, and therefore a limited knowledge.
The "therefore" here Vatke certainly has not learned from his master, wh
more correctly maintains that "he alone can know a limit to be such who is i
some sense already beyond and above it." This inference, however, is of a piec
with the clumsily deceptive argument that "the thinking and knowledge
evil of itself constitutes an evil thought and knowledge." As Vatke by h
principles could only lead us to such abysses as are exhibited in this doctrin
of God's limited knowledge, and of a divine will (as described in the pag
following), which reacts against the divine will of holiness and freedom
he should, at least, have given attention to the views of another, so as n
to misrepresent them as he does, p. 475–477.

† Here BRUCH is by no means consistent, but hesitates between tw
extremes. At p. 162 he says, "The world"—which he immediately befor
describes as "essentially distinct from God"—"is not external to the divin
consciousness, but is altogether included therein." At p. 165, on the contrary
it is said to be "an unsolvable problem how an absolute being can co-exis
with a conditioned or finite being." The problem is certainly unsolvable
when conditioned being is first posited, and the question then asked, how a
absolute being can exist *side by side with it*.

in relation to us,—a foreknowledge which, when this future was realized, would be only a perception of what is present, and when it was past, would be a remembrance? If God's eternal knowledge does not negative the order of time and the succession of events, but embraces the whole together, His knowledge of any event is not only present when it occurs, but in every previous moment on which we may fix our thought. And thus God's *eternal* knowledge really includes what is to us *fore*knowledge.* Are we to regard this relation of any event to the divine knowledge before it occurs as an arbitrary representation? The gift of prophecy, wrought by divine enlightenment in the spirit of man, reminds us that it is not so. But the main point is that it is utterly absurd to look upon God's *eternal* consciousness as a *minus* in relation to a consciousness measured by time.† If *fore*knowledge have the power of necessitating the conduct to which it relates, *eternal* knowledge must possess the same power still *more perfectly.*

Thus it is evident that human freedom cannot be saved by the expedient of regarding God's knowledge as eternal and raised far above the limits of time. Many have certainly imagined that by this the knotty difficulty was solved, because they thus removed the question into a sphere which to us is dark, and where they fancied they escaped from determinate and accurate thinking, and where, therefore, the question no more troubled them. The author of this distinction in Christian theology saw further than many of his modern followers, and therefore

* AUGUSTINE accordingly, notwithstanding his recognition of the supra-temporal character of God's knowledge, is wont, in his later writings, just as in his earlier, to speak unhesitatingly of a PRAE*scientia Dei.*

† Thus STRAUSS (*Chr. Glaubensl.*, § 37, vol. i. p. 570) thinks that "in passing from the idea of a temporal to that of an eternal divine knowledge, this supposed prevision of an action is no more dangerous to freedom than is the perception on God's part of a present act." He should rather have said that, in such a transition, the supposed perception on God's part of an act becomes just as dangerous to freedom as His foreknowledge of it. BOETHIUS likewise regards the absolute present of God's knowledge as a *minus* in comparison with His *pre*science—pr. 6; "*Num quae praesentia cernis, aliquam eis necessitatem tuus addit intuitus? Minims. Atqui—uti vos vestro hoc temporaris praesenti quaedam videtis, ita ille (Deus) omnia suo cernit aeterno.*" It is also overlooked here that our perception of any event taking place before our eyes, strictly speaking, *follows* the event, though only by the thousandth part of a second. Can we say this of God's eternal knowledge?

made no use of it as a means of harmonizing human freedom with the omniscience of God.

This view of the divine knowledge as eternal, serves as an answer to the objections of the Socinians against the possibility of God's unerringly foreknowing our free acts. Joh. Crell, for example, argues as follows :—"Contingent events as future, are still undetermined; God therefore by virtue of the truth of His knowledge, can only know them as *indeterminata et in utramque adhuc partem flexibilia.*"[*] The fallacy of this reasoning appears when we remember that God's knowledge, being eternal, is beyond the bounds of time and cannot be limited to what precedes the free act; on the contrary, it necessarily transcends and includes the act or decision itself. More accurately considered, however, it is evident that in this respect, the distinction between eternal knowledge and foreknowledge in time, does not really affect the question before us. If the Socinian objection recognizes a divine foreknowledge of the future, of the undetermined as undetermined, and the determined as determined, it is surely a merely arbitrary proceeding to refer the divine foreknowledge to those points only wherein the will has still to decide. Why should it not also be referred to those moments when the will has decided? If both stages, that of indecision and that of decision, be the objects of the divine foreknowledge, that foreknowledge recognizes the human will in its transition from the one to the other by self-determination, *i.e.*, recognizes the will *in its freedom*.

God foreknows man's will as free. According to the views of Socinian theologians, as above explained, we find the following formula in their writings :—"God knows man's free action to be free." As they adopt this, its meaning is, God does not foreknow man's free act in its determinate contents. The same formula, however, is used by others in a sense conformable with God''s foreknowledge, and yet, according to the

---

* See the quotations from CRELL's treatise, *De Deo ejusque attributis*, in BAUMGARTEN's "*Untersuchung Theol. Streitigkeiten*," vol. i. pp. 94, 95. Socinus himself argued similarly in his *Praelectiones Theol.*, especially in c. 8, *De Dei praenotione seu praescientia* (*Bibliotheca Fratrum Polon.* tom. i. p. 45), with which we may compare the conclusions arrived at in the preceding chapter concerning the relation of God's *will*, (or as Socinus calls it, *desiderium Dei*) to the future decisions of man, (p. 543, 544).

precedent of Augustine,* as a means of escaping the difficulty concerning human freedom. They have argued from it that the divine foreknowledge, so far from destroying human freedom, is the surest guarantee of it.

We perfectly agree with this proposition, and consider that Anselm of Canterbury was right when he referred to it, as showing that God not only foreknows that a man will sin or will not sin in any given case, but also that he will do so or not without being necessitated thereto.† But though human freedom be really implied in this formula, as we by no means question it is in Augustine's explanation of it in his treatise on freewill, the problem is not solved, but simply stated. For this is the very point in question, Can God with unerring certainty foresee the free acts of his creatures? Can He know them eternally without thus making them necessary? They who (like the Socinians) deny this, will simply explain the formula, "God knows what is free beforehand with unerring certainty," as a *contradictio in adjecto*. Sometimes, however, the expression "what is free" is taken in another sense, when the formula "God wills the free as free" is adopted, in order to reconcile human freedom with God's will, as the sole conditioning cause of what is done. Thus Anselm does in the treatise quoted, quaest. ii. cap. 3, entitled "*Praedestinatio cum libertate conciliatur eodem modo quo praescientia;*" and in like manner, Schleiermacher, in his "*Glaubenslehre,*" § 55, compared with § 49. The two propositions "God wills the free as free," and "God knows the free as free," are used by Schleiermacher in the same sense, namely, that the divine causality, which is all determining and simple in itself, brings about its effects in the sphere of intelligent beings in such a way that these beings are conscious of them as self-determinations. This is a freedom which

<small>*This guarantees man's freedom.</small>

---

* *Dei libero arbitrio*, lib. iii. c. 3, 4; so also virtually *De civitate Dei*, lib v. c. 10, § 2, though in a different way, as is evident from c. 9. Here man's freedom of will is regarded as part of the *ordo causarum*, which is the subject matter of God's knowledge, and the causality of freewill is secured by means of this divine knowledge. But this causality is no more than other finite causes, determinate workings are implied in it, which proceed from it with unvarying necessity.

† *De concordia prescientiae et praedestinationis nec non gratiae Dei cum libero arbitrio*, quaest. i. cap. i., (p. 183 of Gerberon's edition).

possesses reality in relation to other finite causes, but which has none in its relation to God.

We must once more go back to the primary conception of the *divine knowledge*, in order to find the true solution of the problem.

We have already referred to the opinion which considers it prejudicial to the absoluteness of God to attribute to Him *objective knowledge*. They who maintain this, are not satisfied by the statement that the object matter of God's knowledge is not anything independent of Him and co-existing with Him,—if it were, it would certainly exercise an influence upon Him which He has not ordained,—but that God has by an act of His creative will, made this object for Himself, so that His knowledge of it is at the same time His knowledge of his own power, thus to make another being. It is still maintained, that it violates the idea of the Absolute, to attribute to God the consciousness of any Being other than Himself, if as some say, that being be what God himself is not, or as others say, it be not wholly determined by Him in every respect wherein He knows it. According to this, it is not allowable to make any distinction between God's *knowledge* and *will*, His cognition and volition must be commensurate. His thinking and knowledge in this case are in themselves creative, and are therefore one with his will. In so far as God thinks anything, he ordains it to be, not as something distinct from Himself, but as an element of His self-realization in the finite, or as an immanent effect of his absolute causality.

§ 3. GOD'S OBJECTIVE KNOWLEDGE. If denied,

confounds His knowledge with His will,

This view, moreover, can make no distinction in the doctrine of Election between foreknowledge and predestination (*praescientia, praedestinatio*). If it adopt any doctrine at all upon the subject, it must either assent to the Supra-lapsarian theory in its rudest form, as Calvin, Beza, and others advocated it, or resort to Schleiermacher's view which modifies this doctrine by joining to it hypothetically the ἀποκατάστασις πάντων. Augustine shows a profound recognition of the requirements of Christian theism, by not suffering his strict theory of predestination to beguile

and with predestination.

Augustine's distinctions.

him into making it co-extensive with prescience. According to him, the sphere of foreknowledge is wider and more general than that of predestination. Predestination, he maintains, has to do only with what God Himself wills to accomplish, but foreknowledge refers also to what God does not will himself to do.* In keeping with this, Augustine does not reject the idea of a *permissive* will on God's part, he regards it as standing in precisely the same relation to God's *effective* will as prescience does to predestination.†

What then is the real import of the formula that we can attribute to God no knowledge save what is identical with His will, that His will and His knowledge are identical ? It means that, strictly speaking, neither will nor knowledge can be predicated of God ; as Spinoza in his matter of fact way expresses it, " if *intellectus* and *voluntas* belonged to God, they would have nothing in common with man's *intellectus* and *voluntas* save the name,—*non aliter scilicet quam inter se conveniunt canis signum coeleste, et canis, animal latrans.*‡ For the distinction of knowledge from volition is the fundamental element of our idea of knowledge, and if we destroy this distinction, we virtually destroy not only part, but the whole of our idea of knowledge, and cannot speak with any propriety of *divine knowledge*. But the very question we are considering is, how human freedom is to be reconciled with God's omniscience, and such a question can be propounded only upon the supposition that there is such a thing as divine omniscience. He who does not attribute knowledge to God, cannot entertain the proposed problem at all.

If God then be an intelligent and knowing Being, *wherein does his knowledge differ from His will ?*

Difference between God's knowledge and will. Every real volition is a real determining of one's self; it is a conscious causation, the outgo of an *Ego* from its self-contained state of rest in order to posit something actual, either internally or externally. A mere movement of desire which can produce nothing may be called a wish, but it is not a volition. We have already (in the preceding chapter) seen that such a wishing cannot in any true sense be attributed to God.

* *De praedest. Sanctorum*, 19, (x). *De Dono perseverantiae*, 46, 47, (xvii., xviii).
† See *e.g.*, *Enchiridion*, 95, 96. ‡ *Ethic.* i. prop. 17, schol.

But does the same law hold good concerning God's thinking and knowing? To answer this question we must more closely examine a distinction already referred to. It is by an act of His loving will that God eternally begets in thought the idea of the world. But He wills it not only as a thought inherent in Himself, but as something which must actually exist, which must attain the highest reality of which derived being is capable; and the willing of this is necessarily involved in the willing of the general idea of the world as a thought in God. But in so far as God gives to the world an objective existence, there arises another kind of divine knowledge of the world, viz., an *objective knowledge* of it;—there arises, we say, for it follows as a logical sequence, and not in any order of time: for God eternally beholds the world as actually existing, though the world itself is not eternal. This second form of divine knowledge of the world is contingent upon God's will; it is objective, because by creating the world He gave to it objectiveness, and placed it (so to speak) over against Himself.

Here we see more plainly the truth which we had to assume in distinguishing between the creation and the sustaining of the world (vol. i., p. 224), namely, that the world had a *beginning*, though the idea of the world is *eternally* in the divine mind. If we allow that the world obtains an objective existence immediately upon the divine thought of it, according to the maxim, "He thinks and it is done," then this objective existence, though temporal, must be regarded as beginningless. The eternity of the *idea* of the world in God would necessarily involve the eternal *existence* of the world; and so far as the idea in God's mind was realized in time, its eternity would assume the form of limitless duration, if, that is, we cannot allow the world's existence to be the result of a positive *act* on God's part, contingent upon His will, which assigns to it certain limitations. The relation of the world to God would thus be, not that of created dependence, but of necessary sequence arising from the very idea of it in God, and the act of God's will as distinct from His thought would be excluded. But if we consider it, we must see that the world could never have come into existence without such an act of will; it would only have been an unreal reflection of the divine thought, a shadow of the

<small>Creation a positive act of will.</small>

idea cast upon nothing—alike undefined and unreal. The real principle of the world would in this case be not God's will, but that inexplicable deception whereby Absolute Being is supposed to represent itself as something divided and relative;—how, it would be impossible to say, for our apprehension of it would have existence only in and through that deception. If we are to assign to the world a real and substantial existence in time, it must have a definite beginning, and this beginning must have been an act of the *divine will,* of that creative principle in God which has the marvellous power of producing another being.

This creative will of God is certainly eternal, but it wills that its object, the world, shall have a determinate beginning; in other words, that the world and time—for apart from the world as thus created there is no idea of time—shall be limited *a parte ante.** This is no more contradictory than the doctrine which St Paul teaches, that God's plan of Redemption was eternal, while the accomplishment of this plan did not take place till the fulness of time.

Now, in so far as God wills the objective existence of the world, the idea of it existing in His mind is the goal which the world's development ever aims at, and endeavours to realize. This ideal thus becomes a stimulus to the word's development, and explains all the elements and stages of its growth, of which it is the absolute end, however these minor stages may seem to have their end in themselves. God's will being complete and undivided in this ideal, it is our guarantee that the goal will be reached, that the world in its reality will be perfectly co-ordinate with the divine ideal, and that God's kingdom in its completeness shall be realized. Thus the view developed in this work is essentially different from that of Strauss and of many others in the present day. They hold

<small>God's idea of the world the goal of its development</small>

---

* ROMANG, who can recognize freedom as little in God as in man, thinks otherwise on this point. Thus in his *System der natürlichen Religionslehre,* p. 330, he says :—" God's will is ever instantly efficient, and God's thinking is instantly productive, the moment the thought becomes willed; " and therefore it must be eternally so, for Romang regards this divine volition or thinking as itself eternal; and at p. 329, he expressly calls creation an eternal act. We cannot help wondering how (at p. 331) he can, notwithstanding, suppose that the world must have a beginning, a moment of birth simultaneously with time.

that the perfect realization of the world-ideal must be regarded not as a given requirement of philosophy, but merely as a hope or promise of religion. We cannot consider a state of things wherein the divine ideal is partly realized and partly contradicted—a state of things out of which the ideal must gather its *disjecta membra* so as to form itself completely—as in any true sense a realization of the ideal. This realization only takes place when the reality of things comes to correspond purely, affirmatively, and perfectly with the ideal. If, indeed, we look for the realization of the divine ideal in this temporal state merely, it cannot but appear a self-supplanting realization: yet it is not fair to blame Christianity, for that very element whereby it avoids this contradiction, namely, for its eschatology, and the stress it every where lays upon the consummation of all things. This realization of the divine ideal of the world in the kingdom of God may, as far as we are concerned, be still in the distant future and be only the object of hope, and we are not therefore in a position to explain all its elements; but it is ever present to the all-compassing omniscience of God. God's knowledge of the ideal, immanent in Himself, is by no means one and the same with His knowledge of it when realized by the agency of other beings; for the objective realization of the divine ideal, though it cannot enhance the absolute being of God, must be regarded as a progress to something else and to a plurality of things, when compared with the ideal itself as immanent in the divine thoughts.

To say that such a knowledge of something other than Himself which He is not, cannot be attributed to God, because this is conceivable only in the case of a finite Being,* would be really to make the divine consciousness (so far as any mention can be made of consciousness in Him) utterly pantheistic; and then the banishment of Theism wholly from the sphere of

---

* STRAUSS, *Chr. Glaubensl.*, § 37, (vol. i. p. 567), when he adduces the statement of AQUINAS, *Deus alia a se intelligit intelligendo essentiam suam*, yet without concealing the fact that this is qualified in the *Summa* by other statements. It must be allowed that Aquinas vacillates somewhat here: but when BAUR (*Die Christl. Lehre von der Dreieinigkeit*, vol. ii. 655), endeavours to reduce the teaching of Aquinas concerning God, and that of the older Lutheran divines (vol. iii. 341), to the idea of substance or mere substantial existence the thought is so exaggerated that it gives way of itself. It is, however, true that neither Aquinas nor the older Protestant theologians had a thoroughly

modern thought and culture would follow as a matter of course ; seeing that the divine consciousness is looked to as the measure of all truth. Strauss's assertion rests upon that quantitative and extended idea of the Infinite, which, when once adopted, becomes a sword to sever at a stroke the Gordian knots of all problems concerning the relation between God and the world.

<small>God's objective knowledge is not causative.</small> God's knowledge of the world as something objective to Himself, while dependent on His world-creating will, is nevertheless *distinct from* that will, though only in a formal manner. What God's will appoints as an existence distinct from His own being, eternally appears in His consciousness, and forms a part of His knowledge. What He wills to be objective to Him, is regarded by his knowledge as objective, and so far His knowledge has not the least determining influence upon its object matter, but like a mirror, clearly reflects it in its real existence, and as it really is in its minutest details and slightest movements. What is usually called accuracy of perception, or the perfect coincidence and harmony of the representation in the mind with its object, may appropriately be predicated of God's knowledge. But as the perfection of knowledge consists in its perfect correspondence with the object matter presented to it, it is altogether free from any impulse to make its object matter conformable with itself. To the question, therefore, whether God's knowledge of the world, as objective to Himself, does not necessarily imply the creation and moulding of that object, we must give a negative reply. God's knowledge is distinct from His will, for this very reason, that it is not causative in relation to its object matter.

<small>This applied to the decisions of man's will.</small> Now what is true of conditioned Being generally, must especially be true of the human will and its decisions. The fact that the divine knowledge either in the order of time or eternally precedes its object matter, the fact that God knows the self-

<small>clear perception of the divine personality, notwithstanding their maintenance of the doctrine of the Trinity. [In like manner Professor MANSEL quotes Aquinas (*Summa*, p. i. qu. xiii. art. 1), to sanction his theory of regulative morality, and of the unknowableness of God. Though in his notes, Mr Mansel refers to this part of Müller's work, he quite ignores its arguments, and despatches the question of divine foreknowledge with the statement, "The whole meaning of the difficulty vanishes as soon as we acknowledge that the Infinite is not an object of human thought at all."—*Bampton Lectures*, lect. vii.—*Tr.*]</small>

decisions of the human will without waiting for their realization in time, cannot possibly exert any determining power upon those decisions, which it does not possess when viewed simply as knowledge of something objective. The will, whose decisions are all included in God's eternal knowledge, does no choose its decisions, because God knows them; God knows them because they are chosen by the will. Origen affirms this long ago in a passage preserved to us by Eusebius,* χρὴ λέγειν οὐ τὴν πρόγνωσιν αἰτίαν γιηομένων, . . . ἀλλὰ . . . τὸ ἐσόμενοι αἴτιον τοῦ τοιάνδε εἶναι τὴν περὶ αὐτοῦ πρόγνωσιν. In the same way Leibnitz argues that the occurrence in the future of what is contingent now, does not become an absolute necessity through God's unerring foreknowledge of it; † it must be granted however, that the system of Leibnitz cannot hinder the intrusion of this absolute necessity in other ways.‡ Who would ever think of making an unerring prophesy the cause of the event to which it points? Was any necessity laid on Peter to deny his Lord, or on Judas to betray Him, by the fact that Christ, as an unerring prophet, foreknew and foretold that they would do so? If so, Peter might well have spared his tears and Judas his remorse, on account of the sin committed. The true statement of the matter is that Christ foretold these things because he foresaw the fact that Peter and Judas, of their own free and unbiassed will, would betray and deny Him.

It is in this department alone, in relation to the wills of created beings, that the difference between the divine knowledge and Will appears in its true reality and force. As nature, in itself considered, is not possessed of will, nothing in it can be the object of God's foreknowledge, save what is ordained by his will perfectly conscious of its activity and of its design; and hence God's foreknowledge, though even in nature it is not causative, yet includes nothing which does not already exist in His producing will. But in relation to the

* *Praepar. Evang.* lib. vi. 14. We find similar statements made by other theologians,—see Petavius c. 7.

† *Theodicée*, § 36, 37. The theologians of the Wolfian school adopt these conclusions; see *e.g.*, BAUMGARTEN, *Glaubenslehre*, i. 296.

‡ This is strikingly illustrated in the manner in which Baumgarten, following Leibnitz, explains the inner possibility of such unerring prescience on God's part, viz., from His perfect insight of the causes sufficiently adequate to bring about the result foretold. See as before, pp. 90, 98.

decisions of will in the case of created beings, God's will is not determining, because He wills that it shall not be so ; in this department it limits itself to a command, and thus establishes the possibility of a decision opposed to it,—not, indeed, in order that such a possibility may be realized, but that it may be rejected. If, nevertheless, it be realized, there ensues a realization, either in thought or act, hostile to, and contradicting the will of God, yet none the less really present to His omniscience.

God's knowledge and will finally one. While, however, the divine will thus ordains in the freedom of the creature's will the possibility of this contradiction, it must be remembered that in virtue of His all embracing knowledge, God eternally beholds all opposition to His will as wholly overcome in the final goal of the world's development. Volition and knowledge are thus separate from each other in God, in relation only to the temporal development of created personality, and to that extra-temporal self-determining which forms the basis of its development. In principle and in the issue, this separation between knowledge and will is eternally resolved into a higher unity.

Distinction between necessity and certainty. Limborch* and Baumgarten† have already pointed out one important source of perplexity in the decision of this question, concerning the compatibility of human freedom with divine foreknowledge. In popular language, there is great confusion between two different antitheses, *certain* and *uncertain* being usually taken as identical with *necessary* and *contingent*. Limborch rightly attributes this confusion to the fact that, as far as we are concerned in the future, the necessary alone is certain, and he points out with great clearness and simplicity the true distinction between certainty and necessity.‡ Strictly speaking, it is possible that an act may occur otherwise than God

* *Theologia Christiana*, lib. ii. c. 8, § 21.
† *Unters. theol. Streitigkeiten* i. 99.
‡ *Ibid.* § 19, 20. As the distinction is important, I quote in full the principal passage. *Distinguendum est inter affectiones rei absolutas et respectivas. Absolutae sunt, quae rei in sese et in natura sua spectatae tribuuntur. Tales sunt necessitas et contingentia ; res enim in se et natura sua spectata vel est* NECESSARIA *vel* CONTINGENS, *id est, ejusmodi habet essentiam, quae vel potest non existere vel non potest non existere. Respectivae vero, quae rei non tribuuntur in se et natura*

has eternally foreknown it, but it certainly will not be otherwise; for were it otherwise, God would have known that it would be so.

If, indeed, God makes known to any human mind his <small>Hypothetic knowledge of any act, it is quite natural that the necessity.</small> person to whom it was revealed should regard it as necessary; not because of any supposed alteration in the manner in which the act would be brought about, but because he knows that God is omniscient, and that human acts cannot be foreseen by Him save as they really are. This justifies him in the conclusion that man's act must be as God knows them. Hence the forms of expression ἵνα πληρωθῇ, δεῖ πληρωθῆναι, and others of the same kind frequently occurring in the New Testament, especially in the Gospels. If any necessity be implied in them, it is only hypothetically; a hypothetical necessity, which differs from one unconditional, in that it is not causative; and, therefore, the freedom of the act is in no degree infringed. *Hypothetice necessarium est contingens.**

"But we by no means affirm"—many will reply—"that <small>God's Foreknowledge as the *sign*, not the *cause* of necessity.</small> God's foreknowledge, exercises any causative influence upon human conduct so as to make it necessary. We hold that the necessity of what God unerringly foreknows, follows from the fact that nothing can with perfect certainty be known which does not necessarily follow from its causes." This argument brings us back to that Socinian notion of the divine omniscience in its relation to the free acts of men, which we rejected at the outset of this investigation.† If such a view were maintained

<small>*sua consideratae, sed cum respectu et denominatione ad alterum.* Tales sunt CERTITUDO *et* INCERTITUDO, *quae semper includunt respectum ad alterum, qui de re aliqua certus vel incertus est.* [See Archb. WHATELEY's Essays on Difficulties in St Paul's Writings, essay iii. § 4.—*Tr.*]

* Concerning the distinction drawn by the metaphysical school of Leibnitz and Wolf, between *necessitas absoluta* and *hypothetica*, and the application of this distinction to the question before us, see BILFINGER, *Dilucidationes Philosoph. de Deo, anima humana, mundo*, §§ 47, 48, 52, 53, and his treatise *De origine et permissione mali*, §§ 164, 165, 180, 181.

† ROTHE seems strangely to misunderstand the above'statement, when in his <small>Rothe's objections.</small> *Ethics*, i. 119, he applauds the candour with which I renounce the claim of having refuted the argument here urged. The above words refer only to what I stated at the beginning of the chapter, viz., that the inadmissibility of the Socinian limitation of the divine knowledge must be presupposed in our inquiry; and having said this, the few remarks I have added seemed to me a sufficient reply. I did not intend any "presum-</small>

CHAP. II.] RELATION OF FREEDOM TO DIVINE OMNISCIENCE. 223

the question would be, Is God's knowledge of the free acts of
man merely like ours coincident with their occurrence in time,

tuous and disdainful ignoring" of those theologians whom in their place I
esteem as highly as does my honoured friend, but I looked upon the Socinian
argument as one no longer defended in our day. As, however, such a theologian
as Rothe again espouses it, I will not lay myself open to the charge of not
stating the reasons why it must be rejected.

In his Ethics (i. 118–120), ROTHE does not hesitate to attribute to God's
unerring prescience a necessitating influence upon its object
His theory. matter, and he urges against such a prescience of human acts that
it would make God the author of sin. In order to avoid this and
other logical consequences, Rothe maintains that God's foreknowledge, which
(according to him) is identical with his fore-ordained and eternal world scheme,
is nothing more than an eternal vision of the abstract plan—"a formula made up
of indefinite quantities"—designed for the entire course of the world's deve‑
lopment; but that the concrete realization of this abstract plan is left to the
free play of personal and individual action, and is for this very reason not fore‑
known by

Against this separation of an abstract divine knowledge from its concrete
realization, we shall not urge the consideration that a very
Involves the imperfect and limited kind of knowledge is thus attributed to
denial of
guilt. God ; for Rothe would meet us with the Socinian reply that
what is concrete does not at all belong to the possible objects of
knowledge viewed as *fore*knowledge. But granting that the destruction of
human freedom in the case of sin is thus avoided, is the cancelling of guilt
really avoided thereby? Rothe allows that God's plan of salvation is eternal ;
nay, more, that there is on God's part an eternal predestination of certain
individuals, as "indefinite quantities," to the blessings of salvation, vol. ii.
pp. 254, 256. Accordingly, it must be unerringly foreknown of God that sin
would be committed ; and this, according to Rothe's theory—seeing that there
can be sin only where there is will and personality—must be tantamount to a
predestination of certain individuals as persons of whom sin may be predicated.
Not only so, but the human race collectively must be foreknown as the
realizers of this abnormal development. It is to be regretted that Rothe has
not seen fit to show how he explains the manifold contradictions which
variously arise from his own view. In vol. ii. 215, 219, he regards sin as
wholly removed from the range of the divine causation, yet here he clearly
teaches God's predestination of the race to sin as that element in the process
of development which is to be removed, and thus the actual introduction of
evil, as well as its conquest, are attributed to the divine government. And
this, in turn, is a great stumbling-block on Rothe's principles, because he says
expressly (vol. ii. 216), "the individual man and personal being generally
having once unavoidably passed into a sinful state may for ever be entangled
therein," nay, in innumerable cases (see pp. 243-5, 325-7, 322-5) actually are
thus for ever entangled. Indeed, this divine foreknowledge, that the human
race collectively must pass through a state of sin, clearly implies that each
individual must, according to this foreknowledge (=predetermination), have
some participation in sin. But if this be so, sin cannot have its basis in man's
free self-determination, nor be imputed to him as guilt. While,
And of sin. therefore, Rothe may venture to say (p. 230). "No one, least of
all a Christian, condemns himself for ever having had some degree of sin in

224   THE POSSIBILITY OF SIN.   [BOOK III. PART II.

or, more accurately, is it a perception on His part really though momentarily subsequent thereto, and therefore an actual

him," he has on his principles no right to add, "but we do condemn ourselves that we have in us so many and so great sins, far more and far greater than we need have." According to his premisses, Rothe cannot evade the conclusion that sin, so far as it appears as the general destiny of humanity, is an inevitable evil, and that the participation in sin, which (to take the average) is found even in the better sort of men, arises from a necessity in the divine world-plan. This tallies with the reconciliation suggested by VATKE and referred to in vol. i. pp. 392, 397, between the universality of sin and self-imputation in conscience, which violates our moral consciousness as clearly as it contradicts the fundamental truths of Christianity (see below, pp. 250, 251). Rothe indeed attributes to the better class of man a deeper contrition on account of sin, and we allow that this is justified by the earnestness of the moral consciousness as therein evinced. But we cannot attach the least objective weight to this, so long as it is not shown how God's foreknowledge, which, on Rothe's principles, is tantamount to his fore-determination, can necessitate sin in the abstract, without necessitating its concrete realization. Rothe, moreover, gives us no explanation concerning prophecies of those future events which are conditional upon the free acts of men ; *e.g.*, Christ' distinct prophecy concerning His betrayal by Judas, and concerning Peter's threefold denial of Him (Matt. xxvi. 23-25, 34). On Rothe's principles, these free acts could not be the subjects of any certain knowledge whatever while they were still future ; and if they were certainly foreknown and foretold, they were not really free, but must have been necessary (see his *Ethics*, i. 119).

If, on the other hand, we endeavour to maintain the idea of God in its purity, and according to its metaphysical conditions, does Rothe seriously maintain the notion of a progressive increase in the divine knowledge, conditional upon the decisions of the human will ? Nay, more, if man himself has some foreknowledge of the free decisions of his fellow-men, though not an unerring one, are we to regard the divine knowledge as in this respect more limited even than man's ? It must clearly be so, if the future, so far as it is contingent upon human freedom, be perfectly hidden from God. If Rothe shrinks from this assertion, there is nothing for him on his principles but to attribute to God a prescience of our free decisions in the imperfect form of erring probability,—a foreboding and conjecturing which, after all, may err and be deceived !

It also violates our idea of God.

Rothe imagines that God's foreknowledge can only be regarded as "thought" in the narrow and stricter sense of that word, and this thought can only have for its object matter what is necessary (i. 119). Yet he recognizes in God another kind of knowledge, whose object matter is "the free play of created causes," p. 124, and whose clearness and certainty is in no way impaired by this freedom : this kind of knowledge stands in a somewhat similar contrast to God's necessary thought as our empirical knowledge does. But he has still to recognize God's *foreknowledge* of the free acts of man ; to acknowledge that God's knowledge is raised far above the limits which bound our knowledge of what is knowable only by experience. Thus the inquiry must inevitably be involved in a circle, if, to begin with, that be laid down as an axiom which we require our opponents first of all to prove, viz., that the *certainty* of a future event in the divine intelligence essentially involves a *necessity* in the manner of its accomplishment.

transition from ignorance to knowledge? Or is it a knowledge far above and independent of these limits, and free from any such transition? To what we have already said concerning the divine knowledge, we shall simply add the following: Man, by an act of contemplation, knows only events actually before him in time; he may know a future event (if not divinely revealed to him, or, at least, divined by an extraordinary natural power of divination possessed by few), only by *a calculation of preceding causes*. But as an action formally free does not result by any necessity from its antecedents, an unerring prognostication of it is impossible to man; for nothing future can, strictly speaking, be the object of man's certain knowledge. If it be held that God can know a future event as certain only by such a calculation of causes, it must be allowed that He cannot with certainty foreknow any free act of man; for His foreknowledge would be a proof that the act in question was the necessary consequence of certain causes, and not in itself free. If, on the contrary, the divine knowledge be regarded as *intuitive*, we see at once that it stands in the same immediate relation to the act itself as to its antecedents; and thus the difficulty is removed.

Thus we see how important, in connection with this question, is the recognition of the truth that God's knowledge is essentially supra-temporal,—eternal. It is not that the eternity of God's knowledge could deprive it of a determining power supposed to pertain to foreknowledge as such; but because this characteristic of it as eternal, enables us to understand the inner possibility of an all-embracing, all-seeing knowledge.

<small>God's knowledge non-temporal.</small>

BOOK IV.

THE SPREAD OF SIN.

INTRODUCTION.

WE first of all considered SIN IN ITS REALITY, recognized its true NATURE in its inner principle, and directed our attention to the GUILT which attaches to it. Having shown, in the second place, that the VARIOUS THEORIES propounded in explanation of sin are inadequate, we found that the basis of its possibility lay in the FREEDOM of the creature. If, thirdly, we have successfully proved that this freedom in its formal sense necessarily involves the possibility of evil side by side with decision for the good and true, and that this possibility is not incompatible with God's knowledge of the world, and His ever-present and almighty working therein; then, so far as the conception of sin in its origin admits of explanation, the phenomenon of sin has been explained.

Sin, wherever it exists, is a profound discord, and a serious perversion of our inner nature; yet if it only appeared occasionally, or here and there among men—some being afflicted with it and others being free—all we should have to do in order to complete our exposition of the doctrine, would be to trace the development of sin in individual life. But seeing, as is evident, that the case is otherwise, seeing that sin must be regarded as the universal characteristic of human life, a new and by no means easy problem presents itself. The kernel of the problem obviously is the idea of ORIGINAL SIN (*peccatum originale*), attaching, according to the teaching of the Church, to all the descendants of Adam, excepting ONE. The designation, *primitive* or *original* sin, admits of various views concerning its origin in those tainted by it; but, as is well known, ever since the church developed her doctrine of the *peccatum originale*, she has taken it as implying a sin transmitted by inheritance from our first parents to all their posterity, and, therefore, it has been denominated BIRTH-SIN. Unbiassed by church teaching, we have now to inquire how far we can adopt this idea conformably with the results of our investigation thus far, with the facts of experience, and with the doctrinal teaching of Holy Scripture.

CHAPTER I.

THE UNIVERSALITY OF SIN AS A MATTER OF EXPERIENCE.

RELIGION in its true import means an unconditional surrender of one's self to God; and all degeneracy, all variance and perverted development in human life, may be reduced to one universal tendency. It is easy to understand, therefore, how a truly religious sentiment will at the outset be disinclined to ascribe anything to man—viewed in his relation to God, and previous to that self-surrender which it feels to be owing to the influences of divine grace—save sin and guilt. Where this religious feeling co-exists with a torpid moral consciousness, negative views are entertained regarding man's natural state; it is looked upon simply as one of weakness, impotence, and emptiness. But where this sentiment co-exists with a moral consciousness, earnest and profound, combined with a keen sense of the contrast between the principles of selfishness and the love of God, man's state by nature will be viewed in a more positive light, as in all its elements glaring opposition and enmity against God.

1. Extent of Human Depravity.

Intellect seems to confirm what feeling suggests; for all that is in any way a dividing asunder between the Infinite and the finite—God and his creatures—is a stumbling-block to the intellect, involving it in serious difficulties, when it would explain the true relation between God's grace and man's powers of will as co-operating in the

Testimony of the intellect.

work of renewal. If the intellect be allowed to carry on its logical sequences without regard to consequences, and to view the volition of man—so far as it is not acted upon by God, and merely as a form for the realization of His will,—as mere nothingness and sin, all is more simple and plain.

And yet if we follow out this gloomy testimony of religious feeling and unbiassed intellect, we are further off than ever from what the true interests of religion demand. True religion seeks a confirmation in human nature of the absolute reality and importance of redemption, and the possibility of its inward appropriation. The consciousness of these truths implies some recognition of man's susceptibility for redemption, as well as of his great need of it. A belief in man's redemption requires the maintenance of both facts, man's susceptibility and man's need; and, therefore, we must reject not only those Pelagian views which maintain man's capability at the expense of his need, but those approximations also to the Manichaean view which vindicate the greatness of man's need at the expense of his capability. The equally firm maintenance of both facts is all the more necessary, because any special preponderance given to the one tends to the prejudice and depreciation of the other, A capability of redemption without the need would be nothing more than a power of self-restoration; denying man's bondage it would contradict the central idea of redemption. The need of redemption, again, apart from any susceptibility for it, would be a need which could not be satisfied, and which, accordingly, could hardly be called a need in the true sense of the word.

Man's capability as well as need of redemption.

The FORMULA CONCORDIAE of the Lutheran Church in its Article *De peccato originis* having stated the Pelagian, Semipelagian, and Synergistic views concerning human depravity, defines more accurately the extent of this depravity in the following words:—*Haec . . . . dogmata . . . . rejiciuntur, quia verbo Domini docemur, quod corrupta natura ex se et suis viribus in rebus spiritualibus et divinis nihil boni et ne minimum quidem, utpote ullas bonas cogitationes, habeat. Neque id modo, sed insuper etiam asserunt, quod natura corrupta ex*

§ 2. DEFINITIONS OF THE *Formula Concordiae.*

se et viribus suis coram Deo nihil aliud nisi peccare possit.* In the Article *De libero arbitrio*, accordingly, man's inability to take any active part in the work of conversion is defined in the following statements :—*Credimus, quod hominis non renati intellectus, cor et voluntas in rebus spiritualibus et divinis ex propriis naturalibus viribus prorsus nihil intelligere, credere, amplecti, cogitare, velle, inchoare, perficere, agere, operari aut cooperari possint: sed homo ad bonum prorsus corruptus et mortuus sit, ita ut in hominis natura post lapsum, ante regenerationem, ne scintillula quidem spiritualium virium reliqua manserit aut restet, quibus ille ex se ad gratiam Dei praeparare se, aut oblatam gratiam apprehendere, aut ejus gratiae (ex sese et per se) capax esse possit, aut se ad gratiam applicare aut accommodare, aut viribus suis propriis aliquid ad conversionem suam vel ex toto vel ex dimidia vel minima parte conferre, agere, operari aut cooperari (ex se ipso tanquam ex semetipso possit.*† Further on, the unregenerate man is compared in his relation to conversion and renewal to a stock and stone (*nec plus quam lapsis, truncus aut limus*); and he is said to differ from these things only in the fact that, as far as in him lies, he is rebellious, and an enemy to the divine will (*In haec parte deterior est trunco quia voluntati divinae rebellis est et inimicus*).‡

These affirmations concerning the depth of human depravity lead to inferences obviously sanctioning the doctrine of unconditional predestination. Experience teaches that among those to whom the offers of salvation by grace are made, some become partakers of it, and some do not; and this difference cannot be attributed to any distinction of disposition in the human will, if, previous to regeneration, man is utterly incapable of laying hold of, or even of inclining towards, the proffered grace. Wherein, then, can this difference have its basis save in the will of God, who, in cases where the man persistently disdains the offered salvation, has not seen fit to communicate that gracious aid, without which he cannot receive Christ,—yea, cannot do otherwise than reject Him? Thus we are

Lead to unconditional predestination.

---

* *Solida Declaratio*, art. i. (p. 643 Ed. Rechenberg).
† *Ibid.* art. ii. p. 656. ‡ *Ibid.* 662; see also pp. 672, 673.

brought to the *gratia irresistibilis* and the *decretum absolutum* of predestinarianism in its strictest form.

<small>Faith as the condition of redemption.</small> But the *Formula Concordiae* endeavours by all means to avoid such a conclusion as this; and accordingly it maintains the universality of God's gracious will,* rejects the contradictory idea of a two-fold will of God, the one hidden and the other revealed,† and attributes the fact that a portion of mankind is lost, not to the divine foreknowledge or predestination, but solely to man's own perverseness.‡ God's decree for human salvation is conditional upon the relation in which man puts himself to God's grace; and the question is, What is this condition, the *non*-performance of which deprives a portion of the race of the blessings of salvation? This question is not definitely answered in the *Formula Concordiae*, but the older Lutheran theology, in its development of the Lutheran Symbols, declares it to be FAITH in the gospel of Christ, foreseen by God. We shall not here refer to the difficulties which beset this doctrine in its relation to those who have had no opportunity afforded them of hearing the gospel message; but if we consider fully the true nature and life-giving power of this faith, as explained in the evangelic teaching, we are constrained to ask, How can fallen man, possessing a nature so depraved and helpless, of himself beget and exercise such a faith? Such a doctrine goes beyond the Synergistic theory, and accords with a principle distinctively Pelagian; and the *Formula Concordiae*, as well as the Lutheran teaching generally, rejects it. In the passage above quoted from Article II. and elsewhere, the *credere posse* is distinctly denied to the unregenerate man, and everything pertaining to conversion, and especially to the production and maintenance of faith, is attributed to the operations of the Holy Spirit.§

<small>Faith produced.</small> God himself, therefore, must produce in man that condition upon which his election to life eternal depends; and it follows that the non-fulfiment of the con-

---

* *Solida Declaratio*, pp. 805, 818, 819.   † *Ibid.* p. 807.

‡ *Ibid.*, pp. 809, 818.

§ *Ibid.*, art. ii. p. 676 : *Deus* . . . . *fidem aliasque pietatis virtutes in nobis accendit, ita quidem ut haec omnia solius Spiritus Sancti dona sint atque operationes.* This is but one passage out of many that might be quoted to the same effect.

dition must be owing to a want of this divine operation and of the divine will to perform it. In such cases it cannot have been God's will to give the grace necessary for the acceptance of salvation; and thus the *gratia universalis* and the *decretum conditionatum* are again resolved into *gratia particularis* and *decretum absolutum*. By no means, answers the *Formula Concordiae*, for the Holy Spirit does not work saving faith immediately in the man's heart, but indirectly, by the means of grace, especially by God's Word as His instrument; and it depends upon the man himself whether he will use or refuse these means. The *Formula Concordiae*, at the very beginning of its Article *De libero arbitrio*, speaks not only of the Synergistic view, but of the opinions held by certain enthusiasts—the spiritualistic sects of the day—that God converts man by His Spirit alone, without any human means or instruments, and apart from the preaching and hearing of the Word, and it describes these notions as the rocks which the true doctrine concerning the province of human liberty in conversion has to shun.

The *Formula Concordiae*, therefore, rightly affirms, in har-
This leads on mony with the Augsburg Confession,* and the
to Synergism. Smalcaldian Articles,† together with several Confessions of the Reformed Church,‡ that the operations of the Holy Spirit in conversion are carried on by means of the divine Word, and we could have wished that the older Protestant theology had allowed more room for variety in the forms and *media* of the Spirit's working, but does it not necessarily follow, that previous to his conversion, and before the operations of divine grace have been begun in him, man must in himself be susceptible of some bias and desire after the eternal blessings which the Word of God offers? What save such a desire could induce him to give heed to the divine Word? Taking this for granted, it is evident that those to whom God's Word comes can fall short of the salvation which it offers only by their own guilt, namely, by the suppression of that bias and desire. It is no less obvious, however, that on this principle, the statements of the *Formula Concordiae* above quoted, con-

---

* Art. v. xviii. † Par. iii. art. viii.
‡ *E.g. Confessio Helvetica* ii. art. xiv., (Niemeyer, p. 491), art. xvi. (p. 496), *Confessio Belgica*, art. xxiv. (p. 375).

cerning man's utter depravity and the thraldom of his will, must be modified according to the spirit of Melanchthon's Synergism, which it rejects.*

Provisions against this in our confessions.

Against this inference, however, and whatever may follow from it, the *Formula Concordiae*, with the acuteness which distinguishes it, has already provided. It firmly maintains that by original sin man has entirely lost his freedom in spiritual things, and in that sphere of life which concerns his relations to God. But it allows that there remains to fallen man a freedom in outward and natural things, by virtue of which he cannot indeed do anything directly in the attainment of true spiritual righteousness, but is in a position diligently to seek after an outwardly moral life (*externa honesta vita*, called in the *Apologia*, "*justitia rationis*," or "*justitia civilis*").† According to the phase of doctrine adopted in the *Formula Concordiae*, no internal desire for the divine Word induces the natural man to acquaint himself with it as written or preached, because he has within him nothing but disinclination and hostility to that Word.‡ Every inclining, even the very slightest, to the acceptance of God's Word, must be itself the effect of the Holy Spirit's working through the Word. Still, however, it is in the power of the unregenerate man to choose whether or not he will allow himself to be moved to the reading or hearing God's Word by a desire after external honesty or a natural thirst for knowledge.§

* Without of course adopting the formula of the *tres causae conversionis*, and the designation of man's part by the term συνεργεῖν,—for both these express the relation between the Divine and the human in the process, in an exaggerated and distorted manner. The desire or bias in man simply secures his susceptibility of conversion; but this susceptibility is not a cause of conversion, nor is it, strictly speaking, "a co-operating with the Spirit."

† Art. i. p. 640; art. ii. p. 663. The earlier theologians of our Church make a distinction between a *hemisphaerium superius* and a *hemisphaerium inferius* in the sphere of free will in its full import. Free will, they say, has in the natural man lost its freedom in the former sphere, but in the latter sphere, which includes the *justitia civilis* and the like, man still retains *aliquo modo* his freedom. See QUENSTEDT, *Syst. Theol.*, p. ii. c. iii. §§ 1, 7.

‡ Art. ii. pp. 660, 661.

§ Art. ii. p. 671, and elsewhere. The *Formula Concordiae* nowhere defines the nature of this impulse, yet what is said above is clearly implied in its statements. It certainly does not attribute the reading and hearing of the Word to such motives as those named by STRAUSS, *Christl. Glaubenslehre*, ii. 446.

§ 3. THE SUPPOSED CRITERION OF MAN'S SALVATION.

The condition, therefore, whereon the divine decree principally depends, and whereon all decisions concerning eternal salvation or ruin hang, was held to be the use or abuse of the means of grace, arising not from prior inclination or disinclination towards divine things, but from motives which (as the doctrine stated demands) have no merit of their own, nor any necessary connection whatever with the proffered good. But the fact that this inner connection is wanting, renders the supposed condition inadequate. In accordance with the universality of God's gracious purpose—a truth zealously affirmed in the Lutheran theology in opposition to Particularism—the action of divine love is conditional upon an inner surrender on the part of the man himself, and great importance attaches to this surrender. But it is obviously contradictory to attach such importance to a human decision, which is expressly said not to have any moral or religious worth whatever. Man, though fallen, is still a spiritual being, and if he experiences the gracious operations of the Divine Spirit, it cannot be merely mechanically and passively, but by means of a living and spiritual receptivity, which in itself implies activity. If this spiritual susceptibility be wholly destroyed by sin, where should we find any point of union between the old and the new man, or any such guarantee for the identity of the subject in both states, as the idea of redemption in distinction from creation, strictly speaking, demands? If we would exclude the views of FLACIUS and his school, which lead to Manichaeism, it is not enough to maintain, with the *Formula Concordiae*,* that the man's nature is, in a *metaphysical* sense, the same, whether regenerate or still unregenerate, the same after as before the Fall; and that the copious springs of his manifold energies and

Explanations similar to what we have given above occur in AEGID. HUNNIUS, *De providentia Dei et aeterna praedestinatione*, pp. 235, 243, and the theologians of the seventeenth century follow him. Thus QUENSTEDT ascribes to the natural man the power of doing outwardly holy acts, *actiones paedagogicae*, such as attending church, hearing the Word, conversing with others about it, and reading the Scriptures. But following HULSEMANN, he qualifies his statement by saying, that if besides the general desire to know divine things, there be a longing after eternal salvation, or a desire to forsake sin arising from the fear of God, this does not belong to nature, but to *gratia praeveniens*.—*Syst. Theol.* p. ii. c. iii. § 1, 7.

* Art. i. *De pecc. orig.*, pp. 643-5.

talents have not ceased to flow forth in his present sinful state. It is also requisite to preserve the identity of the man as *a moral being*, before and after his redemption; and this is not preserved by a mere ability to desire an *externa honesta vita*, nor by a *liberum arbitrium in rebus civilibus*.*

We must presuppose some basis or connecting link for the process of renewal in the natural man, were it only to account for the fact of his resolving in the first instance to make use of the means of grace. If in his inward and spiritual nature he necessarily resists the gospel call,† while the only promptings to hear it come from his outward and lower nature, wherein he still is free, though in a very limited sense,‡ must not these weak promptings ever be outweighed and overpowered by that inner spiritual resistance?

Requisite to go beyond this.

Experience testifies that of those who do make use of God's Word by reading the Scriptures, and hearing the Gospel preached, all do not attain to a true and living faith. If, then, we would avoid the predestinarian doctrine in its strictest form, we must allow that the entrance of divine grace into the soul is conditional upon something within the man himself. Our dogmatic system, while excluding the Synergistic view as bordering on Pelagianism, contents itself with regarding this inward condition as something merely negative.

---

* The *Formula Concordiae* in one passage seems decidedly to qualify its bare denial of all *vires spirituales* to the natural man; viz., art. ii. p. 657 : *Etsi humana ratio seu naturalis intellectus hominis obscuram aliquam notitiae illius scintillulam reliquam habet, quod sit Deus, et particulam aliquam legis tenet ; tamen, &c.* But if this admission at all modifies the statements concerning man's natural condition and his redemption, it is merely the admission that this spark of knowledge enables the man outwardly (historically) to understand the contents of the divine Word. It is from such conclusions as these that orthodox theologians have developed that strange turn of doctrine, that though the divine image, as they express it, is wholly obliterated in man's depraved nature, some lineaments still remain (*divinae imaginis amissio et quidem totalis, remanentibus saltem quibusdam sive ruderibus sive vestigiis*, says QUENSTEDT, c. ii. sec. i. 25), which form the basis of man's ability in those *actiones paedagogicae*. The Augsburg Confession, in its 18th article, simply denies that man's free will has any power to work spiritual righteousness, without the aid of the Holy Spirit ; nay, the words which follow might be construed as favouring the Pelagian view,—the *aut certe peragere*, I mean, in the quotation from the Pseudo Augustine,—if, indeed, the Confession is to be held responsible for every word of the quotations it makes, whether bearing on the design of the quotation or not.

† *Formula Concordiae*, art. ii. pp. 660, 661–672.   ‡ *Ibid.* art. i. p. 640.

SIN AS A MATTER OF EXPERIENCE.

The *Formula Concordiae*, indeed, does not contain any clear and consistent definition upon this point, but the problem was thoroughly discussed by the theologians of the seventeenth century. Even Gerhard distinguishes between a *nolle privativum* and a *nolle positivum*, and between a *malitia originalis* and an *actualis pertinacia*.* Quenstedt, however, following other theologians, discusses this point with great acuteness.† All here depends upon our rightly distinguishing between the natural disinclination pertaining to human nature as depraved, and stiff-necked persistently cherished opposition to the divine Word. Our depraved nature is always disinclined to the word of God, and its disinclination can be overcome only by the agency of the Holy Spirit, in the form of *gratia praeparans*. But persistent obduracy is an opposition which the Holy Spirit does not overcome, because his working is not irresistible; it must be overcome by the man himself, and the ability to do so resides in his natural powers. By means of this distinction, the apparently contradictory statements of the *Formula Concordiae*,—which, on the one hand, teach that man resists God's Word and Will until God raises him from the death of sin, enlightens and renews him,‡ and which, on the other hand, rejects the affirmation that the Holy Spirit is given to those who resist Him,§—may, perhaps, be reconciled.

Negative condition, capacitas passiva.

The condition, therefore, on man's part, on the fulfilment of which his conversion depends, would be merely a negative one, viz., that he should refrain from wilful and obstinate resistance of the proffered grace; and thus we have the bare notion of a passive susceptibility (*capacitas passiva*) of salvation. But is this condition really so purely negative as at first sight it seems to be? If, prior to and apart from the operations of grace, there be no other feeling in the natural heart toward the divine Word save disinclination and opposition, whenever the Word is presented this opposition must assert itself, and must of itself, and in every case—for what is there

---

* *Loci. theol. loc. de lib. arbitrio*, § 81; *loc. de Elect. et Reprob.* § 139.

† *Syst. Theol.* p. iii. cap. 7, sect. i. 25; sect. ii. 1-3.   See BAIER, *Compar. theol. posit.* p. iii. c. 4, §§ 38, 39.

‡ *Solida Declaratio*, art. ii. p. 672.   § *Ibid.* p. 679.

in the human heart to hinder it?—gradually increase till it becomes obstinate and determined resistance. It is of no avail to say that man's natural opposition is overcome by the power of the Holy Spirit; for as soon as his endeavour to overcome it begins—which cannot be until the Word is presented to the man—He finds the merely natural opposition already increasing and advancing towards obstinate resistance. The consequence would be that no one would be saved. But as this is contrary alike to our experience and our presuppositions, the question arises, How is this enhancement of a natural opposition which the Spirit can overcome, into a resistance which he does not vanquish, to be prevented? It will not do to say that the Holy Spirit Himself prevents this enhancement in the case of those who hear the Word, because we have first to define what that hearing of the man is which conditions the very first entrance of the Spirit into his heart. If it be meant that the fulfilment of this condition is exclusively the work of the Spirit Himself, we are brought back again to the doctrine of an unconditional predestination; nay, considering the contrasted results of the offers of grace, we are led on even to the revolting theory of a twofold will in God. Further, to appeal to outward circumstances and providences whereby many are prepared for the operations of the Spirit, as the means whereby the natural disinclination of the heart is prevented from becoming wilful resistance, is of avail only upon the recognition of some inner susceptibility of the human heart towards the saving designs of these outward providences.

The Lutheran theology is logically driven to the recognition of such a susceptibility in the heart of the natural man for the operations of grace,—a susceptibility which is more than a *capacitas mere passiva*,— in order to avoid the theory of unconditional predestination and the exaggerated doctrine of Flacius. But this necessitates some qualification of the statements above quoted as to the extent of man's natural depravity. For this susceptibility necessarily presupposes, over and above the opposing tendencies of the heart, an element in man which inclines towards the divine Word, and which the tyranny of sin has left untouched. If it be possible to prevent the growth of natural opposition into determined resistance, there must be

A positive susceptibility in man required.

something in the natural man which counterbalances that opposition. Here, too, it follows that moral freedom, or the power of following or despising the higher tendency in our nature, implied in that disposition towards the divine Word, though hindered, and in some cases crushed, cannot be totally destroyed.*

Among our Lutheran theologians, Thomasius in particular Attempted endeavours to vindicate the statements of the explanation of *Formula Concordiae*. He starts from the principle that the natural man possesses no ability in relation to Christ's salvation save a *capacitas* to be converted by God, a capacity of attentively hearing God's Word, provided that by the leadings of Providence he is brought within the range of Gospel privileges. Hereupon the Holy Spirit works within him, and gives to him that positive susceptibility whereby he can either deliberately put the truth from him or yield himself to its power. This susceptibility includes the *motus inevitabiles*, as Musaeus, Quenstedt, and others call them, viz., remembrance of past sin and resolve to forsake it. Thus "it becomes possible for the work of conversion to begin; the power of self-decision is so far restored that further progress can be made, and the whole heart is open to the operations of the Holy Spirit. The beginning of conversion consists in this— the Holy Spirit influences the will to be willing to turn away from sin, and to incline towards God's grace in Christ. This first step is effected" (rendered possible only—according to the above) "solely by the operations of the Spirit as its cause, and yet it is brought about by a conscious movement of the man's own will, which itself again is the result of divine operations. The first impression only is unavoidable and irresistible; the second,

* This argument with its conclusion may be taken as counterbalancing that of SCHLEIERMACHER in his treatise on Election (p. 10, f.), to the effect that the Lutheran doctrine, if logically carried out in its anti-Synergistic positions, involves unconditional predeterminism. SCHLEIERMACHER indeed goes further, and argues with CALVIN that the non-recognition of this predestination must logically lead to Pelagianism. In order, however,to show how the apparent antitheses in our Church's doctrine may coexist, we may refer to Schleiermacher himself, who assents to the Calvinistic dogma only upon the persuasion that it has its corrective in the doctrine of the ἀποκατάστασις πάντων, and who does this clearly in order to avoid the extreme of Manichaeism. Compare, in connection with our argument above, the masterly dissertation of NITZSCH on Original Sin, *Theol. Stud. u. Kritik.*, 1834, p. 2.

the deeper one" (the divine operation ?), "is no longer so. For the man may withdraw himself from this; in virtue of the power of spiritual self-decision in either direction now possessed, he can if he will, resolve to persevere in sin instead of going on from the germ of the new man divinely originated in him to strive against the old." *

It is accordingly the gospel message which produces these movements in the heart, and the attentive hearer or reader of the Word who receives these impressions. But to what is his attention to the Word owing, save to a longing after peace in the depths of his soul, a desire for the harmonizing of that discord which he feels within? If he refuses to give ear to these longings, he will either never read or listen to the gospel, or though reading and hearing it a thousand times he will fail to see its bearing upon his own state. The importance which is attached to attention in the hearer arises solely from the fact of his having this anxious longing; for were the motives prompting him to hear or to refuse to hear the Word, only those of the *justitia civilis*, the fact of God's connecting the hearing of the Word with the possibility of salvation, would be utterly unaccountable, contradicting alike His love and mercy. The impressions produced by the divine message on the heart of the hearer are neither unavoidable nor irresistible; it depends on his inner susceptibility whether he experiences these impressions or not. If we analyse this susceptibility we shall find that it is not fully developed without various divine providences, answering to the germinal sense of need in the man himself before he turned to the Word of God. But we must carefully distinguish these leadings of Providence, which are independent of the Word, from the direct operations of the Holy Spirit, and we cannot allow that they produce the susceptibility in question. It depends, moreover, upon this susceptibility towards divine grace, whether or not the impressions produced will lead the man on to something more. If it be his heart's desire to enter upon a living fellowship with God, God's grace will lead him on by means of the Word to further knowledge; if, on the contrary, he slights the inner impulse towards God, these impressions serve only to estrange him more than before from gospel truth. If with Tomasius,

* *Christi Person und Werk*, part iii. § 1, 465-469 (2nd ed.).

we regarded this inner susceptibility merely as the effect of an impression from without, produced by the Holy Spirit, and conditional upon nothing answering to it in the man himself, we should be obliged—seeing that the *capacitas passiva* is the same in all—to look for the real ground of the difference between the man who cherishes the first effects of the divine Word, and the man who crushes them, not in the men themselves, but in the outward circumstances which in the one case led to the fostering and in 'the other to the suppression of the word received; and thus ultimately we should have to ascribe it to the will or prohibition of God. It would be through God's eternal election that the Holy Ghost begins to work in one portion of those who receive the word—(apart from the consideration that this receptivity itself is said to be the Spirit's work)—and not in another. The twofold and contrasted result depending on the divine will would lead us back to the doctrine of absolute predestination as the cause of the participation of the one in eternal salvation, and of the other in everlasting destruction. If we start back in horror at this Medusa's head of absolute predestination, we must allow that the *capacitas mere passiva* is not an adequate description of man's natural state, but that the divine decree is in some degree conditional upon the susceptibility (*i.e.*, receptivity, which must be clearly distinguished from passivity) of the individual, who can either cherish or stifle religious convictions. At the same time this susceptibility must not be looked upon as a cause of salvation, nor even as a co-operating agent, because there is really nothing for it to effect; it is the power of God alone that works conversion.* Man's entire renewal is in its beginning, progress, and completion, a work of grace, and apart from the saving power of this grace, we can recognise nothing but utter worthlessness and weakness.†

---

* We must be careful not to be led into error as to the meaning of the word susceptibility apart from man's relation to an operative first cause. In the sphere of the finite we have no causes which can of themselves operate immediately upon our inner nature; by an act of will we open our hearts to them or close them against their influence. God's gracious working in man conditions itself primarily by such a decision of man's will, but when the heart is opened to them His operations are not the less consciously immediate in their influence.

† LUTHARDT, in his work entitled *Die Lehre vom freien Willen und seinem*

Thomasius divides the passages of Scripture which he quotes on this subject into two classes. In the one class are those texts which speak of the utter inability of the natural man to become truly good, and of conversion as God's creative work wrought by the Holy Spirit; *e.g.*, John iii. 5; Eph. ii. 1, 5; Col. i. 21, ii. 13; Matt. xix. 26; Jer. xxxi. 18; Ezekiel xi. 19; Phil. ii. 13; Eph. ii. 10; Isaiah v. 21; 2 Cor. v. 17, &c. The other class consists of those texts which represent conversion as a moral work in the man, a movement of his will, and which teach that, where renewal has not taken place, the guilt rests with the man himself, who has withstood the strivings of God's spirit; *e.g.*, Jer. xxxi. 18; Mal. iii. 7; Acts iii. 19, ix. 35, xxvi. 18; 1 Thess. i. 9; 2 Cor. vi. 1; John v. 40; Matt. xxiii. 37; Acts xiii. 46, &c. The natural inference from these texts would seem to be, that the apparent contradiction in the declarations of Scripture witnesses that man's perfect inability to help himself is compatible with his ability to appropriate God's help, and to turn himself to or from divine grace. Even the strongest passages do not contradict this ability; for the "deadness" of the natural man is in one and the same passage, Eph. v. 14, or in different places, Rom.

Texts bearing upon the subject.

Verhältniss zur Gnade, p. 463, well describes this susceptibility. "These stirrings or impulses," he says, "arise so involuntarily or spontaneously (not from any deliberate resolve, but as if suddenly coming upon us), that to the man who feels them they are a kind of call or demand. They present themselves to him as an entreaty or questioning to which he must reply. They show to him the treachery of sin over his intellect, and its fetters upon his will hindering it in its approaches to God, and they operate on his spiritual life, freeing it and influencing it. Thus they make a corresponding decision possible for him. They do not beget or work in him a new volition, nor an active and determinate bias, but they make it possible for him to realise these. They call his attention to his sins and to God's grace. It is a matter of uncertainty whether he will allow his attention thus to be directed. They would lead him to the God of grace. It rests with himself whether he will be led to Him. The selfishness of the natural man resists these inner calls; but grace, which is stronger than this, helps him against the thraldom of self, and makes a free decision for God possible. Grace finds an ally in the natural bias of the man to God, and in his moral strivings. Then follows the contest between the 'new man' who desires to grow, with the 'old man' who will not yield." In another passage, however (p. 457), Luthardt says of these questionings, wishes, and stirrings, "They slumber in the man, and are aroused to action only when the word of grace is addressed to him." He seems not to look upon them as "independent of the decisions of our own will."

xiii. 11; Isaiah i. 5; Hosea v. 13; called also a "sleep" or a "sickness." But Thomasius explains the apparent contradiction between these two classes of texts by saying that "conversion, as a yielding to the operations of grace, is entirely God's act, not produced by any co-operation or act of man ; and yet there is a movement of the man himself." This self-movement simply consists in the fact that the man can either follow or withstand the impulse arising from a natural conviction of his duty to hear God's word. "Thus"—to use the language of Schmid,* "God's word, accompanied by an operation of grace which is certainly irresistible, begets, not at once perhaps conversion itself, but that freedom of will which enables the man, not as before to resist grace, but now to yield to its workings." Here is omitted that necessary alternative which Quenstedt states in the quotation which follows these words, "or to close the heart against its operations," and by adding this, the inconsistency of this view immediately appears. According to it, that which does not peradventure belong to unfallen human nature, but which is first produced as a divine gift, "an operation of pure grace," in those who hear the word in order to their eternal salvation (*i.e.*, the freedom of the will in its power to abjure God or to yield to Him), serves only to plunge into everlasting perdition by far the greater part of those who are called by grace. This view, which can find its sanction neither in Holy Scripture nor in inner experience—not certainly in this, for the very point in question concerns the resisting—is, forsooth, to be received as the final solution of the problem !

Apostolic statements concerning the heathen.
The exaggerated opinion of the Reformers (even of Melanchthon in his earlier life) as to the extent to which moral susceptibility in the unregenerate is destroyed by universal sinfulness, may in great part be accounted for by the fact that they fell into a mistake and confusion which is to be found even in their great teacher on the subject, in Augustine himself, and which, therefore, is the more excusable in them. Observing that humble and self-denying love to God, the true principle of the moral life, is never found save in connection with Christ's redemptive work, they thought that those admirable moral

* *Dogmatik der evangelisch-lutherischen Kirche*, 3d. ed. p. 372.

elements which we sometimes meet with in the unregenera must be ultimately traceable to selfish motives. They ove looked the fact that where love to God was not consciously ma(the highest principle of the moral life, the law of CONSCIENCE ar the stirrings of moral feeling answering thereto,—the συνήδεσθ τῷ νόμῳ κατὰ τὸν ἔσω ἄνθρωπον—may exert a very commandii influence. It must certainly be granted that in such cas the duty of obedience to law is never the ruling princip. But the fact cannot be ignored, that, apart from redemptio man is in some cases influenced purely from a sense of du and its unconditional demand to adopt a line of condu diametrically opposed to the claims of selfishness. This the ἐργάζεσθαι τὸ ἀγαθὸν or δικαιοσύνην, the φύσει τὰ τοῦ νόμ ποιεῖν, the φυλάσσειν τα δικαιώματα τοῦ νόμου which St Peter ai St Paul expressly attribute to the heathen.* The idea *justitia civilis*, by means of which the Reformers endeavour(to explain these cases, is utterly inadequate.† We have i desire to dispute the point if our inquiry, in its unbiass(progress, should lead us to recognize that the original judgme of Protestantism, in its estimate of the heathen world and the natural man, morally and religiously, is in principle and its ultimate bearings conformable with truth. But to defei the particular definitions and premisses by which the Reforme from their point of view arrived at this judgment, is a ta: which no one in our day will undertake who does not wilful

---

* Acts x. 35 ; Rom. ii. 10, xiv. 26. Christ's parable of the Good Samarita Luke x., is also a case in point.

† The question, of course, is not whether this idea of *justitia civilis* adequate, if we suppose it to include all moral elements which can in any c̟ be found where *justitia spiritualis* does not exist ; it is, whether, adopting t sense and limitation which the Reformers attached to it, it is adequate include all those elements. The expression, *justitia rationis* certainly favours more satisfactory explanation of the idea, but the old Protestant interpretaṭi reduces the *justitia rationis* to a mere *justitia civilis*. If, indeed, we enlarge t idea of *justitia civilis* as PHILIPPI does (*Kirchliche Glaubenslehre*, iv. 69), so to make it include the use of the means of grace which produce the *justi*i *s* n*iritualis*, and regard a right application of the *liberum arbitrium*, which exi: in the moral and religious sphere of human life generally, as forming a prepai tory training for the reception of distinctively Christian blessings, an eleme would thus be provided which might explain the transition of the natural m into the higher sphere of the new life. But such an enlargement of the idea c(veyed in the term entirely contradicts the sense in which *justitia civilis* or *ration* is used in the *Confessio Augustana*, the *Apologia Confessionis*, and the *Formu Concordiae*, and by the orthodox theologians of the Lutheran church generally.

shut his eyes to the more comprehensive examination and more thorough Moral estimate of heathendom to which modern science leads us.

§ 4. MODERN THEORIES OF NATURE AND GRACE.

And yet modern science, not indeed in the sphere of history to which we refer, but in that of philosophy and theology, adopts these very terms and definitions,— according to which the natural man has no freedom whatever towards God and His holy will, nor any positive susceptibility for the workings of divine grace,—as truer and more correct in a speculative point of view, and pronounces the synergistic doctrine and all approximations to it as very unphilosophical.

This is, indeed, a very unexpected sanction and help to the narrow doctrine of our Reformers and our church symbols concerning man's natural state, and the worth of all virtue and knowledge to be found among the heathen. Still it would be more than rash on the part of the champions of that doctrine were they to boast of such a confirmatory alliance. Are these philosophic opposers of Synergism, with its remnant of moral self-movement in the will, really in earnest in subscribing to that narrow doctrine ? By no means; for their strong negative assertions, which seem so fully to tally with the old Protestant orthodoxy, will, if closely examined, be found to refer not to the actual condition of the human race apart from redemption, but to the "naturalness" of man in the abstract. They look upon these statements as adequately describing, not human nature in its present fallen state, but human nature merely abstractedly contemplated.* Availing themselves of the

* Even Thomasius seems to favour this view, though the spirit of his theology is manifestly opposed to it. He assumes (vol i. 443) that the point in question concerns man as he is *in himself* (*ex se ipso tanquam ex se ipso*), in his pure naturalness and estrangement from God, apart from all divine influences, and not as experience shows him to be; for as we see him he is already surrounded with divine influences. According to this, even in heathendom, the natural man in his relation to God is already under the influence of prevenient grace, and thus theology forfeits the right to pronounce positively concerning human nature in itself and its power in religious matters. For how could any judgment it might offer be independent of this experience which "does not show us what man by nature is in himself"? The distinction which Thomasius seems to make between inner and outward experience is of no avail; for no inner experience could show us what human nature is in itself and apart from divine influences, if human nature does not now exist, nor is anywhere to be found, thus left to itself and apart from God's gracious help.

idea of the λόγος σπερματικός, as developed in the early Churc and exaggerating the doctrine of prevenient grace, they ca boast of so much that is good, noble, and God-like in th present condition of the race and of individuals which o theologians designated "natural," that they destroy the contra between nature and grace at the very time that they see categorically to hold it. This manipulation of theologic ideas enables them, with the most exact Protestant orthodo? —in opposition to Catholic, Synergistic, and other heresies- to assert the absolute weakness and worthlessness of mar natural state, to attribute every truly religious tendency heathendom to the action of grace, and even to outstrip orth doxy in vindicating the *justitia civilis* as the Reformers unde stood it. Yet at the same time they can take their stand on speculative height from which the antithesis of nature and gra dwindles down into a mere difference in the necessary elemen of human development.

If, however, all that is asserted be that nothing whatev Virtually good can spring from the abstract naturalness deny grace. man, or from human nature alienated from Go and His will, or that "the flesh and what springs from cannot be at the same time an effort of the natural man escape from his sinful state,"* it is obvious that even tl clearest Pelagianism may, without any compromise, allow thi The theology of the sixteenth century in its various phases- Catholic, Lutheran in its different schools, Calvinistic, Socinia in all its affirmations or denials concerning this question- recognises two distinct states differing in time, viz., mar state apart from salvation, and his state as a participator in i man's condition either as separate from the historical Chri or in union with Him; it had no thought concerning tl elements of humanity in its abstract isolation. The real poi at issue lies in the question, whether man in his natural sta be merely (to use St. Paul's word) σαρξ—a fleshly nature, whether besides the principle called "the flesh," he possess another principle which, though restrained by sin, is not whol extinct. This principle may be regarded as σπέρμα τοῦ λόγο without our essentially altering the point in question, provide

* A truth which BAUR in his "*Gegensatz des Katholicismus und Protestant mus*," p. 197, thought it necessary to vindicate in opposition to Nitzsch.

that the idea is not understood pantheistically as an identity of nature between God and man. The σπέρμα may belong to man's own original nature, and as the fall has not utterly destroyed man's moral nature, it may act as a limit to sin's destructive power, and a groundwork for renewal and sanctification. But if these elements of man's unredeemed nature rendering his salvation possible, be regarded as the effects of prevenient grace, what does this opinion lead to? It is well known that Pelagianism attributed even the law to Grace— even man's reason, which raises him above the lower creation, and freewill as the possibility of not sinning,—nay, even our very existence as created out of nothing,*—it attributed all to Grace. But the end in view was not to extol and glorify Grace, it was to do away with the distinction between nature and grace altogether, thus anticipating its full development in Pantheism. The scriptural idea of Grace is very different from this; it is far more definite. What belongs to human nature as a constituent part of it is indeed God's free gift, but it is not GRACE; and, accordingly, the early Protestant theologians rejected the Catholic doctrine that man's original righteousness was a gift of Grace. That divine will and work which Scripture calls Grace presupposes a deficiency in the service and obedience which man ought to render, and is manifestly something *over and above* what sinful human nature can by its own unassisted powers accomplish. We by no means deny that a much more extended range may be claimed for prevenient Grace as an element of Christian doctrine than the older Lutherans were prepared to give to it, but if the idea of Grace be extended beyond the limits here indicated, it will be distorted, and, in its true import, wholly destroyed. In the Babylonish confusion of tongues so rife in our day, the saying ALL IS GRACE is, on the lips of many, tantamount only to the proposition, NOTHING IS GRACE.

Of the *Formula Concordiae* generally, it may be said that though a masterpiece of thorough and careful doctrinal development, it is too much of a dogmatic treatise to answer the purpose and sustain the character of a Church Confession; and this is specially true regarding its treatment of the question before us. It oversteps those bounds of what is clearly defin-

* See AUGUSTINE *De gestis Pelagii*, c. 22. *Opus imperf. contra Jul.* i. 95.

able in a Church Confession, which the other symbolical book of the Lutheran and Reformed Churches have well preserved and it elevates the individually tinged expression of Christia conviction into a standard of dogmatic orthodoxy. If th statements, *hominis naturam et personam . . . peccat originali . . . prorsus et totaliter . . . totam esse coram Deo infectam, venenatam et penitus corruptam,** so that ex s et viribus suis coram Deo nihil aliud nisi peccare possit,* be regarded not as an ascetic, or, at least, colloquial way o speaking, but in a strictly dogmatic sense,‡ every moral elemen in man's natural state is distinctly denied.

We have already (vol. i. p. 210) referred to the fact tha
Signs of goodness in fallen man. there are crimes from which even the most deter mined villain, though but for a moment, shrinks when the temptation to commit them first present itself. Now, this is an undeniable sign that even such character is capable of a still deeper moral degradation. An where this is possible, there must still be some spark of good which, though smothered beneath the ashes of a reckless life is not yet wholly extinct.§ We cannot deny, moreover, tha even a very degraded man can check in some degree the aggra vation of his wickedness, or hasten it wilfully as the case ma be. Even in the lowest depth of moral depravity, the wil though entangled in sin, does not cease to be the ruling centr of the inner life; it still holds its seat—so far, at least, as w can judge of mental states, and provided that human evil ha not been transformed to diabolical—an inextinguishable spark of moral self-determination, a power of choice, however limited between the claims of moral duty and the calls of lust. Anc if this must be allowed in the case of the most depraved o mankind, how much more must it be recognised in the noble specimens of the natural man. So noble is human nature, a

* Art. i. p. 639. † *Ibid.* p. 643.
‡ It is significant of this that a Symbol of Doctrine should base its statement upon an expression in a hymn. The *Formula Concordiae* does this in the passag above given, quoting the hymn :—
" Durch Adams Fall is ganz verderbt
Menschlich Natur und Wasen."

§ *Quamdiu natura corrumpitur, inest ei bonum, quo privetur*, says AUGUSTINE (*Enchiridion*, c. xii.), though in a sense somewhat different, for he here confound metaphysical with moral good.

created by God, that even in its lowest fall and deepest degradation, the lineaments of its high origin, apparent in the power of moral good, cannot utterly be destroyed. We have already shown (vol. i. p. 328) that in Romans vii., the apostle describes, not, as our older theologians almost unanimously supposed,* the state of the regenerate man, but that of the unregenerate, who, as yet, knows nothing beyond the Law. The delineation there given leads to a negative inference only, viz., that the man has no moral power to free the *ego* sold under sin; it is enslaved beneath the law of sin, which rules the outward life. But the deep discord and inward struggle there described, the συνήδεσθαι τῷ νόμῳ τοῦ θεοῦ κατὰ τὸν ἔσω ἄνθρωπον, the θέλειν ποιεῖν τὸ καλὸν, ever hindered in its realisation by the dominant principle of the Flesh —all this surely cannot be called the relation of "a stone" to God's will and law. Any such mere abstract estimate of man's state by nature is necessarily barren and inadequate; it affords no true key to the manifold moral differences and changes of human character. The words in which Neander† sums up St. Paul's description of man's state by nature, are certainly far more in harmony with Scripture and experience. He says:—"Thus Paul describes in the natural man two conflicting principles, the principle of the Divine nature (that kinship with God implied in man's God-consciousness and his corresponding moral self-consciousness, man's moral and religious nature), and the principle of sin;—the spirit‡ and the flesh)—and the

Romans vii.

---

* See CHEMNITZ, *Examen Conc. Trident*, i. 219;—HUTTER, *Loci communes*, 337;—GERHARD, *Loci theol.*—loc. *De imagine Dei*, § 127; *De pecc. actual.* § 42;—QUENSTEDT, *Syst. Theol.* p. ii. c. 2, sect. 2, qu. 9, ἐκδικ. ⁖ BAIER *Comp. Th. Pos.*, p. iii. c. 6, § 4.   For the history of interpretation of this passage, see THOLUCK's Commentary, *in loc.*

† *Pflanzung der K.* p. 680. Compare the remarks of NITZSCH, in his *System der christlichen Lehre*, § 114. The same view is taken in the first half of STEUDEL'S dissertation *über Sünde und Gnade* (*Tübinger Zeitschrift für Theologie*, 1832, p. i. 125), though we miss here an adequate recognition of the limits which affect all the moral acts of the natural man. It is, moreover, to be borne in mind that all mechanical attempts at division between the powers of good and evil in the natural man, and between the work of Grace and human freedom in conversion,—such as SARTORIUS, p. 183, objects to in Semipelagianism and Synergism, and not without cause as to the first—must be avoided as quite out of place.

‡ For the meaning St Paul attaches to this term, as designating the one element in the natural man, see vol. i. p. 329.

former, the original nature of man, is hindered in its development and activity, and even enslaved, by the latter." Man, in his natural state, being destitute of the peace which reconciliation to God secures, and which is his true Inner discord. and normal life, is not at rest, nor self-satisfied. His nature is divided, full of contradiction and disquietude; it cannot help seeking after peace, and it is, therefore, restlessly "tossed to and fro." Peculiarities of temperament, youthful thoughtlessness, special good fortune in outward circumstances, and an uncommon amount of insensibility, may hide from us this inner discord, but it lies hid in the depths of the soul, watching for an opportunity to assert itself; and in innumerable cases it exerts an influence upon the entire life, and even stamps its impress upon the countenance, in lines of care and uncertainty, of unrest and anguish. The utmost, therefore, that the power of moral good in the natural man can accomplish, is not to produce a character conformable with the divine law—this it can in no case do—but to lead him on to humble self-renouncing acceptance of Christ's redemption. Excellent in itself, it may, nevertheless, be transformed into the worst obduracy, if it proudly and in self-sufficiency sets itself up in opposition to the salvation offered.

In his treatise on original sin, in reply to Möhler, Nitzsch § 5. VARIETIES OF MORAL CHARACTER. lays stress upon the fact that there are great differences of moral character in individuals, apart from redemption.* Experience witnesses to these individual differences, and Holy Scripture, in both the Old Testament and the New, fully recognises them. So great are these differences that they make us question whether we are right in including these manifold grades and forms of moral character in one and the same class, upon which we pronounce a condemnatory judgment on account of its inner principle.† Not

* *L. c.* pp. 257, 258.

† Thus DAVID SCHULZ makes use of this distinction, confirming it by a series of quotations and examples from the Old Testament in his *Schriftmässigen Beurtheilung der Lehre von der Erbsünde*, the appendix to his *Christl. Lehre vom Glauben.* pp. 235-237. So also BRETSCHNEIDER, *Die Grundlage des evang. Pietismus*, p. 49. Any one may see that our early theologians recognised this distinction when explaining their doctrine of original sin by referring to HUNNIUS *De providentia Dei*, p. 239, as well as to GERHARD and QUENSTEDT.

only is there a contrast between man's moral life as a partaker of Christ's redemption, and apart from it, but within this latter sphere we find alike those nobler natures that make the spiritual their highest aim, and without difficulty curb the fleshy element, and side by side with them those more common natures which incline to the material, now in reckless libertinism, and now in passive surrender to the service of the flesh. We find men of benevolent, gentle, and kind sensibilities, with a strong love of truth and justice; and hardened and hateful characters, who sacrifice truth and justice to interest. It may always be shown, indeed, that the latter are by far the more numerous, yet the fact remains, that among the unredeemed there are always some belonging to the nobler and more righteous type of character.

We are glad to avail ourselves of the turn thus given to our inquiry by the recognition of this unquestionable distinction, as rendering it unnecessary for us to undertake the sad and unpleasant task of proving the existence of sin in those cases wherein every one recognises its presence. But as to the better and nobler of unregenerate men, the immediate question is only whether sin be in any degree present in their life. This is a simple question of fact, and experience alone can answer it. But any one who has given attention to the testimony of experience in this matter will allow it to be an indisputable fact, though it cannot obviously be argued out by logical induction, that every human life which has passed beyond the term of childish unconsciousness is stained in some degree by actual sin. To assert the opposite, would only be a sign of inexperience and ignorance of life, excusable in youthful enthusiasm towards some who are highly esteemed, but not in men of riper intellect and maturer knowledge.

Sin in the best of men.

Even those theories which fritter away the full significance of sin must allow its presence everywhere in human life. Pantheistic modes of thought, indeed, are ultimately compelled (as we have already seen) from a speculative point of view, to deny the existence of sin as such. But they by no means deny that what our moral sense disapproves as "sin," exists in every human life. Taking, as it does, a wider and nobler view of

This universally allowed.

the world than can theological Rationalism, and therefore more easily adopting the belief in Demonism, Pantheism can the more clearly apprehend and describe evil in its full force as the antithesis of good, and in the range of its power over men. And fancying that it has found the magic spell whereby evil in its very worst forms may be transformed into a necessary element, it has no longer any need to indulge in those *couleur de rose* illusions wherewith theological rationalism so easily hides from itself the real state of human life.

Still, this Deistical and Pelagian doctrine even, which lies Rationalistic at the foundation of our theological Rationalism, view. in the stricter application of the term, cannot help granting the truth of our statement. In discussing this question concerning the universality of sin, it commonly insists strongly upon the differences between glaring violations of duty, gross crimes and vices, and utter degradation on the one hand, and manifold more trifling impurities and ordinary sins of weakness, mixed up, they know not how, with the disposition and conduct of men, on the other. Towards the former it usually feels a lively aversion, and even abhorrence; it cannot tolerate that any one should regard them as owing to natural weakness or deterioration of race under unavoidable circumstances. It asserts the full freedom of the individual to avoid them, and regards them as exceptional. It readily allows that no human life is wholly free from faults and failings of the latter kind, but these it regards as the unavoidable effects of man's finiteness and limited strength, so that no moral reproach can seriously be put upon him.*

But supposing this view to be correct, what would be the What it result? Nothing could be looked upon as, strictly would lead to. speaking, violating the ideal of morality and its claims, save what lay beyond the line thus separating acts of weakness from great offences; and whatever transcends this virtue, so palpably blended with weakness and infirmity, must be excluded from the range of the moral law. But who that really believes in moral truth can rest content with such a

* This view and explanation of the distinction in question coincides with some thoughts of VATKE's, which, however, are usually foreign to him. See vol. i. of this work, p. 397.

doctrine as this? And as often happens now-a-days, in the explanation of a difference not wholly groundless, that is taken for granted which was to have been proved. The very fact that the sin which falls within the line thus drawn is the common experience of human life, so that its existence excites wonder neither in ourselves nor others, is itself the sad phenomenon which we have to consider without explaining it away on the one hand, or surrounding the idea of sin on the other. If sin, in the true idea of it, be maintained, it must be held inviolably true that it is wrong even to move a finger in opposition to God's will. Now, instead of abiding by this principle, the theory I have named argues from the universality of one class of sins, that they must belong to the essence of human nature itself, and denies that sins of this class are sins. It gives that name only to those offences which transgress the ordinary standard, and which more obviously spring from wilful criminality. Can anything be more arbitrary than this standard? Those transgressions indeed alone awaken our abhorrence which manifestly surpass the faults that we ourselves are prone to; but if a mind perfectly pure were among us, he would estimate all untruthfulness and petty selfishness, all harshness and self-exaltation, all want of love and indolence in goodness which we find even among better men, as in the highest degree reprehensible. The universal weakness and frailty of men is only their disloyalty to what is perfectly holy. And he who allows the universality of human weakness and imperfection, must also allow that no human life can boast of freedom from the taint of actual sin, of conduct liable to condemnation in the sight of God.

If we examine facts more closely, experience witnesses that

<small>Testimony of the best of men.</small> even among the better class of men, among those, at least, who are the more honest, we shall hardly find one who would venture seriously to affirm that he had never sinned, at least in direct violation of his conscience. "I look into my heart," says a noble-minded theologian, whose religious predelictions incline to Pelagianism,* "and I see with penitent sorrow that I must in God's sight

* TÖLLNER in his Dissertation upon the division of sins into premeditated and unpremeditated, *Theol. Untersuchungen*, vol. i. part ii. 247.

accuse myself of all the offences I have named:" and he had named only deliberate transgressions: "he who does not allow that he is similarly guilty, let him too look deep into his heart."

We must maintain, moreover, that sins which elicit the more or less distinct warning of conscience, occur as a rule more frequently among the better class of men. The giddy multitude in ungovernable selfishness seldom rise so high as to sin against their conscience, because as far as their depraved impulses are concerned conscience is asleep; their sinfulness usually bears the stamp of rudeness and shamelessness. Moral perception and discrimination usually grow with the awakening force of moral endeavour; but this endeavour, this moral volition, does not in equal proportion become master in its own house. Transgressions spring abundantly from the dark principle of the perverted will still dominant within, but they can no longer pass over the clear bright disc of conscience without intercepting its beams. Hence it is that the man must to a certain extent be morally awakened in order to his attaining that clearer perception of sin on which his salvation depends. His servitude does not begin when first he feels it; but he begins to feel it when first he strives against it. Here we see the twofold bearing of the Law, and of the discord which it produces in human life in proportion as the life endeavours to be one with it. Looking towards the past, it witnesses to the deep depravity of the man who can by sin pervert what was in itself intended for life into a power of death. Looking towards the future, it proclaims the existence and the supremacy of a divine germ in the soul; for the entrance of the law brings the soul into variance with itself, and "puts it to death." "When the commandment came, sin revived and I died." Thus the growing and deepening consciousness of the law results at first in the commission of more *sins against conscience.*

It surely must seem a strange thing, and well-nigh inconceivable from our present point of view, that, so far as experience can judge, no human life which has passed the age of childhood is perfectly free from sins against conscience. It is in sins against conscience that Pelagianism, and modes of thought akin thereto, recognise a perfect guarantee that the acts in question have sprung from the freedom of the will, and that the individual is accountable for them. And herein they are practically right, for the warning voice of conscience before the act seems directly to witness that the deed which ought to be left undone might have been so. And yet this class of sins, this direct and positive evil-doing, seems to be so universal that, on Pelagian grounds, we can hardly avoid the conclusion that it is a necessity of our nature. The contradiction is so obvious that, if they who adopt Pelagian modes of thought adhere to the principle of man's unlimited power of will to resist sins against conscience, there is nothing for them but to deny the fact of the universality of these sins, let experience say what it may.

The moral life of our race collectively shows its true character in the sad fact that it possesses no profound consciousness of its insufficiency and worthlessness in God's sight, nor of its need of a higher power than its own—a divine helper. And while it understands not the radical nature of the disease, or at least of the healing required by the repudiation of its selfish life and the appropriation of a new, a divine principle, it fancies—if it possess any moral earnestness—that it can help itself by its own efforts and its partial amendments. The true cause of this darkness, this perversion of the moral sense with its consequences, lies in the practical principle ruling supreme in man's unregenerate life—in his unsubdued and persistent selfishness. This is the universal characteristic of mankind by nature, and it may coexist, not only with outward rectitude and respectability, but even with earnest efforts after what is virtuous in particulars, efforts which may to some extent be successful while yet the essential principle which rules this state of life remains unsubdued. The fountain of that new life wherein man, disenthralled from self, becomes free in fellowship with God, is still unopened, and the moral *arbitrium* with all its relative freedom and power of self-movement still remains essentially *servum*.

Mankind collectively viewed.

If this be a true estimate of man's moral life, then human weakness and frailty confirm the proverb, suggested not by the Christian doctrine of sin, but by political experience, and ratified by the philosophy of

Sayings implying man's sinfulness.

reason, "Every man has his price."* Or if the maxim is too boldly stated thus, it will hold good if expressed in another form, viz., "Every man has his weak side," and sin has only to overtake him in the right time and form in order by degrees to entangle him in wickedness and crime. The beautiful soul in Goethe's *Wilhelm Meister*, according to her own confession, must have felt that had not an unseen hand shielded her, she might have become a Girard, a Cartouche, a Damiens, or any other monster in sin that might be named; she manifestly felt the propensity in that direction in her heart.† The lovable innocence of youth, especially in woman, may awaken a momentary persuasion that there can be no taint of sin there; and yet there is no charming bloom of human life so perishable as is this. A brief season of confiding companionship with men depraved, yet in other respects her superiors, will suffice to steep this tender innocence, unshielded by a higher power, in the mire of low vulgarity of mind. How often is the remark made, and how seldom felt in its terrible truth, "Not years, nor months, nor days, a moment may suffice to entangle boasted virtue in crimes, the ensnarements of which will sweep it irresistibly along." In Lessing's *Entwurf zu einem Faust*, that is reckoned promptest among the seven fleet spirits of hell which is as quick as the transition from good to evil. Remembering the results of our inquiry thus far, we shall not be likely to question the part that freedom plays in human

* A keen discerner of human character well observes : "Il y a des gens, de qui l'on ne peut jamais croire du mal sans l'avoir vu; mais il n'y en a point, en qui il nous doive surprendre en le voyant." So, too, ARISTOPHANES in the *Plutus*:—

φεῦ!
ὡς οὐδὲν ἀτέχνως ὑγιές ἐστιν οὐδενός,
ἀλλ' εἰσι τοῦ κέρδους ἅπαντες ἥττονες.

Referring to the limitation of the above proverb to mankind apart from redemption as it is understood in the connection where it stands, Dr ZELLER, in his *Zeitschrift* (1847, p. 65) remarks, "the maxim thus taken would be true of our pious theologians." If Dr Zeller will stoop to arguments which remind one of the weapons used by BRUNO BAUER in controversy with "theologians," I cannot prevent him, but I am not certainly obliged to follow him in this style of argument.

† Compare SCHLEIERMACHER's true and able remarks in his *Glaubenslehre*, § 73, 2 (vol. i. 450) ; [and John Bunyan's saying when he saw a murderer led out to execution, "There goes John Bunyan, if it were not for the grace of God." *Tr.*]

virtue; but this virtue and freedom amounts only to this, that the adequate price has not yet been offered in order to bribe it into the thraldom of sin. From this point of view, the security of our virtue against a power lurking within us, whose outbreak would be its overthrow, is at the mercy of circumstances and a matter of chance. Whoever will not allow this, has only to consider what he might have been, if in early life the influences surrounding him had been such as were calculated to poison his mind; or he may study those parts of his actual life when it was not owing to him that wicked inclinations stirring in him did not grow into terrible passions, and that a momentary trifling with a seemingly little sin, did not unwittingly abandon him to a dominion urging him on to crimes he knows not what. By reflections such as these, we may learn better to understand the reason why Christ taught his disciples to pray, " Lead us not into temptation."

§ 6. SCRIP-TURE REGARDS SIN AS UNIVERSAL.

We have been spared* the task of preparing a detailed proof of the fact that Holy Scripture regards the presence of sin in mankind as a universal fact. It is not a question concerning the import of a few isolated texts; the truth runs throughout the whole of the Old Testament, and still more throughout the New. Some modern theologians, who cannot entertain the doctrine that all men are sinners, have taken considerable pains, by means of biblical criticism, to erase this doctrine from Scripture.† But these attempts have been quite set aside by the progress of New Testament exegesis during the past ten years; the critical expositions of the Epistle to the Romans, by men of the Rationalistic school, such as Rückert, Reiche,

* See KLAIBER's *Neutestamentliche Lehre von der Sünde und Erlösung*, p. 47-49.

† BRETSCHNEIDER does this chiefly in his work *Die Grundlage des evangelischen Pietismus*. From Rom. v. 12, however, he infers that it was the Apostle's belief and the witness of experience, "that no man escapes entirely without sin;" but he takes this only as a denial of the notion that man is ever perfect like God, pp. 184, 185. At p. 126 he says : "Nothing distinct from God can possess God's perfection, least of all a being consisting of body as well as soul, such as man. The fact, therefore, that in the best of men there is here and there defect and error of conduct, does not make man wicked," and this shows that on his theory, so far as the universality of sin is admitted, its reality as sin is denied.

Fritzsche, frankly admit that the universality of sin is presupposed in St Paul's writings.

The strongest expressions of the Old Testament, describing the state of mankind universally as sinful, are of such a character as to oblige our postponing the consideration of them until the next chapter. As to other texts, the doctrine cannot be argued from Gen. vi. 5, or Psalm xiv. 1-3; for these passages have not in their primary connection a universal application. The universality of sin is, however, expressly asserted in 1 Kings viii. 26; Psalm cxliii. 2; Prov. xx. 9; Eccles. vii. 20.

That it is presupposed in the New Testament is evident from the fact that Christ everywhere makes participation in the kingdom of God conditional upon transformation of mind or Regeneration; Matt. iv. 17; Mark i. 15, vi. 12; Luke xxiv. 47; John iii. 3, 5. The moral state in which the Saviour finds man is one which thus needs renewal, and if it be maintained that it is otherwise with any, it can only be upon the supposition of some magic worth or power in the external church communion wherein they were born and brought up. The sinfulness of the human race is also implied in those representations which describe the gate to life as strait and the way narrow (Matt. vii. 14), leading out of a state of spiritual death, by the crucifixion of "the old man," Matt. xvi. 24; John xii. 25; Rom. vi. 4-6; Gal. v. 24; and in the fact that Christ began His great sermon concerning the kingdom of God, and the conditions upon which it is attained, with beatitudes upon the poor in spirit and the mourners, Matt. v. 3, 4. Antithesis like these, pervading the New Testament throughout, are meaningless save upon the presupposition of the universal moral derangement of human life. The same truth is implied in Christ's calling his gospel, which was to be preached to all mankind, glad tidings of "forgiveness of sins in his name," Luke xxiv. 47 (John xx. 23). He

Universal redemption implies universal sin.

and His apostles expressly testified that no one could come to the Father but through Him, that there is salvation in His Name only, and that man is made the child of God, an heir of salvation, only by the new birth and faith in Him, John xiv. 6; Acts iv. 12; Mark xvi. 16; John i. 12, 13, iii. 14, 15—declarations which obviously imply the negative truth that man's state universally, apart from fellowship with

Christ, is one which God's holiness pronounces wholly disordered and corrupt. This is also stated very strongly by St John when he says regarding the man who believes not in the Son—not only that "he shall not see life"—but also that "the wrath of God *abideth* on him," John iii. 36 ; clearly implying that he to whom this choice of believing in Christ or not believing in Him is offered, is already the object of God's punitive justice. Holy Scripture, accordingly, represents the objective basis of forgiveness, *i.e.*, the redemptive work of Christ—as something accomplished (as far as its sufficiency and applicability in itself is concerned) FOR ALL MEN ; 2 Cor. v. 14, 15 ; 1 Tim. ii. 4, 6 ; Rom. v. 18 ; Heb. ii. 8. The declarations, moreover, which describe the design and power of Redemption to be for the salvation of the WORLD (John iii. 16, 17, vi. 51, xii. 47 ; 2 Cor. v. 19 ; 1 John ii. 2), imply the same universality of sin, for man needs a Saviour and an Atonement only in so far as he is afflicted with sin and laden with guilt. The fact, too, that all men are sinful and guilty before God is stated in so many words by St Paul, Rom. iii. 9, 19, 20, 23, v. 12 ; Gal. iii. 22 ; and is, moreover, the necessary basis of his whole doctrinal system, so that it would be superfluous to adduce more modern criticisms upon the Pauline doctrine generally, and upon the Epistle to the Romans in particular, in confirmation of it. We would simply mention, in passing, that the Apostle's declarations concerning the negative effects of the law—that "by the deeds of the law can no flesh be justified, for by the law is the knowledge of sin;" that "the law worketh wrath," and "tendeth to death," Rom. iii. 19, iv. 15, vii. 10—are utterly unmeaning, save on that pre-supposition. Christ calls even His disciples, who were distinguished from the bulk of mankind by their hungering after righteousness, and whom He had taken into personal fellowship with Him, "evil"—πονηροί—Luke xi. 13. Not only is he "evil" in God's sight whose whole life is evil, but he also whose life is in the least degree tainted with sin. The petition, "Forgive us our trespasses," which Christ included in the prayer given to His disciples as the expression of their continual relationship to God, shows that He foresaw the continuance of sin as not wholly subdued even among the subjects of His kingdom. St John accordingly exhorts Christians who are in fellowship with Christ, to the confession of their sins—

clearly the sins they commit in their present state as Christians—
and He calls it "self-deception," if they say that they have no sin.

But it is said that Christ expressly admitted that there were
"The whole" beyond the range of Revelation, "the whole,
and the "who need not a physician," Matt. ix. 12, 13
"righteous." Luke v. 31, 32; and St Peter says that apart from
redemption, "he that feareth God and worketh righteousness
is accepted of Him," Acts x. 35. Now, according to th
connection of the passage, "the whole," "the righteous," wh
"need no repentance," must be the Pharisees and scribes wh
murmured that Jesus associated with publicans and sinners
Can it be supposed that Christ regarded them as reall
righteous? If any among the legally righteous who surrounde
Him were truly "whole," and needed not the physician, i
must have been, not the Pharisees, but that young man wh
could say in a truer sense than that of Pharisaism, "All thes
have I kept from my youth." Yet Christ describes hi
shrinking from His requirement as a self-exclusion from th
kingdom of heaven, admission to which his legal righteousnes
could not secure to him. "The whole, who need not th
Physician," were those in their own opinion whole; anc
assuming their standing-point, Christ the Saviour of sinner
the Physician of the sick, says that He could not be this fo
them, so long as they were satisfied with their own righteous
ness (Rom. x. 3).† Luke xv. 5, must be explained in the sam
manner. But as to Acts x. 35, the sense in which th
statements are to be understood as predicated of one apart from
Christ, must be inferred from the fact that Peter proceeded a
once to preach to this God-fearing man "who worke
righteousness," the gospel of the forgiveness of sins in th
name of Jesus Christ, v. 43. From this, and from the rite o
Baptism administered to Cornelius and his household, it is clea
in what sense such an earnest striver after righteousness i
acceptable (δεκτός) to God, *i.e.*, welcome to be received into th
fellowship of His Son. Such a man, "hungering and thirstin

---

* See the true and beautiful remarks of LUECKE upon this text, in his *Com
mentary*, pp. 137, 138.

† We have a striking instance of the manner in which one text of Hol
Scripture throws light upon another in the comparison of Rom. x. 3. with Phi
iii. 4–9.

after righteousness" (Matt. v. 6), may be regarded as one " who is of God " (John viii. 47) ; he is under the influence of a principle in human nature which is Godlike, and which tends to God. But it influences him to hear God's words from the lips of the Redeemer, to keep it, and in the strength of this hearing and keeping, to triumph over the death of the natural life (John viii. 47, 51).

CHAPTER II.

SIN AS A CORRUPTION OF HUMAN NATURE.

§ 1. IMPURITY OF THE HUMAN HEART.

A CALM consideration of the manner in which sin affects us, will suffice to convince us that the notion of its being merely an outward act or omission is utterly superficial and untrue. Even if the beginning of each one's earthly life be considered perfectly pure, it must be admitted that moral acts produce a corresponding moral state, and when a man adopts what is sinful among the principles which guide his decisions, sin is no longer something merely external, but nestles within him, in his very principles of action, and in his feelings. If, indeed, the man's inner nature (according to that notion) were always pure, the first good resolve, earnestly made, would suffice to exclude from his conduct every trace of sin, and it would not be the man himself, but some other nature that manifested itself in his acts. But in proportion as we recognize the untenableness of the notion I have named, the conviction will be forced upon us, that sin is something dwelling within, and that it has its seat, not merely in our conduct, but in our perceptions, inclinations, principles, and feelings.

Holy Scripture also teaches us to regard sin not merely as an occurrence in outward experience, but a disturbance of the inner life, not only as something which enters within us at a certain time, and passes away again (as perhaps Matt. v. 28 implies), but as a permanent defilement and corruption of the heart, manifest in various sinful acts which spring therefrom.

The proofs of this already given (Vol. I. p. 183), may be confirmed by those texts which describe the habitual tenor of the inner life as evil and corrupt ; *e.g.*, Matt. vi. 23 ; Luke xvi 15 ; John xvi. 9 ; Rom. i. 21 ; 1 Cor. xvi. 22; Eph. iv. 18 It is clear from our investigation in Book II., that the Pauline idea of the Flesh, as contrasted with the Spirit, implies the same truth.

In what manner, then, does this element of defilement and corruption dwell within us ? Can it be defined as a combination of certain inclinations, strivings, and principles, and can it be examined by itself, as thus distinct from the pure elements of our inner life ?

It must, of course, be not only possible, but necessary, in idea at least, to distinguish corruption from purity of nature, and sin from what is good in man. And even in actual life, with its character and acts, we fancy that, by a careful self-analysis, we can make the same separation. But the more thoroughly we search ourselves, the more convinced are we that the task cannot be fully, but only proximately accomplished. Fresh elements of impurity are discerned by the practised eye after every separation, and these have in turn to be separated from the manifold inclinations and activities of life, which are in themselves justifiable.* In cases where sanctification has really begun, and where, in spite of many hindrances and drawbacks it may be regarded as the steady development of a new life, of a new divinely-generated personality, sin (especially in men of calm and even temperament) seldom assumes the form of positive and actual transgression. But though no longer manifesting itself in this form, it has by no means wholly disappeared from the life. It may still be inwardly working as a disturbing and troublesome agent, marring the true freshness of moral zeal, and tempting the man, more or less, to resign himself to certain calls and inward promptings, which, though not leading to actual sins, yet somehow beget imperceptibly a

Marginal note: Partly distinguishable from what is pure in us.

---

* Even the Rabinical theology, in its doctrine of the יֵצֶר הרע in the human heart (see Gen. vi. 5, viii. 21), and in spite of the absurdities in which, according to its wont, it clothes the thought, has a better apprehension of sin as deep seated within, than the extremes of Pelagianism in our modern theology. See NITZSCH, *System der christlichen Lehre*, § 106, note 2.

SIN AS A CORRUPTION OF HUMAN NATURE.

state of indolence and selfish weakness, or a prevailing tone of sharpness and bitterness of feeling. In a thousand ways sin would adulterate, mar and spoil, by impure and selfish motives, acts and behaviour which spring primarily from moral impulses. This is usually the way in which sin manifests itself in a life wherein the work of sanctification has been begun.

We must, therefore, recognize an abiding root of sin within us, a root whose shoots and branches may not be wholly manifest, but would be found (did our observation enable us thoroughly to discern them) intertwined in simultaneous growth with all the motives and developments of our life, so that our noblest acts cannot be pefectly pure. If sin, in the case of the regenerate at least, were not an abiding power, exerting its influence on all the activities of life, but appearing only occasionally when any strong temptation occurred, and then disappearing again, every successive entrance of it would be a new fault, suddenly changing the renewed man from perfect purity into a sinner. This, however, is not the testimony of experience, and were it true, it would only hinder serious self-examination, and lead us to desist from searching out and combating the hidden causes from which our sinful actions spring. In this case, indeed, we should have no consciousness of sin, except as it appears in definite transgression, and this is certainly not the experience of Christian life.

Again, if we bear in mind the disturbing and darkening influence of sin upon man's moral discernment and knowledge, and how this dimness and error of moral judgment leads to many unperceived faults in our conduct, how can we presume with certainty to select from this complicated coil (wherein every end is a beginning) the threads that belong to the moral disorder of human life, so as at any given moment to consider the elements of sin purely by themselves?*

Even if we cannot by the minutest analysis discover the least trace of sin, or the slightest unrighteous tendency within us at some one moment of our life, it would not be right for us to conclude that we were then perfectly pure; nor should we doubt the latent power of sin, even where we cannot

---

* To the same effect the *Formula Concordiae* (par. i. cap. i.) affirms:— *Sane affirmamus good hanc naturae corruptionem ab ipsa natura nemo nisi solus Deus separare queat.*

discover any effect produced by it upon the actual state of our moral life at any one point or portion of it.

But let us look beyond single moments or points of our life to the abiding tendencies and peculiarities of character which distinguish those who are sincerely striving after holiness. Contemplating thus their virtues, and not their faults, the remarkable fact presents itself that their virtues are commonly inseparably blended with their faults. So completely have they grown together that the latter seem to be only a different aspect of the former. This cannot shake our faith in the reality of ideal moral goodness, or in the possibility of its embodiment in real life; but it warns us how deep-rooted sin is within us, the noblest tendencies of our life being continually liable to deterioration. Thus strict earnestness degenerates imperceptibly into severity, and gentleness into weakness, energetic activity into imprudent meddling, and calm moderation into careless acquiescence; bold decision, maintaining its own convictions firmly, becomes intolerant narrowness and self-opinionated arbitrariness; due regard to the peculiarities and convictions of others, degenerates into paralysing indifferentism and sceptical indolence; lively trust lapses into haughtiness and presumption, and a wise prudence into cowardice and hesitating anxiety. And as human life is at present constituted, while sowing and cultivating these virtues in ourselves and others, we must ever be prepared to reap with them the tares of their degenerate forms.

Blending of virtue and vice in life.

Modern moralists (especially Tzschirner, in a singular work upon this subject) have searched out an affinity between virtues and vices. What is true in this thought rests upon what we are now describing. Every human virtue has its counterfeit, its degenerate form, which seeks to supplant it; and though totally different in its nature, the deterioration producing this takes place imperceptibly to ourselves and others, like twilight, by slow degrees and easy transitions, so that a slight alteration of a few seemingly unimportant lines transforms the noblest countenance into a revolting caricature. As our organic life is continually exposed to a twofold danger of death,—hypersthenic and asthenic,—from excess of strength

Fineness of the line between the two.

or from debility—so virtue in its earthly development is threatened from opposite sides, from selfishness on the one hand positive and active, and on the other negative and passive; and in resisting the one it is liable to fall into the other. Virtue, like beauty and the higher forms of truth, has a delicate outline. The pure heart would ever preserve this line with ease and certainty, delicate as it is; because it is the simple expression of itself. Sin it is, with its inward penetrating power, which renders it necessary for us ever to be on our guard, lest our neglect on one side or the other should allow bad seed to spring up, the up-rooting of which must, sooner or later, cost us many a hard struggle.

It is worthy of observation, finally, that the practical limitedness of one's own views exercises a narrowing and disturbing influence upon our discernment, and thus increases our perplexity in separating what is evil in us from what is good. How few are there who for a moment hesitate to make their individual onesidedness the absolute standard of their judgment in contemplating any other onesidedness. We daily see how men even of earnest disposition, when advocating with special ardour the moral claims of their own side, are wholly insensible to the claims of the other side, which they ignore; and while very quick to notice the slightest variance with the moral claims of their side, fancy that they see a want of moral principle in those who are only avoiding their partiality. If we are fully alive to this narrowness which biases all moral judgment, and even our self-judgment, we shall feel compelled to give up the idea of accurately distinguishing, as if by chemical analysis, the pure and clear metal from the dross.

Our moral discernment imperfect.

But what has brought us into this disordered condition? We might easily answer this question if at some one moment of our life there had been a transition from sinless purity into the discord of sin. We have already shown that there has been no such transition. We cannot discover any such change in our own experience—and a change of such importance could not occur without our knowledge,—neither can we observe it in others. Man is in sin, he knows not how. Upon the awakening of moral con-

§ 2. ORIGIN OF THIS IMPURITY.

sciousness he finds in himself hostility to its claims. Indeed the discovery of this clashing, this hostility, is usually the occasion of that awakening. The first act of sin presupposes in the man the presence and perception of an opposing obligation. But individual experience of sin intensifies this consciousness, and becomes an element deeply affecting the development of the inner life. Hence it is that children of a more passionate nature and decided disposition generally awake to a definite moral consciousness much earlier than they of less marked character and weaker nature; the deeper shadow brings out to view the sunbeam of conscience more quickly and powerfully from the depths of the soul.

The idea of a first fall into sin in the case of each individual is now-a-days laid stress upon, and we by no means deny that there is truth in it. We have already given our reasons (Vol. I. p. 42) for rejecting the view of our early theologians, who attributed *peccata actualia* to new-born children. Actual sin exists only where moral consciousness awakes; but this consciousness may be veiled in the feeling of reverence for the person of the parent. In the life of every man there must be a moment when the first actual sin was committed, and the form which this first act of sin assumes, and the relation of his free will to the temptation and to the forbidding conscience, must exert an important influence alike upon the person's bias to the sin in question, upon his character as more or less evil, and upon the progress, more or less rapid, of the development of sin within him. And yet this personal fall does not present itself to him as the entrance of a wholly new element into the life of the child, but rather as the development and manifestation of a hidden power, the awakening of a force hitherto slumbering within. Sin does not now begin to exist in him; it now first comes out. It is just in this way that the Apostle Paul describes the falling of the individual into sin, Rom. vii. 8, 9. While speaking of sin as previously "dead," he represents it as needing only the stimulus of its contrast to conscience in order to revive it and to produce every perverted lust; so that this deadness is only a state of fettered activity, wherein the principle already inwardly present has not yet manifested itself in outward life.

And thus the Apostle decided the question so often raised concerning the innocence of childhood. That would indeed be a very rude apprehension of human life and of the Christian doctrine of universal sinfulness which could overlook the great difference between evil as it exists in the child, unconscious and undeveloped, and as it manifests itself in the full grown man, matured, developed, and elevated into a principle. In this the relative innocence of childhood consists. It is not merely that sin is in the child more or less in the form of unconsciousness, nor that the narrowness of his experience, his powers of mind, and his desires, together with his special relationships in life, forbid the commission of serious offences; but the perverted self-seeking volition is really not so strong in him. It is in particular its unacquaintedness with lying and falsehood, and the frank, ready trust springing therefrom, which gives to the innocence of childhood its peculiar character, and which often imparts, even to the germs of perverted inclination and will, an air of *naive* attractiveness. It is to this relative innocence of childhood, to this unquestioning faith, and to this inner capacity of attachment in the child that Christ refers when He makes the disposition of children a pattern for His disciples, and says of the little children, "of such is the kingdom of heaven," Matt. xviii. 3, xix. 14; Luke xviii. 17.* The reference, moreover, is to the moral features of childhood generally, to what childhood is as a rule; for, however inexplicable it may appear to many theorists, an extended observation of children and of childhood cannot ignore the fact that there are exceptions wherein decidedly perverted dispositions—a degree of malice, falseness, and hatred—appear even in the third, fourth, or fifth year of the child's life, which need only more adequate physical and mental power in order to manifest themselves in the gravest crimes.

Some consider that the words of Christ, and the testimony of experience, alike imply something more than I have named; that they indicate absolute innocence and perfect purity in early childhood. If this be so, such an original freedom from every innate disposition to

---

* See NEANDER'S *Pflanzung der Kirche*, p. 700.

sin* must necessarily belong to all. But allowing this, how do these persons explain the fact that all who live beyond childhood are tainted with sin, though of different kinds and in different degrees? Outward causes, deficient education, bad example, the prevalence of corrupt principles in society, &c., may be named in explanation, but these all imply a corresponding evil susceptibility in the child, which is only another name for that corrupt disposition or innate sinfulness. And seeing that these external evil influences are not always present, the still more difficult question would arise,—How is it, that even where outward circumstances are most favourable to virtue, we never find as the consequence a perfectly holy life? This could hardly be guaranteed even were we to carry out the proposal of Socrates in Plato's *Meno*, and to confine children, by nature good (some of them being naturally good, as is there suggested, or all being so according to the present theory), in a fortress, guarding them more jealously than gold lest any one should corrupt them.

But if the freedom of the will be urged as implying the possibility of every one's admitting sin into his originally pure nature, it must be remembered that freedom implies equally the possibility of every one's refraining from any contact with sin. Now, if one portion of the human race were affected by sin and the other not, the freedom of the will might thus furnish an adequate explanation, as the ultimate reason of the fact. But seeing that sin appears in every human life wherein the moral consciousness is awake, freedom will not suffice to explain the phenomenon. Indeed, the presupposition of this freedom really makes the fact more inexplicable; for we must remember that, while implying an ability with equal ease to choose either good or evil, free-will is not the sport of mere chance, but is pledged to a determinate decision by the claims of the moral consciousness.

Feeling the difficulty, those who thus argue have recourse to another principle, namely, that of a Dualism in human nature, according to which the spirit strives upwards, and the sensuous nature downwards towards base things. Or they may prefer to

<small>The notion of a Dualism in human nature.</small>

---

* See the distinction drawn between innate disposition and the mere possibility as implied in formal freedom, p. 30 of this volume.

describe the principle as the weakness of man's fleshly nature, in consequence of which he is unable always to withstand the promptings of the flesh towards what may be forbidden by conscience. We need not here repeat what has already been said about the reduction of all sin to the predominance of the sensuous impulses in man above the spirit. But if it were possible to reduce all sin to this so-called weakness in man as a sensuous being, every one who regards sin as sin, and who believes the maxim that the tree is known by its fruits, and the nature of the principle by its results, must discern in this weakness an evil disposition or sinful tendency in man from which his sinful acts proceed. The only difference between this view and the Church doctrine controverted by it, seems to be, that according to the latter, the disposition to sin possessed by every man, is looked upon as a disturbance or depravation, something foreign to our nature as created by God, and which has come upon it by a fall and a degeneracy; whereas the former finds nothing in this evil disposition incompatible with the good ordering of human nature at the outset, and which might not follow from the necessary laws of its development.* Thus, in order not to admit the fact that impurity has arisen by a fall, it attributes to human nature, to begin with, a principle which violates the Creator's holiness; and moreover, we can no longer see how it can, logically speaking, allow any actual sin, how what it explains as a natural weakness can be regarded as a disturbance.

From what has now been said, it is clear that the notion of the absolute purity of childhood must be given up if the presence of sin in every developed life is to be maintained. The fact must be recognized, that in every human being there is a moral derangement, that an inborn bias towards evil is deep-rooted in human nature as " radical evil ; " while it must at the same time be maintained, that this evil, however deeply rooted, can primarily have arisen only from a voluntary fall, a personal and wilful disobedience.

Idea of absolute purity of childhood untenable.

* See the able remarks of SARTORIUS, as before, p. 85. TÖLLNER puts this alternative somewhat differently, for he recognizes in human weakness a corruption of man's nature, and yet attributes the origin of it to the necessary laws of human development. See his Dissertation upon "taking pleasure in evil," *Theol. Untersuchungen*, vol. i. 1, 97.

These conclusions fully justify the old theological expression
peccatum originale, understanding it as simply
Original sin. affirming the existence of an innate tendency or
bias towards sin in every human being, and apart from the
question whether this bias be inherited or not. This is all that
Luther means when he says that sin is *de natura, de essentia
hominis,* and when he calls sin *peccatum substantiale* or
essentiale. He does not mean that sin is a sort of new nature
possessed by man in his present state, and supplanting wholly
his original constitution ; he simply wishes to affirm strongly,
that before and apart from its realization in will and deed, sin
cleaves to human nature in man's present disordered condition,
and is sure to assert itself in perverted choice and action.*

We may, indeed, differ from Luther in his way of accounting
for this " sinful nature " in man,† but we cannot
§ 3. PHENO-
MENA CON- help granting that a long array of unquestionable
FIRMING THIS facts and obvious phenomena of our moral life and
VIEW.
consciousness are quite inexplicable if sin be not recognized as " the present disturbed constitution of our nature."‡
In a thousand cases we tacitly take this for granted in judging
others ; even those who have denied it in theory have practically to acknowledge it. In our present investigation indisputable facts have urged us on step by step to the recognition of
inborn sinfulness. And many other similar facts might be
named which confirm this recognition. Consider, for example,
the significance of a phenomenon universally felt which we have
already referred to. How is it that whenever a human being
meets us, we know that we have not to do with a holy but
with a sinful nature ? Any one pretending to a moderate

---

* We may therefore venture to call *peccatum originale* man's "nature,"
because it is man's abiding state "by nature," *i.e.,* as he is at present. If we
rightly understand what the expression means, it is quite as harmless as that
phrase "second nature," often applied to habit. See the thorough analysis of
these forms of expression in the *Formula Concordiae,* pars. ii. art. i. (p. 650 of
Rechenb.)

† LUTHER calls this "nature-sin," "personal sin," but AQUINAS distinguishes
the two expressions, understanding by the latter *peccatum actuals.* This seems
to be more correct and fit, yet it will be seen in chap. iv. that we must follow
Luther.

‡ *Perpetua naturae inclinatio, interior immunditia naturae hominum,* as
MELANCHTHON expresses it in the *Apologia,* art. i. pp. 51, 53.

knowledge of men, would pity the man as a good-natured simpleton who expected to work with or by others in the various relations of life without making allowance for the natural *moral weakness of mankind,* the frailty of their virtue, and the possible alternatives arising therefrom. And yet, that very cynical shrewdness which teaches us to regard every one as a rogue, cometh itself of evil. Our duty, of course, is to meet every one upon the common terms of human intercourse, trusting to the rectitude of his disposition, unless we know anything to the contrary; yet we cannot call in question the general testimony of experience concerning human nature. So certain are we of this, that if any one were to assert his own perfect sinlessness, we should at once consider his sinfulness enhanced by overweening conceit and pride, and we could regard no one as an exception to the rule except the man whose whole moral life and character displayed a holiness far above even those who excel their brethren in virtue.

Upon what does this certainty rest? Not certainly upon the notion that sin necessarily belongs to man's nature as man; for such a supposition has already been disproved. By such an account of sin as would make perfect holiness impossible to man, sin, in the true sense of the word, would not be explained, but denied. It rests upon the testimony of experience, and hence it is not found in the unexperienced child, who looks upon any sin which he feels within as something affecting him alone, or as extending only to his playfellows, from whose selfishness he suffers. And yet the narrow range of personal experience is hardly sufficient fully to account for this certainty; and in the previous chapter we had to acknowledge that a logically inductive proof is out of the question here. A certainty which not only a few, but all men, even the most faithful disciples of Pelagius, feel and acknowledge,—a certainty, without which the universality of the mistaken belief in the *a priori* necessity of sin in every human life would be inexplicable, can only be accounted for by the existence of an *inner consciousness* that sin is deep-rooted in the human nature as it now is, an inner consciousness which experience awakens and strengthens by degrees into a settled conviction. The nature of this inner consciousness and its possibility will appear by and by.

If we contemplate the ordinary course of moral development in man, we find it a universally true and acknowledged fact, that toil, effort, and conflict are necessary in order to progress in goodness, while advance in evil is easy and smooth. The seeds of sin germinate and grow in the heart of themselves, and without any care; one has only to go on, carelessly putting no restraint on himself, and he finds himself deeply sunk in sin. But the fact that a man can advance in good only by self-conquest, necessarily implies something in his natural disposition which resists good and inclines to evil. Who that has attentively studied the history of any age, even of our own, has not learned that every noble idea, every holy endeavour, encounters the decided aversion and rude opposition of the masses, and if it is to win their approval, must be sadly misrepresented and degraded. This tragical characteristic of history is sadly reflected even in nature, wherein everything truly beautiful and glorious is but fleeting, while what is ill-favoured and mean has a tenacious life. He who would keep himself unspotted from the mire of falsehood and low practices in this world, must be prepared at any moment to forfeit his fondest earthly wishes, aims, and hopes, yea, his own life also. But this is no easy task; and hence we find the noblest characters whom history presents oftentimes faltering, and in some point or other falling short. Christ Himself had this warfare to carry on, and in suffering He conquered; His death upon the cross, while an act of free self-surrender, if considered in relation to human nature as it is, was an inevitable necessity; He was holy, and therefore He had to die. And the way in which human nature has always treated His Gospel is in itself the strongest confirmation of His testimony as to man's need of redemption.

Proneness to sin in human development.

If the bent of our nature, when we surrender ourselves to it, leads us only into sin and ruin, must we not acknowledge that this evil bias *preponderates* within us, and that whatever tendency towards good we may possess, is restrained and fettered? This is confirmed, even by those who acknowledge the natural predominance of our fleshly nature above the spirit. It is this resistance against what is good in human nature that makes discipline and punish-

Necessity for discipline.

SIN AS A CORRUPTION OF HUMAN NATURE.

ment necessary parts of education. Differences, of course, will arise from varieties of natural temperament, and also from the mystery of free self-determination onwards from its first manifestation ; but, generally speaking, education in every case finds something which must be contradicted and withstood, even the weakest and most morally pliant natures being by no means free from an evil bias. And what a sad, yet undeniable, testimony as to human nature in its present state is furnished in the fact that, while a training which surrounds the youth with sin, and teaches him only sinful principles, leads inevitably to deep depravity, the most careful and prudent moral education often fails of its design !

We are thus brought back to the idea intended to be conveyed when we speak of what man is "by nature," or in his "natural state";—expressions which we have already used. The meaning clearly is, that human life, apart from redemption, is of one definite and universal type or character, moulded to some extent by the unsubdued power of sin. Referring to this "natural state" in the last chapter, we left it undecided whether the universality of sin arose from the voluntary act of each individual in entering upon a sinful course, or whether every one found himself in that condition from his birth onwards. The investigations of this chapter lead us to the conclusion that the latter alone is true. Accordingly, all the testimonies of experience and of Scripture, proving the universality of sin and of the need of redemption, are so many proofs of INBORN depravity. And thus the theological expressions "natural state," "the natural man,"* are fully justified. *Natura* comes from *nasci ;* we call man's sinful

Meaning of the phrase "by nature."

The expression in 1 Cor. ii. 14, rendered by Luther "the natural man," cannot be taken as a *direct* scriptural warrant for these phrases. The ἄνθρωπος ψυχικὸς is a man whose mind and endeavours are absorbed in things outward and temporal (see Vol. I. p. 326) ; the expression taken alone says nothing as to whether all men, or only a few, need renewal before they can attain to fellowship with God, still less does it decide whether the tate referred to is inborn, or whether it begins in the course of life. *Indirectly*, however, it does sanction the theological idea of "the natural man," because it contrasts the ἄνθρ. ψυχικὸς with the πνευματικός (v. 12) ὁ λαβὼν τὸ πνεῦμα τὸ ἐκ τοῦ Θεοῦ and who alone can understand τὰ ὑπὸ Θεοῦ χαρισθέντα ἡμῖν—obviously in Christ. Eph. ii. 3, of which we shall have presently to speak, furnishes a *direct* authority for the use of the phrases in question.

condition his "natural state," because it is that wherein man when left to himself, grows, so long as he follows the tendencies existing within him from his very birth.

The fact that sin is universally to be found, even in the life of those who possess new energies springing up within them through the power of redeeming grace, and who are striving after sanctification, is one of the most telling witnesses as to the depth of sinfulness in human nature. In such a life the dominion of sin has certainly been overthrown, the individual will is brought into harmony with God's will, and this has become the actuating principle. Sin, too, loses its power of progressive development; it is as Schleiermacher aptly describes it, "waning and vanishing,"* the reaction merely of the old life, Eph. iv. 22, 23. We need not, therefore, be perplexed by those aggressive movements which sin sometimes makes in the lives of regenerate men, as if it were about to recover its old sway. As the new life now established within cannot be destroyed, such aggressions only rouse the divine principle within to a more determined resistance; and thus viewing the moral life as a whole, the power of sin is seen to be clearly on the decline. Accordingly that other statement of Schleiermacher's is also true, "sin, in the life of the redeemed, no longer exercises a penetrating power."† It cannot do so, for in the consciousness of the renewed and sanctified there follows upon every sin its own contradiction, and this asserts itself in the outward life. Thus we may easily see how it is that the sinfulness of "the children of this world" will appear pleasing and even attractive to others like them, provided it does not interfere with their interests, because of the unrestrained confidence and careless thoughtlessness which characterises it; whereas the sins of the regenerate never produce this feeling, because their countenance is saddened by the conscious sense of their own self-variance.

Sin in the regenerate.

It is, however, a fact which will not be denied, at least by the regenerate themselves, that those who are partakers of Christ's renewing grace, are never wholly free from sin during their earthly development. They have ever a battle to fight, a careful watch to keep, lest the divine principle within should

* *Glaubenslehre*, vol. i. 460; vol. ii. 225.
† *Ibid.* vol. i. 460.

imperceptibly decline, and the opposite selfish tendency should grow, so as to produce an inner discord difficult to remove, or even the extinction of their spiritual life. This fact, when we reflect upon it, is a very strange and striking one. Nor is it less strange that wherever the work of sanctification is begun it is always accompanied with the consciousness (as if of an inward necessity) that during this life perfect purity and freedom from sin cannot be attained. If sin arose only from a perversion of the will during life, a truly firm and resolute resolve to follow after holiness would in the end entirely destroy all inner discord, for that resolve in the Christian is the fruit of God's grace, and is accompanied by a clear perception both of the end in view and of the hindrances to be overcome. If sin only begins during life how can we be certain that it may not be wholly extirpated during life? Yet every Christian feels this certainty, and it can be accounted for only by the fact that sin is interwoven with our nature from the outset, and that it affects the very form of its development from the beginning. Even in the regenerate man this selfishness, this fleshly mindedness of nature, continually rebels against the holy principles which the renewed will has made its own (Gal. v. 17), and would draw him back again into his former sinful life if he were carelessly to yield to every prompting of his inclinations.

And we must also bear in mind what has already been referred to at the beginning of this chapter, I mean the way in which the unsubdued power of sin asserts itself in the life of the regenerate. On the one hand there takes place an involuntary stirring of some particular affection which occurs before the better nature can prevent it, and on the other hand there is the unperceived or half-recognised admixture of sinful elements in conduct, which, on the whole, springs from a holy motive. The sphere of conscious life is taken possession of by the new, the divine principle; if then the reaction of sin is involuntarily felt, it is evident that, as no decision of will can utterly destroy it, so no decision of will can have primarily produced it. Its seat is in that dark background of "the natural man" out of which the new life in us rises and gradually advances; in other words, it cleaves to man from his very birth.

The manner in which the developed life of man, as we hav
already seen, is spoken of in Holy Scripture, neces
§ 4. WITNESS
OF SCRIPTURE sitates the inference that this inborn sinfulness i
TO INBORN there taken for granted, and indirectly recognized a
SINFULNESS.
a fact. Scripture represents sin as present in ever
human being with the single exception of our Saviour, and thi
involves the truth that there is a germ of sin, a sinful propensity
in every one from the beginning of life. But over and abov
this, sin is expressly described as something dwelling in mai
from his very birth.

Among the texts in the Old Testament bearing upon thi
subject, theologians have rightly regarded Psaln
Psalm li.
li. 5, as the most conclusive. "Behold, I wa
shapen in iniquity" (בְּעָוֹן,*—בְּ denoting the state in which, se
1 Sam. xxix. 7), "and in sin (בְּחֵטְא) did my mother conceiv
me." It cannot be supposed that David (whom we take to b
the author of this Psalm, notwithstanding the arguments o
Paulus, De Wette, Hupfeld, and others, which seem to u:
inadequate) meant something peculiar to his own mother anc
not applicable to the race. Nor can the doctrinal import o
the words be weakened by inferences from other Old Testament passages, wherein a habit or course of action begui
early in life and long pursued is proverbially or figurativel)
described as something practised "from the womb," Ps
xxii. 9, 10, lviii. 3, lxxi. 6; Job xxxi. 8; Isaiah xlviii. 8
There is a great difference between expressions used (as th(
connection shows) merely figuratively, where every one see:
that they cannot be meant literally, and declarations whicl
have nothing figurative about them, but embody a distinct anc
additional thought in the connection in which they stand
Taken by themselves, the words of this passage may be understood in two ways. They may be understood as affirming thal
the mother, in conceiving and in bearing children, is tainted
with iniquity and sin; or that man, from the beginning of his
existence, from conception onwards, is in a state of sin and

* The word עָוֹן is generally rendered "guilt." But as we have already
remarked, in עָוֹן the idea of guilt cannot be regarded as directly and distinctly
included and expressed. It is of course implied in עָוֹן as in every word denoting
sin, inasmuch as sin involves the idea of guilt.

CHAP. II.]   SIN AS A CORRUPTION OF HUMAN NATURE.   275

iniquity. If we adopt the first interpretation, the words, חוֹלַלְתִּי בְּעָווֹן may be rendered (though this would be a very forced rendering), "I was born of one tainted with iniquity," which would imply that bearing children is an act or state necessarily involving sin. And this the second part of the text also could be made to mean; the sin would be taken as predicated of the mother. But such a rendering contradicts the moral teaching of the Old Testament, especially the divine ordinance of marriage in Gen. i. 28. As to the Levitical uncleanness and purifications spoken of in the Mosaic code (Leviticus xv. 18, and elsewhere), nothing sinful is implied in them; their design was simply to elevate the theocratic life and social relations of the people above their merely sensuous life. Thus in Numbers xix. death, and accidental contact with a corpse, involved Levitical uncleanness. We have in such restrictions that Old Testament narrowness (done away in the New) which would keep the sphere of religion and sanctity aloof from the sphere of the natural and material, the sphere designated "common," Acts x. 9. The connection, however, in which the passage in Psalm li. stands contradicts such an interpretation. It would be admissible only on the supposition that the writer's aim was to urge a consideration in mitigation of his guilt so as to obtain the forgiving mercy of God. But the verses following verse 3 are clearly intended to express the greatness of the offences David had committed. Verse 4 describes them as sins against God, and in verse 5 David describes himself as sinful from the very beginning of his life,—the second clause of this verse being an enhancement of the first. As, moreover, verse 5 describes how deeply rooted sin is in our nature, verse 6 naturally leads on to the confession that God "desireth truth in the inward parts," and to the prayer "in the hidden part make me to know wisdom." The second only of the proposed interpretations accords with this.

The passages in the book of Job which most strongly affirm that no one born of a woman can be pure, occur in the addresses of Eliphaz and Bildad, and may therefore (according to the construction and tenour of the drama) be only exaggerations. We can refer authoritatively to chap. xiv. 4 only. "Who can bring a clean thing out of an unclean? not one." This passage alludes not only to an

Job xiv. 4.

inborn, but to an inherited uncleanness. But all that it asserts, if we consider the meaning of the words and their connection, is that no clean thing can come out of an unclean *i.e.*, out of the unclean nature which belongs to man; that all men therefore are tainted with sin. It affirms nothing as to the question, whether the infection be handed down from the beginning of human existence, or whether man at some subsequent time began to be affected by it.

Gen. viii. 21 again still more distinctly refers to an inborn depravity. The declaration that "the imagination of man's heart is evil from his youth," clearly implies that this evil imagination (יֵצֶר הָרַע) is not originated in each heart, but is in it from the beginning. General statements as to the depravity of the human heart are not declarations of a distinct volition of the individual resolving and beginning to be evil; they express a characteristic of human nature in common.

Gen. viii. 21.

As to the New Testament, with the older theologians and with some of our modern divines, John iii. 6 has been regarded as the standard authority for the doctrine of 'man's inborn sinfulness : " That which is born of the flesh is flesh, and that which is born of the spirit is spirit." Taken in connection with what precedes, this declaration of Christ clearly proves the fact of corruption attaching to human nature, seeing that He makes participation in His kingdom dependent upon a thorough renewal, wrought by the Holy Spirit. This universal necessity for a new birth (see John iii. 3, 5, i. 12, 13; Titus iii. 5; James i. 18; 1 Peter i. 3. 23), this beginning and development of a new life implies not only that sin is already present in every human being, but that it has struck its roots deep into the nature which man inherits from his birth. In like manner, the Apostle Paul regards renewal in Christ Jesus as a universal law of human life, and describes it as the "putting off," or "death" of "the old man," Eph. iv. 22 ; Col. iii. 9, compare v. 3; Rom. vi. 3–6. Attempted explanations of these passages, which really explain nothing—*e.g.*, that the old man is "the power of vice, confirmed by habit,"—do not require refutation. Still those words in John iii., τὸ γεγεννημένον ἐκ τῆς σαρκὸς σάρξ ἐστι, do not of themselves speak of this depravity of nature. According to

John iii. 6.

CHAP. II.]   SIN AS A CORRUPTION OF HUMAN NATURE.   277

St. John's conception of the σάρξ, they cannot be taken to mean "that which is generated from the corrupt nature of the parents, must be itself corrupt;"—they evidently refer to the question of Nicodemus in verse 4, and mean " in his natural birth, man obtains only natural life." What this natural life is morally, and how it stands related to the spiritual life, not only as the lower to the higher, but in direct contrast and opposition thereto,—this we can only learn from the general drift of our Lord's discourse.

The Pauline antithesis of σάρξ and πνεῦμα on the other hand embodies, as we have before seen, the doctrine which theologians have endeavoured to prove from the passage in St. John. "The flesh," according to St. Paul, is the active source of all the various forms of sin; it is not something without a man, but is human nature itself as alien from God, and the servant of what is worldly; and holding sway over the whole life, apart from the renewal and sanctification of the spirit (Rom. vii. 5, 14; viii. 3, 9); moral corruption cleaves to human nature as such in every case.

Antithesis of σάρξ and πνεῦμα.

This is as clearly taught in a passage from another of St. Paul's epistles, the bearing of which upon this subject is not generally observed by modern theologians, I mean 1 Cor. vii. 14; "The unbelieving husband is sanctified by the [believing] wife, and the unbelieving wife is sanctified by the [believing] husband; else were your children unclean; but now are they holy." Though the explanation of this passage is not without difficulty, we need not dwell long upon it, for ample light has already been thrown upon it, by the criticism of De Wette* and Rückert.† With them we must take τὰ τέκνα ὑμῶν to mean the children of believers generally. For if it meant the children of those mixed marriages, the statement could not have been urged as a fact, and an argument against those who considered the mixed marriages defiling in their influence; they would at once have objected to it as taking for granted the very point in question. If, therefore, the statement means that Christian children are sanctified by their connection with Christian parents, and that apart from this connection, they would be regarded as unclean,

1 Cor. vii. 14.

* *Theol. Studien u. Krit.*, 1830, part iii., 669.
† *Kommentar zum* 1 Cor., *in loc*.

it is evident that St. Paul regards man's natural life as "unclean" (ἀκάθαρτον) from his very birth. The same inference may be drawn, even were we to refer the statement to the children of mixed marriages. For by his hypothetical words ἐπεὶ τὰ τέκνα ὑμῶν ἀκάθαρτά ἐστιν, St. Paul could never have meant an uncleanness attaching to those children, solely on account of their distinctive parentage, but clearly that inborn uncleanness, which affected them in common with all by nature and by birth, and from which their parentage did not free them.

But St. Paul most fully and clearly describes this inborn uncleanness as influencing man's relation to God in his Epistle to the Ephesians ii. 3. After reminding the Christian converts from Heathenism, of their past thraldom in sin, and of their being quickened from spiritual death by Christ, he says that he himself also, and his own Christian brethren (καὶ ἡμεῖς πάντες), i.e., Jewish Christians, had formerly lived in sin, and he concludes with the general statement, " we were by nature the children of wrath (τέκνα φύσει ὀργῆς) even as others," i.e., Jews and Gentiles, who do not know Christ. We need make only a few remarks on this passage, as the most thorough commentator on this Epistle has an elaborate dissertation upon it, in all the main points of which we agree.* The Apostle speaks of a state, out of which the disciples of Christ had been brought; a state wherein they had been " children of wrath," of course of the divine wrath, and objects therefore of God's displeasure manifesting itself in their punishment. When he further says that they were in this state " by nature" (φύσει), we allow that he did not mean a natural state, as contrasted with one arising from a perversion of will during life, but their state by nature in the sense of φύσει in Rom. ii. 14, that is, as contrasted with their state as Jews, the covenant people, enjoying God's revelations and ordinances, as described in Rom. ix. 4. Thus the unexpected occurrence of φύσει is accounted for;—it was inserted in order to limit a statement which St. Paul was about to make without limitation. But understanding the contrast implied in φύσει thus, the words of the Apostle clearly mean that they (Christians from among the Jews as well as others) were—in their natural state, their inborn character apart from their privileges

Eph. ii. 3.

* Harless's Commentary, pp. 165-180.

SIN AS A CORRUPTION OF HUMAN NATURE.

—the objects of God's righteous displeasure. Herein is contained a thought which forms an additional element of the Scripture doctrine upon this subject. Such texts as John iii. 36; Rom. iii. 19, imply that previous to man's decision, either for or against Christ, there is something in him which incurs God's wrath; other texts of Scripture (especially those last considered), affirm the universality of sin, and show that it is a defilement which cleaves to man's nature from the very beginning of his life. But that this inborn depravity is not only an evil and a sickness, that it entails GUILT on him in whom it is, this we are taught in Eph. ii. 3, because God's righteous displeasure implies guilt in man as its necessary correlative.*

* ERNESTI ("*Der Ursprung der Sünde nach Paulinischem Lehrgehalt,*" vol. ii., pp. 174, 175) declining other interpretations, thinks that τέκνα φύσει in this passage should be taken separately from ὀργῆς, and should be regarded as a parenthetical expression for καίπερ τέκνα φύσει ὄντα. According to this rendering the sense would be, "We (the Jews), though by nature children, were liable to God's righteous displeasure even as others (the heathen),"—*i.e.*, on account of our subjective character, which the apostle had before described. Much, certainly, may be said in favour of this rendering. It cannot be questioned that it is grammatically allowable to take τέκνα φύσει as a distinct expression. The εἶναι ὀργῆς is sanctioned by similar expressions in St. Paul's epistles, and in the Epistle to the Hebrews, *e.g.*: 1 Thes. v. 5, οὐκ ἐσμὲν νυκτὸς οὐδέ σκότους. Verse 8, ἡμεῖς δὲ ἡμέρας ὄντες νήφωμεν (though in the latter the contrast with verse 7 helps to explain the imperfect form of expression, and in the former the antithesis leads us naturally to supply υἱοί);—Heb. x. 39, ἡμεῖς δὲ οὐκ ἐσμὲν ὑποστολῆς εἰς ἀπώλειαν, ἀλλὰ πίστεως εἰς περιποίησιν ζωῆς. But if St. Paul here designates the Israelites τέκνα φύσει, we must supply θέσει to ὀργῆς, and how will this accord with Rom. ix. 4, where St Paul ascribes the υἱοθεσία to the Israelites? It will not serve in answer to this to urge that St. Paul in Rom. xi. 21 calls the Jews τοὺς κατὰ φύσιν κλάδους, for he uses this expression simply on account of the illustration he is making use of, see verse 24. These passages, therefore, are not analogous to Eph. ii. 3, and the meaning which Ernesti here gives to φύσει "belonging to God's people in virtue of His objective choice" (p. 175), "we, in virtue of our ancestry, were partakers of the covenant of promise" (p. 178), cannot be applied to κατὰ φύσιν. It would also be strange upon Ernesti's rendering, that Paul did not distinguish the supposed parenthesis τέκνα φύσει at least by inserting μέν. The train of thought, however, in the passage, seems to me decisive against Ernesti's view. In verses 2 and 3, the Apostle simply extends the statement of v. 1, καὶ ὑμᾶς ὄντας νεκροὺς τοῖς παραπτώμασιν καί ταῖς ἁμαρτίαις, and in verse 4, he introduces the antithesis, ὁ δὲ θεὸς πλούσιος ὢν ἐν ἐλέει διὰ τὴν πολλὴν ἀγάπην αὐτοῦ. * * * ἡμᾶς * * * συνεξωοποίησεν τῷ Χριστῷ. To introduce therefore such a parenthesis as "the Israelites were partakers of the covenant of promise," would be a weakening of the antithesis such as could not be attributed to St. Paul, at least in the Epistle to the Ephesians.

MEYER (*Kritisch exeget. Handbuch über den Brief an die Epheser,* pp. 86, 87,

These words of St. Paul, however, only confirm the conclusion to which we are necessarily led by the undeniable facts of experience, if we bring the true idea of what sin is to bear upon them. Our investigations in Book I., showed that guilt is necessarily implied in the very idea of actual sin. But if from inborn depravity, as the universality of sin testifies, actual sin inevitably springs, we cannot separate man's guilt in God's sight from this depravity. The supernatural birth of Christ also presupposes the impurity of human nature, an impurity from which that life (which was to exhibit a pure and holy manhood), had to be preserved from its very beginning; and hence the expression τὸ γεννώμενον ἅγιον in Luke i. 35, with which may be compared St. Paul's words ἐπεὶ ἄρα τὰ τέκνα ὑμῶν ἀκάθαρτά ἐστιν, 1 Cor. vii. 14.

§ 5. WHAT CONSTITUTES INBORN SINFULNESS.

In endeavouring to define generally wherein this depravity, deep-rooted in human nature, and inborn in every individual, consists, we again encounter that doctrine of sensationalism which we have already discussed. According to it, man's natural sinfulness is really nothing more than the preponderance of his sensuous impulses, and the insubordination of his fleshly nature to his spirit. Michaelis fully advocates and elaborates this view.* We must, of course, grant the universality of this preponderance, and its significance in relation to original sin;

3rd ed.), objects to our rendering of this text as inconsistent with the context and un-Pauline. And yet he speaks of "an inborn principle of sin in man which in its development overcomes his moral will; the mere presence of this however, in the man, does not make him a child of wrath; man becomes this, when the intermixture of the two principles—which takes place in every one— leads to the dominance of the sinful principle." Though the theory of sensationalism in the natural preponderance of the flesh above the spirit as the principle of sin, lies at the basis of this view, it is impossible not to recognize that Meyer here and throughout his Commentaries regards sin as meriting God's wrath. If this inborn principle of sin belonging to man's natural constitution, triumphs in every man over his moral will, and begets actual and damnable sin, this inborn condition must be necessarily linked with sin so as to make the man the object of God's wrath; and this is what the apostle teaches. Or must we believe that what the author himself regards at the same time as universal and as what ought not to be, has the basis of its existence wholly in a decision of the individual will made by every man? Compare PHILIPPI, *Kirchl. Glaubenslehre*, iii. 204-206.

* *As before*, in the section upon " Inborn Depravity of our Nature," pp. 444-550.

SIN AS A CORRUPTION OF HUMAN NATURE.

but it certainly does not explain to us the innermost source of human depravity. Viewing this depravity as something positive, and not as negative merely, we find that it may appropriately be described as uncontrolled selfishness or egoism. This is the universal characteristic of man's natural life; man is by nature, and apart from the affections of benevolence, sympathy, and so forth, which he possesses, an EGOIST; his disposition is to refer everything to himself—his own advantage, pleasure, and satisfaction. It requires pains and toil to keep this natural selfishness within ordinary bounds by considering the general good, and it cannot be wholly subdued save by divine assistance.

We meet with this NATURAL EGOISM—which Pelagianism even would allow were we not to call it a corruption of human nature—in childhood generally, not indeed always in the form of violent passion and self-will, but sometimes under the garb of prevailing passivity and natural softness of disposition and tractableness of character; even in these cases none but a very superficial observer can fail to trace the selfish principle, though modified in its manifestations by natural temperament. An unbiassed observation of childhood, when once the moral consciousness is awakened—for before then no moral quality can be attached to its outgoings—will satisfy any one that in the most tender-hearted and affectionate child there is a tendency to indulge hostile feelings against anything that hinders it in the attainment of its own wishes and desires, and that it is wont thoughtlessly to give way to this impulse provided it be not held in check by other influences, by blood relationship, or judicious tutelage. Even in the best dispositioned children we may discover, in greater or less degree, an element of hatred usually aroused by wounded self-love, and an element of falsehood which in disputes with its playmates, or in answer to its parents or teachers, wilfully sacrifices truth for the sake of self. Experience indeed shows that this self-seeking on the child's part chiefly appears in the gratification of particular affections, and in sensational pleasures, so that these seem to be the excitants tempting it to wrong-doing, and the outward material of its sins; but can this circumstance justify our reducing the principle of selfishness to the excessive strength of particular affections? By no

Inborn selfishness.

means; on the contrary, the predominance of particular affections and sensational desires to which experience thus witnesses arises from a radical disturbance in that other sphere of life which is actuated by the perverted will. Experience, moreover, unequivocally testifies that as human development advances, selfishness shows itself equally in the spiritual nature, and sometimes with such strength as to ignore and suppress the calls of the sensuous nature, and of particular affections. The theory of sensationalism, or of particular affections, is quite insufficient to explain these phenomena.

But in order to understand how it is that this selfish ten-
Negative element in it. dency, deep-rooted in our nature, endeavours not only to overpower, but by increasing degeneracy, even to bring into its service those higher affections which are opposed to it, we must not overlook the *negative* side of human depravity. It chiefly consists in the fact, that the germ of religion in man is not indeed destroyed, for were this so, there would be nothing in his heart by nature save disinclination and enmity against God, but weakened and well-nigh crushed. The Augsburg Confession, while it denotes the selfish tendency in man by the term *concupiscentia*,* describes the negative element of human depravity as *peccatum originis, sine metu Dei, sine fiducia erga Deum esse*. And the *Apologia Confessionis* justly speaks of the perversion of this doctrine by the Schoolmen who dwell chiefly upon the minor infirmities of human nature, *e.g.*, the loss of the *aequale temperamentum qualitatum corporis*, and overlook its more serious defects, viz., *ignorantionem Dei, contemptum Dei, vacare metu et fiducia Dei, odisse judicium Dei, fugere Deum judicantem, irasci Deo, desperare gratiam, habere fiduciam rerum praesentium, &c.*†

That this description of our state by nature, with its inclinations and dispositions in relation to religion, is in the main a true one, the following consideration will show.

In the holiest moments of our life we feel that conscious
True idea of religion. fellowship with God not only produces a perfect peace wherein all the discords of our hearts may

---

* *Confessio Augustana*, art. 2. We must be careful not to confound *concupiscentia* here with the Augustinian use of the word.

† *Apol. Confessionis*, art. 1, pp. 52, 53.

be blended in its harmonizing music, but also fills us with an inner longing after holiness. The natural inference from this is, that according to our true nature, religion is the all-embracing and all-determining principle of our spiritual and temporal life; the principle which, as our powers are developed, should make every new range, every new object its own, and thus beget a rich fulness and multiformity alike of affection and of knowledge. This is manifestly the true idea of religion; it is fellowship with the living and personal God who, Himself unconditioned, conditions all other beings, and therefore is it meant to be the all-prevailing and life-giving principle of our whole existence. But as our life actually is, can we say that religion is all this? The question is not as to partial, though very general hindrances, but as to those only which are universal. All true fellowship with God in feeling, thought, and inward act, involves a continual raising of our spirit out of and above ourselves, above our natural state; it is an upward tendency which must counteract the natural downward tendency in order to realize itself. If we give way to the downward tendency, the issue must necessarily be, that our habits of thought and action will be centered on things temporal— philosophically speaking, on the *here* of the Absolute; and he who will have and love divine bliss merely as "beautiful nature," must content himself with the unlovely naturalness of worldly pleasure. Religion, while in itself inherent in human nature, and embracing all its aims, is ordinarily, as if something extraneous, something extra-temporal (in philosophical language *there* or transcendent), and it is elevated from this position only seldom, and in men of very deep practical piety; it is perfected only in ONE.

The explanation usually given of this fact is, that to us what is actually present is alone perceivable by us. The object matter therefore of religion does not belong to this sphere, and is of course attainable only by abstraction, being as it were far off from us. But this account of the matter can hardly satisfy any one fully alive to the nature of the phenomenon to be solved. We have here to do with the spiritual life only, and the question is, how is it that religion does not preserve that influence which it has in itself, and which we feel it should have? To say, in reply, "what is sensational is the only real

knowledge, and whatever transcends this is a phantom of th
brain," is to argue in a circle, and to make those sensational an
materialistic modes of thought belonging to man in his presen
condition, which are part of the very phenomenon to be explaine(
the principle of the explanation.

This phenomenon is really accounted for by the fact that th
germ of religion in man is weakened and paralysec
and cannot therefore outgrow the sensuous an
worldly impulses, but is suppressed by them. Thi
blunted state of our religious affections contradict
the true ideal of our nature, and yet is entertained therein an
manifests itself outwardly in the same way everywhere. I
hinders the entire course of our religious development. Al
careful moral and religious nurture presupposes this defect
and plans its course accordingly. It feels the religious elemen
to be the noblest in human nature, because it is the tenderes
and the most easily injured, requiring special watchfulnes
and careful nursing lest it be stunted or withered. But it i
not the most exposed to danger because it is the noblest, bu
because it has lost the strength and vitality which it shoul(
have in man's natural life, because this life is one of relativ
estrangement from God.

<small>Faculty of religion weakened in man.</small>

The religious character of the heathen world, as distinct fron
the faiths of the Old and New Testament, has this natura
weakness of the religious affections as its basis. Heathenism
whether in its lowest form as idolatry, or in its higher and mor
cultivated phase as polytheism, is the religion of the natura
man ; human nature, if left to itself, and following its religiou:
impulses, necessarily arrives at one or other of its manifolc
forms. The religious principle has not the elasticity an(
strength necessary to raise the spirit of man above the worldl}
and to elevate him to the one self-existent free and holy God
Hence in its manifestations the outward forces of the world in
nature and in man are confounded with the true Object of the
religious consciousness, of whom man has a dark presentiment
Herein lay the demoniacal charm of heathenism, which was to
the Jews a continual temptation, and one into which they ofter
fell ; a door was here opened for the admission into religion of
the unbridled lusts and passions of the natural life, and even
for their predominance therein. And thus the consciousness of

God obscured in the soul gradually lost sight of its true foe in man's natural life, and even tended in its deep defilement to feed and strengthen the very disease it was intended to cure.

In cases where the germ of true religion retains its true position in consciousness, and yet is unable to conquer the prevailing tendencies of the natural life in the affections and the will, we find that there arises a slavish dread of God. That is indeed a very false, or at least ill-defined, representation which attributes nothing to the human heart in its natural state, but an aversion to and avoidance of God, its primary and natural feeling is a bias towards God, and hence the usual susceptibility of childhood to religious influences. And yet there is in man's natural life an element of secret aversion and dislike towards God, and this arises from the clashing of man's prevailing inclinations and strivings with his inner consciousness of God as the Holy One.

Here we may see what is really meant by the "preponderance of sensuous impulses," which we by no means deny to be an element of man's natural depravity. The expression is of course relative. The strength or activity of the sensuous impulses or particular affections in their natural exercise, cannot in itself be sinful, provided that they do not violate their due relation as subordinate to the higher sphere, *i.e.*, so long as they are perfectly under the control and governance of our consciousness of God and conscience.* But seeing that these authoritative principles within us can only command, that they have not power of themselves to carry out their dictates, that sensuous desires and particular affections assert themselves in opposition to the nobler interests of the spirit, and seeing moreover, that this disorder exists universally in human development, though in different degrees of strength, and in different ways from the very outset, there is also in this sphere—in man's sensuous nature—a derangement and depravation.

[margin note: Derangement of sensuous instincts.]

Thus all the arguments of Töllner and others, to prove that the sensational impulses and affections must be as strong as they in general are in order to fulfil the natural ends of human life, really amount to nothing. We may admit all this, and

* See Bishop BUTLER's *Analogy*, part i. chap. v.; and his *Sermons on Human Nature.—Tr.*

yet as consistently maintain that the tendency of these sensuous impulses to overpower the higher impulses of the spirit, and to rebel against its holy dictates, implies a degeneracy which may be called "natural," only because it is inborn. But he only who starts from the lowest idea of human nature as his principle can regard the corresponding weakness of the human spirit—of the God-consciousness, conscience, and will—as the true and necessary law of human development, and not, as it really is, a degeneracy and perversion. This "natural weakness" of human nature in relation to sensuous propensions and affections is (to repeat an expression already used) its disloyalty to that which it cannot but regard as the standard of perfect Holiness.*

§ 6. DEATH, AND ITS RELATION TO SIN.

As we wished clearly to array the arguments which logically have led us to the conclusions now established we carefully avoided making any reference to a law of our being which impressively witnesses to the power of sin in our human nature,—I mean DEATH, and its connection with the deep-rootedness of sin. It is not that we felt any misgivings as to the reality and logicalness of the connection between sin and death, nor that we under-estimated the importance of this in its relation to Christian truth. But hitherto the considerations which have led us to the recognition of an all-pervading depravity of human nature have been purely ethical and not physical; whereas the connection between sin and death leads us on to that aspect of Christian doctrine wherein natural relations and physical considerations present themselves. These Schleiermacher calls "cosmological questions," and he would put them wholly aside in the stricter exposition of the fact of Christian consciousness. We regard perfect separation of

* In these remarks we see how Müller, in his doctrine of sin, differs from Bishop Butler. Butler (*Analogy*, part i. chap. 5), in answer to the question how creatures made upright fall, says that "it seems distinctly conceivable from the very nature of particular affections or propensions;" and in his theory of Conscience, he recognizes no degeneracy in the moral faculty. Its weakness according to him, is not depravation, but simply an excess or preponderance of sensuous propensions and affections over it. Müller, on the other hand, insists that there is degeneracy on both sides, that while the preponderance of sensuous propensions is a degeneracy, the weakness of the moral sense—the God-consciousness and conscience—is a degeneracy too.—*Tr.*

CHAP. II.] SIN AS A CORRUPTION OF HUMAN NATURE. 287

these elements to be alike unjustifiable and unattainable; but it is true that theology must abandon any speculations about them beyond the teachings of Scripture, and what may with certainty be inferred from the bearings of Christian truth. It must give up the notion of fully answering all the questions which here suggest themselves, if it would avoid unpleasant complications with the natural sciences, in their various branches and phases of development. And yet, be as careful as we may, we can hardly avoid these complications; and when we see theologians, who would be as faithful to the facts of Gospel history and the declarations of Christ and His apostles as ourselves, arriving at conclusions contradictory thereto, as to the connection between sin and death, it is only natural to suppose that diversity of opinion pervading the sphere of natural science (in the widest sense of that term) has given an undue bias to their views. Though these theologians may not, as we do, recognize an element in the physical sphere strongly confirming the moral disorder of human nature, we cannot but think that, having set out with the same fundamental moral principles as ourselves, they will be obliged to recognize the correctness of our main conclusions.

The relation between sin and death has of late been the theme of many able investigations, especially in Krabbe's *Lehre von der Sünde und vom Tode* (1836), and in Mau's *Schrift vom Tode dem Solde der Sünden, und der Aufhebung desselben durch die Auferstehung Christi* (1841); also in Weisse's Dissertation, *Über die philosophische Bedeutung der christlichen Lehre von den letzten Dingen*,* where special attention is given to this subject. We shall therefore be as brief as possible in the consideration of this suggestive and far-reaching problem, the more so as we coincide in all essential points with the views developed by Krabbe and Mau. So far as these two theologians differ, the results of our inquiry will probably be found to mediate between their conflicting views.

Works upon this subject.

If we regard man merely as a sentient being, nothing seems more natural than that he should die. Viewed thus, we recognize an obvious analogy between him and the higher ranges of animal

Death in the lower animals.

* *Theol. Studien und Krit.*, 1836, part ii. 371.

life, organic and sentient. In these, however, the organic process can maintain itself only for a time against the general forces which tend to the dissolution of individual life; its vitality having reached a certain point begins to decline, and at last, if not overtaken by some outward casualty, it dies away, vanquished by those forces.

What is there to make these lower individual existences in nature immortal? They are only exemplars or samples of their species, kind, and so forth, but they possess no individuality of any significance in itself, or worth preserving; they simply serve as instruments whereby the species manifests itself and secures its continuance by the production of others like them. They are insusceptible of any real individuality for this very reason,—because there is no personal centre, no *ego* in them self-conscious, distinguishing itself from others, and assuming certain relations by voluntary self-determination. It is only around such a centre as this that any definite individuality can be formed; such a centre alone has the power of attracting and combining into a harmonious whole the manifold elements which without it would merely co-exist and then be dispersed again in the general tide of things. But when the living creature possesses personality, it stands in a different relation to its species. While the lower existences in nature are merely passive instruments in relation to their species, personal beings can distinguish themselves, not only theoretically by making their species the object of their consciousness, but practically, by a free resolve either to a loving surrender to their species or a selfish abandonment of it.

Man's personality a pledge of immortality.
But as the existence of a conditioned *ego* can be explained only by the existence of the unconditioned primary *Ego*, every self-conscious being not only stands in certain relations to itself and the world, but possesses a consciousness of God, and a bias towards God, which is—*potentiâ*—inborn (see vol. i. pp. 79–81). In virtue of this relation to the absolute *ego*, he is capable of eternal thoughts, of ideas as the principles of what realizes itself in time, and he can determine himself and his actions accordingly. This being the dignity of individual existence as personal, its destiny cannot be merely to be manifested as a

sample of the species, and then to vanish; it has a significance of its own, and a power of imperishable existence, transcending all the forces of nature. PERSONALITY, therefore, by virtue of which man is the offspring of God (Acts xvii. 28), created in God's image, and raised *toto genere*, above all natural existences, is the universal principle of man's immortality. Here the analogy between man and the perishable existences of nature disappears. Were man merely the highest specimen of natural life, the analogy might still hold good. This, indeed, he is if we regard only the physical part of his being and his organic nature; but he is more than this. In him there is blended with this an individual spirit, *i.e.*, personality; and provided that the πνεῦμα retained its position as the determining principle of his being, man could never be subject to the fate of lower existences in nature. It is but natural that a life, whose principle is simply a law of nature, should be overcome by the forces of nature; but that personal and immortal beings die—this cannot be natural, it is a problem that needs explanation.*

Modern doctrine of immortality. The solution of this problem, proposed by the advocates of the modern doctrine of immortality, is well known. Death is only the separation of soul and body: the body sinks into that dissolution to which all matter is destined; but the soul, now separate from the body,—which was always something foreign to it, and an encumbrance hindering its flight,—not only continues to exist with consciousness and recollection, but now, for the first time, in its pure disembodied state, becomes capable of undisturbed bliss and unimpeded progress.

Upon this theory, in fact, death, as the end of our corporeal life, becomes so obviously natural, that it makes birth, as the beginning of this life, completely inexplicable; and the only legitimate answer to the question, why man is doomed to a corporeal existence, which is only a hindrance, and ends in annihilation, is one derived from dualistic principles.

Christian doctrine of immortality. There is less need to argue out the untenableness of this spiritualistic doctrine of immortality, seeing that now-a-days hardly any one undertakes to defend it on the philosophical principles upon which it is

* See the able remarks of WEISSE, as before, p. 293.

supposed to rest, as distinct from the eschatological teaching of Holy Scripture. The Christian doctrine of immortality is indissolubly connected with the promise of a future Resurrection. The purport of this promise essentially is, that the body of sanctified man, destroyed by death, shall be raised again in a glorified state at the end of the present world-development. Here death is undeniably a stumbling-block. If the body, as well as the soul, be destined for an imperishable existence, how comes this destruction of the body in death, accompanied, as it almost always is, with pain and conflict, and being, even when seemingly a placid sleep, an unnatural and violent rending asunder of what had been developed in living unity. Arguing from this unity, the more natural, though still undefined, inference would be, that man having finished his course in this present life, would be translated, not by a destructive separation of body and soul, but by an elevation of his bodily nature to a more perfect state, answering to his higher inner life. Now that this is not the case,—that the transition is effected by a destructive process, the subduing force of which man is utterly powerless to resist, involving as it does the decomposition of the body, and the deprivation of the soul,—this, while ever a source of horror to one's natural feelings, must necessarily be a strange anomaly in the eye of Christian faith.

Thus it is that Holy Scripture views death, representing it as resulting from a moral disturbance, of which it is at once the logical consequence and the punishment. When Holy Scripture speaks of $\theta\acute{a}\nu a\tau o\varsigma$, $\mathring{a}\pi o\theta\nu\acute{\eta}\sigma\kappa\epsilon\iota\nu$, $\nu\epsilon\kappa\rho\acute{o}\nu$ $\epsilon\mathring{\iota}\nu a\iota$ as the result of sin, its reference is generally—not to physical death—but partly to the divided and fettered state of the inner life, and partly to the unhappy existence of the ungodly after death. Let us examine two passages which are evidently parallel, Rom. v. 12, and 1 Cor xv. 21, 22. In the first, death is spoken of as the result of sin, though, taking the text by itself, it may be doubted whether physical death is meant. In the second, physical death and its dominion over the race, is contrasted with the resurrection power of the Saviour, but it is not expressly said that this death is the consequence of sin. If, however, we compare the passages together, we find that each receives from the other the

Scripture view of death.

explanation which perfects its sense. In like manner, the Apostle Paul, in Romans viii. 10, explains the fact of the body being subject to death, even after "the spirit is life because of Christ's righteousness," by a reference to sin—"the body is dead because of sin." This passage throws light upon 1 Peter iv. 6, where it is said of the dead to whom the Gospel was preached during their life-time, that as concerned their death, "they had been judged according to the flesh." Christ's words, too, in John viii. 44, where he calls the devil ἀνθρωποκτόνος, evidently refer to physical death, and its connection with sin as its cause,—as will be further shown in chapter iv., in opposition to another interpretation.

The first two passages named attribute the dominion of death to Adam, and naturally lead us back to the second and third chapters of Genesis. If we compare the penalty of death threatened in connection with the divine command (Gen. ii. 17) with the fulfilment of the sentence after the first transgression (Gen. iii. 16-22), two things are manifest. On the one hand, we find that the death which was to follow the commission of sin, included not only physical death, in the strictest sense, as the moment of departure, but, "the various ills that flesh is heir to," the manifold pains and miseries of our earthly lot; and these are represented as resulting from sin, which ends in death. Thus the well-known difficulty involved in the word בְּיוֹם (ii. 17) is at once obviated: in the very day of disobedience, a life begins, which is at the same time a death.* It thus appears,

<small>Genesis ii. and iii.</small>

---

* And yet I must allow that in taking מוֹת תָּמוּת as referring to physical death only, the explanation offered does not seem to me so inadmissible as many modern critics suppose, viz., "Thou shalt be liable to death as an inevitable necessity." St Paul in a similar way calls the body liable to death σῶμα νεκρόν (Rom. viii. 10). This view, at any rate, is more natural than the explanation which BAUMGARTEN adopts from HOFMANN's work, *Weissagung und Erfüllung*. He takes the threatening of physical death to refer to the very day of transgression, but supposes that between the threatening and the disobedience, a modifying circumstance occurred, namely, the creation of women, and that this hindered the fulfilment of the sentence. *Theol. Kommentar zum A. T.*, part i. p. 43. It seems to meet all difficulties, if we take the "death" of chap. ii. 17, as meaning spiritual death, the unhappy discord and perversion of the inward life, which ensued immediately upon the fall, and showed itself in the feeling of shame and fear which hid from God. Yet apart from the consideration that this interpretation does not accord with apprehensions and

too, that when the serpent, in his subtilty said to Eve, "Ye shall not surely die," this was not a bare lie, but a half truth, and therefore a double deception. But, on the other hand, we find by comparing the two passages, that physical death is the real kernel and gist of the punishment. For the sentence pronounced concludes with the prophecy of death, making this the most important element, by emphatic repetition (Gen. iii. 19); and the account of the execution of the sentence lays stress chiefly upon the fact of man's exclusion from the means of imperishable life (Gen. iii. 22, 24).

Krabbe rightly recognizes the connection between sin and death, as implied in Psalm xc. 7, 9, 11, and in Numbers xvi. 29, 30.* In the former passage the fact that the children of men are "consumed" or "carried away," is described as a manifestation of the displeasure and "wrath" of God, who "sets even our secret sins in the light of His countenance." In the second passage "the common death of all men" (in distinction from the descent of Korah and his company into Sheol), is referred to as the punishment common to all.†

But in order rightly to understand this connection as the Old Testament represents it, we must remember how closely it combines the idea of death and of the under world שְׁאוֹל. Like the shepherd with his sheep, death drives men on into the world below (Ps. xlix. 14, 15) into the silent country where the dead without distinction—wise men as well as fools—rest from the toil and anguish of this earthly life, in a state of shadowy existence, wherein memory and the praise of God are swallowed up in gloom and silence; Job iii. 13, 17-19, xxx. 23; Prov. ix. 18; Isaiah xxxviii. 10-18; Psalm vi. 5, &c. Death thus appears even to the pious man in the Old

views of the Hebrew mind, as manifest in the Old Testament, it has this against it, that in the sentence pronounced—which must correspond with the threatening—no allusion whatever is made to spiritual death. It is evident, too, from what we have said regarding Rom. v. 12, and 1 Cor. xv. 21, that the Apostle Paul did not thus understand the second and third chapters of Genesis.

* As before, p. 98.

† Numbers xxvii. 3, however, seems to me not to bear upon this subject. The most natural interpretation of the passage seems to be that which takes the conjunction in the words כִּי־בְחֶטְאוֹ מֵת as denoting an effect following upon the cause, and thus to take the clause as dependent upon the preceding words, "Our father was not in the company of Korah, so as to have died in his sins— to have suffered death on account of certain sins."

Testament as a heavy calamity, because in looking forward to it he does not think merely of the moment when bodily life ends, but of that charmless and forlorn, yet eternal abode, into which that moment ushers him. Hence the name death is sometimes applied to this abode and state, *e.g.*, Psalm vi. 5, ix. 13.*

New Testament texts.

We cannot expect to find these representations of the older Hebraism adopted fully in the New Testament, for the Old Testament faith itself was gradually raised above this stage of knowledge by the religious principles working in it, and Mau has well described this change.† The general principles certainly of these representations are maintained even in the New Testament; the state upon which they who are justified in Christ enter at death is not the perfection of their being; this they look forward to at the final resurrection; thus even for the righteous there is in death (as will presently appear), somewhat of a retrograde movement. But the state after death which the Old Testament designates שְׁאוֹל, and the New Testament ᾅδης, is no longer assigned to the righteous, but to the rest of mankind as distinct from them, Matt. xi. 23, xvi. 18, Luke xvi. 23; see also the φυλακή, 1 Peter iii. 19. The New Testament calls the abode of the faithful departed "Paradise," and Jewish theology hardly justifies our regarding this as part of Hades; ‡ certainly the New Testament forbids it, for it also describes this state as a "dwelling in the Father's House," Luke xxiii. 43; John xiv. 2. As to the real nature of this state the New Testament not only describes it as a being at home with Christ (John xiv. 3; 2 Cor. v. 8,

---

* Once, indeed, in the New Testament θάνατος is spoken of as a state, Acts ii. 24, but this is an Old Testament allusion. The οὐ πρὸς θάνατον in John xi. 4, may be explained without any reference to the state after death, for a sickness in Christ's judgment was not "unto death," when He knew that the person dying would be raised again in a few days. We need hardly add that the designation νεκροί does not denote this state after death; the departed are called νεκροί, because they are ἀποθανόντες. It is not so easy to decide what St. Paul means by the death which, as the last enemy, is to be destroyed, 1 Cor. xv. 26, —whether he refers to the intermediate state of the redeemed, which shall terminate at the Resurrection, or their dying upon earth, or perhaps both.

† In the work already named, p. 77.

‡ This is BRETSCHNEIDER'S view (*Grundlage des evang. Pietismus*, p. 226); but in endeavouring to trace the Hades of the later Hebraism in the New Testament, he is betrayed into very forced interpretations, *e.g.*, pp. 238, 244.

9; Phil. i. 23), but, in contrast with the state of the dead in Hades, where God cannot be thought of nor praised, it speaks of it as a life in fellowship with Christ, 1 Thess. v. 10 (in the περιποίησις σωτηρίας διὰ τοῦ κυρίου ἡμῶν Ἰησοῦ Χριστοῦ, verse 9).*

When, therefore, physical death is spoken of in Scripture as the result and punishment of sin, we must understand by it not only the extinction of our bodily life, but the state of deprivation and imprisonment (φυλακή) following thereupon.† From the Scripture promises last referred to, we see how far this death as a punishment on account of sin affects those who are in Christ, and how far not. They are, of course, still subject to the evil of physical death on account of sin—τὸ μὲν σῶμα νεκρὸν δι' ἁμαρτίαν, Rom. viii. 10;—but as the intermediate state upon which they enter is essentially different from that appointed to the natural man, and as this state terminates in the ἀνάστασις ζωῆς, the sting of death which affects the very heart of life is taken away; and this sting really consists in the unforgiven sins of the natural life, 1 Cor. xv. 55, 56. The Apostle, therefore, longs "not to be unclothed but clothed upon, that mortality" (the σῶμα as χοϊκόν), "may be swallowed up of life" (by the incorruptible σῶμα πνευματικόν); but he has a good hope

---

* The ζῆν in Christ's words, Luke xx. 38, does not, I think, bear upon this point. For in His argument against the Sadducees the doctrine of the Resurrection is the thing treated of, and the words πάντες γὰρ αὐτῷ ζῶσι may be paraphrased, "God regards them, in view of their future resurrection to life, as living." It would be too great a digression fully to analyse that most difficult passage in 1 Peter iv. 6, containing the words ζῶσι κατὰ θεόν πνεύματι; I will briefly name the results to which a very careful examination of it has led me. It is more closely connected with the thoughts expressed in verses 1, 2, than with the intermediate verses, 3, 5. St Peter would say that the preaching of the gospel would not be in vain even to those members of Christ's church who had died since the Lord had sat down on the right hand of God (ch. iii. 22), and who do not live to see His return (ver. 7); they have received it that, though judged before men in their earthly existence—by death of the body—they live unto God in a heavenly existence—*i.e.*, after the resurrection which will be to them ἀνάστασις ζωῆς. If this interpretation be correct—and certainly it has fewer difficulties than that of STEIGER (on 1 Peter, p. 381), or that of GRIMM *Theol. Stud. u. Krit.*, 1835, part 3, p. 616—this passage does not bear upon our present investigation.

† We must, therefore, agree with MAU when he blames KRABBE for omitting to notice this element in viewing death as the punishment of sin; while, on the other hand, KRABBE is right as opposed to MAU when he maintains the doctrine of Scripture to be that physical death in the strictest sense of the word—the extinction of corporeal life—is the wages of sin.

even if this wish should not be accomplished, because he knows that with him "to be absent from 'the body'" is "to be at home with the Lord," 2 Cor. v. 2-9.*

There is one great difficulty which the inner harmony of Christian knowledge itself suggests against this apprehension of death as the punishment of sin.

Mortality seems natural to man. Death in nature is simply the annihilation of the animal, its return into the universal life of nature. The death of man, on the contrary, is the dissolving of a living union between a reasonable soul and an organized body. Viewing human death thus, in its universality, and as distinct from death in nature, we can easily regard it as the effect of sin. To divide and isolate thus a living unity is the distinctive characteristic of sin. But what is the effect of this dissolution? Body and soul do not both continue to live after their separation, but the body returns to corruption; and when decay begins to show itself in the body, it seems only natural and even necessary for the soul to withdraw itself and to live apart from the wasting organism. But as for the body, mortality would seem, as a matter of course, to belong to it in common with all merely corporeal existences. Are we then to say that in it death has sin for its principle and cause? Is what seems to be its essential constitution to be attributed to sin? This surely cannot be maintained, save upon dualistic principles, opposed alike to Christian ideas of the creation, and to the Christian doctrine of our redemption by the Incarnation of the Son of God.

St Paul's statements regarding man's body. The Apostle Paul, moreover, referring to the material of our corporeal nature, calls the first man ἐκ γῆς χοϊκός, (1 Cor. xv. 48); he describes this earthly body wherein we "bear the image" of our earthly parents as children of Adam, as "sown in weakness, dishonour, corruption," (verses 42, 43, 49, compare the σῶμα τῆς ταπεινώσεως ἡμῶν, Phil. iii. 21), and says, concerning its constituent elements, that "flesh and blood cannot inherit the kingdom of God" (verse 50): yet he does not so much as hint that this constitutional decay of our material nature arises from a prior disturbance therein. In like manner, he distinguishes between the "natural" or animal body, σῶμα

* See NEANDER's *Gesch. der Pflanzung der Kirche*, p. 883.

ψυχικόν which is suitable only for his ψυχή, his lower, finite and sensational life, and the "spiritual body," σῶμα πνευματικόν, appropriate for his higher nature, his πνεῦμα, and fitted to be its organ and medium of manifestation. But according to the whole connection of the passage it is clear that St Paul regards it as the necessary order that in the development of man the animal body should come first, and that it should give place to the spiritual body (verses 45, 46). Hence it would appear that the body liable to death is only a lower stage of development, and not the effect of sin.

The Apostle's statements lead us back to the beginning of Genesis, which he evidently has on his mind. There physical death (as we have already seen) is represented to be the punishment of sin. And yet we there find that from the beginning natural corporeal functions (eating, drinking, &c., Gen. i. 28-30) were ordained for man, which imply the mortality of his bodily nature (compare Luke xx. 35, 36); yea, the very name by which he is called אֲדָמָה אָדָם, denotes his affinity with earth, and the material of which his body is formed is expressly called dust (Gen. ii. 7). Now if these statements imply that the return of our body, "dust to dust," is only in keeping with its primary constitution, there is clearly a contradiction between them and the affirmation of Gen. iii. 19. There we find the sentence pronounced on man representing death as the punishment of his sin, "unto dust thou shalt return;"—and yet in the very same sentence he is reminded of his earthly origin, "till thou return to the ground, out of which thou wast taken."*

Those in Genesis.

The difficulty is solved if we consider the meaning of the "tree of life" in Paradise. The narrative shows that man's possession of permanent existence depended upon his partaking of the fruit of that tree, Gen. iii. 22. If we closely examine the words of this passage, and consider the force of the word גַּם "also," "even," it most naturally implies that man had not as yet eaten of the tree of life. If this be so, we may take this tree of life and the eating of its fruit as a symbol at least

The apparent contradiction removed.

* כִּי מִמֶּנָּה לֻקָּחְתָּ GESENIUS has shown that the particle כִּי here is to be taken not as casual "for," but as a relative "from which."

of man's passing into that higher and immortal life which was intended for him, not as a spiritual being simply, but as a being made up of body and spirit. This immortalizing transition is denied him—as his exclusion from Paradise with its tree of life symbolizes—on account of sin. The sentence therefore pronounced upon man, Gen. iii. 19, consistently refers to his origin as taken out of the dust, and to the natural susceptibility of mortality in his bodily frame, while at the same time it describes this as a punishment, and represents the dissolution of his body as the effect of sin, it being that which ought not to be. Physical death is implied in man's nature—so far as he is originally χοϊκὸς—as a POSSIBILITY WHICH OUGHT TO BE REMOVED; he becomes subject to it as an INEVITABLE NECESSITY and the law of his being, in consequence of sin.*

Christ's resurrection body.
But in order fully to understand the import of this sad law, we must lift our eyes from the first to the second Adam, in whom our true humanity is blended with sinlessness and perfect holiness. That Christ's corporeal nature before His crucifixion was the same as ours is not only witnessed by the author of the Epistle to the Hebrews (Heb. ii. 14; compare 1 John iv. 2, 3), but is implied in the gospel history of His life throughout. His body was, as to its material, "earthly," (σῶμα χοϊκόν), and as to its organic relation to his inner human nature "natural," (σῶμα ψυχικόν) like ours. But what was the nature of Christ's corporeity after His resurrection? We find the risen Saviour taking pains to convince His apostles, upon His first and His second appearances to them collectively, that He is the same Jesus, and that His body is the same as it was before His crucifixion, Luke xxiv. 39, 40; John xx. 20, 26. The proofs, too, which He gives them of this fact imply the earthly materiality of His risen body. "Reach hither thy finger and behold My hands, and reach hither thy hand and thrust it into My side," were His words to the doubting Thomas, John xx. 27; † He eat with them also, Luke xxiv. 41-43; and this an earthly body alone can do, 1 Cor. vi.

* The Socinian theory is similar to this, but it extends death to the soul. See the full exposition and defence of this in SOCINUS: *Disputatio de statu primi hominis ante lapsum* (*Biblioth. fr. Polon.*, tom. ii. 257).

† It makes no difference as to the bearing of this text whether the apostle Thomas literally obeyed Christ, or was satisfied with the evidence of his eyes.

13. Are we then to suppose that the glorified body, which cannot consist of "flesh and blood," 1 Cor. xv. 50, has nevertheless "flesh and bones," as Christ's risen body certainly had? (Luke xxiv. 39). It is very evident that Christ's body, in His appearances after the Resurrection was a σῶμα χοϊκόν. In the early Church the opposite view prevailed, and the sudden appearing and vanishing of the risen Saviour was appealed to as proving that His body was πνευματικόν. But the facts we have adduced would be on this theory inexplicable, whereas any one who believes in the miraculous in Christ's life—and on this ground only can His resurrection be believed—can easily account for His sudden appearances and vanishing through closed doors, &c., while His body was still χοϊκόν.* It is urged again, that when St Paul names the fact of Christ's resurrection (1 Cor. xv. 12) as the guarantee of the simultaneous resurrection and glorification of believers, he implies that Christ's resurrection body was πνευματικόν. But this is not so; on the contrary, when St Paul contrasts the second Adam with the first, the χοϊκός, and represents Him as the type and pattern of our resurrection, he describes Him as ἐπουράνιος, 1 Cor. xv. 48, 49, and thus he implies that Christ's body did not become the σῶμα τῆς δόξης, in the likeness of which our bodies are to be fashioned (Phil. iii. 21) until His ASCENSION.†

Herein we see the full significance of Christ's Ascension. Christ's death upon the Cross was a necessary part of His redemptive work (Rom. vi. 10); it certainly implies Christ's susceptibility of death, and this indeed is involved in the fact of His corporeity (Heb. ii. 14); but death with Him was not a necessity of His nature, it was an act of free self-surrender, as He Himself declares, John x. 18.‡ But when His sacrificial death was accomplished He rose from the grave with His natural body in order to manifest that very freedom from death which pertains to human nature as such, when it is pure from the

Significance of Christ's Ascension.

---

* We find similar miraculous disappearances recorded of Christ during His public ministry;—*e.g.* Luke iv. 30 ; John v. 13, viii. 59, x. 39, xviii. 6, 7. —*Tr.*

† KRABBE defends at length the opposite view, as before, p. 301.

‡ MAU greatly mistakes the apostle's meaning when he supposes (p. 101) that the ἀποθνήσκειν ἐν τῷ Ἀδάμ, 1 Cor. xv. 22, includes Christ.

CHAP. II.] SIN AS A CORRUPTION OF HUMAN NATURE. 299

taint of sin; Χριστὸς ἐγερθεὶς ἐκ νεκρῶν οὐκέτι ἀποθνήσκει· θάνατος αὐτοῦ οὐκέτι κυριεύει, Rom. vi. 9. If immunity from death did not belong to pure human nature, Christ, as truly man, after rising from the dead with an earthly material body, must necessarily have died again, as the risen Lazarus undoubtedly did. But this immunity is really the power of a progressive development, whereby the susceptibility of death naturally pertaining to human corporeity is removed—ἵνα καταποθῇ τὸ θνητὸν ὑπὸ τῆς ζωῆς. This is indeed a sacred mystery, a mystery which, though we know it by faith, must remain unexplained while we are still in the body; and yet we may suppose that upon the principle of development the change in Christ's risen humanity was not wholly accomplished at the moment of His ascension, but that there had been going on, from the day of His resurrection, a development of His glorified corporeity, which expanded from its bud into its perfect bloom in the Ascension. The process must be conceived of as progressing outwards from within; the spirit gradually penetrated His corporeity, and so moulded it that it became (what in idea it was to be) its pure and perfectly transparent exponent—σῶμα πνευματικόν.

These remarks are in themselves a sufficient reply to the objection that the apostle could not have made Christ's resurrection the pledge of ours (which he does in 1 Cor. xv.) if He had risen from the grave in His earthly material body. The apostle's analogy is fully justified by the truth which he states elsewhere, "Christ being raised from the dead dieth no more:" He rose in order henceforth no more to die.* It is, however, equally plain that Christ's resurrection must not be separated from His Ascension; the Resurrection is the starting-point of a development which is consummated in the Ascension. The Ascension is always included, at least *implicitè*, in St Paul's representations of Christ's resurrection, as the type and pledge of the Christian's resurrection not to an earthly but to a heavenly life.†

* Upon this point, and upon the dissimilarity and difference between Christ's Resurrection and the raising of certain individuals from the dead, *e.g.*, Lazarus, see KRABBE, p. 295.

† A mind unbiassed by modern hyper-criticism will not require proof of the fact that the apostle Paul clearly recognized the fact of Christ's Ascension and its connection with His Resurrection; although the only passage in which the ἀνάληψις is definitively stated (1 Tim. iii. 16) is doubtful as to its genuineness.

Though the resurrection must be regarded as the turning-point, when the glorifying and spiritualizing process in Christ's body began to approach its consummation in the ascension, we cannot limit this process within these two events. It may have been going on gradually, even before His death, without in the least deteriorating from the reality of His earthly body. There is one event indicating this in the gospel history, I mean the Transfiguration, which took place shortly before His Passion;*—a manifestation of the hitherto hidden glory of His body to His most trusty disciples. This was a glory which no one else in His earthly life possesses, because the development we speak of can take place only in a humanity perfectly sinless. In all other men it is hindered by sin, and the possibility of physical death thus becomes a necessity.

Let us now inquire from what sin does death inevitably follow in each individual? It is manifest that it cannot be the consequence of each one's actual sin, nor of the sinful state of each which is produced thereby. Death rules over man not only from the moment when he becomes capable of sinning, but from his very birth, yea, during his existence in the womb. If, therefore, death be at all the result of sin, it (together with what precedes and follows it) must be caused by a sin interwoven into our very nature, so that the universality of death is a weighty witness to the depravity of human nature. The apostle confirms this when he states

Death as the wages of sin.

See Eph. i. 20, 21, iv. 10; Phil. iii. 20, 21. Upon the connection between the Resurrection and the Ascension, see NEANDER *Leben Jesu*, 784; and NITZSCH, *Sendschreiben an Weisse*, FICHTE's *Zeitschrift*, 1840, part i. 47.

* That the first three Evangelists attached great importance to the Transfiguration is evident from the fact that they each of them connect it with Christ's first distinct prophecy of His death. The importance attached to it by the early Church is evident also from 2 Peter i. 16-18. If the solution here proposed of the difficulty named, p. 295, be in harmony with the doctrine of Scripture—which we maintain it is, unless it be disproved—the various arguments adduced by MAU to prove that according to Scripture the susceptibility of death belongs to human nature in itself, amount to nothing. It is surprising that, with all his care and circumspection in treating of this subject, he did not notice this way of reconciling the apparently contradictory representations of Scripture, for the solution in the main is not new. We find it in AUGUSTINE, *e.g.*, *De peccatorum meritis et remiss.*, lib. i. cap. 5,—"*Sic et illud corpus (primi hominis) jam erat mortale ; quam mortalitatem fuerat absumptura mutatio in aeternam incorruptionem, si in homine justitia . . . permaneret; sed ipsum mortale non est factum mortuum nisi propter peccatum.*"

as the destiny of human life that "in Adam all die," 1 Cor. xv. 22, and that "death hath passed upon all men for that all have sinned," Rom. v. 12. If human life derives this sad fate of mortality from Adam, it must cleave to human nature as conditioned or tainted by sin.

The words in Rom. v. 12, ἐφ' ᾧ πάντες ἥμαρτον, cannot fairly be urged against this view. The verb ἁμαρτάνειν certainly denotes actual sinning and not a sinful state; and if the ἐφ' ᾧ be understood to denote the reason or cause of the fact stated in the words immediately preceding, the universal reign of death in the human race would be represented here as the result of the actual sins of men; and in this case the apostle must have overlooked the fact that death reigns over a much wider range than does actual sin. Notwithstanding the acute observation of Rothe* on the opposite side, we must, with Neander,† maintain that ἐφ' ᾧ here, as in 2 Cor. v. 4, denotes a causal relationship,‡ and Rothe himself involuntary recognizes this by rendering the expression by the obsolete conjunction *massvn*, "since." But in 2 Cor. v. 4, as well as in Romans v. 12, ἐφ' ᾧ does not introduce the main reason or cause of the fact, but only an additional subordinate and confirmatory reason, so that it may best be rendered by "wie denn," "wie denn auch," "as moreover."§ St Paul had already stated the main reason of the διελθεῖν τὸν θάνατον εἰς πάντας ἀνθρώπους; we find it in the words, δι' ἑνὸς ἀνθρώπου ἡ ἁμαρτία εἰς τὸν κόσμον εἰσῆλθε, καὶ διὰ τῆς ἁμαρτίας ὁ θάνατος; see v. 15, τῷ τοῦ ἑνὸς παραπτώματι οἱ πολλοὶ ἀπέθανον; and v. 17. St Paul might have concluded the inference "so then death hath passed upon all men" with the διῆλθεν. But he does not stop here, for he wishes to remind his readers that mankind had merited this sad curse on account of their actual sins likewise. Understanding the words ἐφ' ᾧ πάντες ἥμαρτον, thus as an additional consideration over and above what had already been stated, we can easily see how St

* *Neuer Versuch einer Auslegung der Paulinischen Stelle*, Rom. v. 12-21, pp. 17, 18.
† *Leben Jesu*, p. 671.
‡ So also as it occurs in Phil. iii. 12; whereas in Phil. iv. 10, ἐφ' ᾧ is not a conjunction but a relative pronoun with ἐπί, "for which," denoting the purpose contemplated.
§ As in Phil. iii. 12.

Paul might make the general statement without naming the exception to it in the case of dying infants. But if the entire argument of verse 12 rests* upon this one clause of it ἐφ' ᾧ πάντες ἥμαρτον—whether we translate ἐφ' ᾧ as Rothe does "with the qualifying consideration that," or as others do "because,"—St Paul's silence as to exceptions would be quite unaccountable, for these would at once occur to his readers, and would totally destroy the force of his argument.†

Several commentators, however, suppose that the 13th and 14th verses are closely connected with this last clause of the 12th verse, and this would be a serious objection to our view of it as merely subordinate in the apostle's argument. But this close connection has not been shown. Verses 13, 14 do not apply exclusively either to the actual sinning of all men nor to the general fact of sin penetrating the whole development of the race; they speak of sin in the widest and most general sense of the word, without reference to any special kind of sin. The most natural construction would be to take the two verses as far as 'Ἀδάμ, not as an answer to an objection, but as a parenthesis enlarging upon verse 12; and the γάρ of verse 13 confirms this view. The apostle had in verse 12 affirmed the universality of sin, *implicitè*, in the words καὶ οὕτως εἰς πάντας ἀνθρώπους ὁ θάνατος διῆλθεν, and explicitly in the words, ἐφ' ᾧ πάντες ἥμαρτον. He then goes on to remark in passing: "Sin was in the world prior to the Mosaic legislation" (a fact which might be overlooked) "as well as after it; but men were not wont to impute sin to themselves if there was no distinct law against them. Notwithstanding this, however death reigned from Adam to Moses, even over those who had not, with Adam, transgressed a positive law." The words ἀπὸ 'Ἀδάμ μέχρι Μωϋσέως και ἐπὶ τοὺς μὴ ἁμαρτήσαντας ἐπὶ τῷ ὁμοιώματι τῆς παραβάσεως 'Ἀδάμ are only a more definite repetition of the words ἄχρι νόμου, ver. 13. The statement ἄχρι νόμου ἁμαρτία ην ἐν κόσμῳ is confirmed by the words ἀλλ

---

* Rothe, as before, p. 38.

† See THOLUCK's defence of the rendering "because," in the 5th Ed. of his Commentary on the Romans, p. 232. Yet he translates the expression "in as much as," because he recognizes the main reason of the universality of death as given in the preceding clauses, p. 234. PHILIPPI also in his Commentary p. 166, adopts the rendering "because," supplying to the verb ἥμαρτον "*Adamo peccante*," p. 168.

SIN AS A CORRUPTION OF HUMAN NATURE.

ἐβασίλευσεν ὁ θάνατος ἀπὸ Ἀδὰμ μέχρι Μωϋσέως, &c., in opposition to the usual non-imputation of sin where there was no actual law; the dominion of death even before the giving of the law proved that even then sin was in the world.

So far, then, in Rom. v. 12, from contradicting the doctrine that death ensues in consequence of that sin which has penetrated human nature, that the main clause of the verse, as distinct from the subordinate one, directly refers thereto as the reason for the reign of death throughout the race.

We may sum up the results of this investigation, and more accurately define them, in the following sentences.

In a twofold sense, the consequence of sin is death. On the one hand, there is spiritual death, the inner Summary of discord and enslavement of the soul, and the misery ensuing therefrom, to which belongs that other death—ὁ θάνατος ὁ δεύτερος, Rev. ii. 11, xx. 6, 14, xxi. 8;—an outward condition corresponding to that inner slavery. This death, the spiritual death—thus deferred in its outward realization as the second death by the plan of redemption—can only occur when man has rendered himself liable to it by actual sin; this is evident from Rom. vii. 9, 10; James i. 15. Numerous texts of Scripture describe this death as the consequence of sin, particularly in the first phase of it—Luke xv. 24, 32; Rom. viii. 6; 2 Cor. ii. 16, iii. 7; Eph. ii. 1, 5; Col. ii. 13; James v. 20; 1 John iii. 14; Rev. iii. 1;—and in the other phase of it as the second death—Rom. viii. 13; 2 Cor. ii. 16 ("death unto DEATH"); vii. 10. Both phases of this spiritual death are represented together in Rom. vi. 16, 21, viii. 5; 1 John v. 16, 17. The Church of Christ is wholly free from this death, having nothing more to do with it. Death, on the other hand, is the effect of sin deep-rooted in human nature, inasmuch as it is an outward paralysis and dissolution—physical death; yet not merely the moment of dying, but the state of fettered and gradually decaying existence during life. Scripture speaks of this death in both its phases; John vi. 49, 50, viii. 21, 24, 51, xi. 26; Rom. v. 12, 14, 17, 21; 1 Cor. xv. 54-56; 2 Tim. i. 10. The bondage of this state is, in the case of believers, inwardly destroyed in its bearing upon the spiritual life, and the moment of dissolution is to them an enhancement of their higher life, and is therefore the object of their desire, Phil. i. 21 ; 2 Cor. v. 8. But in its bearing upon their physical nature, death is an interruption of its development, a retrogression, not only for the moment of dying, but for the state ensuing, a chastisement which even the redeemed, "whose life is hid with Christ in God," must endure, because of the depraved human nature still clinging to them. As in this life, therefore, so also after death, they wait for "the redemption of the body," and its freedom from the bands of death at the resurrection, when "the manifestation of the sons of God" will be realized in its fulness, Rom. viii. 23, 19, 21. The great importance attached to the doctrine of the resurrection in the eschatology of the New Testament in the case of the saved, as well as of others, would be wholly inexplicable, if we did not recognize this preceding and intermediate state of deprivation.* They, too, must bow in this respect to that universal law of human development, which is the result of sin, namely, that as man must reach the goal of moral excellence, not by an uninterrupted ascending, step by step, but only by stooping to the lowest self-abasement,—only by an inner death (Rom. vi. 2, 8 ; Col. ii. 20, iii. 3), so as regards his physical nature, "the corn of wheat" must "fall into the ground, and die," if it is to live (John xii. 24 ; 1 Cor. xv. 36);—a law to which, in its physical bearing, Christ himself became subject, not for His own sake, but for our redemption. There are a few texts, lastly, in which the word death seems to include all the meanings now enumerated, Romans vi. 23, viii. 2.

Let us now endeavour more accurately to discover wherein the deprivation attaching to the state of the redeemed between their death and their resurrection consists. This is specially referred to in those words of St Paul, 2 Cor. v. 3, εἴπερ (according to Lachmann, which I adopt as the true reading instead of εἴγε), καὶ ἐνδυσάμενοι, οὐ γυμνοὶ εὑρεθησόμεθα. In chap. iv. 16, the Apostle had said "though

The intermediate state.

---

* See WEIZEL's Exposition, which in part agrees and in part disagrees with that given in an earlier edition of this work, in his Dissertation upon the primitive Christian doctrine of Immortality ; *Stud. u. Krit.* 1836, part iv. 913. Also KERN's Dissertation on Christian Eschatology, *Tübinger Zeitschr. für Theol.*, 1840, part ii. 13.

our outward man perish, yet the inward man is renewed day by day;" and in close connection with this he proceeds in chap, v. 1, to reason that " if this earthly house "—the natural body of 1 Cor. xv. 44—" be destroyed, we have an eternal, a heavenly habitation, whose maker is God"—*i.e.*, the resurrection body. He then expresses his longing for the full possession of this heavenly house, a longing answering to that Criticism of spoken of in Rom. viii. 23, for the glorious redemp-
2 Cor. v. 1-4. tion of the body. Christ is the Saviour not of man's soul alone, but of his body also, ὁ κύριος τῷ σώματι, 1 Cor. vi. 13, 14; compare Rom. viii. 11. But the Apostle, hoping himself to live unto the second coming of the Lord, describes this " putting on " the heavenly house (the resurrection body), as an ἐπενδύσασθαι, verse 2 (see also 1 Cor. xv. 52, 53), and then he adds the qualifying clause, " if indeed we also shall be found clothed and not naked," in the Day of the Lord. The clause standing in this close connection with ἐπενδύσασθαι is evidently intended to qualify it, to show that the Apostle's hope in this respect was not certain; it would be realized if the Day of the Lord found him among the living, among those still clothed with the earthly body,—if death had not already unclothed him —compare ἐκδύσασθαι, verse 4.* If this be the true meaning of ver. 3, then ver. 4 stands in close connection with it. We take

* According to this rendering the aorist ἐνδυσάμενοι, instead of the perfect ἐνδεδυμένοι is an anomaly, yet one often found in good Greek; see the examples quoted by ROTHE in his Commentary on Rom. v. 12–21, from Buttmann and Bernhardy. We find parallel expressions even in St Paul's own writings; neither in Eph. vi. 14, nor in 1 Thess. v. 8, does he refer to the momentary act of putting on the breastplate, but to the permanent wearing of it, yet he uses ἐνδυσάμενοι in both places (στῆτε ἐνδυσάμενοι—νήφωμεν ἐνδυσάμενοι). Still less can the absence of ἀλλά before οὐ γυμνοί warrant RUECKERT's rejection of this rendering (see his Commentary, p. 146), for we have similar forms of expression in Rom. ii. 29, ἐν πνεύματι, οὐ γράμματι, and 1 Cor. iii. 2, γάλα ὑμᾶς ἐπότισα, οὐ βρῶμα. Whatever difficulty there be in the καί (in my opinion it implies an ἡμεῖς), tells equally against every interpretation which adheres to the reading ἐνδυσάμενοι as upon external and internal grounds the true one. To read as RUECKERT does ἐκδυσάμενοι, because this occurs in a few minor MSS. and Patristic authorities, is hardly in keeping with the just principles of criticism. The interpretations given by LANGE (*Biblisch-theologische Erörterungen, Stud. u. Krit.*, 1836, No. 3, 742), and by NITZSCH (*System der christlichen Lehre*, 404), appear to me—so far as I can understand them, and they are not very clear—to make the Apostle state a self-evident fact, viz., that ἐνδυσάμενος is not γυμνός, and to misinterpret the meaning of the preceding verse, which obviously refers not to a provisional re-embodying of souls, but to the resurrection body.

it with Rückert to be "an explanatory repetition of the statement less clearly expressed in ver. 2." But the explanation depends upon the clause in ver. 3 qualifying the Apostle's wish. The main reason of his "groaning in this tabernacle," is already stated in ver. 2, viz., a longing for the glory of the completed kingdom of God—" to be clothed upon with our house which is from heaven." But another and subordinate reason—ἐφ' ᾧ—is the natural fear of death, a wish as to the manner in which bodily life should end—οὐ θέλομεν ἐκδύσασθαι, ἀλλ' ἐπενδύσασθαι. This also obviates the difficulty of the αὐτὸ τοῦτο in ver. 5, which Rückert considers unsolvable—and justly, according to his rendering of the passage ; the αὐτὸ τοῦτο is the transition into the perfection of glorified human life which St Paul has in view throughout the passage, verses 1–4, as the main object of his desire. It is to this that "the earnest of the Spirit" given to believers (ver. 5) evidently refers.

The Apostle, therefore, in ver. 3 attributes to the soul during the intermediate state between death and the resurrection— (while there is such a state, for they who live unto the coming of the Lord shall not experience it)*—a γυμνὸν εἶναι clearly as regards their corporeity. Other New Testament writers express the same truth when they speak of the departed in the intermediate state as ψυχαὶ or πνεύματα, 1 Peter iii. 19 ; Rev. vi. 9, xx. 4 ; Heb. xii. 23. This, of course, implies that the soul turns in upon itself, that there is a hindrance and limit to its outgo and the exhibition of its life ; and this is indicated in the καθεύδειν in contrast with the γρηγορεῖν of this earthly life, 1 Thess. v. 10 ; 1 Cor. xi. 30 ; though this expression also must be qualified by the ἅμα σὺν χριστῷ ζῆν. But the γυμνότης does not warrant the assumption, which would variously involve us in the greatest difficulties—that the soul in the intermediate state is utterly destitute of any corporeal medium, that the individual retires into an existence merely, and in the narrowest sense, spiritual.† Some organ of self-manifestation will certainly be left to the Ego in death, though it must be one wherein the

* The fact of those who are alive at the coming of the Lord being thus freed from the pain of death, which is the universal law of fallen humanity, will doubtless be a compensation to them for the additional trials and sufferings to which, according to Holy Scripture, they will be exposed through the increased dominance of human wickedness.

† *Geistige* ; see vol. i. 327.

full reality of human life cannot yet appear, and one which is imperfect in comparison not only of the σῶμα πνευματικὸν, but also of the earthly corporeity, involving a relative "unclothing" of the soul.* To show in some degree how such a clothing of the soul is possible after its being unclothed in death we may, as Weisse does, adopt the notion of the "nervous spirit" or the sympathetic system; but theology, as well as philosophy, must allow that upon this subject nothing certain can be affirmed.

CHAPTER III.

The Doctrine of Hereditary Sin.

§ 1. STATEMENT OF THE PROBLEM.

The investigations of this Fourth Book have led us on from the fact of the universality of actual sin to the recognition of a sinfulness interwoven into the very nature of man. But this natural tendency to sin, however deeply it may be rooted in us, cannot be rested in as an *ultimatum* beyond which doctrinal inquiry does not care to go. We cannot rest content with this; for if we would not deny the reality of sin as sin altogether, we must, while allowing this natural and universal bias towards it, firmly maintain that sin does not spring from human nature according to its true ideal.

The Western Church in its theology solves the problem of a sinfulness which, while contradictory to human nature, has yet become natural and constitutional by the dogma of HEREDITARY SIN. We have already seen that we may adopt the name *peccatum originale* as descriptive of this sinfulness; let us now inquire whether the designation *peccatum haereditarium* be equally admissible.

The dogma, in the early Protestant form of it, may be stated

* This statement in some degree modifies and corrects the opinions which the author urged in an earlier dissertation on the subject in the *Stud. u. Krit.* 1835, No 3, 785, in opposition to the view put forth in FICHTE's thoughtful treatise, "*Die Idee der Persönlichkeit und der indeviduellen Fortdauer.*" See on this question the remarks of NITZSCH, *System der christl. Lehre*, p. 401; and of LANGE, *Stud. u. Krit*, 1836, No. 3, p. 700.

thus :—God created man in His own image; that is to say, He endowed human nature in our first parents with original righteousness (*justitia originalis*) which consists of holiness of will and wisdom of understanding. These glorious attributes so belong to human nature that if they fail its purity is lost.* God, therefore, endowed man with these, not simply as a personal possession, but with the intention that if he faithfully preserved them he should transmit them by generation to his descendants, in such a manner of course that they should possess the disposition or capacity of spontaneously manifesting these attributes.† But by disobedience against the divine command man fell, was rejected by God, and not only lost the divine image, but tainted his nature, both body and soul, with a lusting after wickedness. This loss of the divine image and this permanent evil inclination is handed down from him to all men " descended from him by ordinary generation,' and hereditary sin consists of these two elements, the one negative—*defectus justitiae originalis*,—the other positive—*concupiscentia*—the inexhaustible source of all actual sin. Hereditary sin is by no means to be regarded as a mere misfortune or an evil involving no guilt; being truly SIN, it makes every man from the outset of his life actually guilty in God's sight, and exposes him to eternal condemnation. Hereditary sin is at the same time and essentially hereditary guilt.

We have already (chap. i. of this Fourth Book) considered the statements of dogmatic theology concerning the extent of this inborn depravity, and the degree in which those statements are modified by Scripture and experience. We have now to examine and to test the dogmatic teaching of the Church regarding the relation between hereditary sin and the conception of guilt.

Hereditary guilt logically inferred.

Setting out then from this last-named theological statement —" hereditary sin is essentially hereditary guilt,"—it is clear that this rests upon the principle that wherever there is sin

---

* This is in opposition to the Roman Catholic view of a *pura natura*, which is regarded as distinct, at least in thought, from the *justitia originalis* as *donum supernaturale et superadditum*, so that after the loss of the *donum superadditum* the *naturalia pura* remain.

† This follows inferentially from the statements of the *Apologia Confessioni* art i. p. 51.

CHAP. III.]   THE DOCTRINE OF HEREDITARY SIN.   309

there must be guilt; and further, that the present constitution of human nature, whence actual sin of necessity springs, must itself be regarded as sinful. This second proposition is logically proved by the categories of condition and consequent; and the first, viz., that sin and guilt are correlatives, we have already seen (Book I. part ii.) to be equally well grounded, according to the true conception of guilt.

If, however, sin and guilt are correlatives, we may argue inversely that if we cannot possibly attach guilt to the individual in relation to certain acts and states, those acts and states cannot be really sinful. The question is whether the dogma that hereditary sin is hereditary guilt be secure against this reverse inference from its own principles. Guilt cannot be predicated of existences merely natural, but only of personal beings; for a personal being alone can be regarded as the real author of its acts and states. Where there is no personality, and consequently no freedom of will, there can be no power of primary self-determination; what seems to be a self-determining, if traced back to its true source, is resolved into action necessarily determined. Acts and states, in themselves evil, can be regarded as involving guilt only when they primarily spring from the self-determining of the Subject. But if the Subject be merely the medium or instrument for determinations coming from another power—from a force of nature or another person—these acts and states cannot be imputed to him as guilt, unless by some previous act of self-determination he had allowed this power to exert a determining influence upon him. Now the dogma of hereditary sin teaches that the inherent sinful tendency of our nature necessarily leads us on to all kinds of actual sin, according to the canon, *semper cum malo originali simul sunt peccata actualia*,* and, moreover, that this inherent liability to sin, in its universality, is solely the effect of the first act of sin on the part of our first parents. But if this sinful tendency be in us solely through the act of others, and not through our own deed, *they* and not *we* are responsible for it, —it is not our guilt, but our misfortune. And even as to

Margin note: Unjust reversing of this argument.

---

* *Melanchthon* lays down this canon in his *Loci*, in the beginning of the chapter *De peccatis actualibus*, and the theologians who follow him usually adopt it, particularly in their doctrine concerning baptism.

actual sins which spring from this inherent sinful tendency, these are not strictly our own, but the acts of our first parents through us. Why then should deeds which are only apparently ours be imputed to us as actual sins for which we are to be condemned?

Thus the law of necessary connection between sin and guilt, which if we take *sin* for granted, leads to the inference of guilt, threatens, when we deny the existence of *guilt*, to destroy the reality of sin. Christian dogma demands that personal guilt must be maintained as attaching both to inherited sinfulness and to its fruits in our life; and so far as we have yet seen, there is no way of reconciling this with the contradictory conclusion now argued out.

This recoil of the consciousness of guilt against the idea of hereditary sin is so obvious, that the opponents of the Augustinian doctrine, from Pelagius downwards, have considered it their main argument. But it is equally obvious, that they only have a right to condemn the Christian doctrine on this point who are able to furnish a better explanation of the universality of sin as co-existent with individual responsibility. If, on the contrary, all they can do is to deny the fact of the universality of sin for the sake of maintaining the guilt of the sinner, or to derive sin from the essence of human nature, and so to destroy the notion of sin and guilt altogether, then the Christian doctrine has clearly the preponderance of truth on its side, seeing that it endeavours to solve the apparent contradiction by theory of hereditary sin and hereditary guilt, in which the same contradiction reappears. For the most inadequate explanation of a contradiction between two principles equally established is, so long as it maintains both intact, much nearer the truth than an attempt to do away with the contradiction by denying either of the conflicting principles.

A theory, however, which has been adopted by very many deep thinkers in the Christian Church for the past fifteen centuries, and which has been recognized in the Confessions of the Evangelical Church, claims from us a closer examination, both as to its nature, and the principles which lie at its foundation.

This theory in modern times has variously expressed itself somewhat in this fashion.* It is a very shallow and abstract

---

* See, for example, the exposition of this view given by SARTORIUS, *Die Lehre von der heiligen Liebe*, part i. pp. 103, 104.

THE DOCTRINE OF HEREDITARY SIN.

The inner principle of the Dogma.

way of contemplating mankind if we merely regard them morally as an aggregate of single and isolated individuals, having no mutual dependence or connection with each other, save what may arise in their progressive development from discipline, teaching, and example. A more thorough estimate enables us to recognize (beneath this separation into so many mere atoms) *a solid and substantial unity*, out of which each individual life grows as from its native soil. It is also a very superficial notion to suppose that the individual is morally moulded by the community to which he belongs only so far as he voluntarily allows himself to be so. The fact is, as he grows up he is unconsciously affected by its moral tone and standard, its inclinations and interests, its mental views and peculiarities, so that even when he decides and acts in this or that manner with perfect self-consciousness, these social elements (having penetrated his inner life) exert a co-determining influence upon him, whether he be aware of it or not. If the associations in which he lives be not artificial and optional, but natural and fixed, the individual may be said to be born to those very associations. Thus, notwithstanding the unity of the human race, the Caucasian has different moral perceptions and moral character from the Negro, the Germanic race from the Slavonian, and so on. But the individual not only receives a distinctive impress by means of education and custom, he is inherently biassed and moulded by the moral character of the community to which he belongs.

The point in question, indeed, concerns a bias or tendency which is not distinctive of one community, but is common to the race. Hereditary depravity, though common to all, is in its nature a disturbance, something not in humanity to begin with, but something which has arisen; and if the fact of its having arisen subsequent to man's creation be harmonized with the fact of its universality, nothing can be more conceivable than the doctrine that it began with our first parents, and by their fall from God. But if by the fall depravity has penetrated into the very essence of our species, then—however variously it may be embodied in individuals—it must manifest itself not as something foreign to them or communicated from without, but as rooted in their

The organic view.

very nature, and springing therefrom as at once *the character of the species* and the property of the individual in the fullest sense of the word, and penetrating all the decisions of individual life. This is the truer view of this relation; for it apprehends both sides (the species and the individual) in inseparable unity, and is as akin to love as it is to speculative discernment; whereas it accords only with an abstract understanding on the one hand, and egoism on the other, when the individual will not recognize himself in his sinfulness as a member of the species, when he is not sensible of the stream of its life in himself, side by side with his hindrances and troubles, but demands a separate and personal reason for his guilt, apart from his being one of the race,—another way of accounting for it which shall enable him to realize it. Experience, moreover, teaches us repeatedly that vices propagate themselves in certain families from generation to generation, not as acquired practices, but as evil principles and inclinations; and yet those who are liable to them cannot conscientiously justify themselves when they consider them.

Far be it from us to deny that there is some degree of truth in this view of sin, which we may call the "organic" or "substantial" view, just as the espousers of it call ours "an atomic and subjective view." Though we cannot agree to all its conclusions, we must acknowledge that the fundamental principle which it insists on—viz., the hereditary transmission of a sinful tendency—must have its place in every theory of sin which would not be partial or inadequate. And though we have presented this doctrine in its most modern form, it would not be difficult to find what is parallel to it (though on the basis of another philosophy) in the older Protestant theology. We refer particularly to the formula—*natura corrumpit personam*, whereby that theology, following Anselm of Canterbury, Odo of Cambray, Alexander von Hales, and Thomas Aquinas, expressed the *peccatum originis originatum*, hereditary sin and its power; as the counterpart of which they added the other formula, *persona corrumpit naturam*, as answering to *peccatum originis originans*,—the Adamic fall and its consequences.*

Espousers of it.

---

* Hence the following formula may be inferred, *natura a prima persona* (or *a primis personis*), *corrupta, corrumpit ceteras personas.*

In contemplating this view as it has now been sketched, we
must first of all remark that the categories
"individual" and "species," have not, properly
speaking, any place in the sphere of mind; they
belong only to the sphere of nature.* However strong the
term whereby we designate the union subsisting between the
individual and the species, this union must, after all, be a
dependence of the former upon the latter. And this dependence very clearly presents itself in the question before us.
Original sin must be regarded as a character belonging to the
constitution of the species ever since the fall, and abiding
essentially the same throughout all stages of human development. This universal feature of the species is embodied, with
as inevitable a necessity as are its other general characteristics,
in every human being born according to the course of nature,
and thus it is individualized. Yet in such a manner that,
whatever be the determinateness of the species implied in
original sin, its *general character or constitution* only belongs
necessarily to the individual. This general constitution is
what we have here to do with.

Categories of species and individual.

Now we do not feel ourselves warranted unhesitatingly to
pronounce it impossible that imperfections of natural consti-

---

* SCHALLER, in opposition to Strauss, makes the same observation in his work, "*Der historische Christus und die Philosophie*," p. 34, though we cannot agree with him in his mode of applying it. He thinks that "in the sphere of nature the individual represents only one aspect of the species, because it does not combine all its features; and there are other aspects presented in other individuals which supplement it, and make up the universality denoted by the species. In the sphere of spirit, on the contrary, the individual person knows himself,—*i.e.*, he exists as complete in himself, and does not need to be supplemented by another,—and he knows the species as embodied in himself." If this means that the imperfect representation of the species, by individuals, and the consequent need of individuals supplementing each other, be peculiar to the sphere of nature as distinct from that of man, our investigations in the last chapter lead us to maintain the opposite. Even in the highest ranges of nature among the lower animals, the distinctions which appear in the species, so far, at least, as they do not constitute new species, but pertain to the individuals as such—apart from differences of sex—are superficial and unimportant, and cannot necessitate a relation of the individuals to one another, in order to supplement each other. It is only when the individual possesses a distinctive character of its own—*i.e.*, in the sphere of personality—that this enlarging or supplementing is required, through the consciousness of representing the species onesidedly and imperfectly; in this sphere only does the individual maintain any fellowship with the rest of his species.

tution and state, pain, for example, and physical evil generally, are inherited by the individual, simply as the result of the general disorder or imperfection of the species. The principle of God's justice forbids our regarding physical evil, in every instance, as merited punishment. Indeed, such a notion is forbidden by the well-known fact that other sentient existences in nature suffer pain as well as man,—unless, indeed, we adopt some eccentric opinion, such as the transmigration of souls. Indeed, if we could regard sin simply as suffering, and moral evil in the same light as physical, it might seem conceivable that, as the individual has a sinful nature from his birth, this sinful nature reveals itself from the first awakening of consciousness with the same necessity as the corrupt tree brings forth evil fruit. But let us bethink ourselves what we have here to do with. The question is, how man is to be accounted guilty; in what way he has power to destroy his title to fellowship with God, in whom alone is his life, and to make himself liable to God's righteous punishment. That being only can be guilty who possesses an inner centre of independence, the power of primary self-determination either to surrender self to God or to turn away from Him. Thus only can he be really answerable for what (though it be his actual state in this life) he still ought never to have been.

These inadequate to explain man's guilt.

Thus the idea of guilt, according to its true nature, leads us on beyond the distinctions of species and individual, to the fact of personality. We have already seen (vol. ii. p. 289) the self-dependent significance of personality in relation to the species generally, and this alone is the principle upon which the awful burden of guilt can be based.*

Personality alone is the basis of guilt.

Those who think they can maintain the Scripture doctrine of original sin without reference to this principle of personal self-decision, argue out the guilt of the individual in original sin from the fact, that he cannot withdraw this sin from the elements of his life, and that he would not be himself

* We see accordingly that those theologians who consider the old dogmatic theory on this point complete, and as not needing extension, do not properly distinguish between "individuality" and "personality." See the exposition of Sartorius referred to, p. 310.

(according to the determinateness of his particular nature) if this sinfulness had not been in him from the beginning as a co-determining principle of his development. Or they appeal to Augustine's well-known words, *non inviti tales sumus*, and explain the hereditary guilt of mankind by the fact that the natural man does not feel original sin in him as a power which constrains and fetters him,—obliging him to sin in spite of his unwillingness and resistance,—but that he freely surrenders himself to its promptings, so that original sin and its activity are a *voluntarium* in him.

But this is only a description of the manner in which the depravity of the species manifests itself in the individual ; all that is proved is that this takes place naturally, because sin is rooted in his very constitution, not as an injury coming upon him from without, but as a natural bias and tendency, insinuating itself into all the elements of our life. But the idea of guilt involves the element of causation by an act of self-decision ; it has for its foundation that *freedom* which implies the possibility of being and doing otherwise, and which excludes not only force, but inner necessity (in a metaphysical sense). If, therefore, individuals are subject to that depravity which cleaves to the species, by virtue of a necessity wholly independent of their self-decision, in this case—though this depraved nature which they inherit be ever so closely interwoven into their individual character, and be freely cherished and fostered by them in their outward acts—they cannot be held accountable for it ; it must be imputed to the nature of the species, and to him alone who first introduced it. A freedom which merely excludes compulsion, and which consists in the coincidence of individual inclination with impulses towards determinate acts, must be recognized even in the lower animals ; and if the possession of this kind of freedom only warrants us in holding men responsible for the disturbance belonging to their individual life, we must also hold the wild beast of the forest responsible for the thirst for blood and fierceness pertaining to its nature. This mere freedom of inclination cannot guarantee man's self-appropriation of original sin apart from the determining force of the depraved nature belonging to his species, because in this free inclination towards sin, this determining

Freedom implies more than inclination.

force shows itself in all its magnitude. The power of natural depravity would be far less strong if the inclination and effort of the individual were *opposed* to it; and, indeed, we generally look upon its dominion as at an end when the man begins voluntarily to resist it.

<small>Teaching of Scripture.</small> Some there are who call our thus insisting upon personal self-decision as the basis of guilt, a "moral atomism;" but if it be so, Holy Scripture itself is equally chargeable with it. Mankind, in relation to sin, are not there regarded merely as an aggregate mass; a distinction is made within the species between the children of light and the children of darkness, and this distinction is represented as dependent upon an act of self-decision, and as being ultimately decided at the day of judgment in the case of each individual separately, and according to the character of his life in God's sight. If Christian theology, therefore, in harmony with the teaching of Scripture, is to retain in its *eschatology* the conception of guilt in all its reality (as implying a personal act of self-decision towards damnable sin), it must not, in its *anthropology*, weaken this conception. Each individual person is (as the very word denotes, if the term may be applied to any thing in the world) an indivisible and complete whole, and in this sense is an ἄτομον, and a distinct part of the essential elements of the world cannot be regarded as a mere mode or affection of something else. We say again, we by no means overlook the element of determinateness of nature in human sin, and the relative dependence of each individual upon the natural basis, out of which he develops himself. But when that very part of his sinful nature which breaks through these limits and rises above them to a higher self-dependent relation (and herein consists the guilt of personality on account of sin) is regarded as part of that basis of nature, when this determinate nature is made, not only an element, but the sum-total of sin—this partial and mere organic view leads to a naturalistic theory of sin, which endangers not only the doctrine of a final judgment, but of personal immortality generally.

Does Christianity really teach that humanity in its natural state (in Adam) is nothing more than natural existence,— a kind of life which is capable of personality, but not as yet possessing it, and obtaining it only in Christ? If so, we must give up the notion of responsibility in the sphere of man's natural life, because the basis of personality necessary thereto is still wanting, and we must content ourselves with maintaining it in the sphere only of man's regenerate life in Christ. But even here, if we consider the matter, it cannot be retained, because, in this sphere, we cannot speak of an individual choice between good and evil, but only of a decision for good; and, moreover, because man's passing into this sphere cannot, according to this view, be an act of personal self-decision;—if it were, it would imply a power of personal moral choice in man's previous state by nature. Redemption is thus robbed of its moral import, sin is deprived of its reality, and human freedom, together with the divine image in man, is denied. This doctrine, that man cannot be held responsible for the sin which arises from his state by nature, is not only contradicted by the statements of the New Testament, and, above all, by the proclamation of forgiveness in Jesus Christ,—for where there is no guilt, there can be no sin to be forgiven,—but is equally condemned by the undoubted testimony of conscience. Christianity does not profess merely to elevate one who is imperfect to a higher state of being, but to make reconciliation on account of the most serious variance; and it therefore presupposes an energy of *personal* existence prior to redemption, whereby that variance was caused.

_{Consequences of the merely organic view.}

The proposition that "nature corrupts the individual person" may be taken to mean "nature stirs up the person to corrupt himself by an act of perverted self-determination." But if the formula, as it occurs in the works of our older theologians, mean really that "the person necessarily becomes tainted with that sin wherewith human nature is poisoned," we need not stay to prove the truth of the statement; it is certain in this case that no guilt attaches to him on account of the sin thus belonging to him. A guilt which is said to belong to each individual, simply in virtue of his connection with the species and his participation of its common nature, and without any co-operation on his part, is a self-contradictory notion; unless, indeed, we hold that moral guilt does not imply the production of the sinful act or state by a decision of the will.

It cannot, moreover, be said that love to mankind requires us to deny a principle which the conception of guilt necessarily involves, and still to *impute* sin where the neccessary conditions of just imputation are wanting. True self-knowledge and reflection will lead us to regard the sin of the world as our own, and our sin as that of the world, but it also tells us that this conviction does not arise from a feeling of love,—for if it did, the most Holy One should, above all others, regard Himself as guilty as is the world,—but from the fact of our actual self-conscious and personal participation in the universal sinfulness.

The results of this investigation enable us to estimate the worth of the formula whereby Schleiermacher proposes to solve the problem. He regards original sin, on the one hand, as a sinfulness present in each one prior to any act, and having its origin beyond each man's individual life, and on the other hand, as involving a share of guilt in each in proportion as each one participates in it; so that it may be described as the "collective sin" and the "collective guilt" of the human race.*

Schleiermacher's solution of the problem.

To define this view more accurately, we must remember that the human race does not exist collectively at one and the same time, so that each could influence all, and all influence each, however indirectly, and so that "the sinfulness preceding any act is in each the work of all, and in all the work of each."† The human race collectively extends over a long range of centuries, so that each one exerts an influence only on his contemporaries and on those who come after him; and each is, in turn, influenced only by those before him and his own contemporaries. This consideration is by no means unimportant in estimating Schleiermacher's theory; for it follows therefrom that the share each one has in producing human sinfulness increases the further back we go, and decreases with the advance of human development; so that, if we compare an early generation and a recent one, the sinfulness preceding action in the former must be regarded as causative, and in the latter as only an effect, and the supposed equality of all is at an end.

* *Glaubenslehre*, §§ 70, 71.   † *Ibid.* §§ 71, 72 (vol. i. p. 421).

THE DOCTRINE OF HEREDITARY SIN.

As to the main point, however, in Schleiermacher's theory, the idea of "collective guilt," there is a deep truth herein, though he fails to see it. According to his explanation, it does not solve the problem, but merely describes that collective fact which lies before us to be solved. We find that the individual by no means stands alone in his sin, but is in various and complicated relations associated with his fellow-men. While in common with others he shares certain defects of natural constitution, he receives by birth, and transmits by generation, certain modifications and forms of the universal depravity,—pertaining to different ranges of society, and arising from the growth of particular sinful acts into a settled habit or tendency,—and he is influenced during his lifetime to certain sins by his contemporaries, and in turn he himself influences them. The question is, what and how much in this complication of influences is to be regarded as involving guilt on the part of the individual, and how, in particular, those depraved tendencies lying at the basis of all the rest are to be regarded as involving his guilt. When Schleiermacher answers these questions by his theory of "collective guilt," he only restates, he does not solve, the difficulty. He thus calls our attention to the mass of guilt resting upon our race collectively,—but more than this is needed; though, of course, no merely human judgment can decide the exact quota belonging to each, theology has to search out the general principles upon which the participation of each in this collective guilt rests.

Only a restatement of it.

It is not difficult to discover the real reason why Schleiermacher failed in giving an adequate answer to this question. When freedom in the true conception of it is not realized, the idea of guilt is emptied of its significance, and nothing but the name remains. What more than the mere name of guilt is left when the propriety of calling the hereditary sin cleaving to each "his guilt," is made to consist in the fact that "inborn sinfulness grows by exercise out of each one's own activity, that consequently it does not grow without his will, and therefore never would have arisen but by it"?* These propositions

Cause of Schleiermacher's failure.

---

* *Glaubenslehre,* § 71, i. (vol. i. 420). See, as to the last sentence, the observation of KRABBE in his *Lehre von der Sünde und vom Tode,* p. 154.

really form a vicious circle, for as " actual sin neverfailingly springs from original sin,"* the self-activity which enhances inborn sinfulness is itself the necessary fruit of this inborn sinfulness, and is possible only (according to Schleiermacher) upon the presupposition of it. There is, moreover, a fundamental defect in Schleiermacher's conception of personality, the very essence of which is freedom in the sense ignored by Schleiermacher; and hence the view he takes of the relation between the individual and the species in his philosophical and in his Christian Ethics† is very different from that which our investigations here and elsewhere in this treatise lead us to maintain as the 'correct one. It is very remarkable that in his Christian Ethics he thinks he can explain this relation between the individual and the race collectively, so as to establish the self-dependence of the individual without any reference whatever to the principle of personality.

§ 2. MODIFICATION OF THE DOCTRINE. The perception of the insurmountable difficulties which, upon certain pre-suppositions, seem necessarily to beset the theory of individual guilt as involved in original sin, has led to a modification of the doctrine, to which we have already referred, put forth first by the Arminians, elaborated by many later theologians, and now extensively espoused.

This modification represents the dogma of original sin, in its relation to personal responsibility, thus :—The fall of our first parents is allowed to have brought upon the race not only physical but moral disorder and corruption ; so that Adam's posterity are not born in the purity and perfection wherein *he* was created, but are from the beginning tainted with a strong inclination or bias towards evil. This inclination, however, cannot be imputed to mankind as guilt, because without any act on their part, it is born with them, and is in them as a natural evil—as a *malady* pertaining to human nature in consequence of the fall—but not as, properly speaking, SIN. Sin does not begin until the individual, when his moral sense is awakened, yields to the promptings of his corrupt nature,

---

* *Glaubenslehre*, § 71, i. (vol. i. 420).

† See the former in Schweizer's Ed., §§ 157, 158, and the latter in the general Introduction, 58-60.

and thus both pollutes himself by actual sin, and strengthens the bias to evil within him, so that it becomes a dominant propensity and the fruitful source of sinful acts.* Man is answerable only for this *consenting* to the promptings of inborn sinfulness, and for the sinful acts and habits which result from this consent; on account of these he is guilty before God.†

<small>Applied to the solution of the problem.</small> If, as it proposes, this distinction, while limiting the range of human accountability, is really to maintain it more firmly within the limits marked out, it must suppose a power in every one to refrain from this consent. The freedom of the will, though limited by innate sinfulness, cannot in this case be wholly destroyed, and though difficult, it cannot be impossible for man to fulfil the law of God in act and thought so far as he knows it.‡ Though oftentimes unable to withstand the force of his passions

* This is what SCHLEIERMACHER, though on different principles, calls the *peccatum originis originans* of the individual in contrast with the *peccatum originis originatum, i.e.*, his inborn sinfulness itself, *Glaubenslehre*, i. 419. But there seems to be no reason why the latter should not be called *peccatum originis originans*, for it is the chief source of sin, and the former *peccatum originis originatum* because it is produced by inborn sinfulness. Seeing too that *peccatum originis originans* is used, in the older Protestant as well as in the Scholastic theology, to denote the Fall, it is more consistent to retain the old expression used for the distinction, viz., *habitus vitiosus connatus* and *acquisitus* (*peccatum habituale connatum* and *acquisitum*).

† These statements are to be found in the main, even in ZWINGLI's *Fidei ratio*, which he sent to the Diet at Augsburg 1530; and they are further developed by LIMBORCH in his *Theologia Christiana* (lib. iii. cap. 2, § 24; cap. 2, § 1–4; cap. 4, § 1), not, however, without a strong disposition to make the distinction between the depravity of nature, which began with the Fall, and the *status integritatis* one of degree only; "*concedimus appetitus nostros* MINUS *esse puros quam appetitum primorum parentum ante lapsum* . . . . *Adami appetitum* MAGIS *inclinasse in malum quam ante perpetratum peccatum.*" A few of the supra-naturalistic theologians of the latter half of last century adopt this view, *e.g.*, DÖDERLEIN, *Instit. theol. Christ.*, p. ii. §§ 182–188. Among the more recent philosophical and theological treatises upon this subject, that of BOCKSHAMMER, *Ueber die Freiheit des menschl. Willens* (p. 119), and that of STEUDEL, *Ueber Sünde u. Gnade*, and, above all, that of KRABBE, *Lehre von der Sünde und vom Tode* (p. 159), adopt this method of solving the problem; though KRABBE has since retracted his views, and adopted the orthodox doctrine. KERN's dissertation also, *Ueber die Lehre von der Sünde* (*Tübing. Zeitschrift für Theol.*, 1833, p. 30), may be included in the same class, though it is difficult to get at the author's true meaning; this Article, in its second part especially, is most confused and unsatisfactory, an affected attempt after depth of thought and vigour of expression hinders the proper statement and arrangement of the simplest thoughts.

‡ See BOCKSHAMMER, p. 121. KRABBE, 116.

and desires, and to keep his heart wholly pure from the taint of sinful thoughts, yet, according to the view here advocated this is not his inborn state, but one which has arisen and gradually grown by want of fidelity to conscience and earlier consenting to sin.

The problem thus would seem to be solved by the recognition of a sinfulness deep-rooted in human nature to which universal experience witnesses, together with the maintenance (in its integrity) of the sense of guilt which conscience attests. The inborn depravity of every child of Adam pertains to its natural, not its spiritual being, and—so far as *will* can be attributed to natural as distinct from spiritual life—to the natural will; but there is no such thing as an inborn depravity of the personal will upon which responsibility depends—the individual will can become depraved only by a voluntary act.

In testing the tenableness of this view we shall not stay to discuss its incompatibility with St Paul's declarations—especially with Eph. ii. 3. Nor shall we do more than allude to what we have already said (Book III. chap. iii.), regarding the remembrance of an event so important and decisive as the first resolve of the will to sin—a step which, if so decisive, could never be forgotten —and regarding the attributing of so important a decision to the early years of childhood, a decision whereby man's condemnation in God's sight begins anew. The real question is, Does this theory solve the problem which it professes to solve?

The tenableness of this view tested.

This problem is manifestly twofold: *first*, it has to show the possibility of distinguishing between that inborn depravity for which the individual is not responsible and the sin for which he is responsible; and *secondly*, it has to reconcile the fact that no one who has passed the age of moral unconsciousness is free from guilt, with the principle that guilt depends upon an act of free self-decision.

Twofold difficulty of the Arminian theory.

As to the first, it would be easy to distinguish actual sin from inborn sinfulness, if this inborn sinfulness were only a disposition influencing the will to a perverted choice, but powerless of itself to produce movements and changes in the inner and outward life;—a tendency pent up and ineffective in the soul, unless the

(1) *Inborn sinfulness indistinguishable from actual sin.*

will yields to and adopts it in its decisions. But it is not this, nor could it really be so. Even before moral consciousness awakes, and will, properly speaking, begins to act, inborn sinfulness shows itself in various ways, and in acts which seem to all intents and purposes sinful, though conscience and will not being awake, we do not call them sins. Now when conscience and will awake, do these movements and acts of our depraved nature and of perverted impulses suddenly disappear? And if (as the Arminian theory must logically hold) the will is pure in every individual life at the outset, how can it be fettered by any natural corruption? How could it thus be hindered, if it were from the outset, so perfectly lord of the inner and outward life that nothing, save the involuntary organic functions, could stir or vary without its consent? And how easy in this case would it be to be holy, and to keep our entire life pure!

That the working of depravity within does not vanish when the will awakes, is evident when we remember that besides those sins which spring from the direct action of the will, there is a very large class of unpremeditated sins in which the will is not active;—sins especially of haste and weakness (see Vol. I. p. 186). These may, indeed, arise sometimes from previous deliberate sinfulness and neglect of the conflict to which conscience calls us against corrupt desires; but they must nevertheless be regarded as the effect of original depravity. Here we have a confused mass of acts alike sinful, yet differing as to their source; some involving guilt and others not, yet indistinguishable; so that at last our confused consciousness cannot say which are to be imputed to the Subject and which not. Tracing back particular sins to this double source, Krabbe says: "We are only to regard that element as involving guilt which springs from free will, and which co-operates towards the realization of any particular sin; the rest may, indeed, be sin, but it does not involve guilt."* If this be so, we find that we are to blame only partially for many offences of which conscience fully accuses us; but as to any law or principle whereby to distinguish what part of the sin springs from will and what from natural depravity, we have none; unless, indeed, we adopt a further inference from this view,

* As before, p. 167.

presently to be stated, — and, peradvanture, not even then.

Two ways of escape from this embarrassment are suggested. The one is to take sins of premeditation alone as involving guilt, and to regard the rest—not only the stirrings of sinful lust prior to the consent of the will, which Arminiam as well as Catholic theologians are wont to exclude from the category of sin, but sins of ignorance and hate—simply as manifestations of natural depravity, and not, therefore, involving guilt. This would made the range of sins for which we are responsible much narrower than conscience allows. Though the very idea of unpremeditated sin implies that it is not (when about to be committed) the object of the disapproval of conscience, yet after it is committed conscience blames us for it. But even were we to adopt this rule it would not be worth much, for the distinction between unpremeditated and premeditated sin is, as we have seen (Vol. II. p. 68), very uncertain and variable. It would lead, moreover, to that atomistic view which looks upon the erroneous decision of the will as something isolated and transitory, unproductive of any settled habit in the life; for if it does produce a habit, the actions springing therefrom (though unpremeditated) must be traced back to it and be regarded as blameworthy. Krabbe's work generally evinces a deeper perception of the nature of sin, but that expression of his, which we have above quoted, borders upon the atomistic view; for if in any act of sin we are only to regard the free element in it as guilt, man can be held responsible for those sins only which contain a free element; and thus misdeeds of blind passion, for example, would be excluded—and this would be just the atomistic view.

The other way of escaping from the dilemma is to acknowledge the impossibility of separating the two elements of natural depravity and free will, blended as these are in particular sins, and to admit the participation of the individual will, at least negatively, in the strengthening and growth of inborn depravity, so that each one must hold himself responsible for all his misdeeds, without exception. But if this be not a merely ascetic counsel *a tutiori*,—if it be stated as an objective fact,—the question arises, whether the will could have checked the development of inborn depravity, and by withdrawing all encouragement from it, could have prevented its continuance. To answer in the affirmative would be almost to deny inborn depravity in its real power, and to answer in the negative is virtually to undermine the proposed theory.

(2) The universality of guilt.
But the second task which the Arminian view undertakes is to reconcile the fact that every developed human life is stained with guilt, with the dependence of guilt upon the personal self-decision of the will. Its advocates must allow that this is a very difficult problem. For if the pith and marrow of their view lies in the freedom of the will, and its power to refuse to yield to the promptings of the corrupt nature, we might confidently expect that a greater or smaller portion of the human race would have remained pure from voluntary contamination. But this contamination is universal; and consequently resort has to be made to a necessary and hidden law prevailing in man's present state, and deciding his moral condition, while, at the same time, the interests of truth require that the consciousness of guilt, and the freedom of the will (supplying the possibility of resistance) be recognized too.

Reference, indeed, is made to a limitation of the powers of will by inborn depravity, which, without destroying it, makes decision on the side of the moral Law extremely difficult. But if we thus surrender the self-determining power of freedom, and admit this limitation, we must also grant that, in proportion as the difficulty of free decision increases, guilt, in case of sin, diminishes. We thus are obliged, upon the Arminian hypothesis, to give up (in part) the freedom of the will, in order to account for the fact of the universality of sinfulness,—thus weakening the consciousness of guilt;—and yet we have to maintain in some degree the fact of freedom, lest it be altogether lost,—thus leaving the universality of guilt unexplained, and making the proposed concession useless.

It is of no avail to refer to the truth already recognized by us (Vol. II. p. 163) that the origin of evil must be viewed simply as a possibility implied in the freedom of the creature, and not as a reality which is matter of experience. Here the matter to be explained is not the bare fact that man sins and incurs guilt, but that the millions, in whom consciousness is awake, are tainted with sin and guilt,—there being ONE only who was exempt therefrom. By regarding evil simply as the self-willed arbitrariness of freedom in the creature, we can apprehend the *possibility* of its occurrence, but not its realization. Here, however, we have to do with the unanimous witness of innumerable facts, — with a truth remarkably universal in its range, — indicating not arbitrariness, but necessity.

We should also consider the manner in which we become conscious of universal sinfulness. Experience teaches us that sin and guilt exist in human life, but it is too narrow to satisfy us that all men everywhere are sinful. If the idea of free self-decision forbids the universality of sinfulness, and if the view here discussed have no other proof of this universality save an objective and circumscribed experience, the certainty of the fact must be given up, and it must be regarded simply as a doubtful matter: and thus it becomes a doubtful matter likewise whether Christ be the Saviour of all mankind.

§ 3. A VIA MEDIA DEVISED.
To maintain this universality, and, at the same time, to avoid the unpalatable doctrine that by the fall of our first parents all mankind have become depraved and guilty, and liable to punishment, some modern theologians have devised the following *via media*. Not only do they grant that the energies of human nature have been weakened and depraved by the Fall, but they consider this depravity to be the source of the actual sin for which man is himself accountable; yet they do not introduce (as the above view does) any action of free will permitting or preventing the transition from natural depravity to actual sinfulness. Passing over the distinction between premeditated and unpremeditated sins, they take Melanchthon's canon: "*Semper cum peccato originali simul sunt peccata actualia,*" as he himself doubtless meant it, viz., as implying that actual sins spring, by an inner necessity, from original sin. This originally sinful constitution, however, being the consequence of another's sin, is not, they hold, to be regarded as involving guilt; man (they say) is accountable only for those effects of

original sin which are *produced by his own self-activity*, i.e., only for his own actual sins.*

Man's accountability is thus let go.
This theory clearly implies that sin and the need of redemption are universally necessary for mankind; it is, therefore, all the more doubtful whether sufficient care is taken to secure a firm basis for accountability and guilt. Special stress must be laid upon this, because original sin is not recognized as, properly speaking, sin at all; it is said not to involve guilt, because it cleaves to man as something handed down to him from others,

* We find this view already in the Apology of the Remonstrants, where the depravity of Adam's posterity through his fall is not regarded as in itself involving guilt, but as causing "*ut . . . . eadem justitia (originali) destituti, prorsus inepti et inidonei sint ad vitam aeternam consequendum aut in gratiam cum Deo redeundum aut ad viam inveniendum, qua ad vitam aut in gratiam cum Deo redeant, nisi Deus nova gratia sua eos praeveniat et vires novas iis restituat,*" &c.—See WINER's *Symbolik*, 59, 60. EPISCOPIUS (died 1643) the author of the Apology, in his *Institutiones Theologicae*, lib. iv. sect. v. c. 1 and 2, explains this in such a manner as to bring out the unharmonized clashing of the two principles, which LIMBORCH endeavours to obviate in the way indicated above. On the one hand, the *liberrima hominis (cujusque) voluntas* is maintained as the condition of guilt which is *evitabile et vincibile;* and, on the other hand, the effect of original sin is said to be "*ut omnes ac singuli homines nascantur destituti divinae voluntatis cognitione ac proinde impotentes et inidonei ad faciendum ea, quae Deo per se grata sunt, nisi, accedat nova divinae revelationis gratia.*" Among later theologians, J. FR. GRUNER, in his *Institutiones theologiae dogmaticae*, §§ 142, 143, 152—compare §§ 187, 188, —espouses and elaborates this view; MICHAELIS also inclines towards it, especially in his *Dogmatik*, §§ 82, 83, and in his oft-quoted monograph, "*Ueber Sünde und Genugthuung;* and SEILER, in his work *von der Erbsünde*, p. 101. All three bring in the well-known hypothesis regarding the poisonous tree in Paradise, but REINHARD adopts this hypothesis as showing the punishment following the original sin itself, though only in a privative sense;—see his *Vorlesungen über die Dogmatik*, § 83.

WHITBY, in his *Tractatus de imputatione divina peccati Adami*, though starting from different principles, arrives at the same result. He maintains that Adam's posterity inherit an inborn constitution, for which they are not themselves responsible, but which necessarily leads to actual sin; see cap. 1, thes. 1–4. In *thesis* 4 we read, *ea rerum oeconomia*—ensuing upon the fall— *nos passionum impetui et affectuum motibus ita subjicit, ut vix ac ne vix possibile sit nos innocentes legique divinae morigeros per integram vitam perseverare.* He so far adopts the hypothesis of the poisonous tree as to make physical evil the source of moral. Adam, on account of his disobedience, and his posterity by virtue of their natural connection with him, are necessarily liable to physical death; and the fear of death, together with the desire to enjoy life as much as possible, is the source of all sin. In the arguments which Whitby advances in the following chapters against the orthodox doctrine, we find quite enough to refute his own theory.

apart from his own will or choice. Yet this theory does not, like the preceding view, make the transition from original to actual sin conditional upon the free self-decision of a will, which has power to keep itself pure from sin; on the contrary, the transition is said to be necessary, and therefore unavoidable. But if actual sin be thus the necessary result of inborn depravity, the canon must hold good *causa causae est causa causati*, and the Fall must be regarded as the cause of actual as well as of original sin. And if original sin does not involve personal guilt, because it is the doing of our first parents, it follows that actual sin does not involve personal responsibility. The circumstance that the latter is conditional upon our own conduct, and the former not, is nothing to the purpose. If our own action does not spring from a freedom of personal choice, it is nothing more than the particular form or medium whereby the necessary transition from cause to effect is accomplished, and the person sinning, notwithstanding his self-activity, is already determined by the effective principle of the state from which his sinning springs. Actual sin, in this case, would involve no guilt.

The advocates of this view repudiate this conclusion, on the ground that the unerring testimony of conscience obliges us to hold ourselves responsible for our sins. But on this principle they must acknowledge that inborn sinfulness, as the source of actual sin, must be imputed to us as guilt. The condemning judgment of conscience not only applies to the outward manifestations of a depraved nature, but to this nature itself for which also we are responsible. The difficulty arising from the dependence of our sin upon the depraved will of others, applies equally to the outward acts, and to the inner nature; and if, notwithstanding this difficulty, man's responsibility as regards his sinful *acts* be maintained, his responsibility in relation to his sinful *nature* may, with equal propriety, be affirmed.

§ 4. PARTICIPATION OF ALL MEN IN ADAM'S SIN.

In our criticism of these theories concerning the relation between original and actual sin, we are brought back again to a point which we have already found untenable. We must allow that the depravity which all Adam's descendants inherit by natural generation, nevertheless involves personal guilt; and yet this depravity, so far as it is natural, wants the very conditions upon which guilt depends. The only satisfactory explanation of this difficulty is the Christian doctrine of original sin; here alone—if its inner possibility can be maintained—can the apparently contradictory principles be harmonized ;—viz., the universal and deep-seated depravity of human nature as the source of actual sin, and individual responsibility and guilt. The great stumbling-block in this doctrine for our moral consciousness, lies in the fact that Adam's posterity should be held guilty, and deserving of punishment on account of another's sin; the Pelagian principle ever recurs, *Deus qui propria peccata remittit aliena non imputat.* The theories we have considered do not obviate this difficulty. Really to remove it, we must prove that underneath the *alienum* of the phenomenon there lies a *proprium;* we must demonstrate that the will, whose self-perversion in the Fall caused the depravity which precedes all actual sin in Adam's posterity, is at the same time *our own* will, and though dependent in its decisions upon that natural depravity from the very outset of our individual life, is also dependent on its own self-determination. If this can be shown, we shall see at once the necessity of regarding natural depravity with its consequences, as the sin and guilt of those to whom it cleaves; for moral states and actions, springing from an act involving accountability and guilt, themselves involve accountability.

This is the real centre and kernel of the orthodox doctrine concerning original sin ; here, if any where, the difficulties it suggests are solved. At first sight it appears incredible that all Adam's posterity took part in his fall. If it can be shown that this is a paradox pertaining in thought to the relations of things universally, all further perplexities in connection with the doctrine disappear.

It is a striking proof of the acuteness and systematic thoroughness of our older theologians that they recognize this central truth, in all its significance, as the only principle which explains the actual depravity diffused over the whole race of mankind from the fall of our first parents. The early Protestant doctrine represents the connection between our guilt and

<small>Recognized in the old Protestant theology.</small>

Adam's fall as twofold, partly indirect, and partly immediate. The natural corruption which ensues as the consequence of the fall, though at the time it existed only in our first parents, they implanted, by generation, in their children, and these again in their posterity; so that all mankind inherit, from the beginning of their existence, a nature which objectively resists God's law, and makes them guilty in God's sight (MEDIATA *peccati Adamitici imputatio*). But all the posterity of Adam also involve themselves in the guilt of his fall immediately; they are regarded by God as having actually committed the act through which Adam fell (IMMEDIATA *peccati Adamitici imputatio*,—called by the theologians of the Reformed Church *imputatio antecedens*, in distinction from *imputatio mediata* or *consequens*); and they are thus regarded, because they really had part in the act.* This "immediate imputation" has its real basis in the propagation of natural depravity; but Quenstedt recognizes the principle that participation in the penalty of the fall, including the loss of the divine image, and the dominion of depraved lust, depends upon participation in its guilt.†

We thus understand how it was that the older theology (the *Apologia Confessionis Augustanae*, art. 1) could represent hereditary sinfulness which involves guilt, and is the source of further sin, as at the same time a punishment, according to Augustine's view. Among the Arminians,‡ the opposers of the doctrine of "immediate imputation" in the Reformed Church, Placeus § (ob.

Inborn sinfulness regarded as punishment.

---

* *Non posset in nos propagari reatus, nisi praecessisset imputatio actus, quippe qui illius fundamentum est*, QUENSTEDT, § 2, qu. 7 (p. 112); and again, in the same *quaestio*: *Voluntas Adami censebatur nostra; nam primus homo omnium posterorum voluntates in sua quasi voluntate locatas habuit.* QUENSTEDT seems to make out a threefold connection when following BALTHASAR MEISNER (*ob.* 1626) he says (sect. i. th. 30, sect. ii. qu. 7), *tenemur* 1, *participatione culpae actualis; in Adamo namque omnes peccavimus;* 2, *imputatione reatus legalis; stabat enim et cadebat primus homo ut caput, in quo et conservarentur et perderentur concessa dona et privilegia;* 3, *propagatione pravitatis naturalis, quia, in omnes per naturalem conceptionem diffunditur.* This threefold connection arises from Quenstedt's unnecessary distinction between participation in the act, causing guilt and participation in that liability to punishment which the act involves; it, therefore, resolves itself into the twofold *imputatio, mediata* and *immediata*.

† In the 7th *quaestio*, and other places.

‡ See EPISCOPIUS, *Instit. theol.* as before.

§ *Thes.* xxiv. seq. *De statu hominis lapsi ante gratiam*, and *Syntagma thesium theol. in Acad. Salmurensi disputatarum*, part i. p. 209. Many of the

1655) zealously contended against this view; but the orthodox theologians so strongly advocated it, that they ceased to attach any importance to the propagation of original sin by generation, and preferred the theory of Creationism regarding individual souls, to Traducianism, or at least, held it as an unimportant distinction so far as original sin was concerned. From this extreme, sanctioned as it is by the *decretum absolutum*, our Lutheran theology has kept aloof; but it was logically consistent to call hereditary sinfulness—as a condition springing from preceding guilt in the fall—punishment, seeing that the moral corruption into which Adam plunged himself by his fall must itself be so regarded.

The doctrine of the Lutheran theology thus forms a mean between the two opposite extremes. On the one hand is the theory of Placeus, which excludes "immediate imputation," on the ground that the imputation of original sin is sufficiently secured in the natural depravity springing from Adam's fall, and which holds only "mediate imputation."* This theory leaves the most vulnerable part of the doctrine, viz., the imputation of what is innate and unconditioned by the will—the possibility of which is guaranteed by the doctrine of immediate imputation—wholly unprotected, and consequently it has to abandon this and to resort to one of the two theories above discussed.

Opinion of Placeus.

On the other hand is the theory which Thomas Aquinas† advocated, which has since been espoused in Roman Catholic theology,‡ and which found an advocate among the ablest Lutheran theologians in George Calixtus. § This view denies any positive corrup-

Opposite extreme of Catholic theology.

stricter Lutherans too, QUENSTEDT for instance, regard human depravity not indeed as positive punishment, but as the necessary consequence of the Fall.

* *Thes.* vii.-xviii., *De statu homines*, &c., and in the *Disputatio de prima peccati imputatione*, particularly in part i. chaps. iv. x. In the first half of last century this view was current even in our Lutheran theology; see PFAFF's *Instit. theol. dogm., et. mor.*, pp. 236, 237 ; and MOSHEIM's remarks upon the tone of Lutheran theology then prevailing ; *Elementa theol. dogmaticae*, p. 497.

† *Summa*, ii. i. qu. 81. art. 1-3 ; qu. 85, art. 2-4. See also the *Summa contra gentiles*, which gives the view of AQUINAS still more fully ; lib. iv. c. 50-52.

‡ And yet WICLIFFE advocates the doctrine afterwards urged by Protestant against Catholic theologians, declaring that every one has *proprium peccatum originale ;—Trialogus*, lib. iii. c. xxiv.

§ See *Epitome theologiae* by Titius, pp. 66, 67, 71. The thoughts are essentially the same as those of AQUINAS, though the language is stronger, *e.g.*, he calls that *malitia* which AQUINAS and BELLARMINE call *languor*.

tion as the effect of the fall, and maintains only a negative basis of imputation, viz., the want of original righteousness. Sensuous lust (*concupiscentia*) which this theory regards as the material of original sin, having a certain power over against reason and will, is not considered in itself sinful, but as on the one hand the punishment or consequence, and on the other, the occasion or cause of sin. The council of Trent, indeed (Sessio v. 5), says of the regenerate or baptized alone, that in them *concupiscentia* is not strictly speaking sin. It might appear from this, that it was regarded as sin in the unregenerate. But this would involve the Council in a contradiction, for the same Decree teaches that whatever is of the nature of sin, is not only forgiven in Baptism, but eradicated; *concupiscentia* therefore, if it were sin in the natural man, would have been utterly destroyed in Baptism, whereas it is repeatedly said still to exist.* Bellarmine's further development of the doctrine goes to prove that sensuous lust, in its alienation from the higher law of the spirit, is not in itself sinful, but becomes so by a concurrence of the will. Thus the want of original righteousness is the only permanent effect of the fall. When, however, we remember that this original righteousness itself, according to Aquinas and the Romish Catechism, is not an essential element in pure human nature, but is a *donum superadditum*, distinct from its creation, though perhaps given at the same time, the conclusions which Bellarmine arrives at concerning the relation between original righteousness and human nature must be acceded to, viz., *quare non magis differt status hominis post lapsum*

Bellarmine's theory.

---

* The history of the discussions which preceded this decision of the Council seems to indicate that a large majority of its members in answering ANTON-MARINARI'S acute reasonings, endeavoured to prove from AUGUSTINE that besides the *concupiscentia*, which consisted simply in the conflict between the sensuous nature and the reason, and which was not therefore sin, but remained after Baptism; there was another kind of *concupiscentia*, which consisted in the opposition of the will to the law of God, and which, being sin, was eradicated in Baptism. See PAUL SARPI'S *Geschichte des Koncils* (ed. 1621, p. 195). But is it conceivable that the Synod would have attributed this opposition of the will against God's law to new-born children? Had it not just before decided (Sarpi, p. 192) that original sin could not be *ignorantia et contemptus Dei aut certe esse sine timore, sine fiducia in Deum, sine amore divino*, because such *actiones* could not be in newly-born children? just as the *Confutatio Pontificia* argues against the second Article of the *Confessio Augustana*.

Adae a statu ejusdem in puris naturalibus quam differat spoliatus a nudo, neque deterior est humana natura si culpam originalem (the imputed *peccatum actuale Adae*) *detrahas, neque magis ignorantia et infirmitate laborat quam esset et laboraret in puris naturalibus condita.** Thus even the privative element of original sin vanishes, and Adam's descendants have really no defect which does not equally belong to the essence of human nature, the *pura naturalia*. The fact that Bellarmine, like Aquinas, still speaks of a depravity (*corruptio, depravatio*) as distinct from that natural defect, and even of "the wounds of nature" as the consequences of the Fall, in no way invalidates this. For these wounds would have broken out in the essence of human nature itself, had God not sanctified it by the gift of original righteousness, whereby, as by a golden yoke, the resistance of the lower powers, whose source is the fleshy nature, against the higher, was subdued.†
This inevitably leads to the conclusion, controverted indeed by Bellarmine, but advocated by the Catholic theologians Catharinus and Pighius, and which prevailed in the school of Occam, that original sin, as it is inherited by Adam's posterity, is nothing more than the imputation of his disobedience.‡ What, that can properly be called sin, could there have been in fallen human nature, if it had only lost an original righteousness which did not belong to it, and if the restiveness of the desires against the reason be compatible with its purity? And thus the principle that original sin involves personal guilt, has

* *De gratia primi hominis*, c. 5. In book v. c. 15, *De amissione gratiae et statu pecc.* BELLARMINE expressly combats the *sententia eorum Catholicorum qui peccatum originis in quadam positiva qualitate constituunt.*

† See BELLARMINE, as before. That AQUINAS saw this inference is clear from *Summa* ii. i., qu. 85, art. 3. I do not see therefore any real difference between his doctrine and that of DUNS SCOTUS, as the *Dogmengeschichtlichen Lehrbücher von* (*Münscher*) *Cölln*, vol. ii. 134, and HAGENBACH, p. 414, suppose.

‡ *De amiss. gr.*, l. v. c. 16. Compare BAUR's remarks on the relation of this theory to Bellarmine's view, *Der Gegensatz des Katholicismus u. Protestantismus* 2nd. ed., p. 91. BELLARMINE was wrong in treating the theory of CATHARINUS as a private interpretation, and in asserting against him the Decrees of Trent, for as PAUL SARPI shows (p. 192), CATHARINUS not only argued his views in the Council, but succeeded in considerably modifying its decisions regarding original sin. He based the immediate imputation of Adam's sin upon the assumption that God had made a covenant with Adam as the representative of the race. See also CHEMNITZ's *Examen. Conc. Trid.* p. i. 204, BAUMGARTEN's *Polemik*, 3, 501.

nothing to rest upon save the direct imputation of Adam's fall, —an imputation which itself is a baseless supposition. Innocence is to consider itself guilty, and pure nature, as it came from the hand of the Creator, must consider itself as condemned in His sight. Can man believe in that original guilt as really his own, if he finds no inner derangement which he feels to be sinful? No, certainly; on the contrary, he must ever regard that guilt as external and foreign to him, as merely imputed; and the only connection between Adam's disobedience and hereditary guilt, he will feel to be the arbitrary decree of His will whose ways are past finding out.*

The prevailing teaching of our Lutheran theology since the middle of the seventeenth century is far preferable to this, and is worthy of a prominent place in the development of this doctrine. It finds a real basis for the mediate imputation of the Fall in that positive depravity which it maintains to be a disturbance of pure human nature. And it can explain how guilt also can be hereditary on the principle of immediate imputation.

The Lutheran doctrine a mean between the two.

Quenstedt, whom we may regard as one of the chief advocates of the doctrine of "immediate imputation" among our Lutheran Divines,† rightly perceived that in order to explain the manner in which the human race are in that twofold sense guilty through the fall, we must keep in view the twofold relation of ideal and actual union which subsisted between Adam and his

* It is remarkable that the extreme of Catholic Doctrine on this point coincides with that extreme Reformed view which regards all the consequences of the fall in Adam's posterity as a punishment inflicted by the righteous judgment of God. The fact that immediate imputation is kept in the background by the earliest Lutheran Divines CHEMNITZ, HUTTER, and even GERHARD (see also the *Apologia Confessionis*, cap. i. art. 2), may be accounted for as a reaction against this extreme view. Hence, too, we see how it was that AEGID. HUNNIUS—to whom PLACEUS appeals, *De imput. pecc. Ad.*, p. 20—avowed himself against the doctrine of immediate imputation in his *Quaestiones et responsiones de peccato* at the beginning—*Opera lat.* tom. i. 445. Opposition afterwards came from the opposite quarter, and as the Socinian and Arminian denial of all imputation spread, our Lutheran theology learned that if it surrendered the doctrine of "immediate imputation," that of "mediate imputation" could no longer be maintained.

† According to RIVET's *Sammlung der testimonia de imputatione primi peccati* (*Opera*, i. 815), I find that the Wittenberg theologian BALTHASAR MEISNER was really the first who developed this doctrine, and that QUENSTEDT borrows from him sometimes even word for word. I have not, however, seen his *Disputationes de anthrovologia sacra*.

posterity. Adam is, in a twofold sense, the head of the race, he in its natural and its moral representative. Being the natural head of the race, hereditary evil spreads by propagation through all his descendants, and being its moral representative, his sin (as *reatus*), is also theirs. But these two relations Quenstedt will not separate ; for it is only because Adam is the natural head of the race,—or, as he expresses it, *radix et stirps, principium naturale et seminale totius generis humani,*— that he is also its moral representative,—*principium representativum, in quo et conservarentur et perderentur concessa dona et privilegia.**

Judged from this dogmatic theory, the doctrine of Aquinas, in his *Summa contra Gentiles*, must be very imperfect, which bases the imputation of original sin upon the one fact that all men are counted as one in virtue of their sharing the common physical nature which Adam corrupted in his fall.† It is evident that this virtually would lead us back to that naturalistic theory which explains original sin on the principle of the organic unity of the race,—a theory which, as we have already found, destroys the principle of imputation and guilt. It is obliged to allow that Adam's posterity are not *actu* and *personaliter* participators in his fall,‡ and it cannot therefore explain why they should *actu* and *personaliter* be guilty before God in consequence of his fall. To say (as many scholastic and some early Protestant theologians do) that Adam's posterity are individually sinful, not only *potentiâ* but *actu*, is only arguing in a circle. If, again, we base the imputation of the fall upon the fact that when it occurred the whole race or species then existing were our first parents, and that consequently all individuals thereof potentially (or as Aquinas expresses it, *virtualiter*) were present in them, we must hold the race guilty of all the sins our first parents committed, down at least to the time when their children—the next progenitors—were born ; nay, guilty of all

^{Adam the natural head of the race.}

* See *De peccato* sect. i., thesis 19, 20, 30 ; sect. ii., qu. 7.
† *Ibid.*, Lib. iv. cap. 52, i. Compare *Summa theol.*, ii. 1, qu. 81, art. 1.
‡ According to ANSELM's words in his treatise *De conceptu virginali et originali peccato :—In illo causaliter sive materialiter velut in semine fuerunt, in se ipsis personaliter sunt ; . . . in illo non alii ab illo, in se alii quam ille. In illo fuerunt ille, in se sunt ipsi. Fuerunt igitur in illo, sed non ipsi, quoniam nondum erant ipsi.*

the sins of these latter, accumulating generation after generation. Aquinas cleverly meets this objection by saying that it is the first sin alone which corrupts the nature, susequent sins corrupt only the person;* but thus he admits that the first sin, as a turning-point in human history, must have exerted a more corrupting influence than any that followed. But there was no difference in kind between the first sin and subsequent ones; so that its greater corrupting influence must arise exclusively from the supposition that the corruption of nature produced by it was absolute, and this Aquinas by no means allows.† The *in quo* (*Adamo*) *omnes peccaverunt* of Rom. v. 12—even granting this rendering of the Greek ἐφ' ᾧ πάντες ἡμαρτον—is really no argument for the theory of Aquinas; for it would still be undecided whether it referred to Adam as the natural or as the moral representative of the race. Nor is this view confirmed by the statement of Heb. vii. 10, concerning the act attributed to the tribe of Levi as in the loins of Abraham; for Bleek‡ has fully proved that the writer of that epistle simply meant this reference as an *argumentum ad hominem*.

No less imperfect is the other proposed explanation if taken alone, viz., that of immediate imputation, which regards Adam simply as the *moral* representative of mankind, and ignores his *natural* headship. Upon this principle it becomes a matter of mere chance that the blessedness or misery of the race should have been made contingent upon an act of these two individuals in particular. The physical relationship being ignored, we obviously look for some definite compact making them the moral representatives of the rest, and least of all could we regard our first parents as thus appointed, for there was no one besides themselves to appoint them.

Immediate imputation.

And yet we must allow that these difficulties, to some extent, bear upon that more preferable view which regards Adam as both the natural and the moral head or representative of his posterity. Fairly to main-

Adam the moral and natural head.

* *Summa*, ii. 1, qu. 81, art. 2.

† AUGUSTINE does not allow this either, and hence he himself admits (*Enchiridion*, c. 13, 47) that he can offer no satisfactory solution of the difficulty.

‡ *Kommentar zum Br. a.d. Hebräer*, vol. iii. 284. Compare DELITZSCH, *Kommentar z. Br. an die Hebr.*, p. 284.

CHAP. III.]   THE DOCTRINE OF HEREDITARY SIN.   337

tain this we must show that the inner union subsisting between the race and their progenitor involves their willing participation in his primary decision and choice. Quenstedt expresses this union in the strongest terms. Adopting the language of Ambrose and Augustine, he affirms that the whole race existed in the first man, that "he together with all his posterity, were collectively the subjects of the first sin;"* and that "his will included the wills of all his decendants;"† nay, he uses the strange expression that "in our first parents original righteousness was imparted as a gift for their posterity, a gift which would have empowered mankind to obey, not only the command concerning the tree of knowledge, but the whole decalogue."‡ But what is the real basis of this supposed union which thus makes our wills one with Adam's in his sin? Neither theory—neither that of immediate nor that of mediate imputation—taking each separately, explains this; and if we take them both together we are still at a loss, for the union of two inadequate explanations cannot make an adequate one, and the theory of moral headship really depends upon the fact of natural headship. Quenstedt, indeed, lays most stress upon the *caput morale* as the basis of imputation, but how can this supply the oneness of will which Adam's natural headship fails to render? It could do so only on the supposition that Adam was deputed by mankind as their representative in this all-important transaction, and while his natural headship would still be the *conditio sine qua non*, his appointment to this moral headship would be the real basis of imputation. But no one could maintain such a supposition as this; and hence a nominal covenant headship on Adam's part cannot afford that basis which his natural headship fails to render for the immediate imputation of the fall.

In order to maintain Adam's federal headship, as involving the guilt of his posterity, some theologians, both ancient and modern, refer to the divine omni-*scientia media* science, and affirm that God knows that every *Dei.* one else would, if in Adam's place, have acted as he did, and that in virtue of this knowledge, God can justly

Argument from the *scientia media Dei.*

* As before, § 1, thes. 19 (p. 53).   † *Ibid.*, § 2, qu. 7 (p. 112).
‡ *Ibid.*, § 2, qu. 7 (p. 113).
VOL. II.   Y

impute Adam's disobedience to mankind.* Schleiermacher, for instance, grants the universal imputation of the first sin upon this ground—viz., the consciousness that whosesoever lot it had been to be the first, he would have committed the sin.† This arises from his belief in a primitive sinfulness, not consequent upon a fall, but essentially belonging to human nature —a primitive sinfulness out of which actual sin of necessity springs.‡ But if we hold that human nature was originally pure, implying the possibility of evil but not the disposition thereto,—so that the first man possessed perfect freedom to do right, and power to overcome the temptation to evil,—in this case the notion that not one among the millions of mankind who happened to be in Adam's place would have acted otherwise than he, is quite arbitrary and groundless. This could be maintained only by making man's sinful state, which ensued upon the fall, the presupposition or cause of the fall. If it were allowable to refer to some intermediate knowledge on God's part as the basis of imputing the guilt and condemnation of original sin to all men, we might with equal propriety argue that God could justly have introduced mankind at once into a state of misery or bliss, upon the ground of his foreknowledge that certain of them would voluntarily make themselves liable to the one or the other destiny.§

Shall we pause here to consider the glimmering and indis-

* See, for instance, BAUMGARTEN's *Evangelische Glaubenslehre*, vol. ii. 352. SEILER goes so far as to assert that any other man would have plunged the race into greater sin and misery than did Adam; for otherwise God would have chosen that other man, and not Adam, to be the progenitor of the race! (p. 106). Among modern theologians, KERN argues that no one would venture to assert that any other man in Adam's place would have acted differently;— but he thus contradicts what he elsewhere affirms concerning the conditions of guilt.

† *Glaubenslehre*, § 72, 6 (vol. i. 446).   (‡ *Ibid.* p. 445.

§ It is unnecessary to consider the other proposed theories in explanation of the doctrine of original sin as involving guilt, such, for instance, as the reference to the fact that children have often to suffer for the sins of their parents. ZWINGLI and the Arminians have adopted these analogies, but they rightly see that they are examples, not of hereditary guilt, but of hereditary misfortune only. Again, it has been argued that whatever seeming injustice there may be in the imputation of the guilt of Adam's sin to his posterity, this is fully counterbalanced by God's offer of full redemption from that guilt to all men in Christ. See MOSHEIM's *Elem. theol. dogmat.*, p. 498 ; SEILER, as before, p. 101. According to this, God's redemption of the human race would be a redeeming of Himself from an act of injustice to man.

tinct suggestions of modern philosophy, which profess to reveal to us the deep mystery of the dogma of the guilt of all mankind, as involved in Adam's sin? Scientifically speaking, they have no claim to attention until they become more determinate and fixed, so that their true import may be known, and the real difference between them and theories already proposed be seen. A passing glance, however, may give us some idea what help the doctrine may expect from this quarter.

Suggestions of modern philosophy.

In our own day, reference is made to the Realistic view of our ideas of species, as the true key to this doctrine of imputation. "We have only to remember" (it is said) "that it is not any one man, but man in general, the species 'man,' who is supposed to act in the fall, and the determinations which the species there gives itself are, as a matter of course, said to be embodied in all individuals of the species." This seems tantamount to what the older theologians say—viz., that human nature is, at the outset, not only represented, but included and summed up in two individuals; and if they wilfully corrupt their own nature, and burden it with guilt, corruption and guilt become the characteristics of the race in general.* Or it may be taken to mean (as Hegel expresses it) that sin forms part of our very conception of man, that man in sinning realized the conception of himself, and that he must look upon sin, and therefore guilt, as essentially his own. Whichever of these two interpretations we adopt, the conclusions we have already arrived at render it unnecessary to controvert them,

Realistic conception of species.

But there is a third interpretation of the statement now quoted. Göschel maintains that the true significance of Realism—unperceived, perhaps, by the Schoolmen themselves—consists in actual self-dependent personality, as included in the idea of the species "man," apart from and before its realization in

Notion of humanitas implicita in Adam.

* This is really all that the acute Realist, ODO of Cambray, argues from this theory of species, in the Second Book of his treatise *De peccato originali*, when he makes use of it to explain the doctrine of imputation. He rejects the notion that the *universale*, the *species humana*, sinned, and thus changed itself, as absurd; but he says Adam and Eve sinned, and as at the time there was no other human nature or substance but theirs, human nature thenceforward by their sin became corrupt.—*Bibliothecamaxima Patrum* tom. xxi. 232.

individual persons.* Göschel applies this to Christology only; Christ is, according to him, the truly original type of man, the full ideal of humanity, and He is therefore Subject, or more correctly Person; but Adam, on the contrary, "is only the (analytic and synthetic) beginning of an incipient humanity —*humanitas implicita.*"† If we are to attach any distinct meaning to this explanation, and to make it solve the difficulty which the orthodox doctrine involves,—the contradiction, I mean, between what is transmitted to us from without, and what is self-imputed,—we must regard humanity realizing itself in the race collectively, yet personally existing, as the Subject of the fall; and thus we can hardly avoid viewing the narrative in Genesis as a myth, owing its origin to a dark presentiment of that transcendent and extra-temporal event. But this application of the doctrine of Realism, while furnishing a solution of one difficulty, immediately falls into others. If sin, too, be thus a determination of the species collectively by its own deliberate act, tainting the race in all its individual and temporal developments, a sinless Saviour, Jesus Christ, as an historical person is inconceivable,‡ and man's liberation from sin is an impossibility too. Neither, indeed, can man's ever becoming free from sin be conceived of upon this principle, unless we adopted the self-contradictory notion that the first man had determined himself at once as a sinner and as sinless, as the first and as the second Adam. This principle, therefore, being inadequate for the solution of our problem, we need not prove its untenableness on metaphysical grounds,— how the idea of the Species cannot exist eternally as a personal Subject, and yet realize itself in time in individuals.

* *Beiträge zur spekulativen Philosophie,* &c. pp. 58, 100–172.
† *Ibid.* p. 167.
‡ This objection lies equally against the way in which the Scholastic and Lutheran theologians apply the doctrine of Realism to this question, for Christ was *virtualiter* and *seminaliter* in Adam, the progenitor of the Virgin Mary. In order to avoid this difficulty, the Lutherans say "those descendants of Adam, who have sprung from him by *ordinary* generation, sinned in him," but this is evidently a limitation devised in order to preserve the sinlessness of Christ, it has no foundation in the principle of their theory. The realization of this difficulty led HUGO of ST VICTOR, to give up the principle *in Adamo omnes fuerunt originaliter,* as the basis of imputation; see *Tractatus Theologicus,* cap. 31, in the works of HILDEBERT of Mans. Not having HUGO's works, I cite this treatise, for its identity with the *Summa Sententiarum* has been established by LIEBNER.

THE DOCTRINE OF HEREDITARY SIN.

Conclusion arrived at.

Seeing, then, that the theory of immediate imputation does not explain how original sin which is external to the race, can be at the same time its own as involving guilt, we must acknowledge that the dogma as our older theologians asserted it must be given up. Remembering, however, the inward bearing of this doctrine upon religious consciousness, we might expect that its weakness and untenableness would practically appear in the life of the Protestant Church. The theory of immediate imputation cannot satisfy the conviction of conscience that whatever is beyond the range of our power of will and choice, is also beyond the sphere of our guilt. But if the deep-rooted depravity which we bring with us into the world be not our sin, it at once becomes an excuse for our actual sins.* We may easily see the practical danger of this inference in the case of those theologians who, like Michaelis, regard human depravity in this way. And the greater the natural depravity supposed, and the closer the fancied connection between it and actual sins, the more dangerous will this inference practically become.

Protestant hymns.

But the practical religious consciousness of our older Protestantism, embodied as it is in our hymns and devotional books, was able inwardly to apprehend what seemed a contradiction, and at once to recognize inborn depravity as the fruitful source of actual sin, and the personal responsibilty and guilt of each sinner. To express the first of these two truths, it does not shrink from the strong words of the third verse of Lazarus

* The idea has of late been maintained that natural depravity must at the same time be regarded as involving guilt and self-reproach, it being a determination of our own being, and as a relative ground of excuse for actual sin, it being something cleaving to us from without. But this is a manifest contradiction; the ground of our guilt cannot be the ground of our exculpation; depravity is something really affecting us only in so far as it is in us, and it is in us only in so far as we have received it from ¦determining forces external to us. Regarding natural depravity as a determinateness of character in the individual without his will, and therefore mitigating the guilt of actual sin, we must of necessity point out some independent basis of guilt in an act of the individual which is not the consequence of his depravity, if we would not wholly surrender the idea of guilt as involved in that of sin.

Spengler's hymn, "Through Adam's fall, the heart of man, so utterly corrupt," viz.—

> "As we are by another's guilt
> In Adam all defiled,
> So are we by another's grace
> In Christ all reconciled."

But very occasionally, indeed, hereditary sinfulness is referred to as a mitigation of the guilt of actual sin, and a plea for the forgiving grace of God. For instance, in the hymn which begins "Turn back thy wrath," probably by Bartholomew Ringwaldt, the fifth verse runs thus :—

> "With inborn sinfulness oppressed,
> With weakness, want, and death,
> Why should we ever ruined lie
> 'Neath wrath, without thy grace?"*

Religious consciousness, however, universally looks upon what theology teaches to be transmitted as directly and at the same time a *personal* guilt; it excludes the foreign element in original sin by inwardly appropriating it as its own. Thus in its own way it practically solves the contradiction which all aspects of the doctrine involve. And every true development of doctrine will recognize a deep truth in this very fact; indeed, all we have to do in order to be led out of the

---

* Inborn sinfulness is never in Scripture used as an excuse for sin. As to Psalm li. 5 see above, p. 274. In Psalm lxxviii. 39, ciii. 14, the transitoriness and frailty of human life are named as reasons of God's forgiving mercy—in this sense I mean, that were God's grace delayed towards repentant sinners, they would die before it reached them. Gen. viii. 21 seems chiefly to favour the notion of man's depravity excusing sin, but if we compare it with Gen. vi. 5, we find that we can hardly take it thus. Perhaps the כִּי is only a *nota relationis* as in Gen. iii. 19 a, and in this case the words "for the imagination of his heart," &c., are a reason why God might again "curse the ground for man's sake." For the opposite view of the passage, see Cöllns bibl. Theol. i. 238. In the N. T. St Paul seems somewhat to sanction the idea of inherent sinfulness being a palliation of actual guilt in Rom. vii. 17, 20, οὐκέτι ἐγώ ἀλλ' ἡ οἰκοῦσα ἐν ἐμοὶ ἁμαρτία. We should indeed be obliged to view these words thus if they referred to mankind generally. But as we have already seen (Vol. I. p. 198) they describe the condition of a man awakened to a sense of sin and hungering after righteousness; conscious of a variance between his inner will and outward life, until, by Christ's redeeming grace, he is freed from his bondage (vers. 15, 18, 23). The meaning is as follows:—When this variance begins to be felt, our *Ego* is no longer on the side of sin, but on the side of God and His law (vers. 16, 21); it therefore feels the prevailing power of sin as a force external and opposed to it.

labyrinth is to keep fast hold of these inner convictions. But no confirmation of the doctrine as it has hitherto been represented is thus obtained.

§ 5. TESTIMONY OF HOLY SCRIPTURE.
We may, however, recognize the unsatisfactoriness of the theory of immediate imputation, and the still more obvious insufficiency of those other theories which we have considered, and yet maintain the doctrine of original sin as fully assured to us by the testimony of Holy Scripture. Though theology be unable philosophically to explain and harmonize the seemingly contradictory truths, Scripture equally affirms both, viz., a depravity springing from Adam's fall and interwoven with our very nature, which makes all men sinners (Rom. v. 12–19), and the personal guilt of all the descendants of Adam.

Rom. v. 12–19.
The text now named is not only the chief, but really the only New Testament witness for the causal connection between Adam's sin and that of his posterity. This connection is expressly and accurately stated in the words of ver. 12, ἐφ' ᾧ πάντες ἥμαρτον. Older and more modern defenders of the doctrine, in its early Protestant form, alike maintain that though we may not render ἐφ' ᾧ by *in quo* in reference to Adam, but must (with Luther) take it as a conjunction "because," still considering the connection in which it stands, ἐν Ἀδὰμ must be understood with the verb ἥμαρτον.* For death—the old theologians argue—had dominion over new-born and still-born children, who cannot themselves have committed any sin; and the sinning, therefore, which is here said to subject mankind to death, must be participation in Adam's sin. Were we—it is further argued—to take ἥμαρτον as denoting the actual sinning of individuals, death would be represented as the consequence, not of man's connection with Adam—which the οὕτως indicates—but of the actions of each one severally. If, moreover, ἥμαρτον is to be understood of actual sins, the argument of verses 13, 14, to prove that all men share in Adam's sin, seems to be quite out of place.

* See QUENSTEDT, § 1, th. 30 (p. 58). BUDDEUS *Institut. theol. dogm.* iii. ii. 13 (tom. i. 568) ; and more recently a Dissertation on Original Sin the *Evang. Kirchenzeitung*, 1831, No. 49, p. 338.

But is this really the purport of verses 13, 14? The certainty that it is so arises only from our supplying ἐν Ἀδὰμ to ἥμαρτον in ver. 12. We therefore dismiss this last argument; but, while doing so, recognize the force of the other considerations. It would certainly be very strange if the apostle did not give the true gist of the thought in the words ἐφ' ᾧ πάντες ἥμαρτον;—all the more so, seeing that neither the connection of the passage nor the apostolic doctrine generally furnishes an adequate key to his meaning. The two considerations above stated show at least that if ἐφ' ᾧ πάντες ἥμαρτον gives the reason of the affirmation immediately preceding, and if ἥμαρτον means actual ˙sin, the Apostle contradicts the clear testimony of experience and his own teaching. If, however, we take ἐφ' ᾧ in the sense already explained (Vol. II. p. 301), the objections against taking ἥμαρτον in its natural sense, as referring to actual sin, disappear.

While, however, we do not take this particular sentence as explaining the connection of our sinful nature with Adam's fall, there are other parts of the passage which clearly do refer to it. The Apostle's words do not certainly justify us in taking ἁμαρτία to denote a sinful propensity which has come into the world by Adam's act. That there is such a bias in humanity may be inferred from the entire passage, verses 12–21, but it is not expressly taught in this word. We take ἁμαρτία in verse 12, as also in verses 13, 20, 21—as Schmid,[*] Philippi,[†] and Tholuck [‡] do—to designate the generic notion of sin, both the sinful propensity and actual sin (see Vol. I. p. 183).

The statement, therefore, of verse 12, "sin has entered into the world," does not necessarily imply more than the entrance of sin into the will of Adam. But the words "By one man," taken in connection with the inference καὶ οὕτως εἰς πάντας ἀνθρώπους ὁ θάνατος διῆλθεν oblige us to recognize in εἰσελθεῖν εἰς τὸν κόσμον the idea *implicitè* of the spread of sin from one point throughout the world. This follows inferentially also from the connection between sin and death, and the universal reign of death as affirmed by the Apostle, and which he, in verses 15, 17, traces back to Adam's sin. The κατάκριμα,

---

[*] *Exegetischen Bemerkungen über*, Rom. v. 12, in the *Tübinger Zeitschrift für Theol.* 1830, No. iv. 174.
[†] Commentary on the Romans, p. 161.   [‡] *Ibid. in loco.*

CHAP. III.]   THE DOCTRINE OF HEREDITARY SIN.   345

moreover, of verses 16 and 18, which passes upon all men
from one man's disobedience, is clearly death—physical death
in the strictest sense—together with that state of deprivation
and nakedness upon which the disembodied soul enters, wherein
it discerns its inner discord, apart from the distractions and
diversions of the phenomenal world. Most modern critics,
while taking κατάκριμα to denote death, put so much into
the word as to destroy the full force which it has in this
passage as meaning simply death. Rothe* and Tholuck find
in the words of verse 19—" by Adam's disobedience the many
were made actual sinners "—the reason (γαρ) for the statement
immediately preceding.† But if the Apostle intended here to
express a thought which hitherto he had not introduced, we
should have expected a different arrangement of the words,‡
and he would have chosen some other verb than καθίστασθαι, a
word ill-adapted to express and lay stress upon the realization
of an actual fact, at least according to New Testament usage;
for καθιστάναι always (save perhaps Acts xvii. 15) means "to
appoint to an office," "to exhibit in a certain light"—
declarative rather than a causal act—see Titus i. 5; Luke xii.
14, 42, 44; Acts vi. 3, vii. 10, 27, 35; Heb. ii. 7, v. 1, vii.
28, viii. 3; Matt. xxiv. 45, 47, xxv. 21, 23; James iii. 6,
iv. 4; 2 Peter i. 8. If, moreover, we take the first clause of
verse 19 thus, the δίκαιοι κατασταθήσονται of the second clause
must denote an actual becoming righteous in distinction from
justification the δικαίωσις ζωῆς of verse 18, and this, considering
the Apostle's choice of words, would be very unnatural.
Remembering that γὰρ, both in the New Testament and in
the Classics, not only introduces the reason or cause, but also
the explanation or full detail of what has already been stated, §

* *Auslegung der* Rom. v. 42-21 ; p. 150.

† This passage, thus rendered, does not confirm the "immediate imputation"
theory of the older theology, as argued from the actual participation of all
Adam's posterity in his fall. Against such an application of the passage
TAYLOR not incorrectly says, that so far from sanctioning, really contradicts it :
"for had all men sinned in Adam when he sinned, the sin would not have been
'the disobedience of one,' but of millions."—Dr JOHN TAYLOR'S *Scripture
Doctrine of Original Sin Examined*.

‡ FRITZSCHE, *Pauli ad Romanos epistola*, tom. i. 342.

§ ROTHE should not have denied this, for the second usage really glides imperceptibly into the first. The explanation of a true thought serves really to
deepen the conviction of its truth.

we are not warranted in taking verse 19 as a transition to a new thought. What the Apostle says briefly and proverbially in verse 18, he repeats more fully and clearly in verse 19. "By the disobedience of one (as the beginner of sinful development) the many have been declared sinners (as it were before the judgment-seat of God) in that they have become subject to death."

In answer to the question, What is the bearing of this passage upon the doctrine of hereditary sin? we reply, first, it teaches that the universal dominion of death over men is clearly the result of Adam's fall, compare 1 Cor. xv. 21, 22. But while exhibiting death as the consequence of sin, it places the sinning of Adam's posterity in close connection with his fall; and any doctrinal view which denies the influence of this fall upon the development of sin in Adam's posterity is not in harmony with St Paul's teaching. The Apostle does not, however, say that the reign of sin in man's natural life has its adequate cause in Adam's fall; if he believed this, we should have expected him to have fully expounded so important a doctrine, and not to have simply referred to it indirectly in order to bring out to view the plan of redemption in the abundance of its blessings, and the distinctiveness of its realization. Still less does the passage teach that the sin of our first parents is imputed to their posterity, save in so far as death, the consequence of the fall, reigns over all. It intimates, as we have said, that Adam's sin exercises a determining influence upon the sinful development of the race, but as to the nature and extent of this influence it leaves room for many conjectures. That form of doctrine, for example (for other reasons untenable), which attributes to Adam's fall merely a strong inclination towards sin in human nature, is quite compatible with this passage. Against any view which regards the effects of the fall as more restricted than the orthodox doctrine represents, it has been urged that the comparison instituted by the Apostle between Adam and Christ would not be sufficiently complete, seeing that in Christ we have the sole source and cause of our justification and salvation. But it must not be forgotten that the point of resemblance is only in the respective influences of the first and second Adam; the first leading, by

Bearing of this text on the dogma of original sin.

natural development, to corruption ; the second, by spiritual development, to eternal life. The nature and degree of this influence may be very different in the two cases ; indeed, as to its nature, it must be so, for the first Adam is head of his race by virtue of natural propagation ; but the second by the communication of divine powers to the spirit. The early Lutheran theology, in particular, cannot consistently insist upon an exact coincidence in the analogy between the first and the second Adam in their respective relations to the race. It maintains that Christ's righteousness is imputed to others, not like Adam's sin, by way of necessity, but by a free self-decision and appropriation of it by the man himself ; and whereas the fall involves all, without distinction, in sin, guilt, and ruin, Christ's redemption is offered to multitudes in vain.*

In turning to that passage in the Old Testament which the Apostle evidently has in his mind, and which the earliest theologians refer to as affording the main basis for the doctrine of original sin, I mean to the account of the Fall in Genesis iii., we need not enter upon the very difficult and critical question, whether the narrative be throughout historical, because the contrasted dogmatic views which we are here considering are not affected by it. If, indeed, the hypothesis now in vogue were correct, viz., that it is only the philosophizing of some thoughtful Israelite or Oriental concerning the origin of evil, written under the garb of history,† Christian theology could make no use of it. But we cannot adopt this hypothesis, for it requires a much later date to be assigned to the

Genesis iii.

* TOLLNER very candidly and fully discusses this analogy in his Dissertation on Rom. v. 12-19 ; *Theol. Untersuchungen*, vol. i. part ii. p. 82.

† So WINER, *Realwörterbuch*, Article *Eden*. GESENIUS takes the same view in the *Hall. Encyklopädie*, Article *Adam*, and calls it the "mythical," as distinct from the historical or allegorizing view : so also CÖLLN, *Bibl. Theol.* i. 244 ; and TUCH, *Kommentar zur Genesis*, p. 54. Modern investigations, as to the proper definition of the *mythus*, show that this term cannot be applied to a didactic fable deliberately composed by some one. STRAUSS hesitates whether to regard the narrative as a myth or a poem, but he describes it thus :—
"Jehovah, jealous for the privilege of the Elohim to eat of the tree of knowledge of good and evil, punishes man for partaking of its forbidden fruit; and lest he should appropriate the other prerogative of the Elohim, immortality, by a continued partaking of the fruit of the tree of life, drove him out of the Garden." *Christl. Glaubensl.*, vol. ii. 18, 19, 24. The two points in this account are either entirely or partially imported into the Mosaic history : the idea that Elohim had eaten of the fruit of the tree of knowledge is an unwarrant-

narrative than the language in which it is written—allowing the utmost latitude that modern criticism demands—admits. It would, moreover, be very difficult to understand how the profound piety of a Jew, in dwelling upon the sacred traditions of his people concerning the progenitors of the race, could allow him to represent his theorizings as real history; or how, contrary to his purpose, such a misapprehension could arise. That supposition is simpler which regards the narrative as a myth, wherein history and imagination, truth and fiction, are blended. For granting that the existence of a first human pair is not a merely Jewish imagination, but the recollection of a fact, handed down by tradition generation after generation, until it was committed to writing, we could not regard the record as an unmeaning picture of what is true of mankind universally, or of the transition in every one from a state of natural innocence to one of sin and guilt. Even upon this theory we must recognize an historical germ about which elements of fiction gathered during the crystallizing process of national tradition. The coincidence in certain important features between the Mosaic narrative and other oriental traditions concerning the orign of evil, also points to a common historical basis. The Hebrew narrative, moreover, is so much superior to all other eastern myths, and is so interwoven, externally and internally, with the history in the first eleven chapters (as for example, the recurrence of names in the genealogies), which no fair critic would venture to pronounce as throughout mythical, that we may justly consider it to be the purest tradition of the central truth, and the most faithful exponent of its true import. These considerations are confirmed by the testimony of the inspired Apostle, who not only refers incidentally to the Fall, 2 Cor. xi. 3; 1 Tim. ii. 14(?); but recognizes it in his religious consciousness as an historical fact, Rom. v. 12-19; 1 Cor. xv. 21, 22.

In thus recognizing an historical germ or basis in the narrative, Christian theology does not undertake the task of maintaining the historical character of every particular. We can

---

able inference from verses 5 and 22; and as to the tree of life, the narrative expressly describes that as intended for man, chap. ii. 16, 17, and represents him as subject to death on account of his disobedience, chap. iii. 19.

easily understand how an event occurring under extraordinary relations which were destroyed by it, and handed down generation after generation by oral tradition, should gradually have woven for itself from the objects of sense a drapery hardly adequate to represent those primary relations in all their fulness to after generations. Seeing that we cannot distinguish what is merely drapery in the narrative from its original substance, it is far more rational and scientific to confess our present inability, than for the sake of a decisive answer to set up with boasting assurance an untenable explanation.*

Even supposing we took the several particulars of the narrative literally, it contains no hint of a moral corruption of human nature tainting all mankind with sin and guilt from the first moment of their life. The real design of the narrator is clearly to describe the origin not of universal sinfulness, but of prevailing evil, teaching us to look upon the pains and sorrows of our earthly life, and above all, upon death itself, as the result and punishment of sin. He describes this chiefly in reference to our first parents, but verses 16-19 clearly show that the curse pronounced on them is intended for all mankind. The narrative does not necessarily imply the transformation of the first man from a state of perfect purity and freedom from any sinful disposition or bias into a state of dominant sinfulness, but it certainly does most clearly teach that the depravity of man, however it may have originated, has its foundation in himself.

More than this cannot be inferred from the statement of Gen. i. 31, where, after man's creation, it is said, "God saw everything that He had made, and behold, it was very good," nor from the fact that after the fall sin appears in its most awful form in Adam's first-born son, and that in the course of generations the wickedness of man has become so great, that the race is ripe for destruction in the Flood. Does this striking contrast between what man was before the fall and what he afterwards became, warrant the belief in a fundamental change in his moral constitution? We think not. The knowledge which Adam and

Gen. i. 31.

* This is in accordance with THOLUCK's remarks in the 3rd supplement to his work "*Die Lehre von der Sünde und vom Versöhner*," and with those of KRABBE in his *Lehre von der Sünde und vom Tode.*"

Eve obtained by eating of the forbidden fruit is represented as a knowledge of their own nakedness, Gen iii. 7; and this, taken in connection with verse 11, and chap. ii. 25, rather implies a newly-awakened consciousness of a previously existing want, than the entrance of depravity into a sphere of pure existence. And as to the divine declaration in chap. i. 31, that "every thing was very good," it expressly refers to all that God had made, and is quite compatible with the idea of a germ of sin lying hid in man, and having its origin only in man and not in God. It is also plain, that the declaration refers to God's non-intelligent creation as well as to man, so that it expresses the general fitness of every thing for the purpose designed, and not moral good.

Herewith the question arises whether Holy Scripture any where teaches the doctrine that Holiness was the condition of our race at the outset of its history, and that by the first actual sin which he committed man passed out of this into an opposite state of natural sinfulness. We have seen that the account of the first act of disobedience and of man's preceding state given in Genesis, does not present any thing more than an initial state wherein sin had not yet appeared. Our older theology, however, lays the greater stress upon the statements of Gen. i. 26-28, where man is said to have been created in the image of God. This is taken to denote (*principaliter*) a state of perfect holiness and wisdom which our first parents lost by the fall for themselves and their posterity.

Does Scripture teach man's original holiness?

To designate the divine image which man bears in himself in distinction from all other earthly beings, the Mosaic record uses two words צֶלֶם and דְּמוּת, sometimes employing both together, chap. i. 26, and sometimes each separately and alone, צֶלֶם in chap. i. 27, ix. 6; and דְּמוּת in verse 1. Most of the Greek Fathers, and Bellarmine with other Catholic Divines following them. distinguish these two words; they took צֶלֶם (εἰκών) to denote the mental and moral endowments of man; and דְּמוּת (ὁμοίωσις) as meaning the Godlike perfections after which man was to strive. This is a distinction theologically correct; but, exegetically, the early Protestant Divines were right in urging that the words beingused interchangeably elsewhere, when they occurred together they merely strengthened the thought conveyed.*

The Socinians, and to some extent the Arminians likewise, take the divine image wherewith man was endowed, to mean simply his dominion over the creatures.† It must be acknowledged, that in Gen. i. 26, these two things are closely connected. But צֶלֶם and דְּמוּת as they occur in the Old Testament, denote a resemblance in character between the image and its original, rather than in the relation which each bears to something else; and the manner in which the two statements are connected in the 26th verse, as well as their separation from each other in verses 27, 28, goes to prove that they are not identical, but stand in the relation of cause and effect. Man is given dominion over nature, because, by virtue of his creation in God's image, he is superior to nature. The other passages, moreover, where the divine image is spoken of, Gen. v. 1, ix. 6, contain no reference to man's dominion over the creatures; indeed chap. ix. 6 would hardly admit of it.

But while our early Protestant divines were right in rejecting these explanations, their own views concerning the divine image and its loss by the fall have little or nothing to support them in the book of Genesis. Reference, indeed, is made to chap. v. 1, where we read, "in the likeness of God made he him," and then, again, as if by way of contrast at verse 3, " Adam begat a son in his own likeness after his image;" as if implying that after his fall he could no longer transmit the divine image, but only his own. But the most conclusive argument in favour of these views is supposed to be Col. iii. 10, taken in connection with the parallel passage in Eph. iv. 24.‡ The first-named passage alone speaks of the divine image,—as the standard for the Christian's progressive renewal—but says nothing as to its nature save what may be drawn from the expression, εἰς ἐπίγνωσιν, i.e., the *sapientia*.§ But the other text supplies this

---

* See QUENSTEDT, part ii. c. 1, §. 1, th. 9 ; § 2, qu. 4. Also HOLLAZ, *Examen theol. acroam.*, 463.

† *Fausti Socini praelect. theol.*, c. 3, in the *Bibliotheca fratrum Pol.*, tom. i. 539. LIMBORCH's *theol. christ.* I. ii. c. 24, 14.

‡ See GERHARD'S *Loci theol.*—*De imagine Dei in homine ante lapsum*, c. 2, 30, 31. QUENSTEDT, part ii. c. 1, § 1, th. 9 ; § 2, qu. 5.

§ Thus QUENSTEDT ; others, as, *e.g.*, GERHARD, derive *sapientia* as an element of the divine image from Eph. iv. 24.

deficiency, declaring that the new man "after God is created in righteousness and holiness of truth." Seeing that the divine image is thus described as first realized in man's renewal by the gospel, the natural inference is said to be that it must have been lost by the fall. Nothing weighty could be argued against this dogmatic use of the two texts if by the καινὸς ἄνθρωπος κατὰ θεὸν κτισθεὶς and the νέος ἄνθρωπος ἀνακαινούμενος κατ' εἰκόνα τοῦ κτίσαντος αὐτὸν were meant Adam before the fall. But such a reference is obviously excluded, alike by the language of the apostle (especially the νέος ἄνθρωπος ἀνακαινούμενος Col. iii. 10), and by the indistinctness and untenableness of the representation itself. The νέος (καινὸς) ἄνθρωπος clearly denotes the holy life which Christ's redemption produces.* And if this be "the new man," the κτίζειν in both texts cannot mean man's first creation in Adam, but (as in Eph. ii. 10) his second or new creation in Christ Jesus; compare 2 Cor. v. 17; Gal. vi. 15; Eph. ii. 15. Neither passage, therefore, contains any immediate reference to man's primary creation in God's image. Considering the force of the ἀλλὰ τὰ πάντα καὶ ἐν πᾶσι Χριστὸς at the close of the paragraph, the κτίσας may be taken to refer to Christ, and then εἰκών will denote the image of His divine life to be embodied even more clearly and perfectly in the life of His disciples, Rom. viii. 29; 2 Cor. iii. 18. The same thought is more fully expressed in Eph. iv. 24. This interpretation, however, might be admitted, and yet it might be supposed that the image of Christ was that which had been lost at the fall, and that the description given in these two texts of Christ's image in the new man also describes the image wherein man was first created. But it cannot be proved that the new creation in Christ is nothing more than the restoration of the state wherein Adam was at first created. There is indeed a relationship between the two; the divine image wrought by Christ's redemption is the only true realization of the image wherein man was at first created. Man was originally given the one, in order that he might attain the other, if not directly by

[margin: Col. iii. 10. and Eph. iv. 24.]

---

* See for Eph. iv. 24, the Commentaries of OLSHAUSEN, HAARLESS, MEYER. For Col. iii. 10, see those of BAHR, MEYER, BLEEK (Vorlesingen über die Briefe, an die Kolosser, den Philemon, und die Ephesier, 1865). While acknowledging this sense, these Commentators all maintain the reference of the texts to Gen. i. 26.

continuing faithful in obedience and fellowship with God, yet indirectly after his fall by means of redemption. But it is evident that, from the very nature of this relationship, the two are not identical.

If, then, the divine image wrought in the new man by redemption is not merely the repetition of that wherein man was created, Eph. iv. 24 and Col. iii. 10 cannot be taken simply as explanatory of Gen. i. 26, nor can we infer from these passages that the image derived from the creative act of God was lost at the fall. Nor can this loss be inferred from Gen. v. 3; on the contrary, as in verse 1, it is said of Adam, "in the likeness of God made He him," and again, without the least hint of a change, in verse 3, " Adam begat a son in his likeness after his image," the fair inference is that Adam's son also bore God's image and likeness.

Man retained God's image after the Fall. Not only is there no positive proof in Scripture that the image wherein man was created was lost in the fall, but we find statements proving the presence of God's image in man subsequent to his first disobedience. In Gen. ix. 6, the heaviest penalty is ordained to be inflicted for the crime of murder, and the reason assigned is this:—"for in the image of God made He man,"—clearly implying that man still bears that image as the seal of the inviolability of his life. Again, in a similar connection, St James reminds us (iii. 9) that "men" (generic, τοὺς ἀνθρώπους, not τὸν ἄνθρωπον) "are made after the likeness of God." It is clearly a make-shift whereby any arbitrary narrowing or perversion of Scripture might be accomplished, when our early theologians endeavour to bring these texts into harmony with their doctrine concerning the forfeiture of the divine image, by making a distinction between "*imago Dei late sive ἀκύρως and stricte sive κυρίως sic dicta.*" *

The statements of Holy Scripture, therefore, concerning the image of God, wherein man was at first created, give no support to the tenet that Adam by his fall implanted a new principle in human nature which asserted itself in all his posterity and plunged them in sin and guilt.

* QUENSTEDT, as before, p. 3. This cannot be done either by means of the twofold designation צֶלֶם εἰκών, and דְּמוּת ὁμοίωσις, for in James iii. 9, which most distinctly implies that man is still in God's image, ὁμοίωσις is used.

We are not expressly told in the book of Genesis what the image or likeness of God in man really was, but we may easily find it out. After the account of the creation of the various orders of existences in nature by God's almighty power, the creation of man is introduced in a distinctive and marked manner by the declaration of God's resolve to create a being in His own image and after His likeness. This implies that those other orders of created nature were not made in God's likeness. The image of God in man, therefore, must be something which specifically distinguishes him from all other existences in nature. This is manifestly his *personality.** Other beings on earth show forth God's eternal power and Godhead; but those beings only are in the image of God and after His likeness who are a revelation of God; not for others only, but for themselves; who not only are, but know that they are; who are conscious of themselves, and therefore of God also.

<small>Personality is God's image in man.</small>

Accordingly, we find the most conclusive reference to the image wherein man, even according to his spiritual nature, was created, in Acts xvii. 28, 29, where, though the very word does not occur, the thing denoted is clearly meant. Those among our early or more modern theologians who refer this passage to the more general relations of God to all His creatures (to the *concursus generalis*) are evidently in error, for an attentive consideration of the entire connection clearly shows that it refers to the high dignity and destiny of man. It is said of man, as distinct from all other creatures in nature, that "IN God," not only from God, "he lives, and moves, and has his being;" and we have already seen (Vol. II. p. 139) that he can be IN God so far only as he is in the highest sense in himself. It implies that he must be a self-conscious *ego*, a person. And for this very reason he is the offspring of God,—God and man, absolute and relative personality, being a γένος distinct from all impersonal existence. These significant words of St Paul thus indicate the true nature of the divine image in man. The truth that "in Him we live, and move, and have our being," that "we are also His offspring," is stated as a guarantee that we can "feel after Him and find

<small>Acts xvii. 28, 29.</small>

---

* See NITZSCH's remarks in harmony with the above in his first Article of the Protestant reply to MÖHLER's *Symbolik*, *Stud. u. Krit.*, 1834, p. 36, 37.

Him" in His world. In the act of creation generally God wills existence apart from Himself; in producing a being in the sphere of His creation "after his own image," he brings the world, otherwise far removed from Him, back again to Himself. God has willed that man should be like Him, in order that there may be a being capable of holding fellowship with Him; man, therefore, should not let himself be hindered from knowing and loving God as like to himself, by any Deistic or Pantheistic abstractions which would deny him this fellowship. God in creating man made him in His image. There is, therefore, no anthropomorphism when man conceives of God as a being like himself, a Spirit who knows and wills. If, with Pantheism and Deism, we must regard everything that the human mind, judging from its own nature, predicates of God as mere anthropomorphism, God, by creating man in His image, has made it utterly impossible for man to know himself.

The conception of the divine image in man has already been fully developed in Book III. part i. chap. 4, so that we need only call attention to the fact that the declarations of Holy Scripture upon the subject are quite in harmony with our view. If the divine image in man is spiritual personality, it cannot be a merely transitory gift, but is an essential part of his constitution; still possessed by him, though in a state of sin (Gen. ix. 6; James iii. 9), leading to his dominion over the creatures (Gen. i. 26), and fully realised in the image of Christ wrought out in him by redemption (Col. iii. 10).

We therefore retain the *naturalis propagabilis* which our early theology predicates of the *imago Dei* — understanding by *propagabilis* that in every *propagatio* the divine image is transmitted,—but we deny that the *imago Dei* is *accidentalis* and *amissibilis;* for these latter attributes are, even according to the principles of our old theology, incompatible with the former.

As to the theory of man's original state, whereon that early Protestant view is based, we need not here repeat what has already been advanced in other parts of this work against the notion that man, as a personal being, started from moral perfection. We would only call to mind the fact that this conception of *moral* perfection could only be brought about by free self-

Personality does not involve moral perfection.

determination; and that we cannot see how the possibility of evil could have been present from the beginning,—as it certainly must have been, seeing that it was realised,—if man at the outset was endowed with this moral perfection.* This leads us to an inner contradiction discoverable in the earliest theology of the Church. If it asserted (as perhaps Origen does) that the possibility of a fall is compatible with moral perfection, though this would imply a wrong notion of human freedom, it would at least be consistent. But so far from asserting this, it expressly recognises that, in the advance of the redeemed to moral perfection, all possibility of falling away (*labilitas*) is removed by the *confirmatio boni* of God. Yet it does not regard this divine *confirmatio* as something mechanically superadded, and external to the previous development. If it did, every internal moral perfection might be predicated of man's original state, without his being thus raised above the possibility of evil, but the insufficiency of redemption would thus be implied, and the unanswerable question suggested, why did not God bestow this external *confirmatio* at the very beginning, so as to avoid the fall? It does not, however, take this view, but connects the divine decree with the completion of fellowship with God which is brought about by redemption.† Even in this case, however, it must be allowed that the lack of this decree, of this confirmation in moral goodness on God's part, must itself have been a defect in man's original state excluding, not perhaps a negative sinlessness, but certainly all positive holiness as an element of moral perfection. In declining to recognise this, the old theology involves itself in a contradiction but partially concealed by such untenable formulæ, as, for instance, that man in his original state possessed all perfection save confirmation in goodness.

* The recognition of this is implied in the distinction (exegetically incorrect) made between εἰκὼν τοῦ Θεοῦ (צֶלֶם) as denoting man's intellectual powers and ὁμοίωσις (דְּמוּת) as denoting positive likeness to God, holiness and wisdom, which is from the outset the goal at which man must aim.

† GERHARD, *Loci. theol. De vita eterna*, § 75. *Ea ipsa natura sui status non tantum ex lege Dei extrinseca, ut quidam Scholasticorum opinantur, beati erunt i bono confirmati.* QUENSTEDT, as before, part i. c. xiv. § 1, th. 20 (p. 557) See the remarks of GERHARD concerning the confirmation of good angels, *De creatione et angelis*, § 2, qu. 6. Also TWESTEN's *Vorlesungen über die Dogm. de ev. Luth. Kirche*, vol. ii. 325; PHILIPPI, *Kirchliche Glaubenslehre*, ii. 303.

In harmony with the profounder theology of the Middle Ages,* our early divines looked upon "the beatific vision of God"† as the means of this divine strength. And certainly, when man possesses this, sin can no longer be regarded as possible. But this, which is the goal of his perfection, could not have been given to him at first, because the possession of it is conditional upon the fact of his will, which is the essence of personality, being brought into perfect harmony with the divine law. The tender germ of the tree cannot bear the power of the sun's beams until it has first unfolded itself in the darkness of the soil. Man must first of all become matured by communion with an unseen God who is the object of his faith, in order to become capable of the vision of God. The absence of this vision of God in man's primeval state forbids the idea of his moral perfection then.

CHAPTER IV.

The Origin of Inborn Sinfulness.

§ 1. SIN MUST BE TRACED BACK TO AN EXTRA-TEMPORAL ACT.

In the last chapter we considered the contradiction subsisting between those two characteristics of sin which we are obliged equally to maintain, viz., its universality as deep-rooted in human nature, and its guilt as resting upon every one. The question was, whether the Augustinian doctrine of hereditary sin explains this contradiction, and mediates between the conflicting truths. We have seen that it leaves the problem unsolved; while fully recognising the one truth, it leaves the other unexplained. We have also seen that the attempted solutions, by limiting natural sinfulness and its power to pro-

* THOMAS AQUINAS, Summa, part i. qu. 100, art. 2; Confirmatur homo in justicia per apertam Dei visionem.

† GERHARD, as before: Quemadmodum angeli, qui semper vident faciem Patris qui in coelis est (Matt. xviii. 10), sunt in bono confirmati et a peccandi periculo liberati, sic beati, utpote futuri ἰσάγγελοι, perfecte sancti et in bono confirmati erunt per et propter beatificam Dei visionem. See also QUENSTEDT, as before.

duce actual sin, or by transferring all personal guilt to the act of our first parents, fail to reach the root of the difficulty so long as we maintain the propositions: All men are sinners; and, Where sin is there is guilt.

If we closely consider the import of these statements, we shall easily discover the point from which the solution of the problem must proceed. On the one hand we have inborn sinfulness in all men manifesting itself upon the awakening of moral consciousness in actual sin; and yet the true conception of sin as a disturbance, as that which ought not to be, will not allow us to explain this universality of sin as a necessary element in human development. On the other hand, we have to acknowledge the guilt of the person in sin, and this implies (as our investigations in Book I. showed us) that each one must by an act of self-decision be the author of his own sin. Holy Scripture, at least in one passage (Eph. ii. 3) declares that every human being is guilty, as he is *by nature*, and therefore from his birth, and the Church has ever recognised inborn guilt in its practice of infant baptism. We have already seen that it comes to the same thing if we attach guilt only to actual sin, and yet allow that all actual sin inevitably springs from inborn sinfulness. An inborn sinfulness, which makes every one guilty, is itself indissolubly connected with guilt. Thus we are driven to the idea of a sinfulness LYING BEYOND OUR INDIVIDUAL EXISTENCE IN TIME, a sinfulness which either directly or in its consequences involves guilt, and therefore must have its origin in our personal self-decision. It affects our conduct, our entire development from the very beginning, and yet it can only have its origin in our own act.

This the only true solution of the problem.
This would clearly be a contradiction if our personality had no existence previous to our earthly and temporal life, furnishing a sphere for the exercise of that self-decision whereby our moral nature is moulded from the outset. Thus the undeniable facts of human life and consciousness lead us at least to the very same idea to which a careful investigation of human freedom brought us (Book III. chap. iv.), the idea THAT CREATED PERSONALITY MUST HAVE HAD AN EXTRA-TEMPORAL EXISTENCE influencing its life in time. In treating of human freedom we found the sense of responsibility and of guilt in conscience an important

fact; all the more so as the question then was whether, and how far, the freedom of the will explains the origin of evil. But then we had to do simply with the fact of sin in general; how man dare not ascribe it to God, but to himself, as its author, and thus we were compelled to trace back our free self-determining for good or evil into the extra-temporal region of the intelligible or ideal. Having now been convinced, further, that sin is universal among men,—nay more, that it is deeply-rooted in human nature,—it is evident that if we would reconcile this fact with that of individual guilt, a new and stronger necessity obliges us to resort to that sphere. The contradiction between sin's universality and its guilt, as arising from an act of will, disappears, if each one who in this life is tainted by sin has, in a life beyond the bounds of time, wilfully turned away from the divine light to the darkness of self-absorbed selfishness. And thus, too, we may regard the bias to evil in man, according to the Kantian phraseology, as "interwoven with humanity and deep-rooted therein," and at the same time as "caused by ourselves."

Thus the solution of the profoundest problems of our being is not to be found in the facts which contain those problems. The most attentive consideration and most careful analysis of those facts will issue in nothing save the recognition of an inexplicable contradiction. The explanation lies beyond the facts to be explained, and yet so close to them that we have only clearly to realize them in order to discern it. A deep and earnest religious feeling will peradventure think it wiser to leave the mystery of our moral being veiled like the image at Sais; it may regard it as irreverent curiosity when any one ventures to raise the veil, and as the poet says, though in another sense, "to arrive at truth through guilt." And yet all who recognise the twofold fact—the inborn sinfulness of mankind universally, and the personal guilt involved therein—virtually and *implicitè* say the same with ourselves. One has only to adopt the theological dogma of the immediate participation of Adam's posterity in his fall, according to its fair and obvious meaning, or to allow the realistic theory of the fall in its full bearing, and he will logically be obliged to infer therefrom the idea of a primitive fall preceding individual life common to all, and yet in every case personally free.

To exhibit this principle in its fulness and truth it is not enough to state it thus generally, we must unfold it in its complete determinateness. What then is to be guide in doing so? Any unprejudiced examination of Holy Scripture must satisfy us that it says nothing about it, and that no allegorising *ex*positions of Scripture, or rather *im*positions, can afford a clue to it. The reason of this silence we shall presently see. Can we then ascribe to every thoughtful man an immediate consciousness of this original and extra-temporal self-decision, whereby he has become guilty and has given sin a power over him?—a consciousness not only of the fact of original guilt, but of the deed which produced it? We have already touched upon this question (Vol. II. p. 154) in its general bearing, and the answer we then gave was twofold. On the one hand, we stated that an experimental or empirical consciousness of that extra-temporal act is impossible, that we can attain only a speculative or philosophical knowledge of it; and, on the other hand, we referred to the investigation of this Fourth Book, intimating that there are facts indicative of this extra-temporal decision in the consciousness of every thoughtful and earnest man which are tantamount to a remembrance of an original act conditioning the moral character of his present life. We must here explain these statements more fully. An extra-temporal self-decision on the side of evil cannot be the object matter of our empirical consciousness, because, being extra-temporal, it lacks that determinateness, necessary to its being conceived as an act,—its determinateness, I mean, as something actually happening, which has happened and is past. As reflected in our present consciousness, it appears not as an evil *deed* but as an evil *state*, a permanent and sinful condition, and as a state involving guilt on our part, though consciousness does not know that it is the result of any act of our own. And this is just the way in which conscience obliges us to regard sin in our own life. It condemns us not only for our sinful acts, but for our sinful state; not only for a sinful state resulting from our habitual and sinful acts, but for our sinful state antecedent to all acts of sin, and related thereto not as effect but cause. Moral consciousness no sooner awakes than it finds our lives already at variance with its holy law,—

this variance being man's state of nature,—and yet in spite of the universality and seeming necessity of this state, it condemns us as personally accountable. Though it has no immediate knowledge of an extra-temporal fall, it judges and condemns as if it had.

Thus we learn what is to be our guide in determining the contents or elements of that original act of self-decision. Having by speculative reasoning discovered the sphere of being to which the phenomena of our experience and the dictates of our conscience alike point, we may further perceive how the contents of that ideal act are reflected in these phenomena. The only decision possible in that extra-temporal sphere is a decision of WILL. The essence of will, according to any adequate conception of it, is that it cannot *be* perverted, it can only pervert itself. Now, if in entering upon this life there were in the individual will no abiding perversion whatever, its manifestations might not after all be free from disturbance, for external and hindering disorders might have found their way into the lower or temporal sphere; though not itself acquiescing in these hindrances, the will might not be able at once to rid itself of them, and in this case it would be regarded as passively suffering from them until, as the true liberator of human life from its bonds, it had by degrees wholly overcome them. Our moral development would thus be, as it is, one of discord and conflict; but all those whose wills had been firm and steadfast in opposing the disorders of this lower sphere would be free from guilt, and would have no need of expiation or forgiveness.

This non-temporal decision is an act of will.

But this is by no means the testimony of experience. It presents sin to us, not as a natural disturbance unwillingly borne, which vanishes with our development by means of the purity of our will, but as an apostasy of the will itself, which is in league with other impulses. Every man, therefore, in whom moral consciousness is awake, does not merely find in himself an element of sin as a misfortune independent of his will, he finds himself involved in guilt. And thus there attaches to us all, from the very commencement of life, a disturbance of will springing from self-perversion, and this is a prevailing disposition, an habitual state of sin, which, as original guilt and the principle of all further responsibility, is, and can be nothing else than our own extra-temporal doing. Even supposing the phenomena could be resolved into the so-called weakness of will against the promptings of sensuous lust, this weakness could not belong to will as its general character, had it not itself adopted an element of perversion by an original act of self-decision in all men.

<small>Necessitarianism as a witness to this.</small> This accounts for that strong inclination, which the history of theology and philosophy amply shows, to trace back sin as an element belonging to human nature in the true conception of it, and thus to regard it as a necessity. Conscience and religion will ever protest against this, and well they may, for the very notion of sin rebels against it. But speculative theology alone is able to trace the error to its source, and to deprive it of the seeming sanction it obtains from the universality of sin in human nature, by recognising an extra-temporal and free self-decision conditioning the temporal development of mankind at large.

<small>This act of will selfishness.</small> This natural corruption of the will is in its essence that inborn SELFISHNESS to which the *ego* has inclined itself apart from and before all time. We by no means ignore the disorders of man's sensuous nature in all their depth and importance, neither can we deny that this disturbance in one form or another cleaves to man, sometimes as a tendency to sensuous indolence, sometimes as a germ of positive desire and violent passion, sometimes as excessive fear of physical evil, and sometimes as inordinate inclination to fleshly lust. But as to all these forms of depravity,—which may collectively be described as a repugnance on the part of man's sensitive nature to be the organ of his spirit, we have already seen (Book II. chap. ii.), that they by no means constitute the real kernel of sin, that they are merely effects springing from this inner germ which thus shows its nature in a second and derived sphere, an embodiment as it were of the spiritual principle of sin. This non-subjugation of the sensuous nature to the spiritual is not in itself and essentially evil; it becomes so in human nature in so far only as the will of the spirit tends towards good; otherwise it may even become a hindrance to evil.*

<small>* This insubordination of the sensuous nature is innate in every man in one form or another, but each man makes it his own in his own way, by an act of will,—of will perverted by an extra-temporal fall,—and thus it becomes his sin</small>

CHAP. IV.] THE ORIGIN OF INBORN SINFULNESS. 363

As to the extra-temporal and original condition of personal
beings, we cannot predicate of it any other kind
of evil but spiritual evil, for there is as yet no
corporeity in that state. The idea, therefore, which
Kant puts forward (see Vol. I. p. 334), that ideal or intelligible
evil may be defined as " the subordination of the moral promptings of the law to the sensuous impulses," is self-contradictory.
Any one who has not been convinced of this by our criticism
of the sensuous system and the theory of the genetic development of sin (in Book I. part i.) will, if he has followed us in our
argument, have here to allow that the inmost essence of sin, the
evil of evil, is wholly SPIRITUAL. It is because evil is primarily
spiritual in its nature, that mental elevation of any kind can
ever be anything else than a barrier to the power of sin. Man
often falls in the twinkling of an eye from his noblest soarings
and loftiest aspirations to the lowest depths of sensuousness;
and what is still more appalling, at the very moment when his
noblest thoughts and most spiritual aspirations have reached
their highest point, he is in greatest danger (if not under a higher
discipline) of at once passing into a state of diabolical pride and
reckless neglect of holiness, and into crimes of the inner man in
comparison of which the aberrations of sensuousness are the
veriest children's sins.

This non-temporal act spiritual.

Conditioned personality of itself furnishes sufficient ground
of solicitation to a primary and selfish decision. The spiritual
ego or self, which is the created yet extra-temporal germ of
this personality, and without which it would be unsusceptible
of all sanctifying and perfecting love, is the essential ground
of solicitation to a decision which may be evil; but in its
normal position, as the condition and antecedent of love, it
does not cease to be an element of moral good. The possibility of its becoming dominant, of its fall from God, should,
according to the eternal order of things, exist only in extra-
temporal consciousness as something ever to be avoided, and
thus the spiritual *ego* or self would enter its temporal life in a
state of purity. But as this *ego* or self emerges into self-

and forms part of his responsibility. This is my answer to PHILIPPI's objection,
when he urges (*Kirchliche Glaubenslehre*, iii. 107) that I can logically regard only
spiritual lust as sin, because this alone man himself begets, whereas sensuous lust
he inherits naturally.

determination from the (subjectively) undetermined, there is nothing whatever to prevent its primary decision breaking through that eternal order, and realizing the possibility of alienation from God.

Now, seeing that a primary decision of the *ego*, making self the dominant principle, has preceded our temporal life, we can easily understand how it is that so much stress is laid upon the controlling and subduing of self in the progress of life's development. On every hand we are called to self-renunciation and self-denial; from the very first awakening of consciousness this stern call echoes in our ears; our fondest wishes must bow to the commands of others; we must accustom ourselves to rules which we have not made, and must respect authorities the reasons of which we do not see. No self-devised plan of life unmodified by resignation can be fully realized; what we would hold fast to is torn from us by the force of circumstances, and something else is thrust upon us of which we have never dreamed. Not a single work continues our own; as it goes forth from us it becomes variously complicated, and soon begins to appear strange to us,—yea, it may even become a hindrance, opposing our strongest inclinations. In the battle against these opposing forces we realize the truth of the proverb, *fata volentem ducunt, nolentem trahunt;* we can master their power only by yielding to it so far as the inner call of our individuality allows, but the harmonizing of the discord depends upon our trust in the divine guidance overruling all outward circumstances and inward peculiarities, and upon our perception that this subjugation of our own will is a necessary discipline. As unbridled selfishness must ever be thoroughly evil, though its outward acts be in harmony with the rules and morals of civilized society, so earnest discipline and self-denial is the only soil in which virtue thrives, and obedience is the stern and bitter root from which the glorious tree of true freedom grows. In the sphere of morals, no less than in that of art, the beautiful words of the poet hold true:—

<blockquote>
" In vain, in vain do self-willed spirits strive
To climb the lofty heights of purity;
Self-limitation gives the power to rise,
And Law alone can give us liberty."
</blockquote>

Marginal note: Call to mortification of self.

CHAP. IV.] THE ORIGIN OF INBORN SINFULNESS. 365

The question now arises, What is the degree of the will's
self-perversion in the sphere of the extra-temporal? And in answer to this Kant suggests a
twofold possibility.* There may be the open
rebellion of the *ego* ever asserting itself in opposition to
God and His holy law, and determining not to pay any
regard thereto. Or there may be the inconsistency of
assenting to God's will in general, and yet preferring the
guidance of one's own will. The former affirms self alone,
and contradicts God's will; the latter recognises God's will as
well as self, but refuses its demands when they clash with self-
interest.

Extent of this self-perversion of will.

The question, however, can be properly answered by an
appeal to experience only. Kant tells us to ask
ourselves whether, by means of a fixed resolve,
we inwardly feel able to resist the very strongest
temptations to sin (*Phalaris licet imperet ut sis falsus et
admoto dictet perjuria tauro*), and his opinion is, that every
one must confess that he cannot venture to say that in such a
case he might not waver.† But suppose there were some
who took exception to this, and who affirmed that they
would not consent even to the smallest sin, though it were to
escape the most frightful tortures, even these persons would
have to allow that this invincible and heroic virtue did not
belong to them by nature, but that they attained it only by
many a hard inward struggle against self. And this would
be sufficient for the matter in hand. Human nature, in its
noblest as well as its basest specimens, cannot deny that the
maxim which naturally sways it is the utterly base and
ignoble one, " in extreme cases of temptation and danger
sacrifice duty to self-interest." So deep-seated is this principle in human nature, that when any one in extreme cases
acts according to it we rather pity than blame him, because
we feel the frailty of our own virtue; yet this fact cannot
invalidate, it only confirms the judgment which, according to
our past investigations, we must pronounce upon it. It is
just the original decision of will lying beyond the boundary of

Experience alone can answer this.

---

* *Religion inn. der Grenzen der bl. Vernunft*, pp. 31, 32. KANT regards the
higher degree of apostasy as an abstract possibility only, which can never be fully
realized.   † *Ibid.* p. 58.

our present life, which thus embodies itself determinately in this general maxim so natural to us.

<small>Limit of natural depravity.</small> The limit of natural corruption indicated in Book IV. chap. i., may be accounted for upon this principle. This depravity is not a thoroughly deliberate and persistent refusal to obey God simply for the sake of disobedience. We have no ground for pronouncing it self-contradictory to believe that the dominion of selfishness can ever become so absolute in the heart as to extinguish utterly the slightest inclination towards goodness; but we must allow that we cannot form a reasonable, consistent, and clear conception of such a state. The will of the natural man is at variance with itself, and however his depravity may be enhanced by repeated sin and accumulated guilt, this variance still remains as part of his very nature. Our moral development in time begins like the night season, which emerges not from outer darkness, but from a twilight, wherein some gleams of daylight linger, gleams which, after a while, may ripen into dawn again; and hence that irresistible impulse towards light which every moral and religious agency may calculate upon, if it begins its work early enough, and before the "shades of the prison house"* close in. This impulse in man he makes his own, so far as it asserts a barrier beyond which the depravity springing from his original fall is not to go. His will has not utterly rebelled against its eternal rule and standard; this standard still retains its authority, and exerts a counter influence against the dominant principle of selfishness. Hence arises that state of wavering and inward conflict almost universally to be found in the natural man.

<small>§ 3. THIS EXTRA-TEMPORAL SELF-PERVERSION NOT UNIVERSAL.</small> To ascribe such a self-perversion to *all* personal creatures in their extra-temporal state would be to transfer the difficulty into the very sphere wherein it is to be solved. The very task before us is to show the erroneousness of that plausible reasoning which infers the metaphysical necessity of sin from the fact of its universality in this life; or, which is the same thing, to show the compatibility of man's personal

* WORDSWORTH'S *Ode on Intimations of Immortality, from Recollections of Early Childhood.—Tr.*

responsibility and guilt with that universality. But if we transfer the universality of evil into the sphere of the intelligible or ideal, that very metaphysical necessity appears in its most destructive power exactly where it should be overcome and resolved into pure freedom. But there is no occasion whatever to make such a transference, provided that we keep the idea here developed distinct from that other totally different doctrine of a *fall as the cause of finite and individual being*. If we give due weight to the conception of freedom in the extra-temporal sphere, we shall be led to the belief which may be found in the religion of almost every nation, that a portion of the spirit-world has, by original self-decision, formed for itself a moral existence in undisturbed harmony with God, and thus develops its created innocence into free holiness. We may also allow it to be possible that another portion of those created essences have utterly alienated themselves from God, so that all inclination towards good is excluded from their existence in time,

Hence it follows that the religious views so generally entertained concerning ANGELS and DEVILS are not, as some would have us think, the merely imaginary reflection and caricature of our own moral state; this must be acknowledged even by those who, while perceiving the close and important relation between freedom and sin, still think it unnecessary to resort to the idea of an original and extra-temporal state. What Christ and his apostles teach us, though only incidentally, concerning angels and devils, finds its echo and confirmation in the deliverances of our own moral consciousness. It must not, however, be forgotten, that the reason why Christianity interests itself about these beings is the fact of their moral nature and its bearing upon man's moral state, and this is abundantly evident from Holy Scripture.

<small>Scripture doctrine concerning angels and devils.</small>

But if differences of species and varieties of order and rank among personal beings are not, as Origen thinks, consequences of an original fall in the spirit world, but must have preceded any such fall, the difficulty we have been explaining seems again to appear. If we have to allow that all extra-temporal beings belonging to the human species, and in whom the con-

<small>Many even of our own species may not have sinned.</small>

ception of humanity is realized, participated in that original self-decision and guilt, how can we avoid the inference that this guilt necessarily follows from certain elements included in the very conception of humanity? We answer that even here there is nothing to prevent our supposing that innumerable essences of the same order with ourselves did, by their original act, resolve not to realize the possibility of evil, and though we possess no definite knowledge concerning the temporal state and relations into which, in consequence of their holy steadfastness, they were introduced, we believe that it must be in some respects essentially analogous to our own. We do know of ONE human will whose original self-decision must have been in harmony with God's; we know this, because had Christ brought original guilt and the tyranny of sin with Him into this temporal state, His spotless holiness conquering all temptation, and reflecting an inner purity unmarred by any discord, together with the undisturbed harmony of his relations to God, would be wholly inexplicable.

This leads us to the question, To what extent does that intelligible or ideal act affect the empirical facts of our moral consciousness and conduct? It manifests itself, first of all, in the consciousness of an original guiltiness, attaching to our nature in its present state. Our moral consciousness, if clear and thorough, obliges us to regard this guiltiness as a derangement of our temporal nature, and this natural derangement as our guilt, thus referring us to that ideal act. The original guiltiness wherewith that act fetters our present consciousness, is indissolubly connected with our actual bondage. We are actually fettered because our will is by nature bent and divided against itself.

Effects of the non-temporal act on life.

Our investigations will presently show whether, and how far humanity, at the outset of its development when still empirically undisturbed, might have freed itself from this double bondage: it certainly cannot do so in its present state, for the derangement of our natural* (physical and psychical) being corresponds only too fully with the bias of the will. Man cannot

These effects obviated only by Christ's redemption.

---

* For Müller's explanation of this "nature basis," as distinct from the will, see p. 57 of this volume.

THE ORIGIN OF INBORN SINFULNESS.

again, by moral development, get rid of the derangement which subsists between self and life in God, seeing that it has penetrated human nature, and given a bias to every human being from the beginning; all his movements and changes are controlled by that fundamental bias. Man's deliverance from the guilt and power of sin can be wrought only by the merciful interposition of God, who restores the sinner to fellowship with Himself, by the atonement and justification which are in Christ Jesus. And even here there cannot be an annihilation of the past, as if that which had been done could be undone. Man's original decision being the extra-temporal and negative condition of his entire development, is ever the dark back-ground of human consciousness, though by the act of divine grace which appoints an expiation and begins a new life, it exists only as something that has been, and is done away. The sanctified, even when they have attained perfection, will still be the redeemed of the Lord;—not the innocent, in whose consciousness sin has never had any place, but the saved, whose iniquity is forgiven, and whose sin is covered.

Finally, as to the relation of our original and extra-temporal sin to our corporeity and, as corporeity is inconceivable without matter, to our material nature; it is hardly needful to say (for it is clear from the whole tenour of our inquiry) that we by no means entertain the view adopted by Plato, by Philo, and again by Origen, that the body is the prison-house of the soul wherein God has incarcerated it on account of its extra-temporal fall. The various forms in which this theory is held—a theory which is much more in keeping with the spirit of Oriental heathenism than with revealed religion—are based upon the idea that matter is a principle hostile to the realization of conditioned being; and whether we regard it as something independent and distinct from God or as created by God, the difficulty thus involved is the same. Matter is the embodiment of those limits which are inseparable from finite existences and their relations to each other, and thus God, though He may have no immediate relation to matter, has certainly an indirect and no less positive one. Matter is necessary, not indeed for God, who is in His essence relationless and raised high above all suffering (*i.e.*, influence from without), but for conditioned

Relation of inborn sin to our body.

beings. They cannot pass from their purely spiritual state into living and full individuality unless each of them as a spirit, related to God but not yet to other individuals of its kind, becomes objective according to its inherent limits as a living soul in a body, and thus becomes "a nature." Each monad attains the full reality of its being as a member of any organic whole whose parts mutually supplement each other, and not as an isolated atom, relating itself and nothing else to God alone. This mutual relationship is attained only by means of corporeity, *i.e.*, by some material substratum. It is only by thus becoming objective, according to their inherent limitations, that created spirits are able to recognize their inner identity and to distinguish themselves from other spirits. Now, if God wills that they shall have this full reality of existence, He must also will the existence of matter, which is the condition of his reality.

If, therefore, matter or corporeity be necessary to the development of finite spirit from its intelligible or ideal basis, this must specially apply to our earthly and material corporeity. As to the derivations of our corporeal nature from sin, developed so ingeniously by the imaginations of modern theosophic mystics, such as Antoinette Bourignon, Pordage, and Poiret, they will be regarded by ordinary minds as arbitrary dreamings;* but the consideration of the manifold mysteries of our earthly life, from which they have sprung, will lead to a juster estimate of them. Our corporeity, as it is at present constituted, seems very gross and unfitted for the development of the inner man, and the Christian doctrine of the Resurrection teaches us that it may be greatly refined. Nevertheless, we cannot attribute this grossness of our present corporeity to the fall in the spirit world, either as a punishment for that fall or as a discipline of restoration from it. In human nature itself, apart from any fall, there are elements for which our present gross corporeity ($\sigma\hat{\omega}\mu\alpha\ \chi o\ddot{\iota}\kappa\grave{o}\nu$) is needed as the primary basis of its development in time. Possibly it may be the coarser individuality of the human spirit, apart altogether from sin, which requires a corporeity different from that of other beings in the intelligible or ideal world. It is

* See the criticism of these mystical theories in Corodi's *Kritischer Geschichte des Chiliasmus*, vol. iii. part ii.

certainly a marvellous revelation of divine power and glory in creation when, by the charm of His love and knowledge, He can elevate these beings so restricted and pent up by their earthly *nature to a transfigured and angelic (Luke xx. 36) existence—a life which, while a phemonenal glorification of our earthly corporeity retains its distinctive lineaments. By this union of elements which seemed utterly irreconcilable, man becomes in the fullest sense the central being in the universe, and thereby a province of being is secured for the kingdom of God, which must otherwise have remained for ever external thereto and estranged.

When we contemplate the doctrine of Creation and of Redemption in connection with Christology in the New Testament, just as St Paul does in 1 Cor. xv., we are taught two things concerning the σῶμα χοϊκὸν in its relation to the idea of man. It is declared to have been suitable for the outset of human development, but it is said to be inadequate for its consummation; being χοϊκὸν, it has a right to existence only during a transitory stage of the development. St. Paul, by distinguishing it as σῶμα ψυχικὸν from the σῶμα πνευματικον indicats its relative inadequacy for that sphere of our being on which our capability of fellowship with God and our distinctive dignity in the scale of creation depend; and yet he as distinctly declares it to have been God's original design that as the σῶμα πνευματικὸν is the second stage in the course of human development, the σῶμα ψυχικὸν should be the first (verse 46).

The σῶμα πνευμάτικον

We have, however, already seen (Chap. II. of this fourth book) that had sin never entered into the world, man's development would have been different from what it is, and this implies that there are derangements in man's corporeal nature caused by sin. But in order more clearly to understand this we must enter a new field of inquiry, which will reveal to us a second source of inborn sinfulness. There is, as we have already observed (Vol. II. p. 109), a certain charm in being able to trace all the phenomena of life to one principal, and to deduce all human determinations as consequences and manifestations of one original and ideal act. But a fair estimate of the most indubitable facts of experience there enumerated, and the nature of that ideal sphere, and of the original self-determination possible therein, alike forbid our doing this. The history of the human race presents a combination of freedom and necessity, and in the development of the individual, self-determination and dependence are strangely interwoven into an undivided whole. This must be borne in mind when we consider the great end and aim of temporal existence for created personality, fallen or unfallen, namely, to enrich the *ego*, simple at its commencement, with many and varied attributes.

We have already seen (Vol. II. p. 43) that no one is born into the world as man in the abstract, *i.e.*, apart from any personal distinctiveness, but that every one begins his development in time with a natural disposition towards some determinate individuality. We thus reject the notion entertained by some that all human souls are alike at the beginning of their earthly existence, and that they begin to vary only when their development has progressed, through differences of nurture, experience, and circumstances. This theory, if it have any definite meaning, amounts to this: every single soul is born into this world gifted simply with those general characteristics and attributes which are common to the species; the special bias or idiosyncrasy of the individual is gradually contracted afterwards. But even allowing it to mean more than this, allowing it to mean that all individuals are born with a determinate bias—but all with the same, and that this bias is in the great majority of cases crushed by external influences, and in a few only retained and manifested in mental idiosyncrasy, it really amounts to the same thing. For this idiosyncrasy would then be nothing more than the general character belonging to the species, which, however, in the majority of cases, was prevented from showing itself by external hindrances,—these external circumstances being more powerful than the nature common to the species,—the accidental stronger than the essential.

§ 4. HUMAN INDIVIDUALITY.

Our earlier investigations have moreover shown that these peculiarities of character and disposition are not altogether isolated and confined to single individuals, but that they are grouped together. Within the one great whole of the species man, there are many subdivisions or classes, in each of which one common distinc-

Distinctions of race, nation, and family.

tive type is sustained and developed side by side with the general type of humanity; and this determinate type asserts itself amid a thousand lesser deviations and apparent arbitrarinesses, provided, of course, that class is not intermingled with class in the progress of generations. These collective distinctions, to name only the most obvious, are first those of RACE, which are the most comprehensive, secondly, those of FAMILY, which are the narrowest, and thirdly, those of NATION, which are intermediate.

These natural peculiarities of family, race, and nation, are Influence of usually transmitted by parents to their children. parentage. When, therefore, in them the given type, is but weakly expressed, or is supplanted by some other type, it is usually weakened or suppressed in the children, and gradually disappears. This dependence of children upon their parents, not only for their existence, but for the determinate character of that existence, is manifest not only in physical but in mental resemblances, which though variously diversified, are nevertheless unquestionably and strikingly apparent. Not only are physical peculiarities—peculiarities of temperament and the like—thus transmitted, but even given talents are unmistakably handed down from one generation to another, and this is witnessed to us by the succession of artists, of musicians, of mathematicians, of generals, or of statesmen, to be found in the same families.

But how are we to explain the bearing of these distinctive peculiarities of race, nation, and family, upon the individual, distinguishing him from others according to his own natural disposition? There are of course multitudes who, through some interruption hindering the development of character, are mere specimens or samples of the common race, nation, or family; but where development does take place, how do these inherited differences bear upon it? The free will of the individual undoubtedly exercises a determining influence upon the basis of nature within him, but it does this only from the time when it begins to assert itself, and when the natural peculiarities of character are in some degree developed. This basis of nature or distinctiveness of natural character, physically and mentally, cannot be regarded as a mere product of parental peculiarities, variously combined in the several children. In many cases this is very obvious, especially when the child possesses talent which is in neither father nor mother, and which cannot be accounted for as the product of their combined natures. But when less obvious, it is no less really evident, that no new feature of character can be produced by the mere repetition or reproduction of parental distinctiveness of character. That is an utterly mechanical and spiritless theory which would resolve, all qualitative distinctions into quantities of more or less, making the character of the child the sum or product of two other characters. The child's character is in itself original and its own, it cannot be calculated on general principles; it can be known only by a perception quickened by love.

We have already seen that the parents are the agents through whom the influences of race, &c., are transmitted to the individual. This implies two things. An "organ" or agent is not a mere instrument of a general force or power, without any independent influence it possesses a vitality of its own, asserting itself in a determinate manner. But, again, the agent or organ is dependent upon the power whose instrument it is* and which works, not externally upon it, but within it, so as to realize its own unvarying type. We thus see how the power which brings new individuals into existence works by means of the parents, and yet communicates gifts which the parents do not possess. In illustration of this, and as showing how parents, as the organs of a power working in them, may communicate attributes which they do not themselves possess, we may refer to the fact of unmistakable resemblances, both physical and mental, so often traceable between grandparents and their grandchildren, no indications of which exist in the parents themselves.

Nature of this influence.

This effective power, in its all-embracing yet determinate generality, is the generative influence of the species itself, underlying varieties of race, nation, and parentage, modifying itself, and leading to the production of individuals possessing attributes over and above the ordinary characteristics of its race, nation,

Influence of the species through the parents.

---

* JOH. MÜLLER thus expresses the same thought: "Each individual of a species does not merely beget its own counterpart, but herein is subject to the laws of the species in general."—*Handbuch der Physiologie*, vol. ii. part iii. p. 770.

and family. The species itself, having the parents as its instruments, creates in each individual that peculiarity of disposition and talent which marks it off as distinct from every other individual. But the species thus works simply as one of the forces of nature, unconsciously subservient to the divine will. God makes it His instrument in carrying on the world's history, and in raising human development above the tyranny of circumstances and outward hindrances. The progress of historical development depends upon the production of men of strong individuality, who have the power of realizing something positive in a higher sphere of life. In order to this of course something more is requisite than eminent natural endowments; still these form the necessary basis.*

These general and particular characteristics are communicated at the monent of generation. The subsequent de-velopment of the embryo is of far less importance as affecting the character of the new life, which already (notwithstanding its union with the mother's life) possesses a reality of its own, by virtue of which it assimilates what is congenial and rejects what is contradictory to itself. If those forces which produce determinate character acted not in generation, but only by the embryonic development, or even equally by the latter as by the former, it could not be explained how children inherit physically and mentally their father's likeness, or at least why they do not (as we should in this case expect) much oftener resemble their mother. Experience witnesses that the likeness of the father is as frequently and strikingly inherited as that of the mother. This fact cannot be explained by the influence of the father in the nurture and education of the child. For, apart from the error implied in this supposition, that the soul is wholly passive during childhood, and may be moulded at pleasure into any form or character, experience testifies that such striking re-semblances are met with where paternal influence has been out

Time and manner of its trans-mission.

* We see the the profound and suggestive thoughts of STEFFENS concerning the importance of individual character in many of his works, but especially in his *Christl. Religionsphilosophie,* i. 16-61. We need hardly direct the atten-tion of those acquainted with this subject to the difference between the views of Steffens and our own.

of the question. The transmitted peculiarities of the father, moreover, are not only mental, but physical also, and are, of course, most remarkable when they are abnormal in the father himself. We must, therefore, consider generation as the main and decisive moment for the transmission of parental character to the child.

If we consider the development of the embryo from its commencement, it seems very difficult to believe that it can be the bearer of the talents and inclinations of the soul, even from the very outset, when the fact of life cannot yet be proved. But the irrefutable fact that these talents and inclinations are transmitted from the father to the child, warns us against entertaining that merely mechanical view of a first period of purely corporeal existence in the embryo, followed by a union of soul with body (*infundendo*). We should rather regard the connection of soul and body as existing throughout, even while life is wholly latent; for the union of the two is dynamical and inseparable. Physiology has to recognize fructification as working long anterior to apparent life, even in the sphere of animal and vegetable life, and to include this fructification in the category of generation.*

Now, it is an undeniable fact that not only natural and normal tendencies, but abnormal formations,—tendencies to certain bodily diseases and to mental derangement—melancholy and insanity—are transmitted by generation. Nor can we (recognizing this fact) deny that *moral* derangements are transmitted by inheritance from parents to children in the form of evil dispositions. This may particularly be observed in the case of notorious vices. Thus the vices of drunkenness and sensuality, or unbridled ambition and passionateness, when the parents have been subject to them, often reappear in the children in the form of a tendency to like vices. If the children—instead of earnestly resisting these impulses, in compliance with the command of conscience—yield to them, the vices, confirmed by the inborn tendency, will manifest themselves in more terrible strength than in their parents.

Abnormal tendencies transmitted.

---

* See the marvellous facts collected and narrated by BURDACH in his "*Physiologie als Erfahrungswissenschaft*," vol. i. 301.

THE ORIGIN OF INBORN SINFULNESS.

The revolting features of the father's character are thus reflected back to him in the still more revolting countenance and character of his son. Sin, moreover, must attain a certain degree of maturity before it can be reached by the punishments which society, feeling its prevalence, has ordained for it. And hence it often happens that fathers in whom the sin is not yet ripe escape those ruinous consequences which come upon their children with inevitable force. That is, indeed, a terrible declaration—confirmed, as it is, by experience, and by our own convictions concerning the divine law, which will not suffer us to abate one iota of its sternness—" visiting the iniquities of the fathers upon the children, who resemble them in hatred of Me, unto the third and fourth generations," Exod. xx. 5, xxxiv. 7; Numbers xiv. 18.*
Christ himself confirms and explains this when He declares, concerning the generation of His day, that upon them who were filling up the measure of their fathers (who had killed the prophets by the murder of the Messiah and his servants), " should come all the righteous blood that had been shed from the blood of Abel" downwards, Matt. xxiii. 29-35. Here, too, we often find the same phenomenon which we referred to in the natural sphere, namely, that evil dispositions and traits of character in parents, which seem wholly to have disappeared in their children, recur, as if transmitted, in the grandchildren, thus showing that the seeds of that depravity had lain concealed deep in the soil of the individual character.

It is this unconscious basis of nature in man, as we have called it—his physical and psychical nature, as distinct from his spiritual personality—which is efficient in the process of generation, and which forms the link and channel of that degeneracy from generation to generation. Thus, too, human generation must be distinguished from creation, though these

---

* It seems more natural to take לְשֹׂנְאָי (Ex. xx. 5) as referring to עַל־בָּנִים as HENGSTENBERG does (*Authentie des Pentateuchs*, vol. ii. 548), or, as Hengstenberg really intends, to both subjects—לְ meaning clearly " on account of "—than to refer it, as DE WETTE does in his Translation, exclusively to the parents (אָבֹת). Whichever rendering we adopt, it is clear that the children are, as a rule, supposed to resemble their sinning parents, and this is evident from the omission of the לְשֹׂנְאָי in the parallel passages.

two have been confounded by physiologists of our day who, like Burdach, endeavour to supplant the idea of creation by that of generation. The action of the individual is thus taken out of the sphere of conscious self-determination, and regarded as one of the forces of nature subject to a law unknown to itself. But the evil dispositions of the father, equally with those of the mother, are transmitted to the child, and it is, therefore, most natural to attribute this to the act of generation. Psalm li. 5, evidently traces the sinful state of man to this commencement; see Vol. II. p. 274.

This by no means obliges us to regard the intercourse of the sexes as sinful, or to adopt the erroneous views of Augustine concerning the *concupiscentia* as the punishment of the fall; a theory which, under the sanction of his name, was adopted in the Scholastic and even in the Protestant theology. The polluting and poisonous influence of sin has certainly affected this relation, and the fierce violence of sensual passion in many is one of the indications of inborn sinfulness. The bond of union between the spirit created in God's image and man's earthly sensuous nature, while the most strange and mysterious, is the most violable and fragile, it is the point in human nature most exposed to the attacks of sin; and this vulnerability is enhanced in the sphere of the sexes, because here the sensuous and spiritual relations,—the gratification of lust and the relation of person to person,—are so closely interwoven as to involve a stronger incitement to the former, and the degradation of the latter, the spiritual, into a mere means of refined sensuality. And yet, in opposition to the ascetic view with its implied manichaeism, we must maintain the possibility of this sphere even being penetrated with the holy principles of the divine mind. What is sinful here is accidental; what is essential in the legitimate development of this sphere of life cannot be sinful.

Intercourse of the sexes not in itself sinful.

Generation while thus the channel for the transmission of evil propensities, is equally the channel whereby innocent dispositions and traits of character are handed down from generation to generation. Were human nature pure, the mode of transmission would still be the same. Arising as it does from the fact of man's possessing in his earthly development a nature analogous to animal life, it is represented in Genesis, side by side with animal fruitfulness, as the original ordainment of God without any reference to sin (Gen. i. 28, compared with ver. 22; Matt. xix. 4–6). But then it had not as yet any evil propensities to transmit,—nothing but innocent nature and sinless individuality.

Hence, without detracting in the least from the sanctity of marriage, or regarding it as something barely permitted by God for the sake of avoiding a greater evil, we may understand how it was necessary that the Son of God, when he became incarnate, should not be born by ordinary generation. In order that His life might be human He must be conceived and developed and born of a woman; but that it might be from its commencement sinless, a divine creative act must supplant that human act on which the commencement of any new life ordinarily depends.* The Gospel narrative of the virgin birth of Jesus exactly fulfils this dogmatic postulate, and the Christian Church has good reason to maintain firmly the expression of this truth in the early creeds. During its embryonic development the germ of the human life of the divine Son rejected every thing foreign to it, and assimilated only those elements which, according to the laws of organic life, were conformable to it. If, on the contrary, the first commencement—the moment when the existence of Christ's natural individuality was not a self-determining, but a being determined — depended on natural generation, its preservation from the taint of parental sinfulness would not have been a miracle as it is in the supposition of a virgin birth; it would have been a contradiction admitting, and at the same time excluding, the action of the parents in communicating their nature to their child. We cannot, therefore, adopt the theory of Schleiermacher, who holds that the natural conditions of generation were fulfilled, but that a creative power co-operated so as to destroy the sinful influence of sexual activity; † this theory is by no means an improvement of the orthodox doctrine, neither is there anything in gospel history to sanction it.

_{The Virgin birth of Jesus.}

---

* See NEANDER's remarks on the supernatural birth of Jesus, in his *Leben Jesu*, pp. 16, 17.
† *Glaubenslehre*, vol. ii. p. 73.

It is evident from what has been said upon this subject that the moral derangement transmitted by ordinary generation is something universal. It is so because whatever diversities there be as to the degree and character of natural sinful tendencies, such a derangement is universally to be found in the natural basis of human personality. The transference of special dispositions to sin from parents to children is not universal; there are cases in which it does not take place. Hence hereditary tendencies often die out in a family, and he who will not admit this will have to grant that the moral corruption of the race is ever on the increase,—new evil inclinations being ever in process of formation by consent of the will. But beneath these inequalities, as to particular dispositions, there is ever a general derangement common to all transmitted by generation, through which the species asserts itself; and this must ever be distinguished from that corruption of the will produced by an extra-temporal fall. This general derangement must be traced back to the beginning of human history. If it cannot belong to human nature as created by God, it must have occurred then.

The moral derangement transmitted is universal.

There is a threefold primitive state of man : first, his state as conceived in the divine ideal; secondly, his state in the extra-temporal existence of the *Ego;* and thirdly, his state in the temporal commencement of his earthly development. It is of this original state in time that we are now speaking. According to the representations of the book of Genesis and of the Apostle Paul, and according to the results of our investigations, from p. 370 downwards, we must regard this state as at the outset one of *actual* sinlessness, and of undisturbed harmony in the physical and psychical life of man.

§ 5. MAU'S PRIMITIVE STATE IN TIME.

Even the first of mankind are from the very outset of their life in time the subjects of that original fall in the region of their non-temporal and purely spiritual existence, as well as of the guilt incurred thereby. This is the dark abyss whence all human personalities who come into the world arise—with the single exception of the world's Saviour. But as this timeless decision neither does nor can form any part of human consciousness in time, it was in the first man at the outset a latent principle only, which could not come into action until there was a decision of the will in temptation, and in the conflict of opposite impulses.

What was the relation subsisting between the various powers of our nature in that primary Adamic state? We answer, that though as yet undeveloped, they must have been in undisturbed harmony, and not, as Catholic theology asserts, a *naturalis contrarietas et pugna virium et appetituum*, which had to be restrained by a *donum superadditum*. These various powers and affections were of course directed to various objects; but so long as the lower, according to their natural determinations, were subordinated to the higher, there could be no clashing nor strife. Each worked in its sphere according to its law, and in unison with the whole, and the lower impulses ministered to the health and energetic development of the life. But the derangement wherein these instincts and affections became inflamed to passions could only arise from their leaving their proper place as part of the united whole, and asserting themselves alone. The theology of the Middle Ages usually designated this state of innocence as *aequale temperamentum qualitatum corporis*, and the *Apologia Confessionis Augustanae* adopts this expression, but insists upon its inadequateness as a description of man's original righteousness.[*] Our older Protestant divines, while assenting to this, take a somewhat different view.[†] It is clear that a derangement involving the preponderance of the sensuous impulses could arise only from a depravity showing itself in the central will. So long as the will, though containing a concealed variance, consciously persevered in the affirmation of its truth according to God's law, and followed the impulses prompting thereto, the powers and affections of the sensuous life could not do otherwise than render a ready obedience to it, and must have continued in harmonious and happy concord according to the original design of God. The freedom of man in this original state from sickness and death would be in keeping with this.

Marginal note: Man's original state one of innocence.

---

[*] Art. i. pp. 53, 55.
[†] See QUENSTEDT, HOLLAZ, BAIER, BAUMGARTEN, upon the *puritas appetitus sensitivi*, and the *consentus affectuum*, as elements of the *imago Dei*.

For health is the harmony of the several parts of the organic life, the muscular, the nervous, and the reproductive systems; and disease and death, when they are not the mere decline of the vital power, or the consequence of external violence, are owing to the preponderance or "egoism" of some one of these systems thus disturbing their due equipose. Had the will never rebelled against the will of God, man's corporeity, though "natural" and "earthly" ($\psi v\chi\iota\kappa\dot{\eta}$, $\chi o\ddot{\iota}\kappa\dot{\eta}$), would never have lost its harmony, but would have retained it until its elevation to a higher sphere by glorification.

It is evident from our investigations that we must, with Schleiermacher,* attribute to this primitive state of our race "a non-temporal and original sinfulness," but on different conditions and in another sense, for we do not deny that a change took place in the constitution of human nature upon the fall of our first parents. That non-temporal sinfulness did not immediately determine their moral life, but was appropriated by a new self-decision of their will; moral development in the empirical sphere has claims and an importance of its own, and is not merely a shadowing forth of that ideal and original act. The will, indeed, is from the first disordered by the false elevation of the *ego*, and this derangement must sooner or later appear. But being divided against itself, and not utterly alienated from God's will (Vol. II. p. 367), it does not necessarily follow that its derangement must show itself in a fall and an ever-increasing alienation. By a divine order, which is at the same time a plan of grace, presenting to him the conditions of self-restoration, man is brought into the narrow path of earthly development, and is given a law. The pure innocence of his earthly nature, which as yet knows nothing of disorder, makes obedience easy, and within him a divine impulse and the voice of conscience prompt him to submission to the will of God. He must in any case become conscience of a variance within, through the vacillating conflict between contrasted forces; but he may come off victorious in this conflict, and by the habitual practice of

marginal note: Import of man's temporal probation and fall.

---

* *Glaubenslehre*, § 72, 6 (vol. i. p. 445). ROTHE (*Ethik*, ii. p. 216) essentially agrees with Schleiermacher in recognizing the fact itself, and the reason of it.

THE ORIGIN OF INBORN SINFULNESS.

humble obedience he may heal his own heart.* Rothe, when speaking of man's primitive condition, lays stress upon the absence of any educational influence;† and we agree with him so far as this, that we cannot imagine a harmoniously progressive moral development without some such tutelage from beings possessing a mature knowledge of moral relations. If such educational influence was necessary to a pure moral development, instead of inferring that our first parents could not help sinning, we should rather conclude that God's holy love must in some manner have given them this guidance. Human instrumentality is not the only means of instruction, nor can we infer the want of tutelage from the silence of the book of Genesis about it, for no one can regard its account as a full and complete exhibition of man's original state.

The first Adam then might have become in a limited measure what the second Adam really is in the highest sense, the originator of a development liberating the will from its original variance, provided that he had transmitted to his posterity a sensuous nature untainted by sin, and an example of faithful obedience. But he never could have become this had not his obedience to God's will been tested by temptation, and been victorious over the selfish tendency of his own will. This testing element was provided by a positive command given in the form of a prohibition. In itself, the command of God is really a temptation to good, a call to a conscious submission of our will to His; and yet it cannot but awaken the dormant element of self-will to the end that it may be overcome. But as an excitant to evil necessitating a determinate choice, the temptation could come only from a being in whom evil was already present, and who discerned the hidden discord in our first parents between their actual constitution and their divided will. The serpent in Eden, mentioned in Genesis, undoubtedly means a real serpent. It is spoken of as one of the beasts of the field (Gen. iii. 1), and the curse pronounced upon it

Man's temptation.

The Serpent.

---

* While we hold that it was thus possible for our first parents, before the fall, gradually to have freed their wills from the effects of the extra-temporal decision, it by no means follows that this is possible for their posterity, who from the commencement of their earthly life are affected with a depraved naturalness, a physical and psychical derangement, which is the result of Adam's fall.

† *Ethik*, vol. ii. 213.

alludes entirely to its animal nature. And yet statements are made concerning it which cannot be referred to an animal. It seems inconsistent to infer from the subtilty of its words —blending together truth and falsehood with the most refined deceit (verses 1, 4, 5)—that it is not an animal who speaks, and yet to attribute these words to the serpent as the unconscious and involuntary instrument of an intelligent Being.* Internal difficulties beset either theory, that which regards the serpent as an intelligent nature, and that which regards him as merely the instrument of an intelligent nature; the narrative itself does not give the slightest hint that the serpent's words proceed from demoniacal inspiration, indeed, it seems to exclude this supposition, for the curse pronounced (verses 14, 15) is solely applicable to the serpent as an animal, and cannot be explained as if the serpent were a mere tool of Satan, by making it refer to the curse pronounced upon nature generally, or to the slaying of animals who had participated in human sin as enjoined by the Mosaic law. An animal may have to suffer through its dynamical connection with man, because he has committed sin, but this is very different from inflicting a punishment upon an animal "because it has done" something (verse 14), wherein, moreover, it is said to have been only the involuntary instrument of a higher power. The notion, finally, that the speaking of the serpent was a miracle wrought by the devil—apart from the question whether it be reconcilable with the true conception of a miracle—has nothing analagous to it in the whole of Scripture, and there is not a syllable in the narrative itself intimating that it was a miracle.

It rests with theology to analyse the symbolic elements which have gathered round this narrative in the progress of oral tradition, and out of which it has been woven into its present form; and if this cannot be done by means of grammatical and philological criticism, theological considerations and doctrines must be brought to bear upon it.

The being who, by his superior intelligence excites the evil latent in man to action, and thus brings upon him "death and all our woe," can be none other than Satan. That he is meant by the serpent in Genesis is evident not only from the apocryphal book of Wisdom (chap. ii. 24), but also from statements in the New

<small>Satan the tempter of man to sin.</small>

* HENGSTENBERG, *Christologie des A. T.* (2d ed.) vol. i. 5–7.

Testament, viz., indirectly in Rom. xvi. 20; 1 John iii. 8, and expressly in Rev. xii. 9. Christ's words are still more important ἐκεῖνος ἀνθρωποκτόνος ἦν ἀπ' ἀρχῆς, John viii. 44. The interpretation of this by Cyril of Alexandria, now defended by Nitzsch* and Lücke,† which takes ἀνθρωποκτόνος to refer to Cain's fratricide, is by no means so correct as the ordinary explanation, because it does not allow the ἀπ' ἀρχῆς its full force, ‡ and there is not the slightest reference to Satan as the instigator of Cain in the Mosaic narrative in Gen. iv. If, indeed, the death which ensued upon the Fall were only spiritual, we should have to adopt this reference of our Lord's words to Cain's murder; for there would be no such analogy between the Jews who wished to put Christ to death, and the devil who caused man's spiritual death, as that which Christ expresses in the words, "Ye are of your father the Devil,"—even taking into account the statement of 1 John iii. 15. But Genesis iii. (together with many New Testament references) represents physical, not spiritual, death as the effect of the fall. Heb. ii. 14 also, where the Devil is called " him that hath the power of death," refers to physical daath, as is evident from the connection of the expression with Christ's death, and from the words immediately following, which describe the effect of the fear of death in man. It is, therefore, most natural with Hengstenberg, Tholuck, and Krabbe,§ to take ἀνθρωποκτόνος ἀπ' ἀρχῆς as referring to the Fall; and thus the reference of the serpent in Genesis to Satan is confirmed by our Lord Himself.

We do not agree with Schleiermacher when he denies that a self-perversion of the will, beginning wholly from itself, is possible, and consequently that the fall could have been the first beginning of sin.∥ Still there is really nothing in the narrative obliging us to consider the fall as the primary beginning of sin in the strict sense of the word. We have

Derangement of man's nature produced by the fall.

---

* See the Dissertation on the subject—*theol. Zeitschrift von* SCHLEIERMACHER, DE WETTE, *und* LUCKE, part iii. p. 52.

† *Kommentar. zum Ev. Joh.*, vol. ii. 340.

‡ This inadequacy in CYRIL'S explanation is strikingly illustrated by the parallel expression in 1 John iii. 8, ἀπ' ἀρχῆς ὁ διάβολος ἁμαρτάνει, to which THOLUCK directs attention in his Commentary on John's Gospel, *in loc.*

§ *Die Lehre von der Sünde und vom Tode*, 133.

∥ *Glaubenslehre*, i. 430, 432.

already shown (p. 353) that neither the "image of God" wherein man was created, nor God's pronouncing everything "very good," prevents our believing that the fall was only the outward manifestation of a perversion of the will preceding the empirical life of man,—the outgo of an evil already present *in potentia*, which might, indeed, by persevering effort, have been crushed, but which forms the basis of an original moral depravity in human nature. The endeavour of the Tempter was to bring out to view, and into action, this hidden evil. He therefore suggests in the woman's mind a doubt regarding the true import of God's command. And when the woman, in her reply, shows a true understanding of the command, and names the fear of death as the motive preventing disobedience, the master in the art of equivocation denies that this punishment will surely come upon man; and then, as if hinting that jealousy prompted the divine prohibition, he tells her that the effect of disobedience will be a good, the charm of which was well adapted to elicit the hidden selfishness of the will,—"Ye shall be as gods, knowing good and evil." This argument, according to the account in Genesis, was decisive; man fell through coveting undue self-exaltation. It is impossible to say whether any sensuous motive, prompting to disobedience, was blended with this, as Gen. iii. 6 seems to intimate; for we have already limited the historic character of the narrative, and recognized the tree with its fruit to be only a symbol.

The immediate object of the entire narrative is to explain the origin of *evil in general*, and not of sin; and hence nothing is told us regarding the moral consequences of the first sin. Adam's attempt to put the blame upon Eve, and indirectly upon God himself (verse 12), seems to imply that further sins had immediately followed the first act of disobedience. Candidly considering, however, the uncertainty attaching to the interpretation of the text, it is very difficult to decide what is symbolic clothing and what is real fact. But the divine sentence pronounced, verses 16-19, does not threaten man with a life and labour which he must regard as his own perverted doing and guilt, but with sufferings inflicted upon him —sorrow, pain, and death. Considering, however, the following facts,—considering that the dominion of death over man indicated a disorder in his physical and psychical life,—that this disordered state is distinct from the original perversion of the will,—that it manifestly exists in man,—that it is hereditary, and is traceable as a general law from our first parents, as St Paul says, Rom. v. 12 (δι' ἑνὸς ἀνθρώπου ἡ ἁμαρτία εἰς τὸν κόσμον εἰσῆλθε, see p. 344),—we cannot doubt that the fall involved a corruption of the physical and psychical life of our first parents—a derangement of its original harmony, which they transmitted by generation to their descendants, and these again to their posterity.

This derangement, as a naturally depraved constitution, is the same in all, though it is infinitely modified and individualized in the various races, nationalities, and families of mankind. A previous examination has shown us (p. 286) wherein it consists. It is a derangement of the bodily and mental powers ; " a tendency in the sensuous nature to suppress the promptings of the spirit, and to rebel against its holy dictates." This is variously manifest, but it is ever present as a depraved disposition, *i.e.*, HEREDITARY SIN, properly so called ; it is deeply-rooted in every human life, and co-determines its character.

We may now answer the question whether or not hereditary sin is alike in all men. Aquinas thus expresses himself on this :—*Originale peccatum cum sit privatio originalis justitiae in omnibus oppositum habitum penitus tollens, non magis in uno quam in alio esse potest.** While Aquinas thus argues from the very conception of original sin, that it must be the same in all, Limborch argues its inequality from experience. Children are in general, he says, liable to the sins of their parents; and the tendency to sin in them moulds itself according to the temperament inherited. Hence he concludes that children derive their sinful dispositions not so much from Adam as from their parents.†

Is original sin alike in all men?

Now we must allow (as we have already seen) that the particular forms which hereditary depravity assumes differ in different individuals. But it is no less obvious that underlying these varieties there is a COMMON DEPRAVITY, unvarying and universal. An

Specifically the same in all.

---

* *Summa*, ii. i. qu. 82, art. 4.
† *Theologia Christiana*, lib. iii. c. iii. § 4.

essential sameness is traceable amid all variations; the one plain fact of the preponderance of the sensuous impulses which (though assuming different forms that often disguise and hide it) is never absent in any human being born into this world according to the course of nature: and this fact unmistakably leads us back to a derangement affecting the race from the very commencement, and specifically the same in all. Whatever influence the parents have as instruments in the progressive generation of the species, they are not the authors of the sinful disposition which they transmit; they do not create the derangement, but only individualize it—and even this not always, but sometimes almost imperceptibly. Limborch's words, therefore, *Propensionem ad peccandum . . . habent non tam ab Adamo quam a proximis parentibus* are untenable.

Granting, however, that all naturally born are alike tainted with hereditary sin, it is still an open question whether this sinfulness, specifically the same in all, has not different degrees of strength in different individuals.

Yet varying in degree.

We find this to be the case obviously in the developed life of men. We find that the settled influence of the sensuous nature in its herediary inordinateness upon the moral life, is in some cases weakened not only by the divinely implanted energies of the new life, bnt by discipline and law, and even by evil itself—*i.e.*, by its intellectual power springing from another source. In other cases we find that it exerts an uncontrolled dominion. But we are now speaking of the evil disposition as inborn.

How it is in this respect we can discover by experience alone. And experience testifies that hereditary depravity clings to different individuals in different degrees. In proportion as sinfulness increases, succeeding races suffer for the crimes of their predecessors; whole families, nations, and races degenerate, and this degeneracy is apparent in the augmented power of sensuous impulses, and in the reckless passion which governs them. This degeneracy is transmitted in its enhanced form by generation; and it cannot be explained as merely a different form or tendency of the sensuous impulse in the same degree of strength. There can be no doubt that the hereditary depravity of human nature in the races immediately following Adam was not so strong as in subsequent generations; it gradually increased until at length God Himself put bounds to it, and checked it.

The degree of inborn depravity depends on the character of the parents. The strength of this inborn sinfulness depends, therefore, upon the moral character of the parents, to the extent, at least, already explained. As we have already seen, the personal moral character of the individual tends to lessen the derangement of the nature. But this seems to endanger the universality of hereditary sinfulness. The subjugation of the sensuous impulses (it is said) may be so successfully accomplished through the moral character of the parents, that at last inborn sinfulness may be completely eradicated, and the normal condition of human nature restored. This might indeed be the result if the depravity of nature, which secretly and unconsciously works in generation, were completely destroyed by sanctification.* But it is not so; it is only suppressed and subdued; it still remains concealed in the depths of the heart, though for years it has been overcome: and the sanctified man has only to indulge in the feeling of self-security in order again to fall a prey to the very propensities which seemed for ever subdued. Even regenerate parents, therefore, transmit to their offspring this inner derangement, which is the distinctive characteristic of human nature, and which cannot utterly be destroyed; though, together with this, they transmit those virtuous impulses and counteracting limitations which they have cultivated themselves. In every one equally is found that inner variance of will which results from the extra-temporal and intelligible self-decision of freedom. The derangement of the *aequale temperamentum qualitatum animæ et corporis* varies greatly, both in kind and degree, in different individuals.† The argument by

---

* See on this side of the question THOLUCK's remarks in the *Literar. Anzeiger*, 1834, No. 23, 178. AUGUSTINE often touches upon it—especially *De pecc. mer. et rem.*, lib. ii. c. 11, and *Contra Jul. Pel.*, lib. vi. c. 18. See also AQUINAS *Summa*, ii. i. qu. 81, art 3.

† See REINHARD, *Vorles. über die Dogmatik*, p. 311. BAUMGARTEN's opinion, to which THOLUCK refers (*Evangel. Glaübenslehre*, ii. 575), is confused, because he confounds the two ideas, *kind* and *degree*. WEISMANN, also, when opposing the Arminian extreme in his *Instit. theol. exeg. dogm.*, pp. 411, 425, touches upon this question as to the sameness in all of original sin, but does not sufficiently distinguish the different elements blended in hereditary sinfulness,—those which are inborn and those which are acquired in process of development.

which Aquinas supports his statement, that there are no degrees in original sin, shows that he has in his mind a merely privative conception of what that sin is.*

This derangement of man's sensuous, in its relation to his spiritual nature, must not be regarded as a punishment inflicted by God on account of the fall. Several of our older theologians, as we have already seen (p. 330), thus regard it. They consider that Gen. ii. 17 implies this, for they take the death there threatened to be spiritual death. But even if this were correct, which it is not (see p. 291), it would not necessitate our regarding this spiritual death as produced by a positive and punitive act on God's part, and not in any degree as the natural consequences of the fall. It could be God's positive act only as His withdrawment of original righteousness from Adam and his posterity, who (on the theory of immediate imputation) fell with him;—this withdrawment necessarily involving depravation of nature.† But even with this explanation the notion of moral corruption being divinely implanted in human nature, directly or indirectly, seems to contradict the principle that God cannot be the author of evil; and if His withdrawment of original righteousness is necessarily followed by human depravity, the one is the cause of the other. It is quite unnecessary, however, to suppose any positive act on God's part. It is easy to see how the revolt of the will against the divine command is itself enough to produce a weakening of its moral power, and a proportionate dominance of the sensuous nature.

Relation of inborn sinfulness to the Fall.

This depravity of human nature, therefore, was the necessary consequence of the fall in our first parents, and was transmitted by them to their descendants by ordinary generation. It also

---

* Our earlier theologians include in original sin not only the want of original righteousness, but the positive element of inordinate desires, and hence they might—without detriment to their belief that all sins springing from original sin are equally mortal sins—have admitted this distinction of degree. See QUENSTEDT, as before, sec 2, qu. 13. As far as I am acquainted with their works, however, they do not touch upon this question.

† See the *Formula Concordiæ, Solida Dec.*, art. i. pp. 643, 644. *Cum seductione Satanae per lapsum justo Dei judicio in poenam hominum justitia concreata seu originalis amissa esset, defectu illo . . . . humana natura . . . . perversa et corrupta est, ut jam natura una cum illo defectu et corruptione ad omnes homines . . . . haereditario propagetur.*

led to the reign of death; because the gradual development of man's natural life onwards to perfection was interrupted by the sin of our first parents, and by the derangement consequent thereupon of the due balance between the spiritual and sensuous nature. Adam's posterity, moreover, inherit this deranged constitution, because it is in perfect keeping with the moral condition of their will previous to their birth in time.*

Theories as to the origin of human souls. The famous question concerning the origin of individual souls here presents itself, and must be answered according to the principles here developed. If in the TRADUCIAN theory the *tradux* is not a mere continuance of a soul already existing, if the progressive and newly creative principle operative in generation be recognized, and if thus the preposterous notion of a dividing of souls, which the name of the theory seems to sanction, be excluded, there is nothing to prevent our giving our assent to its main principle. All generation of beings endowed with souls is really a generation of souls, calling into existence not only a new life in the physical sphere, but a new psychical principle in the sphere of humanity, and a basis for a determinate individuality. The productive activity of the species is the vital cause of the introduction of new individuals, and the agents of this activity (the *sine qua non* of its productiveness) are the parents, who, according to their individuality, exert a co-determining influence upon the life generated, both as to soul and body. The scholastic theology rejected the Traducian theory concerning the origin of individual souls, through fear that it would lead to materialism. But by its Creatianism it fell into a worse materialism than it thought to avoid. For as it did not deny hereditary sin, and recognized the soul as the seat of sin, it could not help maintaining that souls created by God, in a state of purity, were immediately polluted by union with the embryo body. Thus the material body was made the determining principle, and the soul the merely passive principle.†

---

* Compare with these conclusions what has been said, Vol. I. 150-160, as to the relation of sin in the sensuous nature to its inner spiritual principle.

† This appears very plainly in LOMBARD, *Sentent.* lib. ii. dist. 31, *b.* Some of the Schoolmen, *e.g.*, HUGO of Rouen, in order to avoid this inference, expressly assert the perfect freedom of every soul, and its capability to resist

It is impossible, however, to explain in the same manner the origin of immortal personality in the individual. No mere process of nature could give being to what is distinct from, and above nature,—the spiritual principle in man. Personality, as such, proceeds at the commencement of its temporal existence from its own extra-temporal basis, and the process of nature simply furnishes the basis of its temporal development. This, of course, involves the belief in a theory of pre-existence, but not a temporal and actual *prae existentia* of the soul previous to its life on earth.* We need not prove here what has already been shown (p. 147), that this theory of pre-existence is widely different from any doctrines of emanation or of Pantheism, and that it recognizes Creatianism as its principle.†

§ 6. BEARING OF SCRIPTURE AND THEOLOGY UPON OUR THEORY.

We have thus endeavoured clearly and logically to expound the thoughts which furnish an adequate solution (as we hold) of the problem concerning the origin of sin, as proved in the previous book, and the universality of sin as demonstrated in the present book; and we leave it to the reader who agrees with us in the principles and conclusions from which we started, and which are stated in Book I., to determine for himself whether he can recognize those thoughts as correct and true, or whether he can suggest a better solution of the problem.

the incitations to sin arising from the depraved body. But this is really a surrender of the explanation of sin's universality by hereditary sin; and according to the recognized principle that the soul is the seat of sin, it is virtually a denial of hereditary sin altogether.

* We cannot, therefore, infer anything concerning this pre-existence of the soul from pyschological phenomena often referred to in proof of the doctrine as otherwise held; least of all can we make use of the strange phenomenon that occasionally, when something very trifling perhaps occurs, which cannot have happened to us before, we feel for the moment as if we had witnessed or experienced it before.

† The view of AQUINAS, which DANTE adopts in the *Divina Comedia*, resembles ours in some respects. According to AQUINAS, the *anima sensitiva* is formed by generation, but not the *anima intellectiva*, ("*haereticum est eam traduci ex semine*"), which is created directly by God.—*Summa*, p. i. qu. 118, art. 1, 2. By very ingenious arguments, he endeavours to harmonize this with his doctrine or the guilt of the race in Adam, according to which the subject of depravity is the *anima rationalis seu intell.* See *Prima Secundae*, qu. 81, art. 1 (especially in his answer to the second objection), and qu. 83, art. 1, in the answer to objections 3 and 4.

We have endeavoured to prove, as we proceeded in our argument, that this view, in its main points, is in harmony with the teaching of Holy Scripture. The testimony of Scripture fails us in one fundamental principle of our view,—viz., that concerning the extra-temporal self-deciding of created personalities; but this amounts only to the fact that it is not directly stated in Holy Scripture. Holy Scripture was not intended to give us speculative knowledge; and experience abundantly testifies that it only hinders the fair interpretation of Scripture when the effort is made at all hazards to confirm, by isolated texts and Scripture phrases, what theological investigation has speculatively thought out.* For the sake of historic fidelity on the one hand, and of free thought and philosophy on the other,—above all, for the sake of scientific honour and integrity, it would be well if each department and mode of procedure were kept distinct. Apostolic development of Christian doctrine fulfils one purpose, systematic and speculative theology another. The religious teaching of the Apostles ever has to do with practical Christian life and consciousness, and it by no means derogates from its high prerogative to suppose that there is a speculative element of which it takes no cognizance, but in which Christian truth, if thoroughly thought out, finds its only adequate solution. All that we need prove—and this has been abundantly shown—is that this speculative element does not contradict Holy Scripture, and, moreover, that what Holy Scripture does teach, whether of fact or doctrine, implies and leads on thereto.

This applies to what we may call the *theologoumenon* which we have developed, of an extra-temporal aversion of our own will from God. And yet this theory would contradict Holy Scripture if it derived inborn sinfulness *solely* from this extra-temporal act of the individual, without recognizing in this

---

* In former times, and again in our own day, the words of the Apostle Paul, Rom. ix. 11, in reference to Jacob and Esau before they were born, have been taken to imply their pre-existence, and it has been argued that the reason of the preference, "Jacob have I loved," &c., was based upon their different behaviour in that pre-existent state. But this is a false interpretation, and contradicts the obvious aim of the Apostle in his argument. But it would be equally unfair to argue *against* the principle of an extra-temporal decision, from the words μηδὲ πραξάντων τι ἀγαθὸν ἢ κακόν, for this supposed decision, being the same in all men, cannot in the least affect the argument of the passage.

sinfulness the element of hereditary depravity in the sphere of natural life, and its connection with the sin of our first parents, as St Paul has stated it in Rom. v. 12-19. But such a contradiction of Holy Scripture would be at the same time a contradiction of the most obvious experience. The simple exhibition of our view shows that it is quite free from this twofold objection.

Let us now consider how it stands in relation to the authoritative Symbols and expositions of early Protestant theology. The difference is at once apparent. Protestant theology does not recognize an ideal or intelligible basis for sinful development in time. It even excludes it, for it traces natural sinfulness in all its branches to Adam's fall alone.* And this is not merely an opinion or inference developed from the orthodox theology, it is the definitely expressed conviction of the Reformers themselves, of Luther, Melanchthon,† and Calvin. And as they have insisted upon it in their works, it has been adopted in the Confessions of the Evangelical Church—on the part of the LUTHERAN branch of it in the Smalcaldian Articles (part iii. art. 1) and in the *Formula Concordiae* (art. 1),—and on the part of the REFORMED Church in the *Confess. Basileensis* (1534, art. 2), in the Westminster Confession (art. 3), in the Belgic Confession (art. 15), and in the Heidelberg Catechism (question 7). Still the chief Confession of the Evangelical Church, the *Confessio Augustana*, states this doctrine with such wise reserve that different doctrinal theories, including

Its relation to the creeds and theology of the Lutheran Church.

---

* BAUR, in his *Lehrbuch der Dogmengeschichte*, p. 272, says regarding my "theological theory," that while it is "quite a failure," it is nevertheless constructed out of hypotheses "which sound as if they were orthodox." I have, it would seem, unnecessarily troubled myself to show that this "theological theory" is, strictly speaking, heterodox, and it would be a great pleasure to me to know the articles of the orthodox system with which it "accords." Perhaps nothing was more in keeping with the style of argumentation which that school adopts than the suspicion that I have been aiming throughout at the mere appearance of orthodoxy.

† A remarkable expression of Melanchthon's, at the close of his life, shows that he felt the pinch of the Church Dogma on original sin. On a paper, written only a few days before his death, he notes the question, *Cur simus sic conditi?* as one of the *mira arcana* which we cannot thoroughly know in this life, but which we shall know hereafter. The dogma concerning original sin logically affords no solution of Melanchthon's question, whether we understand it of the creation of the race in Adam, or of the creation of individuals.

the one which we have here developed, may be reconciled with it.* The *Apologia Confessionis* likewise, in its first Article, which is drawn up with great care and precision, contains nothing to exclude the theory of man's inborn sinfulness having an extra-temporal source.

Our theory should not expect, and need not desire more from Church Confessions than this negative sanction which leaves it open for theology scientifically to explain fundamental doctrines. Suppose for a moment that the Reformers had recognized the principle of our view as a link in the chain of theological knowledge;—they had too clear a perception of the province and the limits of public doctrinal tradition in the Church to have allowed its admission into any Confession. It is altogether wrong for Theology to foster esoteric doctrines involving principles either at variance with the fundamentals of Christian tradition, or that give to those fundamentals a meaning quite other than that which an honest historical interpretation assigns to them. By such a course the servant of the Church becomes an adept in lying, and learns systematically to undermine that which he is solemnly pledged to build up. But if the proposed *theologoumenon* confirms the settled doctrine of the Church according to its true import, and so supplements and completes it as to harmonize its apparent antinomies, and to solve the problems it suggests, then its *esoteric* character is perfectly justified. Nay, if Protestant theology itself will not exclude every speculative element— and it can hardly do this without excluding its very heart and soul—its very theology itself—it must contain within its range doctrines of an esoteric character. Speculative theology will unavoidably produce the greatest confusion even where it is in perfect harmony with experimental consciousness, if it tries to popularize itself by inaccurate statements which tear the thoughts from their proper connection; rightly to understand it there must be a degree of philosophical culture, for it belongs to the Schools rather than to the Church.

* Art. 2 : *Docent, quod post lapsum Adae omnes homines secundum naturam propagati nascantur cum veccato, hoc est, sine metu Dei, sine fiducia erga Deum, et cum concupiscentia, quodque hic morbus seu vitium originis vere sit peccatum damnans et afferens nunc quoque mortem aeternam,* &c. It may be regarded as a happy reservation that the *post lapsum Adae* was not augmented to a *propter.*

If we be asked how the Church in her doctrinal teaching is to act in reference to the speculative theory which we have here propounded, we have only to refer to the example of Holy Scripture which Christian teaching must ever keep close to. Neander, in his exposition of the Pauline doctrine, observes that the Apostle, in his Epistles (with the exception of a very few passages), wisely develops man's need of redemption directly from the consciousness of sin as a universal fact of human experience, without tracing its origin further.* According to this example, let the popular teaching of Christian doctrine hold fast by that consciousness which every one who acknowledges the law of God may, nay, must, experience within himself, and it will ever represent the discord in our nature not as an evil for which we are not accountable, but as our guilt, and the guilt of every man. When, again, like the Apostle, it has to enter upon the more exact development of the doctrine of sin, and has to explain our dependent connection with preceding generations, and ultimately with the progenitors of our race, let our teaching keep fast hold of the principle of individual guilt. It will not certainly escape the notice of a thoughtful Christian that there is a seeming contradiction between two truths which sound doctrine obliges him equally to maintain, viz., between sinfulness as an inborn constitution of our nature, and the personal guilt of the individual. But scientifically he may learn that religion does not end with this contradiction, for it recognizes its solution in the extra-temporal basis of created personality. As far as popular teaching goes, this seeming contradiction is the ultimatum; because scientific and speculative knowledge cannot be popularized. In this sphere, therefore, the union of the two seemingly contradictory truths must be treated as a mystery. But if the ordinary understanding refuses to bow before a mystery, the depths of which the most earnest, thoughtful, and patient inquiry confesses that it cannot fully fathom, it will assuredly bring upon itself the punishment of its pride, by falling into the most pitiable shallowness and crudeness in its apprehensions of sin.

---

* NEANDER'S *Planting and Training of the Church*, German Ed., p. 666; Bohn's Ed., p. 422.

APPENDIX TO BOOK IV.

Summary of arguments for a non-temporal choice.

THE derivation of the *peccatum originale* from a fall preceding man's temporal life has met with so much opposition from the highest quarters that I feel myself compelled to add a few remarks, not in the hope of winning over opponents, but in order more distinctly to state the argument.

I have no romantic wish to offer solutions of this great mystery of our being, which will only involve us in further mysteries. If any one can suggest an easier and more conformable explanation — an explanation which views man simply as existing within the bounds of time, and enables us to comprehend his guilt—he will find me a ready listener. But the explanation must be one which does not surrender the truths to be explained. These truths are, on the one hand, the universality of sin in the human race, its deep-rooted presence in the very nature of the species; and on the other hand, personal guilt and responsibility, the origin of sin from the wilful self-perversion of the creature, and not from any necessity, whether freely ordained by the divine intelligence, or existing apart from God. If at any time writers are called to a moral discipline of their thoughts, they are so now. The evil which chiefly threatens us is not political weakness or uncertainty, pauperism or the labouring classes, but the silent sapping and undermining of the moral foundations of human life, which has been carried on secretly for the past ten years, and which now, by a blow from without, even shows itself on the surface. The discipline of thought of which I speak implies chiefly that no place be given to those opinions which would deny man's accountability, to those speculative or non-speculative theories of Determinism which would make excuses for man on account of sin. As for that "logical enthusiasm" which blindly resolves to adopt every conclusion to which its system leads, whether it make the voice of conscience a liar, or the distinction between good and evil a delusion, it is vexation of spirit and ruin; science finds its justification in moral principles alone. The reasons which have led me to seek the origin of sin in an ideal or intelligible self perversion of free-will, I have already stated as clearly and simply as I can. They are chiefly summed up in those contradictory facts of our moral consciousness above stated. Whatever defects there may be in my explanation, however little it may settle of what is undetermined in that transcendental basis of our temporal existence, however many questions it may leave unanswered, I cannot give it up until another explanation which more fully satisfies the facts be offered. If other theories lead to a denial of those facts, I can only regard them as indirect confirmations of the explanation here presented.

Rothe's criticism of our view.

ROTHE, in his *Ethics* (vol. ii. 222-224), takes exception to my view, and thinks that, on his own principles, he can maintain the true conception of guilt,—which he intimates that I have somewhat exaggerated (p. 220). Wherein does my exaggeration of it consist? As far as I can see, Rothe himself agrees with the views of guilt given in this work (Vol. I. 193 *seq.*), and with the conclusions to which our investigations concerning freedom led us in the first two chapters of Book III. (compare *Ethik* ii. 203 ; i. 175). The chief point, according to my view, is to regard man as the real author of that which ought not to be in his acts or condition, on account of which he finds that he is excluded from fellowship with God and liable to punishment. If he be not the real author of his acts and of his state, this exclusion and punishment seem to me inconceivable. ¡But man is not the responsible author of what is wrong in him, if he is logically and unavoidably involved in sin through the progressive development of finite beings. He is in this case only the pitiable instrument whereby sin realizes itself ; God cannot hold him guilty, because His creative power has ordained sin as a necessity in the natural man, inasmuch as the creature cannot pass "from the mere animal to the truly spiritual man," without going through the intermediate stage of the natural or sinful man still encumbered with matter (*Ethik* ii. 216, 217). It avails nothing to remind us of the statement in p. 215, that "the possibility of an actual resistance of evil is always coincident with its entrance into man, so that his consenting to it implies real sin." For while Rothe sets out with the recognition of the universality of actual sinning as an incontrovertible fact which his theory is to explain, he also affirms the unavoidableness of sin ; and if sin's unavoidableness is to be granted, and at the same time sin's universality to be explained, Rothe must allow that the resistance of sin, which he supposes possible, and man's consenting to its yoke, are really nothing more than the *form* in which the necessity of sin realizes itself in the progress of human development, and cannot be any argument or proof of an independent decision on man's part. Sin, being an inward *habitus* in man, must now show itself in sinful acts ; how then could the moment when the knowledge of sin arises nullify, as if at a stroke, the power of the sinful state to manifest itself in sinful act ? Rothe also, at p. 229, limits man's personal guilt and responsibility (in a very untenable manner) to his own sinful acts ; and yet in other places he allows that "evil necessarily maintains its dominion over man," p. 215, and that "man when affected by a sinful tendency, if he cannot evercome it, has only to yield reluctantly to it, as if momentarily vanquished, in order to realize it in action ; and when he decides upon any morally abnormal action, he has only to direct his whole endeavour to an action as little as possible abnormal in order really to commit it." This view of the relation between a sinful state and a sinful act is certainly more correct than that given in the statements quoted above ; but when Rothe himself allows that evil, so far as it is unavoidable, "cannot subjectively be called sin, nor as yet involve guilt" (p. 214), he surely cannot fail to see that whether we look at the state or the act it is altogether uncertain and doubtful how far we are to consider ourselves guilty on account of the morally abnormal elements of our life, and how far we are to regard them as sufferings imposed upon us and beyond our control.*

It seems as if Rothe himself could not avoid the feeling that the weak point in his theory is its not fully recognizing the element of guilt in sin.

* See the remarks already made at the end of Book III., as to Rothe's view of the relation of sin to divine predestination.

Hence it is that he charges me with laying too much stress upon man's guilt in explaining the loathesomeness of sin. "All true abhorrence of evil," he says, "must be based upon its objective nature, and not upon the subjective relation of man to it. . . . That alone is true hatred of evil which condemns and abhors it because it is evil, *i.e.*, because it is diametrically opposed to God and to our own higher nature;—for this reason only is it to be abhorred, and not because it is blameworthy on our part or involves our gilt," pp. 214, 215. I cannot assent to these statements, because they separate things which are inseparable. Our abhorrence of evil, not of evil in the abstract, but so far as it is really in us—and this is the matter mainly treated of in this question—is utterly inseparable from our consciousness of guilt and penitence ; it is so because by virtue of the principle of free will, evil—as opposition of the creature's will against God's will—cannot be understood, unless this opposition have its root in the will of the creature himself. We firmly maintain the truth that no one can even think of this selfish resistance of the creature's will against the moral obligations of God's will without at the same time thinking of guilt. If we do separate—*per impossibile*—responsibility and guilt from moral evil, we have nothing left but natural evil and suffering ; and we may then dwell upon the horror of evil, but it will only be the horror with which we contemplate pestilence or poison—it will not be a moral abhorrence of moral evil. In this case the stronger our horror of sin in us and its ruinous power, the more terribly will the thought grate upon our consciousness that God who is holy love should in His purposes have laid upon that stage of being which we call man such an intolerable burden.

Rothe's view of sin inadequate.

Another dear friend, Dr DORNER, in a thorough review of this work, *Reuter's Repertorium,* 1845, vol. i. 156 ; ii. 140, considers that the main error of my views is that I argue "from an atomistic theory of personal consciousness, and overlook the collective consciousness of the species." He objects, therefore, against my conception of guilt, that it infringes upon an important truth of Christianity : —" Personal consciousness setting itself up for itself alone, apart from the species, and isolating itself from the sin and guilt of the species, seems (if regarded from a Christian standing-point), to be an inferior state of being, nay, to be itself sin" (p. 148). I cannot see how the view developed here can be charged with isolating personal consciousness from the sin and guilt of the species ; for both are distinctly recognized as the sad and universal possession of the species. But I certainly maintain that where there is real guilt, which the person has to answer for before God, it must have for its foundation a free self-decision of the individual, a self-perversion of the person's will. This conception of guilt is based upon Christianity (Vol. I. 238), and Dorner does not furnish any proof that Christianity is opposed to it. Perhaps—(as I might fairly conclude from the fact that my view of guilt, taken as isolation from the species, is called sin)—Dorner's proof is contained in his statement "the highest Christian form of the guilt-consciousness . . . identifies itself in all trust and love with the race and its common guilt" (p. 149). But we have here to do not with a characteristic of the species which it requires truth and love to recognize and appropriate, but one which

Dorner's Criticism.

attaches to us individually at all times, whether we are conscious of it or not. In order to recognize this common guilt we do not need to invoke the aid of fidelity and love towards the race, but the earnestness and candour of the moral judgment. If, on the other hand, we had to allow that the individual partakes of this common guilt through no act of his own, neither fidelity nor love would enable us to discover, in this participation, freedom, responsibility or personal guilt.

Judging from the above criticisms, we might naturally expect to find that Dorner recognizes the guilt of the individual in all its fulness, as implied in the common sinfulness of the species. Strange to say, we find the very opposite. "Man," he says, "does not with perfect consciousness and matured judgment come to the decision which is decisive as to his moral being and destiny until he beholds Christ" (p. 151). "There it is"—if man disdains Christ—"that we are to seek the decisive fall; all other sins are provisional, they decide nothing as yet concerning the man's real character; in themselves they are not damnable if they do not amount to disbelief of the Saviour." Dorner therefore demands as the basis of personal guilt a personal self-decision "distinct from the life of the species collectively," and this is to me (considering the importance I attach to the thoughts of this able critic) a very acceptable confirmation of my conception of guilt to which he objects. In what respect, then, do our views differ? Dorner recognizes in man's natural state no real guilt, no sin which condemns him before God, "but only preliminary sins," because he maintains that the conditions necessary to a personal self-decision do not occur till Christ is presented to the man—because until then the individual is connected with the race. I, on the contrary, cannot think so lightly of man, even apart from redemption and his contact with it, but must maintain that his sin involves real and damnable guilt. This it is which obliges me—in virtue of that axiom which we both allow—to look for a basis of self-decision beyond the range of that seemingly fettering connection of the individual with the sin and guilt of the species. I do not of course deny that the greatest sins are possible only in relation to Christ; but wherever there is a consciousness of the moral law in its boldest outlines, and of its obligation as unconditionally binding, there we have the necessary condition of actual guilt, and this the conscience of the natural man testifies. Can it be a matter of doubt whether this is in harmony with Holy Scripture? I need not quote the various texts which assert this very doctrine, nor the apostolic expositions which imply it, as, for instance, the first three chapters of the Epistle to the Romans. The great blessing which Christ offers to man is reconciliation and the forgiveness of sins, but that reconciliation and that forgiveness clearly presuppose the presence of real guilt.

Defect in Dorner's theory of sin.

It is, moreover, to me also a precious truth, that by virtue of the decree of divine love to redeem mankind through Christ, revealed in the gospel, no man is to perish on account of the sin of his natural state, unless he appropriates it afresh by despising Christ's gospel. This cannot be interpreted to mean that the sin of man's natural state does not imply personal guilt; it is a truth which follows from the universality of God's gracious purpose, and the universal applicableness of Christ's redemptive work. These truths do not at once cancel the guilt of past sin, for man must himself exercise appropriating faith; but they must be recognized in all their solemn earnestness and fulness, and they guarantee that this appropriation shall be made possible to every individual by the presentation to each of the Gospel of Christ.

Whoever, therefore, considers that a perverted self-decision preceding our temporal life is inconceivable, must at any rate maintain alike the UNIVERSALITY OF SIN and INDIVIDUAL GUILT, and must acknowledge the ANTINOMY still subsisting between these two principles (seeing that he assumes the position described above, p. 393, compare p. 359), until perhaps some one else shall offer a more satisfactory solution.

BOOK V.

THE AGGRAVATION OF SIN IN INDIVIDUAL LIFE.

§ 1. INTRO-
DUCTION.
THAT free decision of every personal individual which is the ultimate basis of universal depravity cleaving to man's temporal development, is both original and extra-temporal. But it is not absolute; for if it were it would exclude freedom from the sphere of man's empirical life. The investigations of the foregoing book (chap. i. in particular) have shown us this. In Book III., moreover, we found that there is nothing in our empirical existence, and its relation to that intelligible basis, to exclude freedom from its sphere, or to oblige us to look upon our present life as a state of absolute bondage, or a merely passive reflex of that intelligible and primary decision. A ray of freedom illumines our empirical life, though it be refracted in this medium; liberty manifests itself not only in a transcendental region, but in our present life, though here only partially and limitedly. But our life in time can be a manifestation of freedom in proportion only as freedom really has fair play in it, and as the extra-temporal self-decision so develops itself in it that the motive power of its development is *bona fide* a self-determining from the relatively undetermined. At the same time the will in its temporal decisions cannot destroy the principles which were decided by that original decision and by the fall of the race in Adam; this can only be accomplished by the saving power of Christ's Spirit, who overcomes both the original perversion of the will, and the corresponding discord between nature and spirit in man. All movement and decisions in the natural man's life are carried on within the limits of those principles. But there is still abundant room for very different moral

endeavours which may either limit or enhance the power of natural sinfulness. This involves the possibility of a growth in evil—an aggravation of its power—as the individual's development progresses; an increase implying not only an extension of sinful tendencies already present throughout their several spheres, but an inner aggravation, a weakening of those holy influences which man by nature experiences, notwithstanding the prevalence of sin.

An objective difficulty may suggest itself against the possibility of this enhancement of evil from the very conception of sin as we have already explained it. Every sin is essentially a violation of a practical never-failing truth, of the eternal truth of God's will in relation to man; sin, therefore, may be said to be unconditionally blameworthy. How then can there be any degrees in what is thus unconditionally blameworthy? In reply to this it must be remembered that the eternal truth binding upon man's will is a whole which includes many parts, and as a whole only does it bear the impress of *unconditional ;* its various parts partake of this character only as parts, and may, without any contradiction, be said to condition one another, and to vary in comparative importance (see Vol. I. p. 36). There is no contradiction, therefore, in supposing that all and every the sinful acts and states of man are unconditionally wrong and condemnable, being only different forms of that principle of evil which is the positive antithesis of good ; and yet, at the same time, that they vary in the degree of their blameworthiness, so that an aggravation of sin in the individual is possible.

We have now in this Fifth Book to consider more closely how this aggravation is realized.*

§ 2. GROWTH OF A PERMANENT STATE FROM ACTUAL SIN. The timeless and primary act wherein every human will decides itself begets a prevailing constitution, a moral state—that state wherein we all are born. At first it exists only as a latent potentiality, but it becomes actual upon the awakening of moral consciousness.

There are no sinful acts within the range of this life which

* These investigations are based upon the inquiry concerning the freedom of the will in moral development, Book III. Part i. chap. ii.

have anything like the same influence upon our moral constitution, but some may possess a like determining power in a less degree. Freedom is not a reckless power of the will to load itself with the most shameless crimes, and to relapse again after having committed them to the same state in relation to these crimes. The self-determining of the will becomes itself a settled state; the will contracts a bias to those sins which it assents to, and the element of desire in every sin as the motive of will becomes a prevailing power in the inner life, so that, when external temptations arise, the will of itself inclines to yield. Every kind of sin, being the fruitful source of suffering, contains a terrible abyss which the sinner ever tries to fill by new sins, but tries in vain, for he never finds its bottom.

The power of the divine order and law acts directly upon the wilfulness of man which resists it. Man rebels against the moral law, and God does not prevent, but man still is subject to the natural law of development, and necessarily falls into a settled order and habit in the progress of his sin. Without this order we could not conceive how man could ever be free from sin or attain to settled holiness. The disturbing element having once entered, it must show its true character, for only thus can it be thoroughly removed. As the heavy vapours rise from the earth and fill the air, and are gathered by the sun's beams into thunder clouds, in order that falling again as rain they may purify the atmosphere, so sin must attain a definite form in the life of man that it may be properly combated, and that the strife against it may be prosecuted onwards to a decisive and permanent conquest,—a conquest which is not in man's power if left to himself, but which may be accomplished through redemption, for "if the Son shall make you free, ye shall be free indeed," John viii. 36.

Influence of the divine order upon sin.

Every form of sin to which the will assents, has a tendency to strengthen itself within the man, and to spread, and the first sin will, as a rule, have a succession of similar sins in its

† ARISTOTLE (*Eth. Nicom.*, lib. iii. c. 7,—Bekker's edition, vol. ii. 113–115) shows how the ἕξις springs from the ἐνεργεῖν and the πράξεις in the case of evil as well as good, and how, when it has once been formed, it is no longer under our control (οὐ μὴν ἐάν γε βούληται, ἄδικος ὢν παύσεται καὶ ἔσται δίκαιος), and yet how its effects must be imputed to us and treated as ἑκούσιοι.

train, manifestly because it begins to form a habit in the life. We must, therefore, distinguish between causative sins and sins which are simple effects; though we cannot fail to see that this distinction depends only upon the preponderance of either characteristic. Those sins which are mainly causative, form the epochs of our development when new sin, or a new form of sin makes its appearance in the man's life, and so strengthens the power of sin within him. As, however, all sins, save the original extra-temporal decision, have other sins before them, they can be called causative only relatively,—this being their preponderating character. Sins which are mainly effects, caused rather than casual,—are those which proceed as natural consequences from the moral state, produced by the casual sins. As, however, they contribute somewhat to the strength and permanence of the moral state, they are only relatively effects.* But as the moral state from which they result is produced by causal sins, at least by the primitive sin preceding this life, conscience holds man guilty, not only for his acts, but for his moral state. It makes us chargeable with the very powerlessness of our will; and true repentance, though awakened perhaps by a single sin, will appropriate and mourn over the moral condition of our life as a whole as at variance, through our own fault, with the law of God.

Sins which are causal, and sins which are effects.

In order to understand the production of the sinful state by the sinful act, we must remember the influence which such an act must have upon our physical and psychical nature,—the realm of the unconscious and involuntary within us. It gives the reins to blind desires, and awakens an insatiable thirst. The sin, especially if it be the gratification of fleshly lust, fixes itself in the imagination; a prevailing tone of feeling and bias of the psychical life is formed, so that when bodily or mental energy in any definite employment ceases, evil inclination and

Influence of sinful acts upon our natural life.

---

* SCHLEIERMACHER makes a similar distinction in his *Glaubenslehre*, i. 419; but as to the bearing of this on his dogmatic view, see p. 318 of this volume. We find the same distinction in an interesting work, by the mystic NICOLAUS OF CABASILAS in the 14th century, περὶ τῆς ἐν χριστῷ ζωῆς, which GASS has published. In lib. ii. § 58, 59 of this work, sin is described as γεννωμένη καὶ γεννῶσα ὡς ἐν κύκλῳ. Ὅθεν συνέβαινε ἁμαρτίαν ἀτελεύτητον εἶναι τῆς ἕξεως μὲν τὰς ἐνεργείας ἀπογεννώσης, τῇ προσθήκῃ δὲ τῶν ἐνεργειῶν τῆς ἕξεως ἐπιδιδούσης.

seductive thoughts begin to work, and with the aid of sensation and imagination, lead on the soul easily and imperceptibly to the very threshold of the act; so that it is overcome, and consents before it has begun properly to reflect upon the nature of the act and all that it involves. This is the sphere, as we have already seen (p. 49, 50), wherein habit exercises its power in confining and strengthening sin.

Good and evil stand in opposite relations to formal freedom. What is good and holy, springing from love to God, is the normal truth of the human will, and in coinciding therewith, it has no outward restraint, no limitation or hindrance to its original freedom as a self-determining power; on the contrary, it has herein the highest confirmation. Holiness is, in fact, simply the realization of the formal freedom of the will; that freedom is fully satisfied, and thus passes on to real freedom. The more perfectly the will cleaves to what is good, the more does the man feel himself to be free and master of himself.

Bearing of holiness upon man.

Evil, on the contrary, is in its very nature man's enemy; it is alien to him and to all creatures, seeing that all have their being in God. Though assented to by freewill, it can only create bondage,* " whosoever," said Christ, "committeth sin is the servant of sin," (John viii. 34; compare 2 Peter ii. 19),† the tyranny to which the sinner yields himself takes him terribly at his word. There is but one way whereby formal freedom can become real freedom, and that is the way of holiness; all self-development in evil is self-entanglement, and its goal is utter slavery. Evil therefore ever abides man's enemy, though, as degeneracy advances, and man surrenders himself wholly to it, he ceases to be sensible of its antagonism. As in bodily disease, the cessation of pain is the sign that its power is complete, that the healthy organism no longer reacts against it; so in sin, which is the disease of the soul, man ceases to feel its thraldom when his better nature no longer protests against

Bearing of sin upon man.

---

* St. Paul, indeed, speaks, Rom. vi. 16, of a service of righteousness as well as of sin, but this is only because of the parallelism of the contrast; he simply intends to express the logical consistency with which each character follows the principle it has chosen, whether sin or righteousness, in life and action.

† AUGUSTINE, *Enchiridion*, c. 9 (xxx.): *libero arbitrio male utens homo et se perdidit et ipsum.*

BOOK V.] THE AGGRAVATION OF SIN IN INDIVIDUAL LIFE. 407

it. Its victory is then complete, and it carries man captive under its despotic sway. Yet though its antagonism to what is good and godlike does not directly cause him pain, he cannot help feeling that it sometimes drives him to the extreme of an insensible and half-animal existence, and sometimes drags him hither and thither amid conflicting appetites and passions.

Thus we are led to the conclusion which experience itself illustrates, that the development of sin, as well as of holiness in man, proceeds upon a law of gradual growth. However much one causative sin may involve, a single decision of the will is not enough completely and at once to deprave any one in whom good and evil are still conflicting powers. Though the downward course may be easier, and may lead more rapidly to its goal, it has, notwithstanding, its successive stages. Man could not (even if he wished) pass over them all as if at a bound, any more than he can, when a Christian, by a single resolve become a perfect saint. We may, indeed, imagine the (by no means unheard of) case of a man who has in some degree adopted holy principles, in despair perhaps on account of repeated falls, resolving in some dark moment to give himself over to the devil, and rushing thenceforward into a mad and reckless career of sin. Yet in spite of his horrible purpose, even such a man cannot rid himself of the stirrings of a better nature within him, until, by degrees, perseverance in his mad resolve brings about his utter obduracy.

<small>Law of development in holiness and in sin.</small>

Progress and persistency in evil, however, does not always require such inward movements of resolve. Man may be retained in his evil courses by outward circumstances as well as by his own purpose. The results of his freedom become fetters to his freedom; his choice becomes his fate. A lie, for instance, obliges the liar to lie more presumptuously; hatred awakens hatred in the object of it, and thus, in turn, creates a stimulus for itself. How often does a single act, a seeming weakness or inadvertence, involve its author, in spite of himself, in a labyrinth of sins! Malicious powers seize upon the dark thought hardly expressed, and at once weave out of it an invisible net, in which they entangle the

<small>Enthralling power of outward circumstances.</small>

will, and urge it on with irresistible force to sin;—the seduced falls into the power of the seducer, who knows how to use his satanic power,—after the first hesitating step in transgression, the door closes behind the lost one,—he finds himself compelled to cover crime with crime, and by new sins to strengthen and confirm the works which sin has produced.* One way of return there is, and at every point; but he only can find it who is willing to sacrifice himself—yea, his whole life—in order to save his soul. But while external circumstances connected with the act of sin control its further development, the inner continuity of the sinful state asserts itself, the power of circumstances may hasten the degeneracy, but the inner principle of will must still maintain its deciding power. And if the will does not keep pace in its yieldings to the force of circumstances, a contradiction is apparent between the man's outward derangement and his true moral state.

§ 3. THE DOCTRINE OF VARIOUS STAGES OF DEPRAVITY.

Our Protestant theology, in contemplating the variously modified relations in which the race by nature stands to sin, distinguishes various stages of corruption. Baumgarten must be looked upon as the author of this phase of doctrine,† for it is not to be found in our earlier theologians. But Baumgarten apprehends it in a different way from more recent writers. In contemplating man's state apart from redemption, and under the power of original sin, he distinguishes between a state of security and a state of servitude in the stricter sense, *i.e.*, of servitude realized and felt through the power of the law upon the man,‡ according to the Pauline view. Indeed, he refers to Romans vii. 5, 7-9 as descriptive of the

---

* Thus SHAKESPEARE, in his tragedy of *Macbeth* (act 3), traces with deep psychological insight the manner in which thought becomes sin, and sin leads to sin. GOETHE also, in his *Grosskophta* (a work whose ethical and tragical bearing is not sufficiently recognized), illustrates this fettering power of sin in the home relations of life, in the fate of the niece.

† *Evang. Glaubenslehre*, vol. ii. 579.

‡ It is explained thus in the Dissertation by LITSMANN, *De propagatione et gradibus peccati originalis*, § 54;—a Dissertation usually regarded as BAUMGARTEN'S, but not his, though written under his sanction.

former state.* His idea clearly is man's gradual development and training onwards to redemption ; the law working the sense of servitude in the man is παιδαγωγὸς εἰς Χριστόν ; this is clearly his idea, and he does not refer to man's sinful state in its gradual growth and enhancement. But the way in which these stages of depravity are usually classified by our later theologians, *e.g.*, by Reinhard,† implies a gradual growth of sin ;—the states of servitude, of security, of hypocrisy, of obduracy, are manifestly intended as successive steps in the growth of sin.

To understand the nature of this growth is our topic now.

Three stages of sin's growth. Reinhard clearly regards servitude as the first stage ; ‡ but this seems inaccurate, because the state of servitude is generally preceded by one of unthinking security. The state of hypocrisy, moreover, can hardly be regarded as a separate stage ; it is a feeling which is sometimes found in connection with the state of servitude, but which belongs to the state of obduracy ;— though even here it is not always to be met with. It therefore seems more correct to classify the successive stages thus : The *first* stage is that of relative unconsciousness of the antithesis between the individual's own life and the will of God. This stage includes, on the one hand, that extreme of comparative innocence wherein selfishness seems asleep, and on the other hand, that CARELESSNESS wherein selfishness bears sway, without any qualms of conscience being felt. The *second* stage is that of conscious discord, which cannot be overcome in the natural state by the man's own power ; this implies SERVITUDE in the narrower sense, namely, the knowledge that this state of heart is not a right one. The *third* stage—which ensues upon the second, if it lead not to redemption—is that of OBDURACY ;—of insensibility and

* Concerning the Pauline doctrine of the twofold servitude of the natural man, see NEANDER's *Planting and Training* (German Ed. 686). BAUMGARTEN does not refer to Rom. vii. 14 as descriptive of the state of servitude, but this is because, in common with our older theologians, he regarded that passage as descriptive of the conflict carried on in the regenerate.

† *Vorlesungen über die Dogm.*, p. 325. The successive stages are more correctly described by DÖDERLEIN (*Instit. theol. Christ.* ii. 9),

‡ *Status eorum, qui scientes meliora et probantes ita vi appetituum trahuntur ut deteriora sequuntur.*

callousness, arising from persevering neglect of the warnings of conscience.

Between the second and third stages, which seem rather far apart, we might introduce that condition which is referred to in Rev. iii. 15, LUKEWARMNESS, wherein the inner discord is apparently softened down by weakening the impulse towards holiness, so as to make it somewhat conformable with the moderated sway of the selfish principles. This stage is a sort of capitulation between the holy and the unholy. Though this state, however, is often a transition between servitude and obduracy, it is not sufficiently marked or universal to be made a distinct stage. Obduracy often ensues immediately upon the awakening of conscience, and without the intervention of lukewarmness.

Two difficulties suggest themselves in relation to the final stage, that of obduracy, which is represented in Scripture as a total insensibility to the warnings of conscience, and to the inner consciousness of God.* First, it is asked, whether this state is ever to be met with,—whether such a decided and prevailing opposition to the truth as leads to a condition of utter insensibility, be really conceivable. † It may at once be granted that Holy Scripture, in speaking of obduracy, does not always mean an utter deadness, but only such a suppression of moral and religious feeling as to imply a total disregard of divine calls and warnings, and an insensibility to their importance. Our inquiry, however, concerning the sin against the Holy Ghost will show that the awful state of utter deadness may be realized.

The final stage, that of obduracy.

The second difficulty relates to the fact that the Holy Scripture often attributes this obduracy to the divine efficiency :—*e.g.*, Ex. iv. 21, vii. 3, ix. 12 ; Deut. ii. 30 ; Jos. xi. 20 ; John xii. 40 (quoted from Isaiah vi. 9, 10) ; Rom. ix. 18, xi. 7. The common way of solving this difficulty used to be to explain this reference to divine agency as a Hebraism, by which the sacred writers simply meant to intimate that God permitted the obduracy to

Attributed in Scripture to God.

* This is implied in πωροῦσθαι, but σκληρύνεσθαι expresses a more positive resistance.

† Schleiermacher's objections against this idea of obduracy go to prove that it is inconceivable : see the *Glaubenslehre*, vol. i. 458.

take place. A candid interpretation cannot admit this explanation; neither, however, can it allow that Scripture represents God as the author of sin. We could never take such a view of the inspiration of the Apostles as to suppose that they wavered in their views, now representing man's obduracy as his own doing, and now attributing it to God—and this even in the same passage, *e.g.*, Rom. ix.-xi. We may be sure that their thinking and argumentation is consistent, and that what they say as to God's agency in man's obduracy is quite compatible with the ethical principles they maintain.

We must bear in mind (as has already been shown, Vol. I. 388) that all these passages take for granted a state of sin and guilt out of which obduracy springs. We have not here to do, therefore, with the creation of a sinful state, but simply with the development of a corrupt principle already in the heart. But this development is not only an outgo and manifestation of principles hidden within, but an actual growth in sin, a passing from bad to worse, from stage to stage, till obduracy is reached. Now, it is hard to believe that such a growth in sin could ever be brought about by God Himself. Such a thought is utterly incompatible with the holy purpose of God that sin shall be thoroughly vanquished. The difficulty, therefore, is not explained by any reference to the general law of development, to which sin is subject, by virtue of which each successive stage of sin involved in the man's first resolve, endeavours to assert itself, and fetters the will. The question is not as to the necessity wherewith sin matures and manifests its evil nature in spheres wherein it has once taken root, but as to its spread and its conquest of new spheres.

Holy Scripture very clearly intimates that we must not Examination attribute man's obduracy to God as its Author, as of texts. if He created in the human heart insusceptibility and opposition to His warnings. When in Isaiah vi. 10—a passage often quoted in the New Testament as descriptive of obduracy—when Jehovah says to the prophet, " Make the heart of this people gross, and make their ears heavy, and shut their eyes," the meaning clearly is, not that the prophet is actually and directly to produce these effects on the senses of the people, but that by his preaching of the truth he would produce these effects. And when Christ thanks His Father,

Matt. xi. 25, that He "has hidden His gospel from the wise and prudent," the reference is not to a direct working of God upon the heart to darken it, but to the natural result of the message given Him by the Father to proclaim, in its bearing upon the hearts of those who are wise and prudent. What He gives thanks for is, that it has pleased the Father to make known this Revelation in Christ in such 'a manner that it is hidden from those who think themselves wise, but is understood by the simple-minded ; compare 1 Cor. i. 21, 22. The obduracy of some must therefore be regarded as so far God's work, as it is the consequence of God's dispensations, and results from the revelations of His truth in history.

It is to be observed, moreover, that Holy Scripture never speaks of God's hardening men's hearts save in connection with His revelations through Moses or in Christ. And this shows us what is the real germ of obduracy, namely, the testing power of God's revelation, especially in Christ, which we have already indicated in the other passages we have quoted. No one can withdraw himself from the range and influence of God's revelations without altering his moral state. The idle indifference and disinclination which he shows towards it necessarily grows to positive dislike and a stolid closing of his heart against what is holy and Godlike. If a ray of this light falls upon a man, he cannot, as many would like to do, move out of its range with quiet ease and unconcern ; if he closes his heart to it, he goes on to bitterness and wrath against it.* The means of spiritual healing which the man has perseveringly rejected, not only fail of their saving power, but exercise a contrary influence. Christ has Himself expressed this law in those weighty words, " Whosoever hath, to him shall be given, and he shall have more abundance ; but whosoever hath not, from him shall be taken away even that he hath," Matt. xiii. 12.

Testing power of God's revelations.

* LUTHER gives essentially the same explanation of obduracy in his treatise, *De servo arbitrio*, ed. SEB. SCHMID., pp. 126, 127. But he sometimes describes obduracy not only as an effect of the Divine Revelations, but of God's working within the man, entertaining as he does an original but exaggerated view of the divine *concursus* which reminds us of the later doctrine of Occasionalism ; see Vol. I. 228-230. He speaks of the *concursus* as a *rapers*, whereas the later Lutheran theology more correctly speaks of a *suavis Dei influxus*. Βία ἐχθρόν Θεῷ is the beautiful expression of CLEMENS ALEXANDRINUS.

THE AGGRAVATION OF SIN IN INDIVIDUAL LIFE.

Hence, it follows, that the first beginnings of obduracy are in human freedom; and that the necessary progress which such men make in that callousness, whereby they become the instruments of this fulfilment of the divine plans (as in Pharaoh's case) by their opposition, is a second stage arising from another and special self-perversion of the will. Thus we find it described in a passage, which though not directly treating of obduracy, evidently bears upon it, viz., 1 Peter ii. 7, 8. To the unbelieving Christ is there described as "a stone of stumbling, and a rock of offence, to those who stumble at the word, being disobedient; whereunto also they were appointed." As the preceding connection shows, they were not appointed not to believe the word, but as they do not believe the word, they are obliged to stumble at it. Man first closes his own heart, and then his heart is closed. The hardening of Pharaoh's heart is designedly described in Exodus, first as a self-hardening, Ex. vii. 13, 22, viii. 15, 32, and then as a hardening produced by God,* Ex. ix. 12, x. 20, 27. This is the reason why the early theologians regarded obduracy as a judgment of God.

This leads us to a view often advocated and as often controverted, which is still more general in its bearing, namely, that God punishes men by means of their sins. Augustine, as is well known, adopts this theory, and it found its most zealous defenders among the advocates of unconditional election.† The difficulty involved in this, and it is a serious one, is that punishment is essentially something inflicted upon man and suffered by him, whereas, sin is something done by him and springing from his will. The conceptions of punishment and of sin, seem still

Notion that God punishes sinners by sin.

---

* HENGSTENBERG refers to this *Authentie des Pentateuchs*, vol. ii. 462, but the relation of Pharaoh's self-hardening with God's hardening, as described by him, does not agree with the order of the two in the sacred text.

† The Hattemists (a small sect in Holland towards the end of the seventeenth century) held the extreme doctrine that God never punishes men on account of their sins, but only by their sin. This opinion might always be regarded as the converse of SPINOZA's doctrine,—*beatitudo non virtutis praemium, sed ipsa virtus,* —*i.e.* as Spinoza means it, the denial of recompense. It is by no means conclusive against this analogy, to urge that the sect I have named spoke of a wrath of God arising from the fact that God's purpose in relation to man is not fully accomplished in this life; for this "divine wrath" cannot, upon the theory advocated, be seriously or literally meant.

more absolutely to exclude each other if we thoroughly consider what the purpose of punishment really is. The aim of punishment is to maintain the sanctity of law when violated by sin. It seems as if nothing could be more inappropriate for this purpose than to ordain that the transgressor shall further commit the sin whereby he has already violated the law ; violation is not thus negatived, it is not displayed in the futility of its existence, but it is rather confirmed and multiplied.

If indeed the punishment of sin by sin involves an increase of sinfulness, and an inner growth of depravity, this theory involves a serious contradiction. It certainly could only refer to those sins which we have above described as caused; for being themselves effects, they are not the causes, but only the manifestations of the increased sinfulness. Still we cannot overlook the fact that sin always in some degree, and often in a very marked manner, involves suffering; and this consideration to some extent obviates the second objection we have named. The wretched slavery in which the wilful violation of God's law involves the transgressor is a reaction of the divine order in the government of the world against sin,—a practical demonstration that it is wrong, that it is what ought not to be, —a confirmation of the law in its absolute truth and integrity.

It must at all events be allowed that whatever truth there be in this view of sin, it is after all one-sided and partial. It contemplates sin in that one aspect of it wherein it appears as the consequence of a past act; and it overlooks the fact that in every sin, though it be an effect of former sin, there is an act of will which makes it really sin, and involves its guilt. This theory insists, of course, mainly upon those sins wherein man's ignominy is greatest, wherein he is degraded as a slave of passion and lust, and wherein (in the very commission of them) the man has anything but pleasure, so that he seems a madman, and bewitched. The disgrace and the pain which the very act of sin involves give to it the character of a punishment. And thus it is that St Paul, in Rom. i. 24, exhibits the abominations of utterly depraved lust in heathen life (the ἀτιμάζεσθαι τὰ σώματα αὐτῶν verse 24, the πάθη ἀτιμίας verse 26) as a punishment ordained of God on account of refusing to retain Him in their knowledge and their abandoning themselves to

This a very partial view of sin.

idolatry, without in the least mitigating the enormity of their guilt (verse 32). Those abominations are the results of that law of development to which evil is subject, and that law of development is also God's. The Apostle's statement in 2 Thess. ii. 11, 12, has a somewhat different meaning. There he says concerning those "who believed not the truth, but had pleasure in unrighteousness," that "misled by strong delusion they should believe a lie." But he regards God's part in this progressive deceptiveness of evil as something operative from without. In the development of history, according to God's purposes, evil will be forced to concentrate its inner principle with increasing definiteness, and to combine all the agencies which foster it, so that at length the lie (compare verses 3, 4) and the deceptiveness shall appear with an energy (ἐνέργεια πλάνης, verse 11) which they who are already estranged from the truth will not withstand.*

§ 4. DEGREES OF CULPABILITY IN SIN. We have already seen † that there are different degrees of culpability in sin. This, of course, is true, not only of sins of act, but of sinful habits wherein the sinful element appears as a settled disposition and an acquired facility, an evil tendency and a vicious practice. From a very early period the church distinguished degrees of culpability in both these departments, by dividing sins into MORTAL and VENIAL SINS.

The Reformers themselves and our earlier theologians agreed in rejecting the idea that any sins are, properly speaking, venial, i.e., undeserving of eternal death, and thus it would seem that they rejected the division *in toto*. But while they rejected it as having no place in the sphere of human life in general, they intended to retain it in the sphere of grace,‡ for they distinguished between sins which put an end to the state of grace,—*peccata mortalia*, and those which do not destroy it —*peccata venialia*. These latter must, however, be regarded as essentially mortal sins; they can be called venial, because so

---

* See p. 389, in my criticism of the theory that the universal depravity of human nature was a punitive act of God on account of Adam's fall.

† See Vol. I. 203-205, and SCHAF's remarks in his work upon the sin against the Holy Ghost (1841), pp. 57, 58.

‡ CALVIN speaks of this distinction (*Institut. Christ. Relig.*, lib. iii. c. iv. ₴ 28) in a way which implies that he wholly rejects it.

far as their consequences are concerned, they are forgiven in virtue of the faith which a state of grace implies. But so far as consequences are concerned, the former class also may be forgiven; because faith which, though suppressed by them, is not irretrievable, may again spring up.* If we take the possibility of forgiveness as the criterion, we cannot regard the *peccatum mortale* and the *peccatum veniale* as distinct, unless we reckon those sins only to be mortal which are utterly unpardonable, *i.e.*, that sin which, as far as its consequences are concerned, shall never be forgiven—that of blasphemy against the Holy Ghost. But if, on the other hand, we put unpardonable sin out of the question here, all sins committed by those who are in a state of grace will be either mortal or venial according as we view them. They will be all equally mortal, if we consider the punishment they merit; they will all be alike venial, if we consider the power of divine grace to overcome them. The same, morover, will hold true of the sins of the natural man, so far as they also may be cancelled by forgiveness. As, however, the overcoming power of grace does not belong as an active principle to the natural man, his sins must be regarded according to their objective nature, and to their connection *actu* as mortal sins. But this applies also to those sins of the regenerate which are of such magnitude as to put an end (according to the Lutheran theology) to the working of divine grace as the principle of the Christian life. This theology, therefore, was not so far wrong as it seemed at first sight to be in regarding the *pecc. mortale* and the *pecc. veniale* as different kinds of sin.

The categorical statement that every sin of itself involves eternal death is often understood in a way which makes it incompatible with our Lord's statement, Matt. v. 21, 22. The constitution of our nature in its fallen state is such as does indeed merit eternal death. Its transcendental basis is a mortal sin, involving the guilt of each individual; and in consequence of this no one brings into this life the slightest claim to divine gifts and graces, but according to the strict law of rectitude he merits nothing but punishment. Still the notion that every sin, even the smallest (thoughtlessness or inadvertence, for example, be

Consequences which different sins involve.

* See SCHLEIERMACHER's remarks, *Glaubenslehre*, vol. i. 454.

BOOK V.] THE AGGRAVATION OF SIN IN INDIVIDUAL LIFE. 417

its guilt ever so much mitigated by circumstances), involves the man in everlasting damnation, is a bare logical abstraction of the schools which has no root whatever in life, in conscience, nor in Christian conviction. If it were really acknowledged as true it would do away with all differences of guilt attaching to different sins and different sinners, and would weaken our detestation of deliberate crimes of the greatest magnitude against the holiest commands of God. Such an opinion, however, can only be entertained when each particular sin is regarded as indicative of a sinful condition and a depraved nature. Its error consists in ascribing different degrees of guilt to the state of man viewed as a constitution, and in regarding each particular sin solely as the product of a condition already existing (see Vol. i. 204).

From this consideration it would appear that our estimate of the distinction between mortal and venial sins is even more favourable than that of the older Protestant theology; for if it can be maintained at all we may apply it to the sins, not only of the regenerate, but also of the natural man. As to the division generally it must be said that the characteristics of both mortal and venial sins are very uncertain and varying, and no definite line of demarcation can be drawn between them. Even the same offence will involve different degrees of guilt in different persons, as, for instance, when one person is ignorant but the other knows that the offence in question, though apparently trifling, involves worse offences. The passage, therefore, which gave rise to the distinction between mortal and venial sins, 1 John v. 16, 17, furnishes no criterion of it. The sin there spoken of does not refer to a wide class of sins such as those designated mortal sins. What the sin is is explained in the very name which St. John gives to it—ἁμαρτία πρὸς θάνατον, and by the fact that we are not to pray for it: it is total apostacy from Christ.*

Degrees of guilt depend upon the person sinning.

The difference in the degrees of guilt attaching to actual sins does not, however, depend entirely upon the moral condition of the men who commit them, but depends in part upon the objective nature of

And upon objective circumstances.

---

* See the thorough criticism and exposition of this expression in LUECKE'S Commentary on the Epistle of St. John, p. 306.

VOL. II. 2 D

the offence, and partly upon its inner spring ; whether committed in a state of grace or in a state of sin, and if the former, whether producing a serious interruption of that state. Objectively viewed that offence is the greatest wherein selfishness, the real principle of sin, is most active. And selfishness is most active when the sin directly violates the most fundamental moral commands, or the highest and most universal moral principle. Subjectively, that offence is greatest which is committed with the clearest consciousness of its sinfulness, and with the firmest determination of will to disregard its sinfulness.* But as the resolve to sin often will not suffer itself to be disturbed by the consideration of the objective moral command, and as this implies a higher degree of selfishness, the subjective estimate of the degree of guilt resolves itself sometimes into the objective. The general moral state of the agent modifies our estimate, so far as it leads us to conjecture whether, and how far, he was really conscious of the wrongness of the act. But even this subjective consideration loses its significance when the moral perceptions have been wilfully dimmed by former sinfulness.

§ 5. THE SIN AGAINST THE HOLY GHOST. The New Testament refers to one sin in particular which it describes as utterly unpardonable,—blasphemy against the Holy Ghost, Matt. xii. 31, 32 ; Luke xii. 10 ; Mark iii. 28, 29. A very searching and careful examination of this difficult and wide subject, which furnishes a touchstone for our views concerning the nature of evil, has recently been published,† with the conclusions of which we in the main agree. This renders it unnecessary for us to enter minutely into the question, especially in its bearings upon Scripture and theology, and we shall therefore confine ourselves to its general outlines.

* The strength of the temptation and the difference between a sin only begun and one persevered in and completed—considerations which moral consciousness universally recognizes as important in estimating guilt—may be included under one or the other of these two heads.

† See the work of PHIL. SCHAF, " *Ueber die Sünde wider den h. Geist,*" with which may be compared THOLUCK's thorough dissertation on the subject in the *Theol. Stud. u. Krit.*, 1836, part ii. 401 (also printed in vol. ii. of his Miscellaneous Works), and the remarks of NITZSCH, *System der christlichen Lehre*, p. 300. Also the dissertation of GRASHOF, *Stud. u. Krit.*, 1833, part iv. 935 ; and of GURLITT, *Ibid.* 1834, part iii. 599.

BOOK V.]   THE AGGRAVATION OF SIN IN INDIVIDUAL LIFE.   419

The language of Christ (ὅς δ'ἂν εἴπῃ (λόγον) κατὰ τοῦ πνεύματος τοῦ ἁγίου) put it beyond doubt that He regarded blasphemy against the Holy Ghost as an actual sin. But this does not hinder—nay, it rather implies—that it can only be committed as the extreme goal of a depraved development which has already passed through many stages of sin, of a degeneracy which has reached its acme. If, as Olshausen thinks, Christ's declaration was intended as a warning to the Pharisees before the cup of their iniquity was full, before they reached that extremity from which there would be no return, then Christ Himself alluded to the relation of the sin to a previous development. The sin implies a certain moral state in the person who commits it, the state of total obduracy. If one who has not reached this state should in some fearful moment of despair form the determinate resolve to blaspheme the Holy Ghost, he could not carry out his resolve. For this sin is not a merely external act; it is impossible for a man, as if by the mere magic of certain words, which do not spring from the depth of his heart, to commit the very worst of all sins, and to abandon himself irremediably to eternal ruin.

Blasphemy against the Holy Ghost, moreover, is not represented by Christ as a particular kind of unpardonable sin, but as distinguished from all other sins as the ONLY unpardonable sin (πᾶσα ἁμαρτία καὶ βλασφημεία ἀφεθήσεται τοῖς ανθρώποις). From this we may infer, apart from any other consideration, that the growth of sin in man does not culminate in various kinds of human depravity of which the sin against the Holy Ghost is but one out of many. Sinful development, if not checked by redemption, culminates in every case in blasphemy against the Holy Ghost.

The only unpardonable sin.

What then is the inner nature of this sin? Besides the ordinary interpretations, we may here state that new and contrasted explanation which has of late been singularly espoused. In opposition to the prevailing view, which regards hatred and enmity against the Holy Ghost and His operations as the distinctive feature of this sin, Gurlitt has ably defended the view of this sin which takes it to be contemptuous indifference to every thing good and holy.* According to him it is committed by the man who

Nature of this sin.

* Dissertation in the *Stud. . rit.*, 1834, part iii. 609.

esteems everything which is a revelation of the Holy Ghost in word and life as absurd folly, because he does not believe in the reality of moral good nor in the existence of the Holy Ghost, who is the author of moral good.

If we regard this contemptuous indifference as relative, distinguishing it at the same time (as Gurlitt does) from unawakened carelessness, we find that it very often presents itself in actual life in those "children of this world" who try to persuade themselves that moral and religious truth is only a politic device of clever impostors, or a dream of weak enthusiasts. Gurlitt, however, would not consider them blasphemers of the Holy Ghost, unless they succeed in their endeavour. But if, accordingly, that indifference is to be taken absolutely, we object that it is not possible. The perversion of the will certainly exerts a depraving influence upon the religious perceptions, but it cannot utterly destroy the consciousness of ever valid and practical truth in the human heart. It cannot do so in this life, still less can it in the life to come, when the spirit must know the truth, whether it likes or not, as implied in will, and as the principle of its existence.

Gurlitt's theory untenable.

Here it may be remarked, in answer to an objection easily foreseen, that this consciousness cannot be regarded as a remnant of moral goodness still lingering in the man; for the very reason that no perversion of will can produce absolute disbelief. In considering the existence of moral perceptions in man, we must distinguish between those which are dependent on the will, and those which he possesses independently of it. Moral feelings belong to the former, but the knowledge of the moral law, in its main outlines, and the consciousness of it, as the universal norm of the will, belong to the latter. The most obdurate villain who determines that he shall not be fettered by the law cannot help recognizing that this is wrong, or that it is what ought not to be, when his property or life is wantonly attacked by another. The fact that man has some sense of pleasure and approval when he contemplates the law in its relation to himself, and that the wish that his own life should be conformable thereto is not wholly extinct within him, indicates the moral constitution of his will, its inclination, though slight, towards moral good, and a limit to his subjective depravity. Man's immediate consciousness of moral distinctions, as they present themselves to him, at least in broad outline, as facts of the divine government of the world, is something wholly involuntary, a hold which the strong hand of the Creator has upon him, even in his most violent resistance.

But if, according to the above theory, the acme of sin were total indifference to the moral law, and the extinction of any recognition of it, sin (as has well been remarked)* would finally destroy man's moral nature altogether. And it would consequently destroy itself, and become, by its own working, the redeemer of man from sin. Unsubdued selfishness, indeed, must ever be essentially evil, whether the evil of it be recognized or not; but if the consciousness of sin were destroyed, spiritual personality would be at an end, and the wild lust of selfishness would be nothing more than the ravening of a wild beast.

In considering the sin against the Holy Ghost, we must ever remember that it presupposes a very full and thorough development of the moral consciousness, and we may add of the religious consciousness likewise; because the moral consciousness cannot be fully developed without recognizing the fundamental truths of religion. It presupposes this, indeed, as something experienced at an earlier period in the person's life; but it must have been there for some time, and it must influence the entire subsequent development, however deeply it may fall away again from it, making sins more heinous, wickedness more thorough, and accountability far greater than otherwise they would have been.† Unthinking recklessness, as such, is perfectly secure from the sin against the Holy Ghost. Before a man can possibly commit this sin, evil must thoroughly have taken possession of him by a penetrating and spiritualizing process, whereby its principle is deliberately understood and adopted. Blasphemy against the Holy Ghost is not only the greatest, it is the most spiritual of sins. But according to the conditions of man's earthly development, evil as the antithesis

Side note: What the sin in question implies.

---

* SCHAF, as before, pp. 84, 85.
† See THOLUCK's remarks in the Dissertation above referred to, and in his Commentary on the Hebrews, pp. 264, 363, 3d ed.

of good can attain this intensity only where the inner life has previously been in very close contact with moral goodness.

We cannot, therefore, give up the main features of the old theory concerning the sin against the Holy Ghost.
Its true essence. Its essence is HATRED of whatever is known to be divine and godlike. The blasphemy is the expression of this hatred, but in a much profounder sense than would at first sight appear. They who have attentively observed the depths of human depravity in its more refined and spiritual forms, cannot fail to have discovered the striking fact, that they who have sunk to those depths, can never rest in their hostility to what is holy and divine, but are irresistibly impelled to give vent to it in revilings,—as if they felt a horrible satisfaction in belching forth the most awful blasphemies.

The inner motive of this hatred is unbending selfishness,— selfishness which hates God and His holy law, because it fetters the arbitrariness which would be absolute, and authoritatively demands submission to the divine will. The decisiveness of the opposition consists in the |fact that the man is fully conscious of it, and deliberately persists in it. Self alone will reign, but there are obligations to truth which stand in its way; it therefore endeavours, if possible, wholly to destroy the truth, and fights to the uttermost against its power.

As the corrupt will recognizes its own selfish principle as its fundamental law, it necessarily involves itself in the contradiction of, having to affirm the very negation of moral good as good. At the very outset of the struggle, it must recognize itself as the right, the strong, the dignified, and must describe what it opposes—in spite of its inextinguishable conviction of universal obligation—as that which ought not to be, as a weakness, a mark of cowardice, a slavery.* The sin against the Holy Ghost must be, therefore, the boldest sophistry.

From these remarks it is manifest that it is only another form of the same sin to which St. Paul refers when he represents (2 Thess. ii. 3, 4) the culminating point of man's depraved development as the deification of confirmed egoism. The "man of sin," the opposer of all law (ὁ ἄνομος, ver. 8), in his unbounded

The same sin referred to in 2 Thess. ii. 3, 4.

---

* The character of the Devil, and his maxims, as described by ERHARD, in his so-called "*Apologie des Teufels*," (*Niethammers philos. Journal*, vol. i. part ii. 105), presents many suggestive points of resemblance.

BOOK V.]   THE AGGRAVATION OF SIN IN INDIVIDUAL LIFE.   423

self-glorification, is obliged to maintain this lie (for that he really believes himself to be God no one will suppose),—has to oppose and exalt himself above all that is holy and godlike (ver. 3),—and must systematically make war upon it. He therefore must necessarily be the blasphemer of the Holy Ghost, and signalizes himself as "the son of perdition," *i.e.*, one who has irrecoverably abandoned himself to perdition.

This culminating point of sin, blasphemy against the Holy Ghost, depends upon and is connected with the highest revelation of God; it has become possible only through Christ, and the mission of the Holy Ghost proceeding from Him.

Some of our earlier Lutheran divines insist upon this connection between the sin against the Holy Ghost and God's revelation in Christ, for they hold that it presupposes regeneration.* Most of them, however, do not venture to make this a necessary requisite, but affirm only that the sin implies the knowledge of evangelical truth by the enlightenment of the Holy Ghost.† But this enlightenment cannot be distinguished from regeneration, and the coincidence between the two classes of theologians in their quotations from Scripture illustrative of this sin, shows that they agree. They almost unanimously regard Heb. vi. 3–6 (in connection with Heb. x. 26–31) as one of the chief texts explaining the nature of this sin. And we can hardly doubt that the writer of that epistle had in his mind in this passage the same sin as that which Christ calls blasphemy against the Holy Ghost. His words, morever, clearly show that he is referring to persons who had by regeneration become partakers of Christ's redemption (γευσαμένους τῆς δωρεᾶς τῆς ἐπουρανίου καὶ μετόχους γενηθέντας πνεύματος ἁγίου καὶ . . . . γευσαμένους δυνάμεις μέλλοντος αἰῶνος). No expositor would ever have dreamt of taking these words to denote a merely superficial religious state, had not his theological views obliged him.‡

Heb. vi. 3–6.

---

* HUTTER, *Loci Comm.* De pecc. in Sp. S. pp. 367, 368. QUENSTEDT, as before, sect. 1, th. 96 ; sect. 2, qu. 16 upon the thesis, *Nobis probabilior videtur eorum sententia, qui solis vere renatis, justificatis et renovatis pecc. in Sp. S. adscribunt.* BAUMGARTEN, *Evang. Glaubenslehre*, vol. ii., 618, 619.

† *E.g.* GERHARD, *De pecc. actual.* c. 24, § 109 ; BAIER, part ii. c. 3, § 24; KÖNIG, *Theol. posit.* part ii. § 158; BUDDEUS, lib. iii. c. 2, § 34.

‡ Thus BLEEK seems to regard the passage in his Commentary, part ii. 181, 197; and THOLUCK in his, p. 268.

The idea that regeneration is necessarily implied in the sin against the Holy Ghost involves an important truth. The highest religious consciousness alone is capable of committing the greatest sin, but *that* man alone can possess this highest consciousness who has experienced true fellowship with God. He only can blaspheme the Holy Ghost who has in some degree partaken of his influences. This implies a view of evil as to its nature and conditions widely different from doctrines now in vogue, which look upon evil merely as a weakness or defect in human development, a negative factor in the growth of good, &c. And yet this idea of regeneration, as necessary in order to the sin before us, arises from overstraining a right principle. We have already stated what is required objectively in order to this sin; subjectively it implies a deep conviction previously possessed of the power of God's revelation in Christ, and of the efficacy of God's Spirit among men. If the mind has ever thus been convinced, the higher degree of consciousness is possessed which as a secret force may impel the man who resists the Holy Spirit to persevering resistance, and his sin may be intensified so as to become at last positive hatred of God and of His redemptive work.

The declaration of Christ and the connection in which it stands do not enable us to decide whether He considered that the blaspheming Pharisees had already committed the sin, or whether He meant simply to warn them against it.* He could not certainly have warned them in such an emphatic manner if they had not already been in imminent danger of committing the sin. If, then, the sin presupposes regeneration, these Pharisees must have been regenerate by the Holy Ghost; and some of the older theologians do not hesitate to affirm this; but it is easy to see that such a notion would lead to a very superficial conception of regeneration.†

(margin: What this sin subjectively implies.)

* This is NEANDER's view (*Leben Jesu*, 418), and his view of the connection seems to me the only tenable one.

† See QUENSTEDT, th. 95, p. 77 : *Phrisaei . . . . pro non renatis haberi non possunt, quia per verbum et acceptam circumcisionem, legitima tum regenerationis media, fuerunt regeniti. Imo veritatem divinam eos agnovisse si non aliunde vel solo ipsorum officio et cathedra Mosis, ad quam ipse Christus auditores amandat constare posset.* This view was quite consistent when regeneration was connected with Infant Baptism, and the "sacraments of the Old Testament" were put on a par with those of the New.

The passage in the Hebrews does indeed affirm that the regenerate may fall into that sin, but it does not say that it can be committed by the regenerate alone. Obduracy, as we have seen, implies the objective presentation of the Revelation of God in history : blasphemy against the Holy Ghost, the highest and deepest development of sin, implies the suppression of a movement of the inner life following upon the working of the spirit of grace.

Christ describes blasphemy against the Holy Ghost as the sin which shall never be forgiven. Our earlier theologians, following several of the Fathers and Schoolmen, rightly discerned the true reason of this unpardonableness. It is not that divine grace is absolutely refused to any one who in true penitence asks forgiveness of this sin, but he who commits it never fulfils the subjective conditions upon which forgiveness is possible, because the aggravation of sin to this ultimatum destroys in him all susceptibility of repentance.* THE WAY OF RETURN TO GOD IS CLOSED AGAINST NO ONE WHO DOES NOT CLOSE IT AGAINST HIMSELF. Those who have not closed it against themselves, but who have never in this life had the opportunity of knowing the way of salvation, will certainly be placed in a position to accept and enter upon this way of return, if they will, after their life on earth is ended. This, of course, is true also of those, who though belonging to the more outward sphere of the Christian Church, have never had the gospel in its fulness and freeness presented to them : indeed, we may venture to hope that, in the interval between death and judgment, many serious misconceptions which hindered men from appropriating the Truth in this life will be removed. But while indulging in these hopes we must remember that they also necessitate the possibility that beyond this life man may fall into that unpardonable sin.

Why is this sin unpardonable?

§ 6. THE THEORY OF FINAL RESTORATION.

But if this sin can never be blotted out, and if in virtue of personal immortality evil will ever exist in some, the variance caused by evil in God's universe will never be done away. Here then

* QUENSTEDT in a *quaestio* " *Quaenam sit vera causa irremissibilitatis peccati in Sp. S.* ?" says,—*Distingue inter irremissibile ex parte vel Dei vel peccati in se, et sic nullum irremissibile peccatum datur, et inter tale ex parte personae peccantis, et sic irremissibile est peccatum in Sp. S.*—Sect. 2, qu. 19 (p. 164.)

the question concerning the "RESTORATION OF ALL THINGS" presents itself,—the question whether all beings who have fallen away from God will ever be restored to holy and blessed fellowship with Him. We cannot here attempt a full investigation of this problem; in the few remarks we offer we shall confine ourselves to the bearing of the question upon the human race alone.

It is clear, in the first place, that those theories of an ἀποκατάστασις which represent it as taking place in the interval between death and the general Resurrection, directly violate the New Testament eschatology. Holy Scripture, as we have already seen, teaches that the conflict between the kingdom of God and its foes will become more and more marked as the consummation of all things approaches, and that there will be a final judgment at the end of all earthly history; but upon the theory referred to, nothing would remain to be separated and judged. Arguments, therefore, based upon such texts as 1 Cor. xv. 22, and Romans v. 18, 19, must be put aside; for if these texts sanction the idea of an ἀποκατάστασις πάντων they would place it in that intermediate state. If the idea therefore is to be maintained it must be referred to a period lying beyond the general resurrection.

But even if this be entertained as possible, Holy Scripture cannot be made to sanction the idea of universal restoration, unless we adopt the principle that the final issue of the Divine purposes must coincide with their primary tendency and design; in other words, that God could not arrange His purposes according to the free action of man in relation to them. It is upon this principle only that John xii. 32; Phil. ii. 10, 11; Col. i. 20; Rom. xi. 32; 1 Tim. ii. 4, 6; 1 John ii. 2; and other similar texts can be cited as favouring the doctrine.

Verdict of Scripture;

But if we consider these arguments, derived from the dictates of Christian consciousness concerning the ἀποκατάστασις, no one can reflect upon them without feeling their weight. We cannot, however, regard them as decisive. It does, indeed, seem almost inconceivable that this world's development should terminate with an unharmonized discord,—that any opposition to God's will, in the wills of any of His creatures, should for ever

Of Christian consciousness.

continue. A correct conception of punishment, however, will help us to solve this difficulty. Opposition to God's will does not continue, but is wholly subdued, if the state of the being in whom it is be one of punishment, and if the fettered evil be not allowed to disturb the perfect harmony of the new and perfected world. God will certainly realize his ideal of the world, but we cannot say *a priori* concerning any given individual, that he will be a living member of this perfect realization. "The manifold wisdom of God," Eph. iii. 10, has infinite resources at its command for the attainment of its ends; and if the individual withdraws himself from that position, wherein he would accord with the universal harmony, God's creative plans have otherwise provided that nothing shall be wanting to this harmony. Such an one would be constrained against his will, and by his very opposition, to confirm it.

And yet the idea of divine Love as the highest principle seems absolutely to demand an affirmative har-monizing of the discord, and a positive removal of the variance, so that at the goal of the world's development there shall be no human being unreconciled to God, and unblessed with the smiles of His love. But if this love be regarded as working by way of metaphysical necessity, the development of the moral world and God's providence over it are reduced to a mere process of nature. Our investigations have fully shown that if universal restoration be conceived of in this manner it is inconsistent with the principles of Christianity. Love, in its essence and in its manifestation, implies freedom in those with whom it has to do. Its power is such that wherever there is the least germ of moral life it can develop it;* but it is possible for man to destroy this germ so as to retain no elements within him upon which holy love can work. That theory of course is radically wrong

Of divine LOVE.

---

* If future punishment and final damnation were simply the consciousness of guilt infinitely enhanced, if the life of the lost were one continual experience of moral grief, and if their state were one simply of passive surrender to God's punitive will, this would certainly imply a germ of moral life, which divine love might still unfold. ERBKAM's Dissertation *ueber die Lehre von der ewigen Verdammniss* (*Stud. u. Krit.* 1838, No. ii. pp. 384–494), adopts this view, and develops from it, with great acuteness, the doctrine of universal restoration. The arguments in favour of this doctrine above cited are from ERBKAM, but they are based upon an erroneous conception of punishment, and lead to results which ERBKAM himself would shrink from.

which attempts to explain the antithesis of bliss and misery by a law of beauty, and which argues that some must be eternally lost, in order that the light may be set off by a due contrast of shade; but the mystery of human freedom implies the possibility at least, that some may be eternally lost. It is a fact of experience, that many do actually resist the holiest strivings of divine love; how then can it be impossible for this resistance to be renewed and to be endlessly carried on in a future state? Some hold that continued punishment is conceivable only upon the supposition of continued sin, and even upon this theory, unceasing resistance would involve never ending misery.

Our past investigations furnish a sufficient answer to the objection that the endless damnation of any individual is incompatible with our belief in God's omniscience when He created him. God, it is urged, being a God of love, would not have created an individual whom He foreknew as certainly doomed to eternal misery. We have already fully shown (Book III., Part I., chap. 4) that each individual as created by God, is endowed with the power of realizing, and is intended to realize, the ideal of humanity, and that all individuals are alike in this respect. It is the individual's own act, and seeing that God did not abandon him after that first unhappy choice, his own repeated and persevering act, when he abandons himself to eternal perversity and ruin. The arguments therefore of modern anti-Christian objectors against eternal punishment on the principle of humanity are self-condemned. They simply witness that their advocates have no adequate conception of what human freedom is. Such objectors must satisfactorily reconcile the awful ravages of sin in individual life now—which are matters of experience—with their principle of humanity; and until they have done this, scientific theology need not discuss with them the ulterior question.

<small>Is eternal misery incompatible with God's omniscience in creation?</small>

While universal restoration cannot be established upon internal grounds, Christ's declaration concerning the sin against the Holy Ghost expressly excludes it. The possibility of endless condemnation is involved in the principle of personal freedom; that it is actually realized in any case we can know only by Revelation.

Awful as is our Lord's statement, exceeding great and precious
hopes lie hid within it. The words πᾶσα ἁμαρτία
καὶ βλασφημία ἀφθήσεται τοῖς ἀνθρώποις may of
course denote either a future fact or a possibility only; but there
is nothing in the connection which obliges us, and therefore
nothing that justifies us in departing from the ordinary force
of the future tense as expressing a future fact. We may
therefore take our Lord's word as referring to a time when
all the sins and blasphemies of men, save the sin against the
Holy Ghost, shall be forgiven. Our Saviour does indeed say
in the same discourse (Matt. vii. 13, 14), of the way of life,
" few there be that find it," and of the gate " that leadeth to
destruction," " many there be that go in thereat;" but the
destruction here spoken of cannot be taken as necessarily
synonymous with eternal damnation, and many may "go in
thereat " in this life, many may be lost as far as their state
here and for some period after death is concerned, who shall
finally be saved. Again, as to the words οὔτε ἐν τούτῳ τῷ αἰῶνι,
οὔτε ἐν τῷ μέλλοντι, we cannot fairly take the latter alternative
phrase as merely synonymous with οὐδέποτε. Of all the Rabbinical parallels which Wetstein adduces, there is but one, that
from the *Cod. Hasidim,* wherein the expression εν τῷ μέλλοντι
can be taken for οὐδέποτε; in all the other references it has a
distinctive meaning, and it may have this in the one doubtful
citation. Consequently, our Lord's declaration clearly refers to
the forgiveness of sin in the αἰὼν μέλλων. But the αἰ ὼν μέλλων
does not mean the time and state immediately ensuing upon
death, but the period when the kingdom of the Messiah shall
be fully realized and revealed,—the period which follows the
resurrection and the judgment. Christ's words, therefore,
inspire the glorious hope—not in the unbelieving, for they
despise Christ's word, but in the Christian—that in the world
to come, in far distant aeons, they who here harden their
hearts against God's Revelation, and can expect only a verdict
of condemnation in the day of Judgment, shall find forgiveness
and salvation.

But while Christ's words thus favour the doctrine of Final
Restoration up to a certain point, they explicitly deny the
universality of the ἀποκατάστασις. Divine love draws all to
itself who do not resist its holy influence; but the stiff-necked

and disobedient who perseveringly bind themselves to that which ought not to be—to evil—are cast away like dross by the great " refiner and purifier " of the world, now that it has become the perfected kingdom of God, now that, having completeness in itself, it requires not the discipline of moral evil. As the goal of sanctification is a perfection of moral goodness which shall for ever exclude the possibility of evil, and yet be the outgo of the highest freedom, so the development of evil ends in a state wherein unwillingness to goodness has ripened into inability, wherein personality, persisting in alienation from God, has become absolutely petrified in sin. This is " the worm that never dies, the fire which shall never be quenched." This is the selfishness which will not humble itself that it may be exalted, which will not die that it may live ; hatred indeed, but impotent hatred, furiously raging against God, yet compelled to acknowledge Him as the almighty Creator of all.

CONCLUSION.

THE end of our exposition of the doctrine of Sin leads us back to its beginning. If EVIL did not exist,—evil which is not a transitory element in the progress of the world's development, but abiding through the persistence of the obdurate will for countless ages,—the great problem of the world might be solved on purely theoretic principles. Religion is not dependent for its existence upon the fact of sin ; apart from sin the soul of man would still need a more lively and spiritual knowledge than Spinoza, for example, could give it; though it might, in this case, rest content with Spinoza's principle that we may overcome the world by contemplation. Evil is the rock on which this doctrine falls to pieces ; for no one can overcome sin by mere contemplation. A man may indeed learn to look upon sin as a necessary element in the world's progress, but in so doing, so far from recognizing evil in order to vanquish it, he would be denying it in order to become a slave to its power. Yet there is a knowledge which conquers evil ideally, though it be not as yet really destroyed—a knowledge which is attained by practice : "If ye continue in My word, then are ye my disciples indeed, and ye shall know the truth, and the truth shall make you free," (John viii. 31, 32). Religion, in one aspect of it, is a theory, but the true principle of it is practice, the inmost action of the soul. Yet this is the very point face to face with evil—where religion alone can solve the unsolvable variance of our being—this is the very point where the apparent variance between philosophy and religion is transformed into a sure and abiding harmony. ONE there is among the sons of men who is perfectly free from evil, and He gives this His freedom to all who are united to Him by justifying faith. As yet they have this freedom not in themselves, but in Him only : their union with Him is not as yet a perfect union with self, they are not as yet themselves perfectly pure and holy, and therefore every realization of union with Him is blended with a new self-surrender. Christian hope looks forward to a day when all that they have in Him they shall have also in themselves. Then the few and broken harmonies, which but now and then we hear, reminding us of the divine order of the universe, will blend in a full and glorious chorus, wherein all dissonance shall be for ever done away.

INDEXES.

I.—HEBREW WORDS EXPLAINED.

	VOL. PAGE		VOL. PAGE
אֱוִיל	i. 163	נוֹאַלְנוּ	i. 93
אָוֶן	i. 243	נֶפֶשׁ	i. 322
אָשָׁם	i. 199–202	נָשָׂא	i. 203
בַּקָּרֵת	i. 245	עָוֹן	{ i. 93
בָּשָׂר	i. 322		(ii. 274
רְמוּת	ii. 350, 351	פֶּשַׁע	i. 91, 93
הָטָא	i. 92, 184	צֶלֶם	ii. 350, 353
חַטָּאת	i. 199–202	קֹדֶשׁ	i. 233
חֹשֶׁד	i. 236	רַע	i. 94, 236
יָסַר	i. 245	רֶשַׁע	i. 94
יֵצֶר	ii. 260, 276	שְׁאוֹל	ii. 292
מוֹת תָּמוּת	ii. 291	שָׁפָל	i. 58
מוּסָר	i. 245	שְׁגָגָה	i. 202
נְבָלָה	i. 163	שָׁלוֹם	i. 236

II. GREEK WORDS EXPLAINED.

	VOL. PAGE		VOL. PAGE
ἄγνοια,	i. 145, 207	γυμνός,	ii. 306
ᾅδης,	ii. 293	δικαίωσις,	ii. 345
αἰτία,	i. 196	δίκη,	i. 246
αἰσχρός,	i. 194	δουλεία,	ii. 12
ἀκηδία,	i. 178	εἰκών,	ii. 350, 352
ἀμαθία,	i. 145	ἐκδίκησις,	i. 246
ἁμαρτία,	i. 90, 184	ἐλεύθερος,	ii. 11
ἀμετρία,	{ i. 146	ἐνδεχόμενον,	ii. 27
	(ii. 344	ἔνοχον,	i. 199
ἄνοια	i. 145	ἐπενδύσασθαι,	ii. 305
ἀνομία,	i. 91	ἐπιθυμία,	i. 157
ἄνομος,	i. 142	ἐφ' ᾧ,	ii. 301, 304
ἄτη,	i. 145, 164	θάνατος,	ii. 293

VOL II.   2 E

434 INDEX.

	VOL. PAGE		VOL. PAGE
καθιστάναι,	ii. 345	πωροῦσθαι,	ii. 410
κατάκριμα,	ii. 344	σάρξ,	i. 321-323
κόσμος,	i. 157	σκληρύνεσθαι,	ii. 410
κρέας,	i. 324	συμβεβηκὸς,	ii. 27
κρίσις,	i. 238	σῶμα,	i. 318-336 / 330
μανία,	i. 145		
μετάνοια,	i. 214		ii. 295-299
ὁμοίωσις,	ii. 350, 353	τιμάω,	i. 249
ὀργή,	i. 247	τιμωρία,	i. 246
ὀφείλειν,	i. 198, 210	ὕβρις,	i. 145
παθη,	i. 157	ὑπερηφανία,	i 143
παιδεία,	i. 245	φιλαυτία,	i. 144
παραβασις,	i. 90	φυλακή,	ii. 294
παράπτωμα,	i. 90	χοϊκος,	i. 318 / ii. 298
πνεῦμα,	i. 326-328		
πνευματικος,	ii. 271	ψυχικὸς,	i. 305 / ii. 271
πονηρία,	i. 145		
πονηρός,	i. 90	ψυχή,	i. 326

III. PASSAGES OF SCRIPTURE INCIDENTALLY EXPLAINED OR ILLUSTRATED.

	VOL. PAGE		VOL. PAGE
Genesis i. 26-28,	ii. 350	Psalms xxv. 8,	i. 93
i. 31,	ii. 349	xlix. 15,	ii. 292
ii. 17,	ii. 291-348	li. 5,	ii. 274-275
iii.	ii. 347	xc. 7, 9, 11,	ii. 292
iii. 1,	ii. 383	Prov. vii. 36,	i. 93
iii. 1-6,	ii. 384-386	xix. 2,	i. 93
iii. 16-22,	ii. 291	Eccles. ii. 3,	i. 323
iii. 19,	ii. 292-296 / 348	v. 6,	i. 323
		Isaiah vi. 10,	ii. 411
iii. 22,	ii. 296	xlv. 7,	i. 236
v. 1,	ii. 351	lxiii. 17,	i. 236
v. 3,	ii. 335	Jer. xxvii. 14-15,	i. 237
vi. 3,	i. 323	Ecclesiasticus x. 15,	i. 143
viii. 21,	ii. 276		
ix. 6,	ii. 353	xxiii. 16,	i. 323
Exodus vii. 13-22.	ii. 413	xxviii. 5,	i. 323
ix. 12,	ii. 413	Wisdom ii. 24,	ii. 384
xx. 5,	ii. 377	Matthew iv. 6-10,	i. 71
xxxiv. 7,	ii. 377	v. 21-22,	ii. 416
Leviticus v. 1-13,	i. 200-202	v. 28,	ii. 259
v. 17-19,	i. 200	vi. 12,	i. 198
xiv. 10-32,	i. 200	vii. 17-18,	ii. 47
xxi. 8, 15, 23,	i. 233	ix. 12,	ii. 258
Num. vi. 9-12,	i. 200	xi. 13,	ii. 257
xiv. 18,	ii. 377	xi. 25,	ii. 412
xv. 22-31,	i. 202	xii. 31-32,	ii. 418-422
xvi. 29-30,	ii. 292	xii. 33,	ii. 61
xxvii. 3,	ii. 292	xiii. 12,	ii. 412
2 Sam. vi. 22,	i. 58	xv. 19-20,	i. 310
xvi. 10,	i. 236	xviii. 3,	ii. 265
xxiv. 1,	i. 236	xviii. 7,	i. 388
1 Kings xii. 15,	i. 236	xix. 14,	ii. 265
xxii. 22,	i. 236	xix. 17,	i. 56-112
Job xiv. 4,	ii. 275	xix. 27,	i. 49

INDEX.

		VOL.	PAGE
Matt.	xxii. 36-39,	i.	109
	xxii. 39,	i.	340
	xxiii. 29-75,	ii.	376
	xxvi. 41,	i.	315
Mark	x. 21,	i.	56
	xii. 29-31,	i.	109
Luke	ii. 34,	i.	131
	ii. 40,	i.	67
	v. 31,	ii.	258
	xi. 13,	ii.	258
	xii. 47,	ii.	92
	xiii. 4,	i.	198
	xv. 5,	i.	388
	xv. 12, 13,	i.	142
	xvii. 10,	i.	57
	xviii. 17,	ii.	265
	xx. 35, 36,	ii.	296
	xx. 38,	ii.	294
	xxiii. 34,	i.	209
	xxiv. 39,	ii.	298
John	i. 2,	ii.	136
	iii. 6,	i.	316
		ii.	276
	iii. 36,	i.	209
		ii.	257
	viii. 32, 36,	i.	74, 165
		ii.	11
	viii. 34,	ii.	406
	viii. 44,	i.	163, 235
		ii.	291, 385
	ix. 3,	i.	388
	ix. 41,	i.	209
	xi. 4,	ii.	293
	xv. 22, 24,	i.	209
	xx. 20, 26,	ii.	297
Acts	x. 35,	ii.	242, 258
	xvii. 20,	i.	207
	xvii. 28, 29,	i.	305
		ii.	354
Romans	i. 21-23,	i.	129
	i. 24,	ii.	414
	ii. 10,	ii.	242
	iii. 19,	i.	199
	iii. 24, 25,	i.	255
	iv. 1,	i.	321
	iv. 15,	i.	104-106
	v. 7,	i.	113
	v. 12,	ii.	290, 301
	v. 13, 14,	ii.	302
	v. 12-19,	ii.	301, 343-346
	v. 13,	i.	104, 105
	v. 20,	i.	104, 105
	vi. 6,	i.	330
	vi. 9,	ii.	299
	vi. 16,	ii.	303, 406
	vii.	i.	183
	vii. 5,	i.	106
	vii. 6,	i.	327
	vii. 8-11,	i.	183
	vii. 7-20,	i.	198

		VOL.	PAGE
Romans	vii. 14-25,	i.	48, 328,
		ii.	247
	viii. 4,	i.	49, 328,
	viii. 7,	i.	106
	viii. 10,	ii.	291
	viii. 19, 21, 23,	ii.	304
	ix. 11,	ii.	393
	ix. 21,	i.	389
	x. 5,	i.	48₁
	xiii. 2,	i.	88
	xiv. 23,	i.	208
	xvi. 20,	i.	385
1 Cor.	i. 26,	i.	321
	ii. 14,	ii.	271
	iii. 1-4,	i.	321
	vi. 13,	i.	318
	vii. 1,	i.	324
	vii. 14,	ii.	277
	vii. 22,	ii.	12
	ix. 12-18,	i.	57
	ʃxi. 19,	i.	388
	xi. 32,	i.	247
	xv. 21, 22,	ii.	290
	xv. 26,	ii.	293
	xv. 28,	i.	121
	xv. 44, 45,	ii.	295, 296
	xv. 44-46,	ii.	371
	xv. 48,	ii.	295
	xv. 55, 56,	ii.	294
2 Cor.	ii. 16,	ii.	303
	v. 2-9,	ii.	295
	v. 3,	ii.	304
	v. 4,	ii.	301
	vi. 14,	ii.	41
	vii. 1,	i.	311
	xi. 23,	i.	325
Gal.	iii. 3,	i.	321
	iii. 12,	i.	48
	iii. 21,	i.	49
	v. 13-24,	i.	321, 327
Eph.	ii. 3,	i.	105
		ii.	278-280
	ii. 15,	i.	325
	iv. 24,	ii.	352
	v. 28-3,	i.	140
Phil.	iii. 6,	i.	48
	iii. 12,	ii.	301
	iii. 21,	ii.	295, 298
	iv. 10,	ii.	301
Col.	i. 22,	i.	324
	ii. 11,	i.	330
	ii. 18, 19,	i.	322
	iii. 5,	i.	332
	iii. 10,	ii.	351.seq.
1 Thess.	v. 10,	ii.	294
2 Thess.	ii. 3, 4,	i.	142
		ii.	422
	ii. 8,	i.	142
	ii. 11, 12,	ii.	415
	ii. 13,	i.	242
1 Tim.	i. 9,	i.	70

436   INDEX.

		VOL. PAGE
2 Tim.	ii. 20,	i. 387
Hebrews	i. 9,	i. 91
Hebrews	ii. 14,	ii. 385
	vi. 3-6, x. 26-31,	ii. 423, 424
	xii. 6,	i. 247
	xii. 29,	i. 248
James	i. 13-17,	i. 234
	i. 14, 15,	i. 157,316 / ii. 303
	i. 25,	ii. 12
	iii. 9, 10,	i. 110 / ii. 353
	iii. 11,	ii. 169

		VOL. PAGE
1 Peter	ii. 7, 8,	ii. 4, 13
	iv. 6,	ii. 291,294
2 Peter	ii. 19,	ii. 406
1 John	i. 8, 9,	ii. 258
	ii. 15-17,	i. 157,158
	iii. 4,	i. 43
	iii. 8,	ii. 385·
	iii. 15,	ii. 385
	iv. 20,	i. 110
	v. 16, 17,	ii. 303,417
Rev.	ii. 11,	ii. 303
	iii. 15,	ii. 410
	xx. 6, 14,	ii. 303

IV.—SUBJECTS MORE OR LESS FULLY CONSIDERED.

Ability defined, ii. 301
Absolute, the, Müller's meaning, i. 17 ; the negative, ii. 133 ; personality, ii. 132, 133
Absorption, theory of the Mystics concerning, i. 121
Acosmism, i. 125
Adam the natural head of the race, ii. 335 ; the progenitor of the race, ii. 338
Adam, the second, ii. 346, 347
Angels and Devils, i. 361 ; Scripture teaching concerning them, ii. 367
Animals, the lower, types of evil among them, i. 380 ; signs of freedom in them, ii. 32
Anthropological theory rejected, i. 304-306
Arbitrariness not freedom, i. 100
Arminian theory concerning original sin, ii. 320-326.
Art, significance of evil in, i. 364
Ascension of Christ, its significance, ii. 298
Asceticism condemned, i. 154
Atheistic frivolity, i. 180
Atomistic theory, ii. 38
Augsburg Confession on sin, i. 261
Augustine, his theory of sin, i. 132, 289, *seq.;* on the infralapsarian view, i. 258; on moral perfection, i. 59, 60; on the contrasts of life, i. 367 ; on freedom, ii. 35-37 ; on Death, ii. 300
Autonomy of the will, i. 72

Balance, as an illustration of freedom, objected to, ii. 21, 31
Baptism, Infant, implying sin, i. 42 ; removing sin, ii. 332
Baur's theory of evil, i. 285
Beginning of the world, i. 224

Bellarmine on works of supererogation, i. 52-54 ; on actual and habitual sin, i. 184
Beza, his view of sin, i. 264, 389
Body, the natural and spiritual, ii. 297, 298 ; Christ's resurrection, ii. 298 ; relation of original sin thereto, ii. 369
Boethius, his advice concerning evil, i. 29.
Bradwardine of Canterbury, i. 259
Bretschneider's view of freedom, ii. 13

Calculation of moral conduct impossible, ii. 64, 66
Calling in life, choice of, ii. 6
Calvin's theory of the *decretum absolutum,* i. 107 ; concerning guilt, i. 264
Character defined, ii. 40 ; formed by the will, ii. 47, 59, 61
Chastisement, i. 244, 247
Childhood, sins of, i. 42 ; ii. 71 : awakening of conscience in, ii. 264 ; innocence of, ii. 265-268 ; selfishness of, ii. 281
Choice, power of, in the lower animals, ii. 33
Collision of duties, i. 36
Concursus, scholastic doctrine of, i. 229
Conscience, i. 31, 37, 80, 210-212 ; implying law, i. 71 ; as a standard, i. 208 ; awakening of, i. 305; tenderness of, ii. 252
Consciousness of God, i. 80 ; of guilt, i. 210
Contingency, ii. 26
Contingentia mundi, ii. 137
Contrasts in life, i. 359-366
Corruption of human nature, ii. 259-262
Covetousness, i. 161, 162

INDEX. 437

Creation, i. 127, 224; distinct from providence, i. 222; ii. 134
Culpa and *dolus* distinguished, i. 197

Daub's theory of evil, i. 408; ii. 175
Death, ii. 303; in the lower animals, ii. 287, *seq.*; the wages of sin, ii. 300; man's body before the fall liable to, ii. 295, 296
Deformity as distinct from evil, i. 193
Degrees of guilt, i. 203-206; ii. 90-92
Depravity, limit to, i. 211; ii. 366; inborn, ii. 280; how transmitted, ii. 375
Devil, the, his existence denied, i. 283: prompts to action, i. 362; his maxims concerning sin, i. 398; the tempter in paradise, ii. 384
Descartes, his *cogito ergo sum* a tautology, i. 17
Determinism described, ii. 42; its theory of will, ii. 43
Development, moral, ii. 54; two principles of, ii. 56; epochs of, ii. 63
Distinctions of nation and family, ii. 372
Dualistic theories alien to the spirit of our times, i. 407; self-contradictory, i. 412
Duty, meaning of the word, i. 67; different from law, i. 68; to one's self, i. 141
Dschelaledin the Mohammedan Mystic quoted, i. 366

Education must take sin into account, ii. 65, 271
Eternity, idea of, ii. 150
Ethics, a system of, based on love, i. 124
Evil, the fact of, i. 28; alien to our nature, i. 30; natural, i. 240; sometimes a means of good, i. 375; radical, i. 336; awful activity of, i. 379; dependent on good for its existence, i. 413; self-destructive, i. 417; texts which seem to attribute it to God, i. 236
Eudemonism, i. 164
Extra-temporal existence of man, ii. 358; nature of this existence, ii. 360; silence of Scripture no argument against it, ii. 393-396
Extra-temporal decision of man, ii. 73, 147 *seq.*; 361, 366

Fall, account of it in Genesis mythical, ii. 383-386; in each one's life, ii. 264
Fallen man, goodness in, ii. 246
Faith, the condition of redemption, ii. 230
Falsehood, i. 162-164
Father, influence of, in transmitting sin, ii. 375

Fichte, his principle concerning self-love, i. 139; his explanation of evil, ii. 95
Flacius, his views, i. 409; ii. 233
Fleshly lust is selfishness, i. 169
Foreknowledge of God, ii. 204; analogies to it among men, ii. 205
Folly explained, i. 181
Formula concordiae, its statements concerning original sin, ii. 228
Fortuitousness, ii. 27
Freedom works on, ii. 2; identical with holy necessity, ii. 9; formal, ii. 14, 22; elements of, ii. 30; essence of, ii. 26, 140; phases of belief in, ii. 61; *in aequilibrio*, ii. 69; of God, ii. 142

Generation, sin transmitted in, ii. 374
Gifted men, the most tried, i. 382
God, His name, ii. 114; the author of the law, i. 80; not the author of sin, i. 216, 234; His nature and essence, ii. 129, 132
Good, activity of, i. 337
Goethe, his Faust quoted, i. 308, 362; his Grosskophta, ii. 408.
Government, forms of, ii. 7
Guilt, what it implies, i. 195; words for it in Scripture, i. 199; descriptions of in the classics, i. 217; Hegel's theory of, i. 397; universality of, 254, 258

Habit, law of, ii. 48; distinguished from disposition, ii. 49; from act, ii. 60; of sin, i. 182
Hamann quoted, ii. 161
Hardening of the heart, i. 275; Pharaoh's, ii. 412
Hattemists, the, ii. 413
Hatred, i. 170, 172; against God, i. 172; overrides selfishness, i. 175
Hase's argument against absorption, i. 123
Hegel's theory of evil, i. 390; summary of his philosophy, i. 393; his fundamental error, i. 402; his witness to Christianity, i. 406
Heathenism, ii. 284
Herbart's saying concerning freedom, ii. 16, 73; his Determinism, ii. 52, 59
Hereditary sinfulness, how transmitted, ii. 307, 377
Hugo St Victor, saying of, i. 130
Hymns, the theology of, ii. 341

Image of God in man, what it consists in, ii. 350, 354; retained after the fall, ii. 353
Immortality, argument for, ii. 74.
Imprudence, i. 182

438 INDEX.

Imperfection of the creature, i, 271
Imputation, doctrine of immediate, ii. 341
Inconceivable, meaning of the word, ii. 167
Inconceivableness of sin, ii. 174
Indifferentism, ii. 18, 20
Individuality of character, ii. 45
Injustice, i. 169
Instinct of self-preservation, i. 152
Intelligible freedom, ii. 80
Intermediate state, the, ii. 304, *seq.*

Jacobi's polemic against the moral law, i. 190 ; his view of freedom, ii. 19 ; his horror at the thought of endless duration, ii. 149
Jerome on the being of God, ii. 129
Jesuitical morality, i. 55 ; maxims, i. 191
Judgment, the final, i. 238

Kant, on the autonomy of the will, i. 72, 74 ; his view of the origin of evil, i. 334 ; his doctrine of transcendental freedom, ii. 78, 80 ; his nobleness of mind, ii. 81 ; his dualism between the ideal and the concrete, ii. 82 ; his main error, ii. 85
King, Archbishop, on the origin of evil, i. 290 ; ii. 18, 20
Krabbe's theory concerning inborn sinfulness, ii. 323

Lactantius on the contrasts of life, i. 366 ; on the existence of God, ii. 129
La Mettrie, his theory of Determinism, ii. 42
Law, the Moral, i. 32 ; its loftiness explained, i. 33 ; the Mosaic, i. 38; ii. 58 ; its source in God, i. 86
Laws of nature, i. 82
Leibnitz, his law of fitness, i. 21 ; his theory of the source of evil, i. 272, *seq.;* ii. 156 ; his Theodicèe, i. 280, 281
Lex aeterna, notion of a, i. 102
Libertas in aequilibrio, ii. 21, 22
Love, the real principle of the law, i. 109 ; presages of it in nature, i. 114 ; akin to faith, i. 116 ; pathological and practical, i. 122
Love to God, what it includes, i. 117 ; the foundation of all love, i. 133
Luther's view of *contritio*, i. 214; of providence, i. 221, 228 ; of original sin, ii. 268 ; of divine assistance, i. 263
Lying systematic, i. 166

Machiavelli's Prince, i. 182
Malebranche's theory of occasional causes, i. 229, 230 ; his view concerning degrees of guilt, i. 203, 205

Manichaeism, i. 409
Melanchthon's definition of sin, i. 203 ; of original sin, ii. 268 ; on divine assistance, i. 262
Milton referred to, i. 388
Möhler's view of works of supererogation, i. 52
Monograph, the Dogmatic, described, i. 26
Mother's influence on her offspring, ii. 375
Motives, ii. 51, 54
Mystics, their theory of love, i. 119

Nature, signs of sin in, i. 381; meaning of the term "by nature," ii. 268, 271
Nature and grace, modern theories concerning, ii. 245
Naturalness, meaning of the term as used by Hegel, i. 391
Necessity, metaphysical, i. 101, 396 ; moral, i. 395; external, ii. 6; internal, ii. 6, 7 ; distinguished from certainty, ii. 221

Obedience, spontaneous, i. 41
Obduracy, ii. 409, 410 ; God not the cause of it, ii. 412
Occasional causes, doctrine of, i. 229
Old Testament morality, i. 256
Omnipotence of God, ii. 181 ; Schleiermacher's view, ii. 182 ; implies the power of self-limitation, ii. 195
Origen, his theory of evil, i. 257 ; his doctrine of pre-existence, ii. 76, 77, 158
Original sin, ii. 268 ; its relation to the body, ii. 369 : not a punishment, ii. 390
Original innocence of man, ii. 381

Pansatanism, i. 269
Pantheism, its theory of speculation, i. 9
Parentage, influence of, upon character, ii. 373
Passavant's analysis of will, ii. 145
Passion, i. 156
Pelagian view of freedom, ii. 37 ; of God's foreknowledge, ii, 203, 212
Perdition everlasting, ii. 75
Persian dualism, i. 411
Perfection, Christian, i. 56
Personality, elements of, i. 76, ii. 139 ; divine, ii. 132 ; human, ii. 139
Philo, his theory of transcendentalism, ii. 76
Philosophy and religion, i. 23
Plato, his view of guilt, i. 217 ; his theory of evil, i. 95, 145, 196, 278

INDEX. 439

Plainness of bodily features no proof of sin, ii. 109
Possibility, meaning of, ii. 29 ; of evil, ii. 27, 144
Placeus, his doctrine concerning original sin, ii. 331
Power, love of, i. 169
Pride, i. 167-170
Privative, evil as, i. 286
Providence, i. 219, 232; Arminian theory of, i. 231
Protestant spirit, what it really consists in, i. 27
Prayer of Eastern mystics, i. 121
Punishment, divine, i. 241 ; sin is not, ii. 413

Quenstedt on sin, i. 60

Radical evil, i. 336 ; ii. 80, 267
Realism, the doctrine of, applied to the fall, ii. 339
Redemption implies guilt, i. 251 ; its universality implies the universality of sin, ii. 256, 257
Reformers, their explanation of sin, i. 144
Religion, true idea of, ii. 282
Repentance differs from the sense of guilt, i. 213
Restoration, final and universal, ii. 425-427
Rights, i. 170
Retribution, i. 240
Ritter on God's relative will, i. 266 ; his theory of freedom, ii. 3, 4
Rothe's theory of speculation, i. 11-17 ; his theory of evil criticised, i. 146-148 ; his denial of the world's beginning, i. 225 ; on the conceivableness of evil, ii. 176
Rückert, his lines upon the end of poetry, i. 385

Schelling's theory of enthusiasm, i. 377 ; his speculation concerning God, ii. 96 ; his theory of evil, ii. 96 ; of freedom, ii. 102; his dualism, ii. 100 ; his limitation of Kant's theory, ii. 105; what he means by *Ungrund*, ii. 179
Schiller's Wallenstein quoted, ii. 65
Schleiermacher's view of sin, i. 45 ; of freedom, i. 51 ; on the origin of evil, i. 341, *seq.*; his system of ethics, i. 51 ; his theory concerning Christ's birth, ii. 377
Schmid's theory of freedom, ii. 94
Scripture, its relation to philosophy, i. 6 ; ii. 393
Scotus, Duns, his doctrine concerning law, i. 97 ; concerning fredom, ii. 19

Scotus, Erigena, his doctrine of preexistence, ii. 77
Second sight of the Scotch, ii. 205
Self-consciousness, its limits, i. 78
Self-determination explained, i. 80 ; ii. 140
Self-deception, i. 163
Selfishness, i. 134 ; the essence of sin, ii. 362
Selfish isolation, i. 136
Self-love, distinct from selfishness, i. 138 ; three stages of, i. 141 ; enjoined in Scripture, i. 140
Sensuality one with cruelty, i. 176
Sexes, relation of, in marriage, sinless, ii. 378
Serpent in Genesis, ii. 383, 384
Shakespeare referred to, i. 386 ; ii. 408
Sin, its nature, i. 42 ; definitions of by Lutherans, i. 44 ; inner principle of, i. 134, 136 ; etymology of the word, i. 89; testimonies regarding it in the classics, i. 145 ; its slavery, ii. 406 ; gradual growth in, ii. 407-409 ; hereditary, ii. 376 ; against the Holy Ghost, ii. 418-422
Sinfulness, sayings which imply its universality, ii. 253
Sinlessness of Christ, i. 181, 195
Sin and trespass offerings distinguished, i. 199-203
Sins of the emotions, i. 177 ; of the intellect, i. 178 ; of infirmity, i. 187, 205; of ignorance, i. 206 ; against conscience, ii. 68 ; mortal and venial, i. 204, ii. 408
Social life, levelling influence of, i. 160
Sophocles, his view of guilt, i. 218
Space necessary to finite existence, ii. 93
Speculation, what it is, i. 7 ; true starting-point of, i. 17 ; guarantee of truth in, i. 20
Speculative theology, its relation to Scripture, ii. 393
Stapleton quoted, i, 60
Strauss's description of the fall, ii. 347
Spinoza, his idea of God, i. 9 ; ii. 134 ; his theory of evil, i. 283, 294; his view of freedom, ii. 8
Supererogation, works of, i. 52

Time, its beginning, i. 226, *seq.*; necessary to finite existence, ii. 93 ; not a limit to finite spirit, ii, 94 ; its relation to man's knowledge, ii. 207 ; to God's, ii. 208
Trinity, doctrine of the, ii. 122, 136
Tree, poisonous, in paradise, ii. 327 ; of knowledge, ii. 347
Transcendental freedom, ii. 73, *seq.*

Unpardonable sin, what, ii. 422

INDEX.

Vatke on the necessity of evil, i. 392, 395
Virtue, delicate outline of, ii. 263
Virtues and Vices, affinities between, ii. 262
Virgin, birth of Christ, ii. 379
Voltaire, saying concerning him, i. 95

War, legitimacy of, i. 363, 384
Whitby, his theory of the fall, ii. 327

Weisse, his view of freedom, ii. 130
Will, defined, ii. 23; and freedom distinguished, ii. 25; enslaved, ii. 25; testimony of language concerning, ii. 51; begets motive, 53
Will of the people should not be law, i. 88; ii. 7

Zeller a necessitarian, ii. 130
Zeruane Akerene, i. 411

ERRATA.

Vol. I. pages 16, 17, *for* Des Cartes, *read* Descartes.
,, page 29, note, *for* Philosophae, *read* Philosophiae.
,, ,, 100, note, *for* Abtail, *read* Abtheilung.
,, ,, 102, line 21, *for* passes, *read* bases.
,, ,, 114, line 8, *for* lay, *read* by.
,. ,, 122, note, *for* des, *read* der.
,, ,, 144, note, *for* Le a. Dratiae, *read* De a. gratiae.
,, ,, 149, line 15, *for* self, *read* self-love.
,, ,, 157, line 23, *for* one in, *read* one.
,, ,, 171, note, *for* Greuzen, *read* Grenzen.
,, ,, 231, line 16, *for* dogmatical, *read* dynamical.
,, ,, 257, line 20, *for* casuality, *read* causality.

THE END.

www.ingramcontent.com/pod-product-compliance
Lightning Source LLC
Chambersburg PA
CBHW071139300426
44113CB00009B/1017